DATE DUE

DE 15 '99			
NO 12 '02			
AG 5 '04			
DE 17 '0			
DE 6 '05			

DEMCO 38-296

MEXICO CITY

WORLD CITIES SERIES

Edited by
Professor R. J. Johnston and Professor P. L. Knox

Published titles in the series:

Forthcoming titles in the series:

Other titles are in preparation

MEXICO CITY

Revised Second Edition

PETER M. WARD
*Department of Sociology and
Lyndon B. Johnson School of
Public Affairs, The University
of Texas at Austin, USA*

JOHN WILEY & SONS
CHICHESTER • NEW YORK • WEINHEIM • BRISBANE • SINGAPORE • TORONTO

Copyright © 1998 by John Wiley & Sons Ltd,
~~~~ ~~ne, Chichester,
D19 1UD, England

)1243 779777
+44) 1243 779777
rvice enquiries): cs-books@wiley.co.uk.
v.wiley.co.uk or http://www.wiley.com

ven Press. Copyright © 1990 Peter M. Ward

may be reproduced, stored in a retrieval system,
electronic, mechanical, photocopying, recording,
scanning or otherwise, except under the terms of the Copyright, Designs and Patents Act 1988
or under the terms of a licence issued by the Copyright Licensing Agency, 90 Tottenham Court
Road, London, UK W1P 9HE, without the permission in writing of the publisher and the
copyright owner.

Other Wiley Editorial Offices

John Wiley & Sons, Inc., 605 Third Avenue,
New York, NY 10158-0012, USA

WILEY-VCH Verlag GmbH, Pappelallee 3,
D-69469 Weinheim, Germany

Jacaranda Wiley Ltd, 33 Park Road, Milton,
Queensland 4064, Australia

John Wiley & Sons (Asia) Pte Ltd, 2 Clementi Loop #02-01,
Jin Xing Distripark, Singapore 129809

John Wiley & Sons (Canada) Ltd, 22 Worcester Road,
Rexdale, Ontario M9W 1L1, Canada

Library of Congress Cataloging-in-Publication Data

Ward, Peter M., 1951–
    Mexico City / Peter M. Ward. — Rev. 2nd ed.
      p.   cm. — (World Cities series)
    Includes bibliographical references and index.
    ISBN 0-471-97529-X
    1. City planning—Mexico—Mexico City. 2. Urban ecology—Mexico—
Mexico City. 3. Mexico City (Mexico)—Economic conditions.
4. Mexico City (Mexico)—Social conditions. I. Title. II. Series.
HT169.M42M498   1997
307.76'0972'53—dc21   97–22251
                                                                 CIP

British Library Cataloguing in Publication Data

A catalogue record for this book is available from the British Library

ISBN 0-471-97529-X

Typeset in 10/12pt Garamond from authors' disks
by Mayhew Typesetting, Rhayader, Powys
Printed and bound in Great Britain by Biddles Ltd, Guildford and King's Lynn

This book is printed on acid-free paper responsibly manufactured from sustainable forestation,
for which at least two trees are planted for each one used for paper production.

For Victoria, for colluding in not taking no for
an answer, and for honouring me by saying yes

CONTENTS

PREFACE AND INTRODUCTION TO THE SECOND EDITION

The 1990 edition of *Mexico City* was the first in the World City series, and it generated considerable interest and complimentary reviews. A year later it was published by the Consejo Nacional de Cultura y Artes in paperback and that, too, gave me particular pleasure, since as I stated in the original preface it was the first book about contemporary Mexico City to be published in English, and I saw this as a way of giving something back to Mexico. Whether either version sold a large number of copies I doubt; certainly I have not been inundated with publishers' requests for reprint runs nor with royalty cheques, but most of all my satisfaction has derived from knowing that I managed to write a *good* book, one of which I could be proud. The real additional buzz and warm glow has come from kind remarks that people have occasionally made, and from letters – quite out of the blue from people I don't know, and probably will never meet – saying how much they enjoyed it. By and large we academics are not used to such expressions and kindness, but rather scan the journal reviews, keeping the good ones, praying that no-one will see the bad ones, and wondering when and how we can get even!

One of the nicest compliments came late in 1991 when I met anthropologist Frans Fontaine, a curator at Amsterdam's Royal Tropical Museum. He was in the process of mounting a major exhibition for the museum about Mexico City, which ultimately, brilliantly recreated room by room a sense of Mexico City: a store in Tepito; a typical room of a tenement (*vecindad*); a roof top (*azotea*) complete with washing hanging out to dry; a street market, and so on. Indeed, the entrance to the exhibition and the ticket booth was that of the entrance to a Metro station. However, in order to research and prepare for the exhibit he had to spend several months in Mexico City. Most graciously he thanked me for my book and indicated that it had been helpful in the formative stages, but what he had most empathized with was the personal aside that I included in the original preface. This describes how I have come to view Mexico as a mischievous genie that can be both playful and dangerous, and that just as my exasperation and fear are about to become uncontrolled, the genie gently puts me down having taught me not to take Mexico or him for granted. It taught me patience and some considerable humility, and reminded me of Rodolfo Usigli's comment that 'In Mexico you begin life again every day'. Anyway, Fontaine told me that soon after he arrived in the city he also began to experience its frustrations; so much so that he placed a message to himself on his bathroom mirror reminding him each morning to 'Remember the Genie!'. That particular anecdote meant a great deal and gave me enormous pleasure, for which many thanks.

The first preface, rather like the introductory lines above, was designed to offer a brief personal statement about my own involvement and passion for the city. That is why I have decided to retain the original preface intact, and I hope that readers will continue to read it as a personal statement from me. However, I want this second preface to be different, and I regard it much more as an important introduction to the second edition. Like the chorus of a Greek play, it seeks to tell the story so far, and to act as a prelude to what we are about to see. Whenever the reader begins a section of this book, I hope that they will glance first at the following few pages in this Preface, which offer an overview of recent changes in Mexico and Mexico City.

Ordinarily one might expect a second revised edition to stand alone and to speak for itself. That won't work here, for while much of what I wrote less than a decade ago still stands, it needs to be contextualized and read against a new and very different backdrop that is Mexico in 1996–1997. It has been said that 'the past is another country'. In several important respects Mexico today is another country, even compared with the one which provided the backcloth to my analysis of Mexico City in 1989, published in its first edition in 1990. That is why I am especially pleased to have the opportunity to extensively revise this volume, and why it is desirable that the second edition comprise rather more than an update of new data and the names of new actors. Although the changes to Chapters 5–7 are less extensive, the remaining chapters have all been substantially revised.

Mexico is another country in several important respects. *Economically* in 1989 the country was on the cusp of an economic boom, and therefore this edition is quite unlike so much of the previous one, which focused upon recession. Inflation was brought down to single digits, and GDP grew at over 2 per cent per annum between 1989 and 1994 (and remained positive in *per-capita* terms) before it collapsed late in 1994/early 1995 due to a sharp decline in capital reserves, a botched devaluation leading to a further loss of confidence, and the immediate withdrawal of massive capital investment which had been placed in short-term high-yielding bonds that were guaranteed in dollars. Not for the first time in recent history the country woke up to find that it was broke. Nor was it the first time that an incoming president (Ernesto Zedillo) had to pick up the pieces, as he discovered that, whatever other intentions he may have had, his presidency was hidebound by the imperatives to regain macro-economic control, repay the bail-out $50 billion loan guarantee package orchestrated by President Clinton in 1995, and try to achieve some level of economic recovery inside 3 years before the mid-term elections in July 1997. A comparison of Zedillo's inauguration address on 1 December 1994 with the dramatic change in content and prioritization of his policies only a month later puts these changes into sharp relief.

Like the rest of the country, Mexico City was hard hit by these economic changes. While this was something of a *déjà vu* for the bulk of the city's working class population, many of whom had learned before how to cope with austerity packages of wage restraints, hikes in the cost of staples, and rising rates of unemployment, for the middle classes this was something both different and unprecedented. Unlike previous devaluations, the primary effect of which was to devalue their savings, this one was a double whammy. Not only did it devalue savings (where these were in *pesos*), but the spiralling rise in interest rates on credit (which early in 1995 approached three digits) hit the hardest, since the middle classes, like the country, were in hock. Unlike most working class citizens, the Mexican middle classes held mortgages, bought cars and other consumer durables on credit, ran up extensive credit card debts, had children in private schools, depended upon the private sector for (uninsured) medical care, and so on. Their reaction was reminiscent of Dariel Fo's playscript *Can't Pay, Won't Pay*, and the so-called *Barzón* movement was formed. (A *barzón* is the yoke strapped onto oxen.)

This debtors' movement was particularly strong and vociferous in Mexico City, with its larger proportion of middle classes, its large small-business sector (which had proliferated during the previous 6 years), and its high profile within the media and principal means of communications. People remonstrated with the government, deposited their car and house keys on the bank counters, thus effectively reneging on their contracts, and threatened widespread default on mortgage repayments (in fact, although many suspended payments pending government action to reschedule loans, this was eventually achieved through an excellent and well-regarded programme). However, images of the *Barzonistas* (especially well-heeled Mexico City housewives from Los Lomas and the rich apartment district of Polanco, and from suburban residential areas such as Pedregal) became a regular feature of national and international television news. By July 1997 the movement claimed 600,000 members and was a significant force in the anti-PRI vote that was registered in mid-term elections for Congress and for the Federal District governorship.

Mexico City also experienced other profound economic changes during this period that were specific to its particular economic structure, which are discussed in detail in Chapter 1. Briefly, since 1986–7 industrial expansion in Mexico has intensified in export-orientated manufacturing growth located in new plants both in the border region and in provincial cities. Mexico City's economic base was rapidly restructuring – away from industry and towards service and commercial activities, both of which expanded fast. Former president Salinas aimed to convert Mexico City into Latin America's principal centre for the provision of financial services, and together with Mexico's entry into NAFTA on 1 January 1994, intensified the city's emerging role as financial centre and commercial capital. The stock exchange boomed, short-term fast-return investments flowed in, and extensive shopping malls were planned and constructed, now including major US franchises, only for the process to be thrown into sharp reverse in 1995. Other cities suffered also, but it was Mexico City where the effects were felt most heavily.

Politically, too, Mexico as a nation has changed dramatically, and the political–administrative structure of the Federal District itself has gone through several transformations, which are discussed at length in Chapter 3. The most important broad changes have come in the electoral process itself, which has become more transparent, cleaner and a little more fair (although equity of opportunity remains a contested issue between the opposition parties and the dominant Partido Revolucionario Institucional (PRI)). A series of electoral reforms between 1989 and 1996 have paved the way for more democratic elections, the apparatus of which is no longer directly controlled by the governing party. The political culture of suspicion (*cultura de la sospecha* as it came to be known from 1988), which many – myself included – imagined would take at least a generation to overcome, has largely dissipated. Notwithstanding heavily contested elections in which party protests led to subsequently overturned results, particularly during the Salinas administration (1988–1994), credibility in elections has substantially improved. Previous safeguards and anachronisms, such as the 'governability clause' which guaranteed the PRI majority control and the ability to control the legislative process, have recently been set aside. Of specific interest to me in this book is the anomaly whereby Federal District residents (just over 50 per cent of the total metropolitan population) did not elect their city council and chief executive (mayor), but were governed by a presidential appointee or *Regente*. This anomaly was finally removed in July 1997 (see Chapter 3) when the Federal District elected a governor and candidates from an opposition party (PRD) to run the city. The powers of the Representative Assembly (first elected in 1988) were increased, and it became a formal legislative body, also dominated by the PRD for the period 1997–2000.

There are other important ramifications of these political and electoral changes. There has been a liberalization of the press and the media, with less direct or indirect government control and influence over the content of publications and programming. Today, the press is more likely to be objective, and is free to be more critical of government actions without fear of reprisal. The level of debate and the quality of reporting has improved, although the majority of the media remains closely associated with the government. Several new newspapers have emerged in Mexico City – most notably *Reforma*, which is an offshoot of the well-respected independent *El Norte de Monterrey* – and the elegant *Mexico City Times*, published daily in English.

Perhaps the most important political change, however, is that the PRI's virtual monopoly on government is now broken. In 1989 the National

Action Party (PAN) broke the total dominance of the PRI control of state government in Mexico when it won Baja California. The newly created (1989) Party of the Democratic Revolution (PRD) also began to make major inroads, winning a large number of mainly rural municipalities. Since 1989 both parties, but most notably the PAN, have gone from strength to strength. Indeed, they have now begun to challenge the PRI's dominance in federal elections, depriving the governing party of its outright majority in Congress in the July 1997 mid-term elections. As of September 1997, opposition parties govern more than half of the national population at state and local levels, and attention now focuses upon the presidential and federal elections in the year 2000. Between 1989 and 1997 the PAN, in particular, had major success by winning control of city hall in all of the major metropolitan areas (except in Mexico City, where until 1997 there were no direct elections), as well as governing in six states (including Baja California, which it won again for a second 6-year term in 1995). All sights were set on the July 1997 mid-term congressional elections and particularly upon whether an opposition party would win the governorship. Unlike elsewhere in Mexico, where recent elections have effectively crystallized into either PRI–PAN or PRI–PRD races, Mexico City always promised to be a three-horse race, since both the PAN and the PRD had major victories in large-population metropolitan municipalities in November the previous year. And so it proved: but it was the leftist PRD rather than the PAN that swept to victory in the governorship elections. Overall the PRD significantly advanced its national position, achieving 26 per cent of the vote in the congressional elections, coming very close to the PAN (27 per cent) and challenging to be the second-most important party after the PRI. No longer can I claim that Mexico City comprises a 'government without democracy', as I did in the first edition.

Demographically, too, Mexico City has changed in several surprising and unexpected ways. It is no longer the largest single city in the world, having been edged out by São Paulo (Tokyo–Yokohama, New York–New Jersey were always larger, but both were a coalescence of two cities). This 'demotion' in its status as the world's largest city has occurred partly by sleight of hand, and partly by genuine demographic change. The sleight of hand occurred when the statistical bureau (INEGI), supported by the Population Council (CONAPO), declared the 1980 census to have been an inaccurate count of the metropolitan area's population, suggesting that in reality those estimates should be reduced by one million, and giving a 1990 census of 14.7 million.

While some significant overcount appears to have occurred in 1980, there are clear indications that demographic processes in Mexico City have indeed changed markedly. The overall growth rate has come down by almost a percentage point to 1.5 per cent per annum; the city centre is losing population and only the outermost suburbs continue to show significant growth rates. Indeed, CONAPO now insists that Mexico City is a net exporter of population, with more people leaving the capital than migrating into it. Moreover, the age structures depicted by a broad-based pyramid in which just over one-third of the population is less than 15 years of age has begun to truncate, as the baby boomers move through the pyramid and become workers, parents and ultimately middle- and old-aged. Although still some years off, coping with a progressively older dependent population will become one of Mexico City's major challenges. The over 65 age group is expected to double in size between 2000 and 2020 (to around 8 per cent of the total population).

In land-use terms, the built-up area covers approximately 1500km², although the total area covered by the 16 Federal District *delegaciones* and the 27 municipalities that are now included in the metropolitan area cover some 4500km². Today the not-so-distant peripheral areas of Chalco (east) and Tecamac (north-east) and beyond continue to be the pressure-point areas and the battleground for expansion. However, there are important land-use changes now occurring in older established areas of the city as these densify and become more mixed and threatened by blight. Most significantly, the oldest central areas of the city are experiencing population and job losses, restructuring, acts of God (earthquakes), and so on. Mexico City now has an inner-city 'problem', the nature and extent of which will be analysed in an entirely new section in Chapter 2 of this second edition.

Decentralization and the loosening of traditional Mexican centralism is another important change that is very recent. Conceived in part by assassinated presidential candidate Luis Donaldo Colosio, decentralization, reform of the state and the creation of a New Federalism (with greater responsibilities and autonomy being accorded to the states), have become the watchwords of Ernesto Zedillo since he stepped into Colosio's shoes as candidate, and since he became president. As mentioned at the outset, Zedillo's ability to pursue these policies as forcefully as he might otherwise have intended was diluted by the imperatives of the economic crisis. Nevertheless, there has been a significant loosening in the level of Mexico City's former centralism.

For the first two years of his presidency Zedillo stepped back from playing such a dominant role in the national congress and in the PRI. He has sought to overhaul the Supreme Court and the judiciary, making these more independent and more credible institutions, with a professional career structure and with new people in senior positions. The structure of the Federal District and the national judicial police forces have been overhauled in an attempt to reduce corruption and their informal ties to drug conglomerates. In 1996, almost one-third of the judicial police were fired from one day to the next, and since then the leadership has been systematically replaced.

Many of these initiatives are being emulated in the 32 states through state judicial reforms, the strengthening of legislatures, and so on. Revenue-sharing to states and municipalities has increased slightly (from 18 per cent to around 22 per cent), and federal lines of expenditure are ostensibly being decentralized as 80 per cent of social development funding shifts to local (state) control (although, in fact, initial evidence suggests that federal agencies continue to retain a large degree of discretion). States are now empowered to levy certain new or additional taxes in an effort to strengthen local revenue creation. Responsibility for education and health care are actively being transferred to state government, intensifying and completing the process begun in the previous two *sexenios*, albeit without enthusiasm in many cases. Thus, some of the power is beginning to shift back towards the sovereign states. In part, this power has been wrested by the success of the opposition in breaking the orthodoxy of power relations exercised by the PRI and in challenging the Executive, whose 'metaconstitutional powers' have traditionally offered him enormous influence far beyond those mandated by the constitution. In part, they also reflect Zedillo's belief that the country will be more effectively run and managed if greater power and responsibility is given to locally elected governments. Widely described as a policy of New Federalism, this may perhaps be more correctly interpreted as less of a strategy and more as a pragmatic adjustment and fine-tuning to economic and political processes already entrained.

However one views it, New Federalism is impacting upon Mexico City in several respects. It helps explain why Zedillo quickly cut through previously agreed and legislated proposals, and insisted instead upon direct election for the mayor of Mexico City. It is leading to downsizing of the federal bureaucracy (at least in sectors such as education and health) as these federal agencies' principal functions become increasingly normative. By shifting the pressure for problem resolution back to the states, decentralization promises to remove some of the heat from protest groups camped out in Mexico City's central square, or *Zócalo*. Moreover, it is encouraging a greater degree of population decentralization as employees move to new job locations. But mostly it is reducing the attraction and need to be in Mexico City in the first place, thereby deflecting or retaining growth that might otherwise have occurred through migration. The old adage that '*fuera de México, todo es Cuautitlán*' (metaphorically, 'outside of Mexico City, it's all the boonies') is neither economically nor politically true today. States and cities are experiencing greater autonomy and, as they prove themselves and gain greater experience, those demands for autonomy may be expected to increase.

Finally, compared with 1989, Mexico City seems like another country in so far as *personal security* and *crime* are concerned. This is probably the most retrogressive and unfortunate change that has occurred, notwithstanding the police and judicial reforms just mentioned. Of course, these reforms were designed to respond to rising lawlessness, but in some cases they have actively contributed to the problem by casting adrift former policemen who have now turned to gangsterism. Ten years ago Mexico was one of the safer large cities of the world, where one could, within reason, walk and ride the streets without undue cause for concern. That is no longer the case. While car theft, pickpocketing, and women being 'goosed' or hissed at were always endemic, muggings, burglary, armed robbery (individuals and banks), kidnappings (and not only of the mega-rich), rape, enforced armed robbery withdrawals from cashpoints, and so on, were neither common-place nor endemic. Today they are, and most city residents have their own stories to tell, many of which are truly horrific. Drive-by taxis are no longer safe, and tourists are increasingly encouraged to do what most of the Mexican middle classes do: use hotel limos or call by phone for a taxi so that the driver and vehicle dispatch are logged. Many office buildings may only be entered after extensive security checks and with a pass. Banks are heavily guarded by multiple armed security carrying automatic weapons and deliberately placed outside the building, where it is hoped that they may dissuade would-be bank robbers. Gone are the days of a single security guard inside by the door designed to prevent the robbers from getting away, rather than from getting in in the first place.

Moreover, violence has become political. Until 1994, when presidential candidate Colosio was killed in Tijuana and a few months later PRI party secretary Francisco Ruiz Massieu was gunned down in Mexico City's downtown, top-level political violence in Mexico's cities was virtually unheard of, and was almost never visible. However, Mexico has become increasingly significant in the transport and distribution of drugs emanating from Colombia and elsewhere and being smuggled into the United States. Mexican drug rings have increased their scale of operations and their control over the distribution process. This has made them enormously powerful locally in Mexico, with untold capacity to suborn judicial and state authorities. As their influence has grown, so too has their presence threatened to permeate the highest echelons of government. Compared with 10 years earlier, a major difference today is the increased scale of the power and financial influence of the drug lords on the one hand, and on the other, the growing demands from the United States for bi-lateral collaboration in drug interdiction, tied to US 'certification' of each country's efforts to tackle drug production and distribution. This has obliged the Mexican authorities to step up and harden the line taken, but it has entailed a high cost. There are indications that drug barons are behind some of the politically motivated violence in Mexico, and that they are behind the long list of brutal slayings of law-enforcement chiefs and judiciary officials. Mexico City has seen a number of such murders in recent months, as have certain states that are in the front line of drug movement into the US – Baja California, Chihuahua and Tamaulipas (all northern border states).

At the other extreme of the country, on the southern border, the Chiapas rebellion in early January 1994 has also had its repercussions upon Mexico City since that time. While the war has largely been contained within

Chiapas, and negotiations have proceeded slowly between the Zapatista army (EZLN) and the central government almost continuously since the original outbreak, both the initial success of the EZLN and the rash of bombings in Mexico City in mid- to late 1994 have further heightened the sense of instability that exists within the country.

For these and other reasons, polls show that security has become the overwhelmingly important issue for Mexico City's population at all class levels, but especially among the middle and upper classes. Until 1997, the Federal District city authorities, delegated and appointed as they were, proved largely ineffectual in their fight against this wave of violence and crime. Now that the governor is elected for the Federal District, he (Cárdenas) will have to act decisively and effectively if his party, the PRD, is to stand a chance of re-election in 2000. (He will be ineligible given Mexico's constitutional clause which prohibits back-to-back re-election.)

Adding to the unease, Popocátepetl, Mexico's snowcapped volcano some 60kms to the south-east of the city, is no longer quiescent. It became active again in 1994, and in June 1997 the latest in a series of minor eruptions sent a thin layer of dust across the city. However, in many other respects Mexico City remains the same country and the same terrain. One gains reassurance from seeing the same waiters and bell boys in restaurants and hotels, in seeing one's favourite buildings and monuments (albeit sometimes from fresh perspectives as roads are opened up or as buildings disappear and new public spaces are created), and there are sufficient new and exciting building projects going on to enhance the sense of movement and dynamism which has always been an important feature of the city, even in recession. However, the freedom to walk those streets without the fear of being accosted, except by itinerant street sellers, is over.

Many of the aforementioned profound changes have been analysed and described in much of the new literature that has emerged about both the city and the nation. I have tried, wherever possible, to include those references in the bibliography and to refer to these works throughout the text. Moving to live in Austin, Texas, as I did in 1991, and since having the privilege of directing the University's Mexican Centre between 1993 and 1996, I have had the opportunity to be much more actively engaged in Mexican affairs and current events – much more than was ever the case when I was living in England, when visits tended to be more fleeting. Much of my most recent research has focused especially upon political change and governance in Mexico – touching directly and indirectly upon many of the issues outlined above. Yet while I have been in Mexico City approximately once every 6–8 weeks for meetings, ironically I have had less opportunity to add greatly to active research and fieldwork in the city, which informed the first edition in 1989. Fortunately, however, I have the work of others upon which to draw and, of course, a large tranche of official documents and government data to interpret. Nevertheless, I feel that even though I may not be as familiar with the contemporary nooks and crannies of the City and its low-income settlements as I once was, my understanding of recent events in Mexico is much more nuanced. This, above all, will allow me to write a *'good'* second edition.

Peter M. Ward
Austin, Texas, USA
July 1997

PREFACE TO THE FIRST
EDITION (1990)

When you travel to Mexico City go POSH (port out, starboard home). Ask for a window seat on the left-hand side when you fly into the city's international airport; and sit on the right-hand side of the plane when you leave. That way you will get a marvellous view across the city as the aircraft takes a flightpath down the west side, before turning and banking across the south of the city to land in the east. At nighttime, or if the pollution is not heavy, you will see everything. Flying out of Mexico City towards the north-east there is less to see, but with a starboard window seat you will certainly see the swathe of irregular settlement that is Netzahualcóyotl, where over one-and-a-half million of the city's poorest people live. Craning your neck and looking south, you may also get a view of the snow-capped volcanoes of Iztaccíhuatl and Popocátepetl, and, if you've stayed long enough, you may even be able to pronounce their names correctly.

However, many people come to Mexico City with some trepidation. This is not surprising in the light of the adverse publicity that the city receives. In the early 1970s I wrote a paper in which I described the pollution levels in downtown Mexico City as the equivalent of smoking two packets of cigarettes a day – as it was put to me by one expert. Rather like a Chinese Whisper this 'fact' has reappeared many times in the international press, often in exaggerated form. Would that reporters followed my other work so assiduously. Nevertheless, I still feel a little guilty about identifying this 'fact', and I hope that the more serious analysis in this book may go some way to setting the record straight.

One of today's buzz words is 'megacity' (over 10 millions), and Mexico City with almost 15 million in 1990 is certainly mega-big. Undeniably it has enormous problems: of population size and growth, poverty and under-employment, inadequate housing and servicing, pollution and traffic congestion. For the tourist this does not make it a terribly pleasant or comfortable city to visit. My advice would be to spend 3 days in the city and do the obvious sites, but if one is sensible and reasonably sensitive, then it is not a particularly dangerous city. Nor is it an easy city in which to live permanently. People often challenge me and ask, 'Would you want to live permanently in Mexico City?'. 'Hell, no!', I reply, but then nor do I want to live in London, New York or any other large metropolitan area where many of the same hassles and problems apply.

But for some reason – perhaps because it will shortly be the largest city in the world – Mexico City attracts attention and publicity. *Time* magazine (2 January 1989) describes the city as 'the anteroom to an ecological Hiroshima' and as an 'urban gas chamber'. This is grossly irresponsible reporting. Owing to temperature inversions in the Central Valley, pollution is likely to be especially severe at the beginning of the year, prompting the authorities to initiate such drastic measures as to stagger school hours, ban cars with particular license plates from being used one day a week, etc. These may be *ad hoc* measures, but often, also, they are considered responses that city authorities and citizens undertake while seeking to remedy the problem in the longer term. Call it muddling through if you wish, but it is these state-initiated responses that are an important element of evaluation in this book.

My aims in this text are to offer a serious analytical account of the nature of the urban structure of Mexico City, and to provide an accurate diagnosis of why it exists in the first place. I examine Mexico's recent economic development strategy in Chapter 1 as this, more than any other factor, determines the dynamic of Mexico City's emergence, and of its poverty. Rapid population growth, and often-uncontrolled spatial expansion, are analysed in Chapter 2, as is the spatial segregation between rich and poor. Chapter 3 analyses Mexico's political structure and, in particular, evaluates the rationale for existing political and managerial structures and their capacity to respond to the city's needs. Transportation policy and planning experience in general are examined in the following two chapters. Both exemplify well the way in which decisions are taken in Mexico: behind closed doors and with low levels of public debate and involvement. However, the rationality, nature and outcomes of city policy in the fields of access to land for self-build, and access to urban services and health care (Chapter 6), suggest that, while the city's administration has become more technocratic and sophisticated in matching policy to needs, it has done so in ways that are politically convenient to the maintenance of the *status quo*. Social control is the order of the day, not a political commitment to improve conditions as rapidly, and as efficiently, as possible. Finally, in Chapter 7, I show how the city's architectural structure reflects both the city's evolution and its philosophies, and in so doing helps to reproduce inequality and ideology.

This idea of reproducing and sustaining inequality is a central theme throughout the book. I show how the spatial structure, as well as the architecture and architectonic processes, recreate, and in some cases intensify, poverty. The same applies through the systems of delivery whereby urban resources are distributed and people's needs are met. These systems act to accentuate stratification patterns and to resist other forms of organization, solidarity and collective action. Indeed, I will show that the very management structure of Mexico City has evolved and is designed to head-off social unrest and to retain political control for the government and its party (the PRI). However, the election results in 1988 and the breaking of the PRI's stranglehold over the electoral process, particularly in the Metropolitan Area, raise important questions about whether the city's political structure can survive by making minor concessions, or whether it must be completely reconstructed. In short, I argue that genuine empowerment of the city's population, together with a party-based political agenda for the city's future development, is required if the city is to thrive. The alternative is survival through policies that will comprise more of the same (i.e. muddling through). I do not write the city's epitaph in Chapter 8. There is some cause for optimism, and much to applaud in recent policies.

My own personal involvement with the city began in 1973, when I embarked upon research for a Ph.D. Soon after arriving in the city I moved into one of the many peripheral squatter settlements in order to analyse at first hand the process of self-build. Since that first year I have returned to the country many times to conduct further research, to attend conferences, to adopt a child, to advise successive governments, to lie on beaches, etc. Although the city is too large to know like the back of one's hand, I know it better than any other in which I have lived. Whether as researcher, adviser, tourist or supplicant, the country and the city have been enormously kind to me. I hope that this book is one way of giving something back.

Living in Mexico, and particularly in its capital, can be an exasperating and sometimes a frightening experience. I often visualize the country as a mischievous genie who plays with you until you think you can stand no more. Then, just as you feel you are about to die or break down, or get on the first plane home, the genie puts you down – gently. It is as though this is a way of teaching you respect for nature and for a country that is volatile, and sometimes violent. Not everyone is so lucky. Periodically disasters such as the gas explosion in Azcapotzalco in 1983, and the earthquake in 1985, result in a huge loss of life. Personally, too, I have lost too many close friends to take the genie for granted.

It is a country to which I feel very committed. Yet I had always been slightly disappointed (and surprised) that, although much has been written about Mexico City in journal articles or chapters to books, there was no serious or comprehensive academic text on its contemporary development – with the exception of the recently published *Atlas de la Ciudad de México* (DDF/Colegio de México, 1987). Even this superbly informative study fails to provide an integrated analytical view, written as it is by over 80 different authors. Thus, when invited to contribute an early volume to the 'World Cities Series' I jumped at the opportunity. I was especially eager to write a good book: one that was both analytically strong and perceptive. I wanted it to reflect the essence of the city: its guts, its frustrations, its violence and its beauty. I wanted to show that, while not an easy city to live in, the consequences are less dire than some would contrive to have us believe, and although heavily engaged in the city and committed to it, I wanted this book to be as objective as I could make it. As a scholar I was determined to describe the city as I saw it, even if the result was to offend those with whom I have worked, and whom I admire. I hope they will respect this intention and forgive any errors of fact or of interpretation that may have arisen. Responsibility for the errors are, of course, mine alone.

Above all, I wanted this book to be enjoyable to read, so that it reflects some of the fun and pleasure that I had in the making of it. Although it carries a lot of data and statistical material, I have tried to avoid jargon or concepts that would make it impenetrable for the lay reader. Although designed for the specialist student, I would like to think that Mexican politicians and officials, newspaper reporters, analysts of all kinds, and perhaps even the occasional tourist might read it and be stimulated by some of the discussion.

PMW,
6 November 1989
Cambridge, UK

ACKNOWLEDGEMENTS

As I indicated in the original Preface above, this book and its revision is the outcome of 20 years' involvement with Mexico City as researcher and sometime resident. It is impossible, therefore, even to begin to acknowledge all those who have contributed information, ideas and criticisms throughout such a long period. Inevitably, those thanked here are likely to be those most recently embroiled in the making of the book.

Several funding bodies should be acknowledged for having financed research at some stage. Specifically, the UK Overseas Development Administration financed the research project entitled 'Public intervention, housing and land use in Latin American cities' (PIHLU) which I co-directed with Alan Gilbert between 1978 and 1982. The British Academy supported two separate periods of fieldwork in Mexico City in 1982 and 1984. The Nuffield Foundation also supported a visit in 1986. The bulk of the actual writing was done during sabbatical leave early in 1989 while I was a stipendiary Visiting Research Fellow at the Centre for US–Mexican Studies at the University of California, San Diego. Between 1989 and 1993 I held two major research awards to continue my work on Mexico and to direct or co-direct major research projects on land markets and residential land prices (UK ESRC), and on 'oppposition' and local governments in Mexico (US National Science Foundation). Many other foundations have supported recent work: *inter alia* the Ford Foundation (Mexico City), the Mellon Foundation, the Public Research Institute of the LBJ School of Public Affairs, and the University of Texas which gave me Faculty Research Assignment leave during the spring semester, 1997. I am grateful to all institutions and to anonymous referees who throughout have been prepared to back my proposals financially and intellectually. Responsibility for the views expressed in this book is mine alone, and those views do not reflect those of any funding body.

In Mexico, many institutions have assisted in one form or another. The *Instituto de Geografía*, at the National Autonomous University in Mexico City, provided an office and a physical base for fieldwork in 1978–9. My period as an adviser in the Human Settlements Ministry (SAHOP) provided a unique insight into the inner workings of government and planning in Mexico, and I should like to acknowledge the support I received then and subsequently from Arq. Roberto Eibenshutz, ex-director of the Population Centres' Directorate (SAHOP) and of FONHAPO. I also thank Noemí Stolarski, a colleague and friend from that time. I benefited, too, from an invitation to advise the reconstruction agency (RHP) in 1986, when it was engaged in the most dynamic period of its earthquake rebuilding programme.

At Cambridge, I am indebted to various people in the Department of Geography: Mike Young, Lois Judge and Ian Agnew in the drawing office, and Dennis Blackburn in the photographic department. He is to be congratulated for improving the appearance of my (often) poor-quality photographs which are included in this volume. Thanks, too, to Jean Lucas, my secretary at Fitzwilliam College, Cambridge, for putting up with the 'midden' that was my office during the latter stages of production of the manuscript.

At Texas I am grateful to my student Nicolás Pineda Pablos, who spent several weeks during the summer of 1996 scanning the text of the first edition into a state-of-the-art PC and software package, my old BBC machine with its 24 000 bytes of RAM having been (somewhat) by-passed by the tide of cyberspace. He is also to be thanked for having prepared the new voting maps for Chapter 3. At the LBJ School of Public Affairs, I warmly acknowledge the ongoing support received from my administrative assistant Debbie Warden, whose efficiency appears to know no bounds, and helps to protect my time as well as me from myself and from my own inefficiency. Similarly I owe an enormous debt to my research collaborators on other ongoing research projects: Gareth Jones (University of Swansea), with whom I have been engaged in research into Mexican land-price behaviour and public policy, as well as housing and land-market methodology, and Victoria Rodríguez, with whom I shared research into local governmental and political change in Mexico. While both topics would appear to be somewhat tangential, both proved to be central in improving my understanding of contemporary processes in the country and in the City.

I am also indebted to the large number of individuals who have assisted me at some point or other with my research, not least the householders, agency personnel and private architects and professionals whom I interviewed, sometimes more than once. In particular I should like to thank Arq. Javier Caraveo, one-time Director of Planning in the Federal District. Our many discussions always proved most illuminating and I hope that my interpretations about planning reflect creditably upon some of the major advances that his group managed to implement between 1980 and 1983. I should also like to thank two of his team, Arq. Carlos Tejeda and Arq. Jorge Gamboa (the Planning Chief in 1989), for the numerous conversations we have had about the city, its architecture and its politics. Among my former UK colleagues I should like to thank Alan Gilbert, with whom I co-directed the PIHLU project. Many of the arguments about land and servicing emerged jointly in our earlier work, and I am grateful to him for allowing them to be reproduced and extended here.

The bulk of the writing of the first edition was undertaken between January and April 1989 in California. My warmest thanks go to Prof. Wayne

Cornelius, the Director of the Centre for US–Mexican Studies, and to all his staff for making my stay at La Jolla so pleasant, stimulating and productive. My thanks go to other Visiting Fellows at the Centre who put up with my often apparently 'off-the-wall' questions about the city which, interjected *à propos* of no particular conversation, must have struck them as odd at best and, at worst, extremely eccentric. It was fun being a part of that group, and I hope that some of the enjoyment rubbed off in the text. In Texas I (finally) wrote this second revised edition while on a Faculty Research Assignment in the spring semester, 1997.

For the First Edition, thanks to my beach, which was a source of stimulation and invigoration, and to Crockett and Tubbs who, often twice a night, helped while away the hours before Victoria came into my life. Victoria is my wife, my friend, my colleague, (sometime) co-teacher, co-researcher and co-author. Friends may be forgiven for wondering how we manage with lives that overlap so, but in truth Victoria makes it remarkably easy. As before, to her I dedicate this book.

Cambridge, UK, November 1989
Austin, Texas, March 1997

1

THE PARADOX OF DOMINANCE YET DEPENDENCE: THE LOCAL IN THE NATIONAL IN THE GLOBAL

CITIES WITHIN A GLOBAL SYSTEM

Urban development has traditionally been analysed at two levels (Johnston 1980; Badcock 1984). First, the role of urban centres within a wider urban system: their commercial and administrative functions as 'central places'; their functions as *entrepots* as new lands were colonised; their position within the settlement hierarchy, and in particular their position in relation to some notion of a rank-size rule of urban settlement. The second level of analysis has traditionally concerned the nature of the urban place itself: its land-use structure; the socio-economic attributes of city populations and their behaviour; residential structure and housing markets. Increasingly, too, interest has grown in the role of the local state in mediating the allocation of urban goods. While there was always implicit recognition that these two levels were inter-related, until the 1970s few analysts sought to explain that relationship. Changes and processes within the city were explained largely in relation to the qualities of the city itself, and not as part of the outcome of the operation of a wider logic of national and international processes that, to a greater or lesser extent, shaped city development.

These analytically limited and limiting notions began to change broadly from the 1970s onwards. As is so often the case, however, the 'new' approach overreacted and overstated the relationship. Dependency theory in its earlier formulations emphasised the conditioning effect of 'metropolitan' capitalist expansion in the core (principally Western Europe) upon the Third World, which was cast as the 'periphery' (Gunder Frank 1967; Dos Santos 1970; Amin 1974; Wallerstein 1974). Primary products were extracted from the periphery and shipped to the core economies, where surplus value was added as they were converted into manufactured goods for export or for local consumption. Because the periphery was 'dependent' and under metropolitan hegemony (often through colonialism), the terms of exchange were unfavourable to the newly penetrated countries. This led to them being actively underdeveloped. Since the 1970s this account has been viewed as both crude and inaccurate (Palma 1978; Roxborough 1979; Corbridge 1986; Lehmann 1990), not least because it failed to explain why certain areas had developed quite successfully (Argentina for example), why certain areas remained locked into pre-capitalist forms of development, and why, if the periphery was subject to an overall conditioning relationship, the experiences of regions were often so different (Roberts 1978, 1994; Gilbert and Gugler 1992).

The fact that experiences on the periphery were so different offered an important clue in analysing 'dependent urbanisation' (Castells 1977). Certain sorts of product have a greater propensity to generate urban linkage effects. Temperate agriculture in Argentina, for example, and coffee production in the south of Brazil led to the development of a broader system of urban centres, and to a wider distribution of wealth between them. Conversely, 'enclave' economies such as mining towns, most plantation economies and so on generated few multiplier effects, and offered little opportunity for wider socio-economic mobility (Furtado 1971). An excellent example of the way in which different types of production systems may shape town development is provided by Balán (1982) for late nineteenth-century Mendoza and Tucumán, two provinces at the periphery of Argentina. Mendoza's economy developed around wine production on small holdings, while Tucumán produced sugar on plantations. Both provinces developed significantly during the period and their principal cities were prosperous and well serviced, but because Mendoza's productive base was oriented towards wine it generated numerous multiplier effects: corks, bottling plants, etc. This created a more diversified and dispersed settlement pattern than was the case in Tucumán, where the focus around plantations and sugar mills led to greater concentration, a restricted economic base, and greater inequality of income distribution.

Thus we have begun to recognize that while broad conditioning relationships imposed by international capitalism are important, it is their *engagement* with the local economic, social and political structures that is all important in determining the shape and nature of dependent urbanization. For the researcher this is precisely what makes it interesting. As Harvey stated long ago (1973: 232) 'global metropolitanism is embedded in the circulation patterns of the global economy . . . different city forms are contained within that economy'. Strangely, though, we have not come very far in our analysis of the relationship nor of different city forms. The focus of study has, quite correctly, been upon the changing nature and logic of capital accumulation processes internationally, and how this is restructuring relations of production on a *global* scale. Increasingly, finance operations and, more importantly, production itself, are being put 'offshore' where tax restrictions are less onerous, and where labour is cheaper (Dicken 1986a; Sklair 1989; Herzog 1990). The deskilling of the production process has facilitated the use of labour (often female) in the Third World. The organization of this process is vested in transnational corporations whose headquarters are in so-called 'World Cities'; their research and development operations are in removed high-amenity locations associated with major seats of learning or technological advance, while actual production is no longer wedded to skilled labour or specific materials supply, and may be located where labour is cheap and passive (Sassen 1991, 1996; Knox and Taylor 1995). As Harvey (1987, 1989) has argued, in terms of time, accessibility and costs of transfer of capital, information and goods, the world has shrunk as capital accumulation processes have become much more 'flexible', capable of switching sectorally and spatially as conditions demand (Martin 1987). This is the so-called New International Division of Labour or NIDL (Henderson 1986).

Of course, not all cities and countries are locked equally into this arrangement. Certain nations – the Newly Industrialized Countries (NICs) – have successfully created export-oriented manufacturing industries around which they have developed rapidly. Others have not. Having spent two or three decades developing an industrial strategy constructed around import-substituting industrialisation (ISI) in order to reduce their dependence upon advanced capitalist economies, many countries have found it difficult, or have been unwilling, to adjust to export-oriented growth. In Latin America, Brazil, Mexico and to a lesser extent Argentina have made the adjustment and achieved technological advance in different ways (Gwynne 1985), but the most successful examples remain the East Asian 'Gang of Four' (Singapore, Taiwan, Hong Kong and South Korea). Mexico's initial export growth has developed around certain investment sectors in which it has a comparative advantage (oil and petroleum-derived products) and around its export-processing zone along the border with the USA. These latter in-bond (assembly) industries have led to the establishment of over 2000 factories and 500 000 jobs (Sklair 1988, 1989; Wilson 1992; Gereffi 1996).

Although we now have a more accurate idea of what, precisely, is important in driving the settlement process internationally, few have studied the impact that these processes have upon Third World cities. Thus there is a danger of repeating some of the intellectual errors of the dependency school: i.e. thinking that we understand the conditioning process, so the outcomes are predictable. The aim must be to verify the relationship and, once again, to analyse how it engages with local structures. We should be cautious about making generalizations such as those relating to World Cities (Friedmann and Wolff 1982), which suggest that certain large emerging metropoli (e.g. Mexico City and São Paulo) fulfil control centre functions in the 'semi-periphery', similar to World Cities such as Los Angeles, New York, London and Frankfurt in the core. Neither Mexico City nor São Paulo exercise anything like the international or even sub-regional importance that World City status proposes. They are among the world's largest cities, but economically, financially, technologically and in terms of information processing, they are not among the most important (Sassen 1991; Knox and Taylor 1995).

Similarly, too, the processes associated with the much vaunted 'globalization' must be analysed in so far as these impinge and interact upon local, regional and national structures. While the world has become a smaller place, experiencing time and space compression, the overarching impact of the economic change and information accessibility will be mediated by local political and social structures. Globalization does not mean convergence to a common form, any more than dependency did. It is the engagement of global processes upon national and regional structures that will shape both the nature of local processes and their outcomes, and these will be different spatially and socially (Cox 1997).

The urban process

The second level of urban analysis concerns individual city structures. The question becomes one of explaining the changes that an individual city experiences. Most recent research has tended to emphasise as the *leitmotif* of city development its function either as a centre of production or as one of consumption. Obviously a city fulfils both functions, but it is a question of where the emphasis is placed, and in both cases the role of the state is a critically important determinant of city processes. Since this volume is specifically about Mexico City, I do not propose to address the debate head-on although some of my findings may relate to it tangentially. There are many other specialist texts which do justice to the topic (Castells 1977, 1979; Saunders 1979, 1986; Harvey 1985). My purpose in this volume is to analyse the way in which inequality is reproduced through existing city structures and through state action.

Castells' work has focused upon the city as a unit of consumption. For him, it is the way in which the city 'reproduces labour power', particularly through public and private investment in a broad range of services which he calls the 'means of collective consumption'. There are problems with this term, as well as with his rather artificial separation of production and consumption functions (Pickvance 1976; Harloe 1977; Saunders 1979), but Castells' work was analytically attractive, especially in relation to the Third World, because it provided an alternative basis around which class consciousness might emerge and class struggle might be organized. Classical theory of revolution, of course, was built upon an extensive industrial proletariat which did not exist in developing countries and was fast disappearing in advanced nations as well. He identified the provision of the 'means of collective consumption' (cf. the means of production) as the locus around which conflict would evolve, increasingly with the state cast in the position of protagonist responsible for providing the means of consumption (Castells 1979: 18). In effect this politicizes the issue and brings to the forefront state intervention and response to social conflicts that arise.

Harvey's (1985) work, in contrast, emphasizes the logic of capital accumulation processes by different income groups, and identifies different forms of urban development that result from fundamental contradictions arising in the process of capital accumulation, and in particular overaccumulation crises. The point is that this leads to capital investment flowing out of the 'primary circuit' (of production) into alternative circuits of capital accumulation such as the secondary circuit, which includes the 'built environment for production'. This embraces infrastructure, transportation, investment in the provision of electric power, etc. Capital may also be invested in the 'built environment for consumption', which includes housing, pavements, parks, etc. Often investments fulfil both productive and consumption functions (Lojkine 1976; Saunders 1979, 1986). However, given the large-scale nature of many of these investments, their 'lumpy' nature, etc., there is a tendency for capitalists to underinvest in the built environment for production and consumption. Instead, it is the finance market and often the state which takes on investment in large-scale projects. This switch of resources requires a credit system to be created, controlled by financial and state institutions which play a mediating role between the primary and secondary circuits of capital accumulation (Harvey 1985). They play a crucial role in affecting the volume and direction of capital flows and cannot, therefore, be excluded from a study of urban development processes (see also Lamarche 1976). The tendency towards overaccumulation is a contradiction arising from the competitive nature of relations between members of the capitalist class, and it dictates a cyclical nature of capital flows into the secondary and tertiary circuits. These investment cycles are argued to have different 'wave' lengths or periodicity (Gottlieb 1976; Harvey 1985).

The shift or 'switching' of capital into the built environment leads to a 'displaced class struggle' (Harvey 1985) which Harvey sees as essential for social change and for resisting the 'violence' that will otherwise be visited upon working-class populations in cities. Thus, as with Castells, urban politics move to centre stage (Saunders 1979, 1986). However, while the potential for conflict exists, so too does the propensity for state intervention to defuse, co-opt or ultimately repress working-class movements – as will be demonstrated throughout this book.

FROM BOOM TO BUST AND BACK AGAIN: MEXICO'S RECENT ECONOMIC ROLLERCOASTER

In this section I want to sketch out the backcloth to Mexico's recent economic performance, to concentrate primarily upon the nature of economic structural change in recent decades and identify the objectives and outcomes of economic management since 1970. This will provide a context in which Mexico City's growth and predominance may be analysed.

Economic change before 1970: the years of the 'miracle'

The economic and social upheaval caused by the Mexican Revolution during the second decade of the century gave rise to one of the most stable and

TABLE 1.1 Growth of gross domestic product, 1941–95

Sexenial period	GDP % annual growth rate during *sexenio*	GDP % growth rate per capita *sexenio*
1941–46	4.7	1.9
1947–52	5.3	2.6
1953–58	6.4	3.7
1959–64	6.1	3.4
1965–70	5.7	2.9
1971–76	5.1	2.4
1977–82	5.3	3.0
1983–88	1.7	−0.1
1989–94	2.5	0.6
1995 (est.)	−6.9	na

Source: Zorrilla-Vázquez 1996: 114–15.

arguably least oppressive societies in Latin America. Yet it is also one of the most unequal. Neither rapid economic growth between 1940 and 1970, nor enormous expansion in oil production during the late 1970s have significantly changed levels of income inequality, although both processes have generated major changes in the nature of economic activity.

In the short term the Revolution (1911–18) caused enormous disruption. Population declined; the traditional élites were overthrown and replaced by recently formed interest groups, some of which were regionally based while others were tied to different sectors of economic activity; finally, the breakup of agricultural estates led to a period of virtual anarchy in rural areas, causing production levels to fall. Except for manufacturing, which recovered quite quickly, economic performance during the 1920s and 1930s was sluggish. This was partly an outcome of worldwide depression and the decline in export earnings from precious metals. It was also a result of inadequate foreign investment which had been discouraged by the radical stance taken by President Cárdenas (1934–40) after he nationalized oil production and actively pursued a programme of Agrarian Reform. As well as being a hero in his own time, Cárdenas' policies laid the foundations of much of Mexico's subsequent political and economic development (Aguilar Camín and Meyer 1993).

Although the development of an industrial base during the *Porfiriato* (1876–1911) and the social and political transformations that evolved from the Revolution constitute the origins of the Mexican 'miracle', its fruition only came after 1940. Between 1940 and 1970 the Mexican economy grew at over 6 per cent annually and at more than 3 per cent annually per capita (Table 1.1). In certain sectors such as manufacturing it was significantly higher. Hansen (1974) explains this phenomenal growth as being due to several factors. First, political stability was achieved during the 1930s and institutionalized in a single governing party (the PRI, discussed in Chapter

3). Second, public financial institutions such as the Banco de México and Nacional Financiera became the vehicles for large-scale state support and intervention in economic development. In the early period (1940–50) these institutions underwrote the development of basic industries, while later they directed investment to infrastructure such as electric power and railways. Other state interventions were also important and helped stimulate rural to urban migration – necessary to supply adequate cheap labour to the cities. Third, changes in the social and psychological make-up of the élite and the new opportunities for socio-economic mobility enhanced development.

How extensive was this development? In agriculture, production rates grew very fast at the outset, but dropped back to average 4.3 per cent between 1950 and 1960 and 2 per cent in the last 5 years of the 1960s (Scott 1982: 77). By 1970 there were clear indications that agricultural production was in crisis. The production of certain staples was falling behind demand, guaranteed prices for basic foodstuffs had declined in real terms, and land was increasingly being turned over to export crops and to cattle rearing (Tello 1978: 15–20; Heath 1985). However, state response was ineffective since much of the assistance and the new techniques associated with the 'Green Revolution' favoured larger, more commercialized farming units (Cockcroft 1983: 165–73). Increased production levels were especially marked in the highly capitalized sectors of sugar, coffee, market gardening and cotton. The latter, alone, contributed 18 per cent of commodity earnings abroad. Yet despite the pressures working against them, small-scale peasant farmers still generated 40 per cent of the corn crop. Indeed, overall production on *ejidos* kept pace with that on private farms, although the former concentrated much more upon the production of staples (Hansen 1974). Nevertheless, the overall effect of agricultural development during this period was to reduce the opportunities and viability of the smallholder. Between 1950 and 1960 the level of landlessness rose from 2.3 million to 3.3 million (Hansen 1974: 81), and the proportion of the total labour force employed in agriculture declined from 65 per cent in 1940 to 39 per cent by 1970. Similarly, its share in gross domestic product (GDP) declined from 23 per cent in 1950 to 16 per cent in 1960 to 11 per cent by 1970 (Tables 1.1 and 1.2; United Nations 1980).

It was in industrial development that the 'miracle' was most pronounced. Manufacturing grew at over 8 per cent annually (Hansen 1974: 41). Import-substituting industrialization complemented investment in activities that produced goods for export. The state intervened to enhance Mexican competitiveness abroad by devaluing the *peso* in 1949 and 1954 and by holding down wage increases. Foreign investment in Mexican industries was stimulated by providing infrastructure, by tax incentives for new firms, by low rates of tax generally, and after 1965 by special concessions in the US–Mexican border zone which made it highly profitable for US companies to establish industries in that area using Mexican labour.

TABLE 1.2 Economic growth, prices and purchasing power, 1970–95

Year	Percentage increase in GDP over previous year[a]	Percentage GDP per capita (rate of development)[b]	Inflation: percentage increase in CPI[c]	Purchasing power over previous year[c] percentage variation for:	
				I	II
1970	6.9	3.5	7.0	10.8	2.7
1971	3.5	0.1	5.3	−5.1	−0.1
1972	7.9	5.0	5.0	12.6	0.5
1973	8.2 — 5.1[e]	4.9 — 2.4[e]	12.0	−6.2 — 16.1	−5.2
1974	6.3	2.8	23.8	9.9	−4.5
1975	3.0	2.4	15.2	0.9	1.2
1976	2.1	1.2	15.8	11.6	0.7
1977	3.4	0.5	28.9	−0.9	−0.8
1978	8.3	5.2	17.5	−3.4	−2.9
1979	9.2 — 5.3[e]	6.2 — 3.0[e]	18.2	−1.1 — −7.2	−1.1
1980	8.3	5.4	26.3	−6.6	−3.7
1981	7.9	5.1	28.5	1.0	3.8
1982	−0.6	−3.1	57.6	−0.1	0.7
1983	−5.3	−4.8	101.7	−22.0	−22.8
1984	3.7	0.7	65.5	−9.0	−7.1
1985	2.7 — 1.7[e]	0.3 — −0.1[e]	57.7	−1.2 — −18	−2.8
1986	−3.1	−2.9	86.3	10.5	−5.9
1987[d]	1.4	−0.1	131.8	−6.0	−1.9
1988	1.3	−0.5	114.2	12.7	−1.3
1989	3.3	1.5	20.0	−6.6	9.0
1990	4.4	2.6	26.7	−9.1	2.9
1991	3.6 — 2.5[e]	1.9	22.7	−4.5 — −13	4.9
1992	nd	nd	11.9[r]	nd	nd
1993	nd	nd	8.0[e]	nd	nd
1994	3.1[f]	nd	7.1[e]	nd	nd
1995	−7.0[f]	nd	51.7[e]	nd	nd
1996 (est.)	−6.9[e]				

Notes: I, minimum salary; II, wages in manufacturing industry; CPI, consumer price index; nd, no data.

[a] Source: GDP figures are calculations by the author based upon IMF *International Financial Statistics*, various volumes. 1987 estimates are from the Economist Intelligence Unit, *Country Report – Mexico*, No. 3, 1988.

[b] Source: Banco de México, *Indicadores Económicos* 1965–1982, August 1984.

[c] Source: Banco de México, *Cuaderno mensual, Indices de precios*, No. 75, July 1984. CPI calculations by the author. Percentages show price rise over previous year.

[d] 1987–95 data compiled from Lustig 1992: 40–41.

[e] Zorrilla-Vázquez 1996: 135.

[f] Handelman 1996.

This very successful period of economic growth had widespread repercussions upon both the total population and its distribution. Total population increased rapidly from 19.6 million in 1940 to an estimated 81 million in 1987. Also, Mexico became primarily an urban country. The proportion of the national population living in urban areas (defined as more than 10 000 people) rose from 22 per cent in 1940 to 42.3 per cent in 1970, and today stands at around 55 per cent (Scott 1982: 53; Brambila Paz 1992).

Yet, despite the impressive rates of economic growth recorded, the distribution of incomes has not altered significantly. Indeed, it appears that the early phase of rapid economic growth was achieved at the expense of growing income inequality. Measures of inequality show an increase during the 1950s when the position of the poorest income groups deteriorated (Makin 1984; Aguilar Camín and Meyer 1993). In the 1960s the lowest 40 per cent of the economically active population earned only 11 per cent of the national income and there were pessimistic forecasts that this situation was unlikely to alter appreciably during the 1970s (Navarrete 1970). In fact some recent progress has been made. The level of income inequality has declined (from a Gini coefficient of 0.551 in 1956 to 0.503 in 1977; Makin 1984: his Table 2.6). With the single exception of the lowest paid 10 per cent, all income groups have improved their position in absolute terms. However, if the fruits of economic growth have trickled down to a limited extent, they have fallen mostly into the laps of the middle- and upper-middle-income groups. The Mexican 'miracle' appears to have resulted in a redistribution of incomes in favour of these middle-income groups at the expense of the top and bottom sectors (Hansen 1974). Income distribution in Mexico remained one of the most unequal of all Latin American nations (Weisskoff and Figueroa 1976).

Moreover, by 1970 the high social costs associated with economic development were beginning to surface. Wage levels and employment conditions were worsening and the 1970 census revealed enormous levels of deprivation among large sectors of the population. There were also political consequences: growing alienation among the intelligentsia; increasing unrest in rural areas; and the first signs of a groundswell of public protest in low-income areas of the cities. In particular, the disturbances of 1968 and 1971 were key signals which demanded adjustment to the policies that had previously sustained the so-called period of 'stable development' and heralded a period that was, perhaps optimistically, referred to as 'shared development' (Teichman 1988).

'Boom, bust and belt-tightening': instability and austerity during the 1980s, revisited in the 1990s

Economic management and crises 1970–1996 In order to tackle some of these problems, incoming president Echeverría sought to assert the directive role of the state in the national economy and created or revitalized a large number of state enterprises in the fields of production, distribution and welfare (Tello 1978; Needler 1982; Goulet 1983). Public sector expenditure in social welfare increased significantly in real terms. Wages were increased and tax reforms were proposed, as were other actions which sought to favour working classes at the expense of the private sector (Tello 1978). Inevitably many of these proposals encountered strong resistance from élite groups (Cockcroft 1983), but they failed, ultimately, not because of that opposition but rather as a result of a combination of national and international factors. The promise of gradual structural changes to the economy foundered, and the period emerged as one of disequilibrium and erratic economic expansion.

Although the overall economy continued to grow at a satisfactory rate during the 1970s (at an average of 5.9 per cent of GDP between 1971 and 1980), it has not been a smooth passage (Padilla Aragón 1981: 14). Whereas between 1963 and 1970 the growth of GDP per annum never fell below 6.3 per cent, the period 1971 to 1980 saw it fall below 6 per cent on several occasions (Table 1.2). Four 'depressions' figure prominently: the first began late in the administration of Díaz Ordaz and reached its worst point in 1971; the second began in 1973, but its impact did not really become discernible until the latter part of 1974 and it culminated in a near 100 per cent devaluation of the *peso* just before Echeverría left office in 1976. The economy did not pick up again until López Portillo reflated in 1978 and thereby abandoned policies imposed by the IMF as conditions for its support. Unfortunately, the spurt of economic development in the late 1970s was short-lived and failed to touch, in any appreciable way, the underlying structure that had contributed to the earlier crisis.

A third 'depression' emerged as the economy overheated, bringing about further devaluations and IMF intervention in 1982–3. This marked the beginning of the so-called 'lost decade' of the 1980s, so-called because between 1982 and 1989 the per capita GDP growth was rarely positive, and was mostly negative (Table 1.2). Moreover, the purchasing power of real wages declined even more markedly. Real minimum wage levels dropped by over 45 per cent, and while most employers moved off the statutory minimum as the baseline wage for many of their workers (paying rather more instead), real wage levels fell dramatically across the board in most cities during the period (Ward *et al.* 1994). Only in 1989 was a significant improvement recorded in manufacturing wages, although the statutory minimum continued to lose ground in real terms (Table 1.2; Dussel Peters 1996). The fourth 'depression' would come late in 1994 after several years of economic growth during the Salinas presidency. However, before examining the nature of that crisis in detail, it is necessary to backtrack a little and examine what was to become both an important reason for economic recovery, as well as a key factor in Mexico's next collapse: investment capital.

An ongoing problem for Mexico has been one of attracting investment capital for growth. In the past, national investors withdrew their money to the United States whenever they became uncertain about economic performance or when a devaluation threatened. Official sources estimate that

US$33 billion left the country as capital flight between 1975 and 1981. In 1984, Mexicans held $20 billion in foreign accounts (Chislett 1985:12). This helps to explain why Salinas tried so hard to strengthen the Mexican stock exchange, especially through privatization of some 'star' performers, and why they offered treasury certificates and bonds at preferential rates and why they guaranteed them in dollars. These options were so attractive that national investors started 'switching' their investment portfolios out of real estate (where it had been fairly safe) into the riskier but potentially high-yielding stock exchange (Jones *et al.* 1993).

The first 4 years of the Salinas administration were wedded to a major neoliberal economic recovery plan built around privatization, the tearing down of tariff barriers and free trade, which began in 1986 when Mexico entered GATT, and then was immediately prioritized by Salinas, who approached President Bush about a US–Mexico free-trade agreement. The plan included restructuring towards export-oriented manufacturing growth in certain key areas (automobiles and auto parts especially) and manu-facturing production for the home market, which required large-scale capital goods imports and the attraction of foreign capital. The most dynamic manufacturing branches since liberalization were dominated by either trans-national corporations, monopolies or domestic oligopolies (Dussel Peters 1996: 81).

Traditional sectors (agriculture and smaller national industries) were left to fend for themselves as best they could, although some protection was afforded to the agrarian sector by progressive implementation of the tariff reductions made compulsory once Mexico entered the North American Free Trade Association with Canada and the US (formally on 1 January 1994). Deregulation of the Agrarian Code in 1991–92, which freed *ejidal* land for purchase or for joint ventures, was also designed to free-up the sector and make it more amenable to new investment and restructuring (Austin 1994; Cornelius *et al.* 1994; Gates 1996).

Huge inflows of capital were attracted by new short-term high-yielding Treasury Certificates (CETES), and subsequently by Treasury bonds (*tesobonos*) which were guaranteed in dollars, or into the stock market (approximately 70–80 per cent of total investment according to one source, with 15–20 per cent going into direct investment in what might be termed productive areas (Zorrilla-Vázquez 1996: 61)). This, together with the high-profile privatization programme built around the 'star' performer of tele-communications, allowed the government to cover its heavy balance of payments deficit (about 6 per cent of total GDP in 1994), as well as to build up major foreign exchange reserves which were derived from the import of capital goods designed to support restructuring and export-oriented industrialization on the one hand, and on the other, to support a major social welfare program (PRONASOL) designed to 'cushion' the Mexican population from the adverse effects of austerity and the social costs that restructuring and neoliberalism would entail (Lustig 1992: 58–9; Cornelius *et al.* 1994). As Lustig points out, the critical thing was to turn around the balance of payments deficit by turning the inflow of capital goods into productive investment.

The inflow of this easy money raised the capital account balance from an estimated US$8.16 billion in 1990 to almost $31 billion by 1993, offering a deceptively rosy picture of an economy which was becoming increasingly vulnerable given its susceptibility to capital flight the moment there was a loss of confidence. Until the Chiapas uprising and the assassination of PRI presidential candidate Colosio early in 1994, however, there was little that suggested a loss of confidence; in fact quite the opposite. The economy and stock market were bullish, NAFTA approval was on fast-track, the President was extremely popular and was admired at home and abroad, and after the success in the 1991 mid-term elections, the PRI governing party was expected to retain its position of dominance while conceding some electoral and gubernatorial space to the opposition. Economic reform was being followed by political reform (Roett 1993; Rubio 1993). Unfortunately, much of this buoyancy proved to be a *chimera*, and after 5 good years for Mexico and for Salinas, 1994 was a bad one which would close with the worst economic crisis that Mexico had faced in recent history.

Some authors view the regular presidential renewal every six years as a positive advantage, allowing a clean break to be made, and new commitments to be forged (Purcell and Purcell 1980; Whitehead 1980). Echeverría was able to distance himself from the former economic model and shift direction. The accession of both López Portillo (1976) and De la Madrid (1982) allowed them to appear as conciliators between the government and the private sector, and the simple fact of their accession did much to restore public confidence. President Salinas, too, after his narrow (and some would say dubious) victory in the 1988 elections, pledged to continue to modernize the economy and to undertake fresh initiatives to modernize the government party and to embark upon electoral reform (Cornelius and Craig 1991). Traditionally, too, this renewal has provided overall stability to the system by allowing for the imbalances of one regime to be redressed in the subsequent one. This helps to explain the shift back and forth from broad political right to broad political left that has occurred in Mexican politics since the 1930s until the mid-1980s (see Figure 3.1), but which came unstuck thereafter, alienating many and leading to the split that ultimately led to a new party being formed. De la Madrid, Salinas and now Zedillo are strong technocrats without previous electoral experience, and on the political right in their macro-economic policy (Centeno 1994; Handelman 1996).

The crises themselves appear to be in part at least an outcome of the Mexican system of mandatory change of government every 6 years, and reflect the instability that arises during the final year whether due to heady largesse in matters of public policy during the final months of any administration, or to the political pressures upon the incumbent to 'clean the slate' and carry out any measures that are likely to be unpopular (such as devaluation) before the new Executive takes over. This was a feature of the handover in both 1976 and 1982, although it was not in 1994, when neither Salinas nor his Treasury secretary (Aspe) were willing to do what was necessary to manage a modest devaluation without promoting a loss of confidence (as they probably could have done). Whether through vanity, or political ambition that would have been sullied by a devaluation (Salinas had his eye and heart set on being the Executive Director of the newly created World Trade Organization), or from bloody mindedness (Aspe had been a prime contender for the presidential nomination himself), we will probably never know, but Zedillo's administration had to embark upon the devaluation, which it did some 15 days after the inauguration, but which was botched by not having secured the support of principal players in Washington and on Wall Street, and by trying to do too little. Immediately there was a sense of confusion and a loss of confidence, which spiralled as the government and the president dithered over Christmas 1994, sacking the newly appointed Treasury Secretary and generally failing to take control.

One view which appears to hold up well in explaining some of the internal dynamics of jostling for power within the cabinet is that all presidents are committed to economic expansion from their fourth year onwards, if not before (Whitehead 1984). Policies of economic austerity oblige the state to make deals with those social groups that are likely to suffer most and upon which, ultimately, they depend for their legitimacy (e.g. the unions and the poor), but such agreements can only be expected to endure for 2 or 3 years, after which growing unrest demands some degree of reflation. Also, interministerial competition associated with the struggle to win the nomination for the presidential succession itself creates strong spending pressures which the incumbent is unable to prevent (Teichman 1988). By 1984 there were already signs of growing unrest and of unwillingness on the part of the trades unions to continue to cooperate. Thus it appeared that some degree of reflation was underway. However, this failed to materialize given, first, the intensity of the crisis; second, the lack of available funding for a reflationary programme; third, the further cut in oil prices and the second 'round' of austerity measures enacted in 1985; and fourth, the personal determination of President De la Madrid to 'break the mould' and to succeed where his predecessors had failed, namely by applying a brake upon expenditure throughout his term in office. Even the intense competition for the government party candidature in 1986–7 did not lead to any significant reflation.

Salinas did not need to reflate since he had kick-started the economy in 1989, but one does see major political movements occurring in personnel relating directly to behind-the-scenes competition for the succession: Colosio's move from being head of the PRI to a new superministry that would take over the PRONASOL social welfare expenditure, the firing of one or two other senior ministers who were pressing their case too strongly and challenging the president, and so on. Zedillo's administration looks set to be similar to that of De la Madrid, given that any significant real growth will be a major achievement and will have to be invested to good economic as well as political effect. Moreover, he has already stated his intention not to hand-pick his successor as party candidate, and the PRI voted recently in its (1996) General Assembly that the presidential candidate must have held elected office before running for the presidency. Thus, for several would-be contenders in the cabinet there is now no possibility, and aspirants in future will no longer be able to seek directly to win friends by embarking upon major spending programs mid-term, as has frequently been the case in the past.

However, it would be wrong to suggest that these crises are merely a sexenial phenomenon: external and internal factors are also important. The international recession and rising prices from 1973 onwards, a growing balance of payments deficit, inflation, and the transfer of capital out of the country, were important factors which contributed to undermine the economic strategy of the Echeverría administration. Similarly, the effects of inflation, over-extended public sector expenditure and a growing balance of payments deficit (partly induced by the enormous purchases of foreign technology for the exploitation of oil resources and for industrialization) led to spiralling indebtedness from 1978 onwards. When at the end of 1981 Mexico was obliged to cut the price of its oil by 8 dollars a barrel in line with other oil-producing countries, the country found itself suddenly broke. In effect the depressed price of oil meant a loss of 10 billion dollars in earnings during the first half of 1982 (Cockcroft 1983). Much of this anticipated revenue had already been earmarked and spent. Similarly, when investors lost confidence after the December 1994 crisis, they emptied their portfolios or prepared to do so at the next short-term rollover of the Treasury bonds. After Salinas' lies, or at the very least his being 'economical with the truth', about the foreign exchange reserves available in late 1994, Mexico found itself unable to meet prospective withdrawals in the first 6 months of 1995. Again it was broke, and this time the support came directly from the US and from the international agencies which put together a rescue package of 50 billion dollars. In effect this guaranteed Mexico's ability to meet its creditors' demands should the bonds be called in.

In part these crises reflect mismanagement, corrupt practices, and bad luck. The 1981 drop in oil prices was not foreseen and Mexico was totally overextended and so could not expand its production levels. In 1982 the costs of debt servicing alone amounted to over one-half of the revenues derived from exports. President Salinas was successful in diversifying the export economy away from oil production towards manufactured goods, thereby reducing this dependency. (Ironically this is one of the few areas that has gained from the 1994 devaluation as a result of cheaper exports and more competitive pricing of its goods.) However, he badly misjudged and mishandled the investment strategy, allowing it to flow into areas that were not directly productive and upon terms which left the country vulnerable to large-scale withdrawals. Also, having won the election for Zedillo in August, he failed to take appropriate action to devalue in the last months of 1994, paving the way for a smoother transition. There seems little doubt that the combined shocks of Chiapas, the political assassinations, and the pressures of bringing the PRI to a successful election in August, had a profound effect upon Salinas and that in the latter months his judgement became clouded and self-serving. Just as he rightly took much of the credit for inspiring Mexico towards fast-track NAFTA and economic restructuring (like it or not), so, too, he must personally bear much of the blame for the crisis that occurred as soon as he left office.

There is also mounting evidence of large-scale corruption and ties with drug barons. Salinas' brother is in prison on charges of unexplained enrichment of over US100 million dollars, alleged to have come from kickbacks for services, for privatization contracts, money laundering and deals with drug rings. He is also alleged to have been heavily involved in the political assassination of PRI Secretary General Francisco Ruiz Massieu in 1994. For his part, the former president languishes in self-imposed exile in Ireland, his reputation destroyed. Much of the blame for the PRI's drubbing in the July 1997 elections and for the PRD's and Cárdenas' phoenix-like rise from the ashes has been blamed upon Salinas since both he and the PDR had been consistent in their criticism throughout the Salinas presidency.

With the exception of De la Madrid, who was rather unpopular throughout his mandate due to the austerity straightjacket in which he found himself and which he sought to uphold, all recent ex-presidents have been vilified upon leaving office. Despite being one of the most popular presidents since López Mateos in the early 1960s, Salinas' last troubled year and the economic crisis that he foisted upon his successor have made him one of the most unpopular ex-presidents ever. Ridiculed publicly by street vendors selling Salinas masks with elephant-size ears, the sense of betrayal is palpable throughout Mexico. Trusted and believed in by most Mexicans, the depth of the crisis, the levels of corruption of members of his family, and the alleged involvement of his brother in politically motivated assassinations, have made him the lightning rod for people's anger.

This crisis hit more widely and more intensely than any of the previous ones, the major difference here being the dramatic increase in interest rates during 1995, which for a time ran at 90 per cent, forcing small businesses and middle-class families into economic collapse. Unlike working class Mexicans for whom austerity and adjustment packages were nothing new, the expansion of credit facilities among the middle classes left them often impossibly exposed once interest rates rose steeply. Moreover, while most people recognised the importance of the $50 billion bail-out guaranteed loan put together by the United States and the principal international organizations in May 1995, there was widespread criticism (in Mexico as well as abroad) that this was targeted to guarantee investors withdrawals from Mexico – i.e. foreign investors were privileged above the immediate hardships of the Mexican population. Of course, the Zedillo government felt obliged to take steps that would reassure international investors past and present in order to reduce the haemorrhage of capital and to retain some possibility of future growth-inducing investment, but this alienated the middle classes, who had come to depend upon credit and were now faced with bankruptcy and default. The *barzonista* movement was born (a *barzón* is a yoke). Throughout Mexico, street demonstrations protested against the government's policies and demanded that Salinas be brought to justice. At the forefront were well-heeled men and women not usually associated with public demonstrations.

In Mexico City, in particular, the crisis has also fuelled a spate of bank robberies and a sharp rise in burglaries, more specifically armed robberies of individuals as they walk the streets, dine in restaurants or ride the city's taxis. This lawlessness and the incapacity of the police to respond has further alienated the middle classes, which are now voting for the opposition in ever increasing numbers. For the governing party the race is on to stem the tide, but this is proving difficult in an economic environment which offers little short-term hope, and with an executive who, until early 1997 at least, appeared unwilling to assert and impose a strong sense of leadership.

Sectoral performance 1970–1996   Since 1970 the various sectors of the economy have been affected in different ways. In terms of its contribution to GDP and its relative importance as an employer of the economically active population, agriculture has fared particularly badly, although its decline began much earlier than the 1970 cut-off point considered here. The industrial sector, and in particular manufacturing, has grown sharply both in terms of its contribution to GDP (from 31 per cent for industry in 1965 to 40 per cent by 1983) and in the employment opportunities that have been created. In recent years, of course, petroleum has reinforced the contribution that this sector makes to GDP, although it generates relatively few jobs. Services and commerce have always been important, and since the 1960s have contributed over 50 per cent of GDP. However, this significance in absorbing labour has increased dramatically over the same period: from 27 per cent of the economically active population in 1960 to over 43 per cent today. Much of the growth observed in services has involved the creation of 'genuine' jobs in banking, large-scale commerce, etc. However, it also includes the atomization of jobs within the tertiary sector: in activities such as small family businesses, individuals stalls, lottery ticket sales, and so on.

In manufacturing there has been a significant shift in emphasis and a concerted effort to move away from the United Nations ECLA-inspired models of import-substituting industrialization which, it was widely recognised, had failed to generate sufficient jobs and was leading to an increase in dependence upon imported technology, capital and raw materials. Instead, investment during the 1970s focused upon industries which utilize locally occurring natural resources, such as food processing, mining and petroleum production and petrochemicals (Needler 1982), complemented increasingly since the mid-1980s by export-oriented manufacturing growth. Early in this period an attempt was also made to extend 'backward' industrial linkages by developing machine tools and the production of other capital goods, themselves often dependent upon steel. However, at least in the short term, this process has threatened to increase Mexican dependence, since much of the 'seed' technology is developed outside the country (Cockcroft 1983). According to one source there was a nine-fold increase in production goods imports during the 1970s, which led to the dramatic rise in the public sector debt (Cockcroft 1983).

The important point to recognize here is that, while overall economic expansion occurred during the 1970s, it has been a stop–start process and was mainly concentrated within the industrial sector. While this generated considerable employment, particularly in manufacturing, the largest growth area as far as jobs are concerned has been in the service sector. The expansion of the public bureaucracy during the 1960s, and especially in the 1970s, was another important feature of the changing structure until the mid-1980s, when austerity obliged major cuts in public expenditure and the government bureaucracy began a process of downsizing as parastatals were closed down and as ministries were consolidated. These attempts to shrink government and to make the bureaucracy more efficient continued under Salinas with a major sell-off of formerly state-owned enterprises. In total the privatization process has involved some 950 state and parastatal enterprises, diverse trust funds and other agencies, as well as the banks, which had been nationalized in 1982 (Lustig 1992: 105; Zorrilla-Vázquez 1996).

Exports as a proportion of GDP grew from 3.7 per cent in 1970 to 8.2 per cent in 1980 to 11.5 per cent in 1990 and to 25.5 per cent in 1994. This huge increase reflects the dramatic change around in Mexico's development strategy during the 1980s. Analysed by sectors, one observes a sharp reduction in the role of petroleum and other extractive industries which was the leading sector of exports in 1980 when it comprised almost 70 per cent of export revenues, being overtaken by manufacturing goods in 1990. The latter more than *tripled* its relative importance in the following 4 years, so that by 1994 manufacturing comprised 84 per cent of all exports (21.4 per cent of GDP). This is a dramatic switch from dependence upon oil revenues in the late 1970s and early 1980s to export manufacturing a decade later. As we will observe later, the petroleum industry has suffered from gross underinvestment since the late 1970s, but potentially Mexico now has two major export platforms upon which to build its future development.

The increase in manufacturing generated employment in export industries, especially in the *maquilas*. The population employed in the sector grew from around 100 000 in 1980 to just over half a million by 1992. Notwithstanding this sector's growth, it in effect cushioned what would otherwise have been a decline in employment in manufacturing. In absolute terms the economically active population employed in industry at the end of the 1980s was the same as at the beginning, although as a proportion of the workforce it declined from 11 per cent to 9 per cent (Salas, 1992: 96). Inevitably these processes have had major repercussions upon prospects for employment and wage levels both nationally as well as in Mexico City, points to which I return later.

The impact of oil production   Within this sharply contrasting economic performance, oil has been both a boon and a bane. While the rapid rise in known reserves and the dramatic increase in production allowed López Portillo to reflate the economy, it also led ultimately to economic collapse. Knowledge about the extent of known reserves was a carefully guarded secret from 1974 onwards. At the end of the Echeverría period reserves were set at 6 billion barrels; López Portillo updated this estimate in 1978 to 20 billion, and again in 1979 to 40 billion (Whitehead 1980). In 1982 Mexico's reserves were set at 72 billion barrels and an eventual level of 250 billion barrels was thought not beyond the bounds of possibility. This would place Mexico not far behind Saudi Arabia in the oil-producing league (Cockcroft 1983). In the past decade, however, PEMEX has consistently announced a decline in its estimated reserves as a result of low investment in well-drilling and exploration. Earlier estimates are considered to have been inflated, and have declined from 72 billion barrels in 1984 to 63.2 billion barrels in 1995 (Grayson 1995). The reserves to production level have declined from 56.8 years to 48 years.

At the outset of the boom in petroleum production the government expressed its firm intention to avoid squandering revenues from oil. It did not wish to encourage consumption of expensive consumer durables; nor was it prepared to bail-out the purchase of food imports on an ongoing basis. In the rhetoric of the day, oil was a national patrimony to be shared by all and to be used to generate long-term development. This conflict between 'expansionists' and those who urged more caution became the locus around which intense inter-ministerial infighting occurred between 1978 and 1981 (Teichman 1988). Ultimately the forces of caution (these included De la Madrid as the then Minister of Programming and Budgeting) won and got the head of PEMEX (the state-run petroleum company) dismissed, but not before he had driven up production levels, contracted huge debts against future oil revenues, and silted away a large fortune for himself and other cronies. Thus, the damage was done. Little wonder, perhaps, that De la Madrid, once he was President, went after the ex-head of PEMEX and had him imprisoned for embezzlement.

The original idea was that no single country was to receive more than 50 per cent of total exports in an attempt to avoid the dangers associated with overdependence on a single source of foreign earnings. As a consequence a production limit was set of 1.5 million barrels per day throughout the 1980s (Cockcroft 1983). Yet this was later raised to 2.2 million barrels and production at the end of 1982 was scheduled to reach 2.7 million (Needler 1982). Work to expand port development to cope with much higher levels of oil production also suggested that in the future these production ceilings would count for little. Moreover, despite the guideline about a maximum level of exports to any single country, by 1981 more than four-fifths was going to the USA. The crux of the problem was that Mexico needed the money: the only way out of the spiralling indebtedness was to increase oil production. Also important, however, was external pressure from the USA to provide increasing amounts of oil and gas for its own consumption, thereby allowing that country to conserve the rate at which it was obliged to exploit its own reserves. The substance of that pressure was the threat to withhold financial credit.

Oil production also fuelled the crisis in another way. Inevitably, perhaps, almost all of the technology required to extract the resource had to be purchased from abroad. This meant that PEMEX was spending far more than the profits it was bringing in. By mid-1982 it had accumulated a foreign debt of $25 billion: one-third of the nation's total (see Whitehead 1980; Cockcroft 1983).

Production levels during the 1990s have been at around 2.6 million barrels of crude oil per day, of which approximately one-half is exported. Petroleum's leading role as an export earner was eclipsed during the Salinas period when export-oriented manufactures took over as the leading earner. In 1995 PEMEX generated 12 per cent of the merchandize exports, 28 per cent of all government revenues, and 6 per cent of GDP. It remains a key component in Mexico's economy, and the Zedillo government has continued to resist pressures to open up-stream (production) activities to outside competition. These pressures intensified during negotiations over the US$50 billion bail-out package, which many thought might be the opportunity to force Mexico to open up the PEMEX monopoly. This was resisted, although it seems that some of the production revenues may have been offered as collateral on the loan.

Nevertheless, PEMEX desperately requires further investment capital in order to extend its exploration, to modernize production, and to invest in new petrochemical plants. The latter area – petrochemical industries and gas production and distribution – is being opened up to private investment.

Under legislation passed in April 1995, Mexican and foreign companies may build new gas pipelines provided they receive permission from the Energy Regulatory Commission. The aim here is to attract much-needed investment as Mexico seeks to shift from a dependence upon oil-fired power (electricity) generation to gas-fired (Grayson 1995). Yet, the widely expected privatization of the secondary petrochemical sector did not occur in 1996. While plans were far advanced and the strategy was for PEMEX to demonopolize 61 of the state-owned plants, these plans were shelved in 1996 when strong opposition emerged in Congress. In some ways this was only a pyhrric victory for legislators, since the new law still allows private capital investment in *new* plants, yet the principal aim was to find fresh investment for the older outmoded plants. Symbolically, though, Congress's refusal was important, showing that the jewel in the crown for privatization – PEMEX – is still not up for grabs.

The problem of indebtedness The absolute size of the public debt had grown inexorably since the mid-1970s and by 1982 had come to account for a large slice (around 46 per cent) of public expenditure. This rise reflects the growth of new credits, the effect of devaluations, and high interest rates in the USA. By 1984 Mexico's foreign debt totalled 97 billion dollars which, along with Brazil, was the world's highest. More immediately the problem was one of servicing the debt, and when in 1983 De la Madrid announced that Mexico was going to find it difficult to meet even the interest payments, further interim credits were provided. A large proportion of actual debt repayment was rescheduled, but the interest repayments were especially onerous during the De la Madrid years, given that growth was so low or non-existent. The total debt (federal and private) continued to rise to $104 billion in 1990, to $136 billion in 1994 and to an estimated $153 billion in 1995. The public debt represented the lion's share of the total, being around 62 per cent in 1994, although this represents a considerable decline from the 80 per cent level in 1985–88, and the difference has been taken up by substantial increases (absolute and proportional) in the private and bank share of the debt (Lustig 1992; Zorrilla-Vázquez 1996). In 1985 the total debt represented 87 per cent of GDP, declining to average around 40 per cent during the 1990s. In 1995 it jumped to an estimated 72 per cent (Zorrilla-Vázquez 1996: 127).

Some attempt has been made to raise revenues through taxation. Echeverría initiated higher rates of income tax and raised the efficiency with which they were collected. However, the relative contribution made by income tax compared with other forms of tax (oil, imports, etc.) fell from 51 per cent to 33 per cent between 1979 and 1981 (Padilla Aragón 1981). Moreover, López Portillo raised the thresholds at which income tax was payable and imposed value-added taxes so that the net effect of tax reform under his administration was to produce a more regressive structure

(Needler 1982). Later, his successor further increased the rates of value-added tax and extended them to all but basic subsistence commodities. As part of the austerity measures advanced in March 1995, VAT was increased from 10 to 15 per cent. Moreover, subsidies on many commodities and services have been phased out or substantially reduced during the Zedillo administration.

The impact of boom and bust upon employment and wages   The pattern of growth and contraction that I have described had an important impact upon access to employment, the opportunities for economic mobility and the value of real wages but, as I have shown, this period also saw a shift in the structure of the Mexican economy, particularly in relation to the nature and scale of activities carried out within the industrial and service sectors. The imposition of austerity measures in 1982 and 1995 seriously affected government expenditure and wage levels. The changing nature of employment and wages, therefore, were a response to all of these factors and are not simply an outcome of the rate of economic expansion. The important questions to ask here are whether the poor benefited significantly from the changes induced since 1970, and whether these changes were from the oil bonanza of the late 1970s or from economic restructuring and privatization during the Salinas years.

For several reasons the broad answer to these questions is no. The Mexican workforce is increasingly vulnerable to international economic changes. The level of labour utilization in Mexico is low compared with most other Latin American countries (around 27 per cent of the population in 1970 and 34 per cent in 1988), and has actually declined from 39 per cent at the beginning of the century. According to some authors this suits capital in so far as it represents a 'reserve army' of labour that may be maintained without cost and absorbed when required, as well as functioning to keep wage levels low, to weaken attempts at labour mobilization for improved conditions, etc. (Cockcroft 1983; but cf. Roberts 1994). Labour can be regularly hired and fired according to the amount of work available, or to ensure passivity of the workforce, or to avoid contractual obligations required for 'permanent' employees. Workers are also arguably 'superexploited' not simply by being paid low wages, but also by an increasing intensity of work and by an extension of the working day (Cockcroft 1983). Vulnerability is further heightened by the growing use of capital-intensive technology in industry that generates less employment per unit cost investment – arguably an undesirable trend given Mexico's youthful age structure and the estimated 800 000 new jobs required each year to cater for those entering the labour market for the first time, and to allow for the growing participation of women within the economy (Mexico, SPP 1983). For the 1970–90 period it is estimated that the annual shortfall was 385 000 jobs, which further fuelled the growth of underemployment and the informal sector as well as pressures for illegal migration to the United States – met by increasing resistance and border controls in that country (Bustamante *et al.* 1992).

Vulnerability also arises from the fact that so much recent industrial investment comes from outside the country. Increasingly we may conceive of an international division of labour whereby transnational companies utilize the relatively cheap labour available in Mexico and effectively decide the workforce's livelihood. This is not a feature unique to Mexico; it is a familiar enough problem in the UK, but Mexican workers are more vulnerable than their British counterparts because the level of dependence upon external companies is greater and because their activities are often limited entirely to the assembly of imported goods. There is considerable truth in the maxim that when the USA sneezes, Mexico catches cold.

Unemployment Unemployment has shown a clear tendency to increase during the periods of economic depression identified earlier. In 1974–5, 1982 and 1995 many factories were closed down temporarily and others went bust, as did many small-scale businesses. There are few good data available that describe unemployment or underemployment at a national level, although one estimate suggests that early in 1975 more than 4 million workers were affected (amounting to 25 per cent of the economically active population; Padilla Aragón 1981). It is estimated that in 1984 approximately two in every five Mexicans did not have full-time employment. Between 1981 and 1983 the rate of urban unemployment nationally rose from 4.2 per cent to 6.3 per cent, and declined thereafter to less than 3 per cent during the 1989–90 'boom' (Lustig 1992). In 1995 it rose again to over 7 per cent (Pastor and Wise 1997: 434). In reality, of course, actual underemployment is much higher.

There is some evidence to suggest that families today are consciously adopting a strategy to maximize their employment opportunities. It has been argued that in rural areas many peasants have become 'proletarianized' and now work as waged labour on large-scale commercial farms but also utilize family labour in subsistence farming or in handicrafts to survive economically (Cockcroft 1983). There is evidence for an intensification of this 'proletarianization' process in the agriculture sector as an outcome of deregulation of *ejido* land ownership in 1992, and as protective tariffs are gradually lowered post-NAFTA (Gates 1996; Cornelius and Myhre 1997). Multiple earning strategies have long been utilized in the *maquiladora* industries in the north, which employ a large female workforce. There are suggestions that similar patterns may be observed elsewhere and that they may have growing relevance for urban areas (Pommier 1982; Tuirán Gutiérrez 1992; González de la Rocha 1994).

Neither should we assume that, given a choice, people automatically opt for employment in the formal sector: an industrial job for example. Recent labour market studies in Guadalajara, which has a tradition of 'outwork' in clothing and shoemaking, suggest that some self-employment or employment in the informal sector may maximize the household's earning power (Arias and Roberts 1985; Chant 1991; González de la Rocha 1994). Also, during periods of wage restraint, informal sector activities are not subject to the same restrictions as formal employment: prices and fees can be raised more readily to meet inflation. Although it might be sensible to have one household member employed in an industrial enterprise, thereby enabling the family to qualify for social security, it may be economically and socially more convenient for other household members to work 'casually' (González de la Rocha 1988).

Nevertheless, it does appear that during times of crisis, when workers are shed from the industrial sector, they seek employment in the tertiary sector. Indeed, if they are to work at all, there is no other alternative. In Mexico City, for example, tertiary-sector employment expanded between 1974 and 1978, not all of which can be explained by an expansion of civil service jobs (Pommier 1982).

Inflation and wages The whole of the 1970–88 period is epitomized by rapid price inflation, finally brought under control by the Salinas administration. Between 1971 and 1978 it averaged 15.2 per cent annually, in contrast with 2.8 per cent between 1959 and 1970 (Padilla Aragón 1981). From 1977 it has spiralled to 25 per cent per annum (1977–80) and to almost 100 per cent in 1982 and 1983. It declined in 1984, but overshot the 40 per cent target for that year. However, considerable success was achieved through the Social Pact (a prices and incomes agreement) in bringing down inflation from 159 per cent in 1987 to 20 per cent in 1989 and to single figures in 1993–94. The 1995 crisis saw inflation rise sharply to just over 52 per cent.

Part of the success in controlling inflation was wage constraint. Generally speaking the lost decade was a period of severe wage reduction in real terms, with significant improvement coming only with active growth in 1989–94. This pattern of general decline with occasional periodic attempts to restore real wage levels is the pattern of the past two decades. Although real wage levels were restored in 1974 to above their previous highest level, the purchasing power declined sharply after 1977 (Table 1.2; see also Bortz 1983). Maximum wage increments (*topes*) allowed for workers were negotiated by the government and the unions between 1977 and 1980 and again in 1983, but these fell far below price increases over the same period.

In Mexico the traditional means of protecting the value of real wages has been one of regular (usually annual) revision of the daily minimum wage. In times of rapid inflation or after a devaluation, minimum wages have been renegotiated, but have usually resulted in an erosion of purchasing power. They take a month or two to introduce, while in contrast prices are raised overnight, bringing about short-term hardship. Since late 1982 there has been some call from organized labour for the introduction of a 'sliding scale' whereby wages are automatically adjusted every 3 months to take account of price increases (Bortz 1983; Garavito Elías 1983). During the early months of 1983 the government was lukewarm in its response to the idea. Although it was never admitted publicly, a sliding scale adjusted automatically every 3 months would have reduced the bargaining strength of the government in its relations with labour. Also, from the government point of view, faced with appeasing the IMF, a decline in real wages was both anti-inflationary and provided a windfall to capital, whose production costs were thereby reduced. Nevertheless, as a concession to the unions, the Ministry of Labour agreed to allow the Minimum Salaries' Commission to meet 'as often as required'. In fact, however, the value of the real minimum wage was so seriously eroded that few employers used it as their modal baseline for wage setting: in effect most would pay 1.5–2 minimum wages. Real (i.e. adjusted for inflation) minimum wages rose by 16 per cent under Echeverría (when they were the standard wage for approximately 70 per cent of the economically active urban population), but declined by 7 per cent under López Portillo, by 18 per cent during De la Madrid's administration, and by a further 13 per cent under Salinas (Zorrilla-Vázquez 1996: 126).

Manufacturing real wages also declined during the 1980s but improved significantly between 1988 and 1994 (Pastor and Wise 1997: 433). If real wages are standardized to 100 in 1988, then they were 119 in 1992 and a little higher in certain categories of manufacturing production (automobiles, basic petrochemicals, etc.; Dussel Peters 1996: 80). Nevertheless Mexico's poor and worsening record of inequality in wage distribution that was registered during the 'miracle' and into the 1980s has been sustained despite the apparent growing prosperity during the early 1990s. Gini coefficients for family income in 1984 and 1992 show a further deterioration and a shift to greater inequality (0.429 to 0.4749, Zorrilla-Vázquez 1996: 116; see also Pastor and Wise 1997: 425). In some respects we should not be surprised, since Salinas' programme of restructuring was deliberately accompanied by a poverty alleviation program (PRONASOL), and was predicated upon the time-worn ideas of trickle-down economics. So far as waiting to see the benefits is concerned, most Mexican workers continue to hold their breath.

MEXICO CITY'S CHANGING ECONOMIC STRUCTURE

The limits of Mexico City

Throughout this book by 'Mexico City' or the 'Metropolitan Area of Mexico City' I mean the contiguous built-up area shown in Figure 1.1. Thus I will not usually include municipalities whose urban areas are not contiguous (such as Teotihuacán to the north-east of the city). For the time being these form part of a separate 'Metropolitan Zone' which is not quite the same as

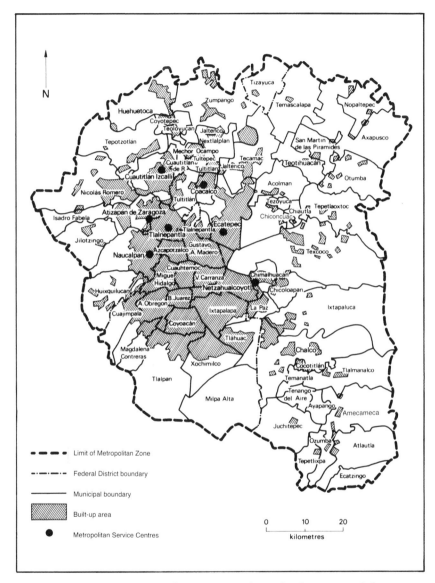

N

Limit of Metropolitan Zone

Federal District boundary

Municipal boundary

Built-up area

Metropolitan Service Centres

0   10   20

kilometres

FIGURE 1.1 Political limits of Mexico City, the Federal District and the 'Metropolitan Zone'

the Metropolitan Area, although the two spatial entities are fast converging as the city continues to expand outwards. Thus the definition of what constitutes Mexico City is not fixed. It cumulatively absorbs outlying political entities, as will be demonstrated in the following chapter. Indeed, using criteria of built-up areas, travel times and average density of 20 people per hectare, CONAPO has recently revised its definition of the metropolitan zone as now including the Federal District and 38 municipalities, one of which (Tizayuca) is in the extreme north and forms part of the State of Hidalgo, the remainder being in the State of Mexico. In essence their definitions comprise all the area indicated in Figure 1.1, except those municipalities in the extreme north-east (beyond San Martín de las Pirámides) and beyond Chalco in the south-east (CONAPO 1996).

Within Mexico City the 'Federal District' is a political unit created in 1928 which, as I shall describe in Chapter 3, enjoys a unique administrative status within the confederation of Mexican states. Internally it is divided into 16 political–administrative units called *delegaciones*, which are identified on Figure 1.1 and on most subsequent maps. Parts of the built-up area of Mexico City extend outside the Federal District into the surrounding State of Mexico. Here, as in all states, municipalities form the political sub-units. Autonomy of the municipality is an important element within the Mexican Constitution, and while in practice in the past it counted for little, since 1983 and the reform of Article 115, this tier of government has become much stronger and more autonomous (Cabrero Mendoza 1996; Rodríguez 1997; Ward 1998).

Reference to the 'inner-city' or downtown area loosely refers to the four central *delegaciones* of Miguel Hidalgo, Benito Juárez, Cuauhtémoc and Venustiano Carranza. In the past this area was also often referred to as the 'City of Mexico', but in order to avoid confusion this study will not adopt the term. I will return to discuss some of the specific characteristics of the inner city in Chapter 2.

The city's national dominance: the local in the national

The impact of national economic growth between 1930 and 1970 was felt disproportionately in the capital city. Indeed, public policy acted to further concentrate industrial production in Mexico City throughout this period. The city was especially favoured in its access to electricity generation, oil and other power sources and products for petrochemical industries, the provision of water and drainage facilities and, last but not least, it was the focus of road investment programmes (Garza 1986). As a result of these state-led investment programmes, the rate of return on industrial goods was systematically higher in Mexico City than elsewhere (Garza 1986). However, Garza concludes that although industrial location in the Metropolitan Area offered many micro-economic advantages, it presented major obstacles and problems when viewed from a national perspective. Specifically, it generated all sorts of diseconomies for the city's population (pollution, long journeys to work, high costs of basic goods, etc.), and it also accentuated the regional inequalities that exist between the capital city and the provinces.

Mexico City, with slightly less than one-fifth of the national population, always exercised a position of paramount importance in the national

TABLE 1.3 Gross domestic product generated by the Metropolitan Area of
Mexico City, by sectors 1940–80

	Mexico City's gross domestic product in constant (1950) *pesos*				
	1940	1950	1960	1970	1980
Agriculture	30	28	37	54	105
Percentage of national product	0.6	0.3	0.3	0.3	0.4
Percentage of all sectors	0.4	0.2	0.1	0.1	0.1
Industry	2286	3378	10 509	16 086	34 619
Percentage of national product	33.7	27.1	42.7	30.9	30.8
Percentage of all sectors	32.6	27.2	39.1	28.4	30.0
Transportation	576	1038	2184	2775	4788
Percentage of national product	66.6	62.2	60.0	58.1	34.4
Percentage of all sectors	8.2	8.4	8.1	4.9	4.2
Services	4118	7983	14 128	37 816	75 826
Percentage of national product	40.9	46.0	44.0	49.0	50.5
Percentage of all sectors	58.8	64.2	57.2	66.6	65.7

Source: *Sistema de cuentas de México. Producto interno bruto por entidad federativa, año 1980*, Dirección General de Estadística, SPP.

economy. The proportion of national GDP created within the city grew from 30.6 per cent in 1940 to 36 per cent by 1960, after which it roughly levelled off at between 37 and 38 per cent (Puente 1987; Huerta García 1993). In certain sectors its national importance is even more pronounced: in transportation until 1980, for example. In services, too, around one-half of the total national product generated by the sector is created in the Metropolitan Area (Table 1.3). The same is true for manufacturing industries. Although slightly less than one-third of all industry production in 1980 took place in the city, this included 48 per cent of all manufacturing activities (Garza 1987). The decline in the proportion of total industrial production registered since 1960 (Table 1.3) reflects the rising importance of alternative industrial centres elsewhere in the country and has shown further decline during the 1980s (Huerta García 1993; Rowland and Gordon 1996). However, the predominance in manufacturing remains (Table 1.4), although there has been an important decline in the total numbers employed in the sector in the Metropolitan Area since 1980 (from just over one million to less than 750 000 in 1988; Rowland and Gordon 1996: 181).

Moreover, these high levels and steady increases since the 1930s are not only relative, but also reflect a dramatic absolute increase from a total city GDP of 7010 million (constant 1950) *pesos* in 1940 to 115 338 million *pesos* in 1980. In effect, city GDP has doubled in real terms every decade, broadly paralleling national expansion. Inevitably this growth generated a huge demand for labour especially in manufacturing and in services, much of

TABLE 1.4 Evolution of Mexico City's manufacturing industry 1930–80

	1930	1940	1950	1960	1970	1980
Number of establishments (%)	6.8	8.7	20.0	29.9	27.9	29.5
People employed (%)	19.0	24.6	25.0	46.0	41.9	46.9
Total earnings (%)	32.9	36.7	44.1	41.1	51.3	48.0
Capital investment (%)	22.6	29.3	35.5	37.8	42.5	ND
Manufacturing contribution to GDP (%)	28.5	32.1	40.0	46.0	46.8	48.0

Source: Garza 1987: 101.

which was met, initially at least, through provincial-to-city migration (see Chapter 2).

Broadly, there has been a shift away from industrial and manufacturing production towards services since 1960 (Table 1.3) and this 'tertiarization' of the city's economy has intensified during the 1980s. In 1975 industry and services generated 30 per cent and 61 per cent of GDP, respectively; by 1985 these proportions had declined to 26.5 per cent in the case of industry, and risen to 67 per cent in the case of services (Villegas 1988). A similar decrease is observable in the case of people employed in industry, which declined relatively from 43 per cent of the national total in 1975, to 36.5 per cent in 1985, to 31 per cent in 1988 (with the absolute decline in numbers noted above by Rowland and Gordon). In 1994 the estimated industrial employment was down to 24 per cent of the national total (CONAPO 1996: 1).

The most important industrial activities undertaken in the city are the manufacture of clothing and furniture (and repairs), publishing activities, the production of rubber, plastic and metal goods, and the assembly and repair of electrical goods. The most important branches by total number of employees are metal products, machinery, etc. (27 per cent of personnel and 25 per cent of total value), and chemicals and plastics (18 per cent of personnel and 25 per cent of value), closely followed by foodstuffs (16 per cent of personnel and 18 per cent of value), and textiles (17 per cent of personnel and 10 per cent of value). The bulk of these transformation industries are orientated towards the local market: consumer durables such as food, drinks, shoes, petrol and gas refining, etc. Only 35 per cent of those employed in industry produce goods which have no intrinsic orientation towards the local market (Camacho 1987). The important point to recognize is that most of this production is for a national and local market rather than orientated towards global markets. While there has been some expansion of *maquila* types of industry in the Metropolitan Area, other areas remain much more important, most notably those in the northern Mexico–US border zone (Sklair 1988; Shaiken 1990).

The Metropolitan Area may be divided into a series of three 'rings' (see Chapter 2), surrounding a central city core (with 13 per cent of the total population in 1990): a first ring of the surrounding *delegaciones* and municipalities immediately adjacent to the Federal District (49 per cent of the total population), a second ring of more outlying *delegaciones* and less adjacent municipalities in the State of Mexico (32 per cent of population), and a third ring comprising in essence the outlying, fast-growing municipalities (7 per cent of population). The location of the different types of industrial activity varies within the city. Overall between 1980 and 1988, with the exception of the third outer ring, industrial growth rates declined between 12 and 17 per cent (Rowland and Gordon 1996).

The Federal District and its inner areas are increasingly orientated towards non-durable consumer goods industries, while the outer areas and the metropolitan periphery are more directed towards capital goods and the production of consumer durables. Industry has a declining role in the city overall, with two areas hit hardest: the central area with its small-scale enterprises (Monnet 1995), and the second ring, which includes some of the larger industrial closures in Tlalnepantla (14.4 per cent and 17.2 per cent reductions in the two areas, respectively, between 1980 and 1988; see Table 1.5). Overall, the greatest gains are in services, with a 3.8 per cent average growth rate during the period 1985–88. In 1988 almost 58 per cent of all services were concentrated in the central area, and within the centre their share increased while commerce and industry declined (Table 1.5).

Manufacturing in the first ring occupies around 50 per cent of the total city share, and within that ring, its importance has dropped marginally (−3.3 per cent) with slight gains in commerce and services. Of all the zones this was the most stable internally during the period. The second ring, on the other hand, appears to have taken a particularly hard hit, declining by 7 per cent overall, and by 10 per cent in manufacturing jobs. Services increased by 6 per cent, but from modest base levels. The third ring was the only area to show an actual growth of jobs (+33 per cent), but the total remains modest (46 759), and internal shifts in sectors showed increases in commerce and services, with a loss in manufacturing (Table 1.5). In short, there are some interesting adjustments taking place spatially, which not only reflect overall trends, but also the nature of the industrial and manufacturing structures that exist in each sector, and their capacity to adjust to deteriorating economic conditions during the late 1980s. Unfortunately, corresponding data do not exist for the boom years 1989–94.

If manufacturing growth has declined, services and commerce annual average growth rates have been generally positive: services grew 3 per cent between 1985 and 1988 (cf. the decline of manufactures of −4.7 per cent), while commerce grew just over 1 per cent. Increasingly these are distributive, professional and administrative services (Sobrino 1992). Those serving local markets appear to be moving out of the city centre towards the first and second ring areas, while 'high tech' services such as electronics, publishing and printing are making a comeback in the central city area (Aguilar Martínez 1993).

TABLE 1.5 Metropolitan employment by sector and by city zone, 1985–88, showing gains and losses within each zone

Zone	Total		Manufacturing		Commerce		Services	
	1985	1988	1985	1988	1985	1988	1985	1988
Centre City[a]: Total numbers employed	666 506	649 185	211 033	176 350	222 366	220 931	233 107	251 904
– % of total share (column per cent)	37.8	37.9	24.5	23.6	43.4	41.7	59.7	57.6
– % employees in zone (row per cent)	100	100	31.7	27.2	33.4	29.5	35.0	38.8
– % change in zone between 1985 and 1988		-2.6		-4.5		-3.9		+3.8
First 'ring'[b]: Total numbers employed	753 776	731 199	414 917	376 539	213 980	216 791	124 879	137 869
– % of total share (column per cent)	42.7	42.6	42.8	50.3	41.8	40.9	32.0	31.5
– % employees in zone (row per cent)	100	100	55.1	51.5	28.4	29.7	16.6	18.9
– % change in zone between 1985 and 1988		-3.0		-3.6		+1.3		+2.3

Second 'ring'[c]:							
Total numbers employed	308 709	287 907	216 611	173 506	63 613	73 122	25 485	41 279
– % of total share (column per cent)	17.5	16.8	25.2	23.2	12.4	13.8	7.3	9.4
– % employees in zone (row per cent)	100	100	70.1	60.2	20.6	25.4	8.3	14.4
– % change in zone between 1985 and 1988		−6.8		−9.9		+3.8		+6.3
Third 'ring'[d]: Total numbers employed	35 110	46 749	18 683	21 636	12 403	18 741	4024	6382
– % of total share (column per cent)	2.0	2.7	2.2	2.9	2.4	3.5	1.0	1.5
– % employees in zone (row per cent)	100	100	52.3	46.2	35.3	40.0	11.4	13.7
– % change in zone between 1985 and 1988		+33.0		−6.1		+4.7		+2.3

Source: Adapted from Rowland and Gordon 1996.

[a] Includes the four central *delegaciones* of Benito Juárez, Cuauhtémoc, Miguel Hidalgo and Venustiano Carranza.

[b] Includes the following *delegaciones/municipios*: Alvaro Obregón, Azcapotzalco, Coyoacán, Gustavo Madero, Iztacalco, Ixtapalapa, Cuajimalpa, Naucalpan, Netzahualcóyotl.

[c] Includes the following *delegaciones/municipios*: Magdalena Contreras, Tlalpan, Xochimilco, Tlahuac, Tlalnepantla, Chimalhuacán, Ecatepec, Atizapán, Coacalco, Huixquilucan, La Paz, Tultitlán, Atenco, Cuautitlán Izcalli.

[d] Includes the following *delegaciones/municipios*: Milpa Alta, Cuautitlán de Romero Rubio, Chalco, Chiautla, Chicoloapan, Chiconcuac, Ixtapaluca, Nicolás Romero, Tecamac, Texcoco.

The important points to recognize are first, a sharp decline in industrial and manufacturing production and jobs in Mexico City, even though in absolute terms the number employed remains substantial. Second, there is a sharp trend towards expansion of the tertiary sector, but this is not in the form of 'petty' informal-sector-type jobs. Much of the expansion in commerce and in services (especially) are in what might be considered formal sector positions.

The changing nature of the urban labour market

Mexico City constitutes one of the largest single labour markets in the world, with over 7 million economically active people within it (Jusidman 1988). According to one study, approximately 37 per cent of those working in metropolitan areas in Mexico were classified as being in the informal sector, which comprises those activities – usually small scale – which carry only small or minimum levels of capital investment and involve low levels of productivity. Moreover, wages are low and personnel engaged in the informal sector are usually not covered by social security or other forms of public welfare protection. In Mexico, self-employed workers may contribute into the social security system but, given the lower levels of benefits they receive, relatively few opt in. Since the 1970s, general understanding of the nature and organization of the informal sector has tended to emphasize the importance of its close connectedness with, but domination by, the formal sector (Bromley 1978). Even informal sector activities such as garbage-picking are often tightly organized and closely tied into the formal sector in terms of the recycled inputs they provide on terms set by the latter (Birkbeck 1978; Castillo *et al.* 1987).

In Mexico City there is a clear trend of inter-related expansion and contraction of the two sectors, with the formal sector growing at the expense of the informal sector during times of economic growth and buoyancy (e.g. 1978–81), and the latter growing as a result of the spare capacity in the labour market during periods such as 1983–7. The proportion of workers employed in the informal sector grew from a low of around 34 per cent in 1981 (when there was actually a labour shortage in unskilled labour for construction, cleaning services and even in some manufacturing industries) to almost 40 per cent in 1987 (Jusidman 1988). This was a result of workers being shed from one sector to another, as well as a tendency for an increase in the participation rates of those members of a household who work (especially women) during periods of economic crisis and declining real-wage levels. Nationally the participation rates of the economically active population increased from 43.6 per cent to 51 per cent between 1970 and 1980. In Mexico City they have always been higher, but they also show a tendency both to increase (47.6 per cent to 53 per cent) and to fluctuate (around a low of about 53 per cent) when times are hard

TABLE 1.6 Per cent of economically active population in Mexico City, by principal worktype and by sex of employee, 1970–80

	1970			1980		
	Total	Men	Women	Total	Men	Women
Professional	10.18	9.69	11.34	11.82	11.01	13.37
Bureaucrats/directors	5.14	6.04	3.07	2.11	2.70	0.99
Administrative personnel	11.59	12.85	22.56	17.01	14.31	22.20
Commerce and sales	11.03	11.18	10.67	10.18	10.36	9.83
Service workers	21.15	15.71	33.68	15.18	12.89	19.60
Agricultural workers	2.41	3.13	0.75	0.85	1.11	0.35
Workers and artisans	31.05	38.14	14.71	26.91	32.81	15.56
Unspecified	3.24	3.25	3.22	15.93	14.81	18.10

Source: Oliveira and García 1987: 145.

and the extra income-earning activities of women, children and the elderly become especially essential to survival (Oliveira and García 1987; Jusidman 1988). The increased rates of economic participation have been especially noticeable in the State of Mexico municipalities between 1970 and 1980 for both men (from 70 per cent to 76 per cent) and women (from 18.6 per cent to 27.6 per cent) (Oliveira and García 1987).

As well as more male and female workers entering the workforce, there have been important structural changes in Mexico City's labour market since the 1950s (Muñoz and Oliveira 1976). Although the overall proportion of those employed in the tertiary sector has not changed greatly, the activities that these personnel fulfil have probably become more 'productive'. Although the data displayed in Table 1.6 at first glance suggest some decline in the importance of service jobs between 1970 and 1980, this is almost certainly due to the larger number in the 'unspecified' jobs category (Oliveira and García 1987). Many of these workers are in the tertiary sector, which the same authors argue continues to absorb around 50 per cent of the total economically active population (Oliveira and García 1997). The absolute expansion of jobs in the tertiary sector is not directly related to migration and a proliferation of urban marginality, nor does it demonstrate rising underemployment (García et al. 1982; Benería 1991). As pointed out earlier, these are genuine jobs, the creation of which is associated with rising tourism and the expansion of service activities associated with industrial change and consumerism, which have intensified since 1988.

Within the tertiary sector, too, while female participation in the labour market is increasing, there also appears to be a segmentation process operating once people are in employment. Patterns of wage inequality between men and women, for example, do not appear to be the result of prejudicial hiring and firing of women relative to men, but are associated more with the allocation of tasks once in employment. Men are more likely than women to be in the 'public space' where their access to tips and higher wages rates is enhanced (Chant 1991).

During the 1970s employment and unemployment changes closely reflected the national economic fortunes described earlier. Within the Federal District the cycles of unemployment associated with economic decline are quite clearly identified (Pommier 1982). Unemployment reached its height in 1977 (at 8.4 per cent of the active population) and dropped regularly thereafter to less than 5 per cent by mid-1980. It rose again in 1982 and 1983, and again in 1995. Compared with men, female workers are particularly vulnerable to unemployment, as are migrants and those workers entering the labour market for the first time (Muñoz *et al.* 1977; Pommier 1982). Certain districts like Netzahualcóyotl have particularly high levels of unemployment and underemployment. Although there was an important rise in unemployment and work was not easily come by during 1977–8 and 1982–3, the situation was almost certainly better in the capital than elsewhere. Also the rate of female participation in the economy of the Federal District is almost twice the national average (García *et al.* 1982). In part this has come about by the expansion of *maquila*-type industries established in Mexico City over the past decade.

Nevertheless, wages are not high. Despite the fact that the majority enjoy regular employment, most are poorly paid. According to one sample, 41 per cent of those employed earned the minimum wage or less, while 60 per cent earned less than twice the official minimum wage (Muñoz *et al.* 1977). Today the minimum wage is no longer an appropriate baseline, but the average wage in Mexico City remains at around US $8.00 per day.

Getting by in Mexico City: survival strategies of the urban poor

At a national level access to social security coverage is unequally distributed both spatially and socially (Ward 1986). Although Mexico City residents fare much better than their provincial counterparts, there are important variations in access across the city – as I shall discuss in later chapters. Also, as I pointed out above, there are important temporal changes in the economic welfare of the city's population which lead to important shifts in economic participation rates, work strategies between sectors and so on, but on a day-to-day basis how do they survive? How do those without social security protection, for example, meet one-off payments such as the costs of a midwife to attend the birth of their children? How can they afford to bury their dead? These may appear to be extreme examples, but they are just a few of the problems that low-income people must regularly confront in Third World cities.

The strategies which poor people adopt to overcome these difficulties have been recognised implicitly for a long time but they have only recently become the subject of detailed study. Few low-income families possess sufficient savings upon which to draw in times of crisis. If hard cash is required and cannot be borrowed from friends or kin, then the alternatives are the pawn shop (assuming that one has an object worth pawning), or loan sharks who charge very high rates of interest. Some households belong to an informal credit system (*tanda*) in which an agreed amount is contributed weekly and each household takes turns to receive the pooled amount. In the event of an unexpected crisis suffered by one member, the group may allow that individual to swap their turn and take that week's savings.

Given a lack of savings and facing job loss or declining real wages, people may respond in a variety of ways. First, they go without. Children drop out of school (or never go in the first place) and take on some sort of employment. People stay ill: stomach complaints go uninvestigated and untreated; minor treatable illnesses become chronic. Meat, if it ever figured in the weekly diet, disappears altogether and is replaced by cheaper but less nourishing substitutes. Likewise leisure pursuits that cost money are dropped. Finally, shelter costs are minimized: cheaper rented accommodation is sought; others squat and construct dwellings made from recycled throwaways. Those who have achieved some security of land holding and through self-help have improved their dwellings to a basic level must suspend consolidation, and may even lose their plot of land through failing to meet repayments.

A second strategy involves adjustments at the household level (Selby *et al.* 1990; Chant 1991; González de la Rocha 1994). Nuclear households may be extended by the inclusion of brothers, sisters, in-laws, married children, etc. Extended family structures offer greater security in that they are likely to have more members engaged in paid employment, so if one person loses their job there is still some income from other sources. Extended family systems also have other advantages, such as mutual child care which allows more adults to work outside the home (Chant 1985, 1991). In Mexico City there is evidence to suggest that the average household size rose from 5.8 to 6.2 in the three-year period 1985–88, and was only noticeable among low-income households. The hypothesis proposed to explain this is that these were strategic adjustments designed to help overcome the social impacts of the crisis (Tuirán Gutiérrez 1992).

Multiple employment strategies in both nuclear and extended households frequently aim to ensure that members are represented in both the formal and informal sectors, thereby enjoying the benefits of both. Having at least one member in the formal sector will usually ensure special health care benefits for the whole family; having others in the informal sector can mean higher earning capacity. During times of wage restraint those working in the public and private sectors may suffer an erosion of purchasing power, while self-employed workers in the informal sector can more readily raise their prices to match inflation (Arias and Roberts 1985; Roberts 1994).

Third, the poor may seek support from a wider social network that embraces kinsfolk, friends and neighbours. Individual circumstances vary of course, but these networks are often critically important sources of credit, food, child care, moral support and accommodation (Lomnitz 1977). Networks may be formalized through godparent relationships (*compadrazgo*) created around a range of events such as confirmation or graduation as well as baptism. Occasionally, economic obligations may be so onerous that better-off families whose support is constantly sought by kinsfolk are forced physically to remove themselves from the residential group in order to reduce the demands upon them (Kemper 1974).

Finally, an important source of welfare protection is patronage from one's employer. To some extent traditional relationships between workers and a patriarchal head of a family enterprise have disappeared as factories and stores get bigger and are run along corporate lines. However, many workers in small firms still go to their boss if they need financial assistance. Similarly, domestic servants and retainers frequently expect their employers to help them and their families in times of difficulty. Usually this involves a loan, cash handouts, medication and payment to visit a private doctor. Middle-class patronage of this nature is rarely analysed or taken into account. Yet it is important both in quantitative terms in the level of protection and assistance it offers, and in ideological and political terms in so far as it reinforces the dependency of one social group upon another and sustains the continuance of discretionary patronage that pervades the social system in Latin America.

DECENTRALIZATION: ATTEMPTS TO REDRESS MEXICO CITY'S PREDOMINANCE

Thus Mexico City presents a dual face. Internationally it is highly dependent, forms part of the global semi-periphery, and has relatively little clout. In some respects its impact and role within the international economy is less important than minor cities such as Santa Cruz in Bolivia, or Medellín in Colombia; both centres of cocaine production and distribution. Yet the paradox is that at a national level it is all powerful and all dominant. In 1990 its 15 million inhabitants comprised approximately one-fifth of the national population. The Urban Development Plan of 1978 highlighted the two extremes: Mexico City on the one hand; and on the other, some 95 000 settlements with less than 2500 inhabitants. In particular the aim has been to stimulate the growth of intermediate-sized urban centres within integrated functional systems (Mexico SAHOP 1978). Politically, the Federal District is the seat of government, and power is heavily centralized in the Executive and in federal agencies and ministries. Mexico City has also enjoyed a privileged access to employment opportunities compared with most other urban centres. In 1980 the Federal District alone received 54 per cent of all private investment (Makin 1984). In terms of consumption of electricity, transport, water and public utilities, those living in the city are heavily subsidised (Bazdresch 1986).

In the area of social welfare facilities the city does better than the provinces. The Federal District has three times as many doctors per capita than elsewhere. The number of people covered by some form of social security is twice as high as the national average. School facilities are better in the Federal District and children are not only more likely to attend school, but also to complete the various stages of schooling. Similarly, the lion's share of investment resources for public housing have been directed towards the Metropolitan Area. Between 1963 and 1975, for example, 58 per cent of the public housing units constructed for the poor and for lower-middle-income groups were built within the Metropolitan Area (Garza and Schteingart 1978).

Therefore it was not surprising that people flocked to the City (although migration has long since been displaced by natural increase as the primary determinant of growth). The impact of the economic crisis upon jobs in Mexico City, and the slow expansion of economic opportunities elsewhere, meant that the rate of in-migration slowed during the 1980s; so much so that the latest census data suggest a net migration loss to the metropolitan area (see Chapter 2). Although in the past most Mexico City residents were loathe to leave the city, notwithstanding the quality-of-life horror stories to which I alluded in the original (1990) Preface, it appears that since the late 1980s there is a greater willingness to move to the provinces if the opportunity arises.

Chilangos rule OK?

People born in the Federal District are known as *chilangos*. In Mexico the use of nicknames for people is very common and rarely ill-intentioned or taken badly. However, for many in the provinces the term *chilango* is increasingly associated with antipathy and resentment. As a Federation, Mexico has, until recently, looked to different states for its national leaders, and although the centre benefited more than anywhere else, so, too, did those regions from which top leaders and camp-followers were drawn. Part of the problem today is the emergence of a new, more technocratic élite educated (if not born) in the capital and whose origins and loyalties are less regionally oriented. Moreover, as noted above, the Federal District is beginning to export people as a result of public-sector efforts at decentralization to provincial towns and as middle-class intellectuals decide that the diseconomies of the city no longer offer professional and personal attractions as they did in the past. However, the resentment traditionally felt in the provinces about Mexico City's preferential treatment is nothing compared with the tension and anger expressed today against many *chilangos* who are perceived to be taking housing and jobs which ought, by rights, to be destined for local people. They are also accused of driving up land and housing prices, and generally acting with arrogance and a lack of sensitivity. *'Sé patriota – mata un chilango'* (Be patriotic – kill a *chilango*) is a sad, but not uncommon, piece of graffiti to be found in provincial cities.

Decentralization programmes

In addition to arguments relating to greater equity and a reduction in regional disparities, there are various other reasons why decentralization programmes have figured prominently in government rhetoric in recent years. The need to contain the growth of Mexico City and to deflect migration to alternative 'growth poles' was one motive, as was the desire to move towards a more 'log normal' distribution of urban population (Mexico SAHOP 1978). Better utilization of national resources and the industrial development of petrochemicals, together with the need to stimulate growth in towns and cities throughout the territory, informed the Industrial Secretariat's Development Plan of 1979. Politically, too, in the provinces, where the government party (the PRI) had traditionally been very strong, several major cities were captured by the right wing opposition party (PAN) and the image of the PRI had become rather tarnished. By the late 1970s and early 1980s there was a perceived need among government supporters for the centre to assist the periphery in its efforts to restore legitimacy to state and municipal governments and to reinforce support for the party apparatus.

The most strenuous efforts at decentralization were made between 1982 and 1988 under the De la Madrid administration, but the concept of decentralization may cover many meanings. Where it embraces some devolution then it may involve a genuine shift in power and autonomy to peripheral regions. However, *deconcentration* may achieve some shift in resources, people and plant, but it does not, necessarily, invoke a shift in the spatial locus of power. It may simply transfer specific faculties to a subordinate person or administrative entity (Rodríguez 1992, 1997). The central superior body retains the possibility of control. Genuine *devolution* of power in Mexico has been resisted, and the main purpose and effects of De la Madrid's decentralization policies were to establish a system which is decentralized administratively but remains centralized politically (Rodríguez 1997). Although the new legislation reasserting the principle of municipal autonomy and freedom offered potential powers of devolution to the grassroots in practice, the initiative was 'hijacked' by state governors who appropriated the power and resources intended ostensibly for the municipality (Rodríguez 1987). Only in the cases of 'opposition' governments, especially those of the PAN, was the chain of command and orthodoxy broken, such that these non-PRI city governments could assert themselves and exercise greater autonomy (Rodríguez and Ward 1992,

1994b). Thus, although there was some slight reaccommodation in the political centre of gravity towards the states, this did not go far enough; nor did it usually percolate down to the municipal level.

Some decentralization of public administration was achieved during the 1980s. The public health system was decentralized, as were several 'light-weight' government departments and institutes (Beltrán and Portilla 1986; Jeannetti Dávila 1986; González Block *et al.* 1989), but the lack of full political commitment to decentralization was laid bare by the government's response to the earthquake in 1985. The worst damage was sustained in the inner city of the capital, and large-scale financing was generated from national fiscal resources as well as from loans through the World Bank. Instead of using these resources to undertake reconstruction outside Mexico City and to relocate those people who had lost their homes, the government opted for the politically less contentious strategy of rehousing the popu-lation *in situ*. Moreover, the financial terms on which rehousing low-income households was undertaken represented another major subsidy. In real terms, cost recovery was minimal on the special fiscal resources generated. The opportunity to use those funds as seed capital for a national housing programme was given up – for political reasons.

Although these changes did not auger well for extensive decentralization, in retrospect De la Madrid's initiatives do appear to have paved the way for genuine decentralization. Salinas also engaged in much of the decentraliza-tion rhetoric during his presidential election campaign, yet there was little evidence in his policy making of an explicit commitment to decentralization. Implicitly, though, his social welfare programme PRONASOL was targeted at municipal and sub-municipal poor communities. In effect this brought in major federal resources to strengthen municipal communities – a policy which was reinforced by major programme loans from the World Bank in 1993–94 (Rodríguez 1997).

The whole issue of decentralization came alive in 1994–95 with President Zedillo's so-called New Federalism program (Zedillo 1995, 1996). While there is little evidence that this constitutes a strategy or a clear set of policies, many of the current administration's initiatives are leading to greater effective decentralization (Aguilar Villanueva 1996; Rodríguez and Ward 1996; Rodríguez 1997). *Inter alia* these include: vertical decentraliza-tion of the health and education sectors to be managed entirely by the states; the shifting of 78 per cent of the *Ramo XXVI* (former PRONASOL) line of funding to be directly administered by the municipalities and states; new tax and revenue creation possibilities for the states; revision of the federal revenue-sharing formula to raise (slightly) the amount redistributed to the states. In addition, one is seeing a horizontal decentralization process as power is shared between the three branches of government (executive, legislature and judiciary) at national and at state levels (Rodríguez and Ward 1996; Rodríguez 1997). In effect this is lessening the traditional overarching power of the executive level, and creating greater opportunities for other powers to come to the fore. The argument is that decentralization has become an imperative if government is to be made more efficient in future, if Mexico is going to be able to respond adequately to the development that it faces, and if the PRI is to have a chance of holding onto the reins of power. In this sense, the aim is to 'retain power by giving it away' (Rodríguez 1997).

Mexico City's national predominance will undoubtedly remain, but important shifts may be observed as its economic dominance begins to decline, and as its population decentralizes and moves towards a period of static growth. The revolution in telecommunications on the one hand, and the decentralization of industrial activity on the other, have made traditional agglomeration economies of a location in Mexico City redundant. Other metropolitan regions are the 'hot' spots. Moreover, the political opening has lessened the dominance of the capital and begun to strengthen the opportunities and importance in the states and municipalities. No longer is life outside of Mexico City like living in Cuautitlán (the boonies). How the city is accommodating to this downsizing – at least of its role – and how far it is able to develop new systems of political management, administration and planning will determine whether it survives, thrives or falls apart. This is the subject of the following chapters.

2

URBAN GROWTH AND THE APPROPRIATION OF SPACE: FROM PLAZA TO SUBURB TO MEGACITY

INTRODUCTION: THE GROWTH OF *LA REGIÓN MÁS TRANSPARENTE*

La región más transparente is the title of a novel about Mexico City written by the contemporary Mexican author Carlos Fuentes. Usually translated as 'Where the air is clear' it describes a clarity and sharpness of light in the Central Valley that was truly remarkable – at least until the early 1960s. Since that time, clear days, when as a daily feature of the landscape one could see 50 kilometres to the distant snowcapped volcanoes of Popocatépetl and Iztaccíhuatl, have become so rare that they are something of a novelty worthy of comment and photographs in the following day's newspapers.

In 1996 Mexico City, with just over 16 million inhabitants, was the fourth largest city in the world after New York/Jersey, Tokyo/Yokohama, and São Paulo (Gilbert 1996: 2). Unlike two of its slightly larger counterparts, however, it is a single city rather than two or more large urban centres which merge into a single metropolitan area (Hauser in Brambila 1987). However, league tables based upon city size do not mean very much. More important are the processes and dynamics of city growth and the effects that these have upon the life chances of its citizens. In the previous chapter I examined Mexico City's role in the national and international division of labour and spelt out the changing nature of job and income-earning opportunities for the city's population. I want now to describe the impact that some of these economic processes have had upon city growth. Specifically, I want to exemplify how social inequality is embedded within the spatial structure of the city. Later chapters in this book will address the extent to which these inequalities are changing in ways that are socially progressive or regressive.

My focus in this book is unashamedly contemporary, but it is important to recognize that Mexico City is not only the largest single urban area on the continent, but is also one of the oldest. Located in an upland basin some 7000 feet above sea level, the Spanish *conquistadores* built their colonial city upon the ruins of Tenochtitlán – the capital of Moctezuma's Aztec Empire. Indeed this was the final phase (albeit one of the most splendid) of several periods of urban or ceremonial-centre development in the Central Valley which has left pyramids in Cuicuilco (now adjacent to the southern peripheral motorway) dating from 400 BC, and at Teotihuacán (some 30 km to the north-east) which flourished around 300 AD (Hardoy 1967). In the final chapter of this book I will return to describe briefly the city's early history. Here I wish only to note the important pre-Columbian origins and to encourage the interested reader to explore that history with others more competent than I (Durán 1967; Calnek 1975, 1976; Sanders *et al.* 1979).

Nor do I wish to dwell upon Mexico City's development during the colonial period, when it flourished as the political and economic centre for New Spain ruled by proxy through a series of viceroys until independence early in the nineteenth century. Thereafter the city was the seat of power for a series of rulers with often dubious and spurious legitimacy, such as the self-imposed Emperor Iturbide 1822–4, the Archduke Maximilian imposed by a French expeditionary force in 1863, and a series of elected presidents, the most notable of whom was Benito Juárez whose death in 1872 heralded the rise to supreme power of the dictator Porfirio Díaz. The latter ruled Mexico with an iron hand between 1876 and 1910 before being displaced by the Revolution (Lombardo 1987; Kandell 1988). From the outset, the colonial city was laid out on a grid-iron pattern as prescribed by the Spanish monarchy and later embodied in the Laws of the Indies established by Philip II in 1573 (Stanislawski 1947). The central plaza was the seat of the principal Council buildings, the Treasury and the Cathedral, while the rich lived in large residences on the main streets running east and north. Once established the colonial city expanded relatively little between 1700 and the mid-nineteenth century, covering an area of approximately 6–10 km² (Morales 1987; Connolly 1988a). It was not until the stability and economic growth of the *Porfiriato* that physical city expansion began in earnest (Rodríguez Kuri 1996). Both the colonial period and the nineteenth century development of Mexico City are the focus of a large number of wonderful pieces of historiography, and I feel guilty about not pausing, at least for a while, in order to explore some of these analyses, many of which have been informed by archives held in my own University here in Texas. However, it is Mexico's recent dynamics that are the focus of this book, and I must simply leave the reader with a number of pointers to some of the texts on Mexico City's pre-twentieth-century development (Arrom 1985; Arnold 1988; Jiménez 1993; Lear 1993; Hernández Franyuti 1994; Rodríguez Kuri 1996; Tenorio-Trillo 1996; Piccato 1997).

From the very earliest settlement to the present day the site has been an impressive one. The Central Valley is surrounded by volcanic mountains, two of which rise 10–12 000 feet above the valley floor. Much of the area was a saline inland lake, and even during Aztec times fresh water had to be brought to the city by aqueduct. Today, most of the lake is gone and once-marshy land is covered by a swathe of low-income settlements. Although smog and pollution restrict visibility across the city, on days that are clear or at night when driving down from mountain passes on the Toluca or Cuernavaca high roads, the sight is spectacular and awesome. I can think of no other place in the world where so much humanity is laid out and visible to the naked eye (see Figure 2.1, satellite photograph).

NATIONAL DEMOGRAPHY AND URBAN GROWTH: MEXICO CITY IN PERSPECTIVE

Before proceeding to analyse that specific humanity, let us take a brief look at Mexico's national demographic development trends which shape the backcloth for Mexico City itself – with one-fifth of the population. Many people, when they think about Mexico's development or underdevelopment, tend to lay the principal cause for sluggish development and poverty upon rapid population increase, and particularly upon high rates of natural increase. In part, this reflects a strong tradition in development thinking during the 1960s which emphasized the need to achieve a 'demographic transition' in less-developed countries similar to that achieved in the late nineteenth century in much of Europe. Failure to achieve a decline in birth rates to match the sharp decline in death rates that resulted from immunization campaigns, better health care and so on, threatened to overwhelm these countries with a population that they could not support. This neo-Malthusian thinking was pervasive during the 1960s and 1970s, and among some circles remains today. This is not to suggest that rapid population increase is not a development issue: it is. But it is not *the* issue. As we have already observed, Mexico's most rapid period of economic growth coincided with the most rapid period of population expansion and migration to cities and to Mexico City in particular (1940s–1960s). In fact, these processes were closely related, particularly the movement of people into the metropolitan areas in order to man (for it was mostly men) the factories established as part of the import-substituting industrialization programme (ISI). People did not move out of the countryside simply because they had little potential livelihood as peasants – this had been the case for many of the younger people for many years. Rather, they moved because the demand for labour in the factories promoted and required their movement. Similarly, an emerging middle class and the need for cheap services created a fierce demand for domestic servants. Young men and women moved to the cities to fill the demand for labour.

Once in place, and saving a moratorium upon marriage or a strict population control policy, urban areas quickly developed a population age structure in which the young parent cohort bases were heavily loaded – to mix metaphors. This potentially fertile population would generate a population structure with a very broad base in the young infant and child-age cohorts. Even if population control measures were adopted and birth

FIGURE 2.1 Satellite photograph of the Metropolitan Area

rates were quickly brought down to the replacement rate, the population was always going to continue to grow, as today's children (already born) have children of their own. It takes approximately 70 years for a young population structure to move into equilibrium, and for zero growth to be achieved. Recognition of this simple demographic fact is salutory and important, since it obliges us to do two things. First, to take appropriate steps in order to create the conditions whereby rates of natural increase will be brought down, and second, to develop policies that will cope with the inevitable expansion that is built into the population structure. Population control does not become the be-all and end-all of urban development or national development policy.

Mexico's demography is both fairly typical of middle-income developing countries, and also encouraging. Many of the data profiles shown in Table 2.1 are typical: (1) high national population growth rates from 13.6 million at the turn of the century to 16.5 million in 1930, 48 million in 1970 and over 80 million in 1990; (2) high birth rates and annual rates of increase from the 1950s to the 1970s; (3) a fast decline in the death rate and rising life expectancy at birth; (4) a population shift from predominantly rural to predominantly urban (cf. 1930 and 1980). As well as being encouraged by improving survival rates of infants and life expectancy, one of the most significant features of Table 2.1 and of Mexico's recent demographic trends is the fast declining rate of natural increase – from 3.3 per cent per annum during the 1960s and 1970s, to less than 2 per cent since 1980 (Benítez Zenteno 1995). Given that Mexico only developed a population policy in the early 1970s this is impressive, and it is in large part due to the responsibility shown by Mexicans to adjust their family size to the changing economic conditions observed in Chapter 1.

In terms of urbanization, by 1970 Mexico was an urbanized country. However, the distribution of the urban population was extremely skewed, with the 'primate city' of Mexico (8.5 million) dominating the next largest two cities of Guadalajara (1.5 million) and Monterrey (1.25 million). In 1978 the National Urban Development Plan (PNDU) identified the magnitude of the problem more in terms of the urban structure than in terms of city size *per se*. On the one hand were the 20 per cent of the national population living in a single city, while on the other, there were over 95 000 population centres with less than 2500 people. The challenge was to develop an urban policy that might begin to integrate population centres into a more structured and efficient system and sub-system of centres. Thus Mexican urban policy since 1978 has sought to control and consolidate the process of development in the largest metropolitan centres, and to encourage and promote the development of so-called intermediate (sized) cities within a series of regional urban systems (Castro Castro 1995; Aguilar *et al.* 1996). This promotion of 100 intermediate-sized cities was opportune since, as I outlined in Chapter 1, the economic imperatives of export-orientated manufacturing growth and

TABLE 2.1 Mexico: national population increase and demographic indicators, 1930–90

	1930	1940	1950	1960	1970	1980	1990
Total national population (millions)	16 553	19 653	25 791	34 293	48 225	66 847	81 141
Population growth							
% annual increase[a]	1.6	1.7	2.8	3.1	3.3	3.3	1.9
Birth rate[b]	49.5	48.1	45.6	46.1	44.2	35.0	29.0
Mortality[c]	26.7	22.8	16.2	11.5	10.1	6.2	6.0
Natural increase[d]	na	25.3	29.4	34.6	34.1	28.8	na
Net migration[e]	na	-3.7	-4.7	-4.1	-3.7	-1.2	na
Growth rate[f]	na	21.6	24.7	30.5	30.4	27.6	22.0
Population dispersion							
Density[g]	8.4	10.0	13.1	17.8	24.5	34.0	43.6
% rural[h]	66.5	64.9	57.4	49.3	41.3	33.7	27.5
% urban[i]	33.5	35.1	42.6	50.7	58.7	66.3	72.5
% small city[j]	na	8.1	9.3	10.8	9.4	10.0	na
% middle city[k]	na	4.0	7.5	11.6	13.3	16.5	na
% large city[l]	na	7.9	11.1	14.9	22.9	26.2	na
Demographic indicators of quality of life							
% illiterate	na	37.21	30.38	34.67	19.81	13.88	9.65
Life expectancy (years)							
Average	36.1	40.4	50.6	58.6	61.5	66.8	na
Males	na	39.5	49.1	57.1	59.5	63.7	na
Females	na	41.5	52.1	60.1	63.6	69.9	na
Fertility[m]	na	na	19.6	19.2	17.6	16.6	15.3
Infant mortality[n]	131.64	125.69	96.2	74.19	68.46	46.6	43.0

Source: Various population censuses.

[a]Average annual per cent increase for the decade. [b]Average annual number of live births per 1000 inhabitants. [c]Average annual number of deaths per 1000 inhabitants. [d]Average annual population increase per 1000 due to births minus deaths. [e]Average annual population increase per 1000 due to migration (negative figures = emigration). [f]Total average population increase per 1000 inhabitants. [g]Average population density in inhabitants per square kilometre. [h]Per cent population in localities with fewer than 2500 inhabitants. [i]Per cent population in localities with more than 2500 inhabitants. [j]Per cent population in localities with 15 000–99 999 inhabitants. [k]Per cent population in localities with 100 000–999 999 inhabitants. [l]Per cent population in localities with more than one million inhabitants. [m]Number of registered births per 1000 women aged 15–49. [n]Number of deaths within the first year of birth per 1000 live births.

maquiladora expansion was being concentrated in medium-sized cities. Intercensal data showing the growth rates show that the fastest growing cities during the 1980s were those of 50 000–100 000 people (5.0 per cent per annum), whereas the large metropolitan areas of over one-million people grew at only 1.2 per cent per annum during the same period. Cities of 250 000–500 000 grew second fastest – at 4.3 per cent per annum (Aguilar Martínez and Graizbord 1992). This suggests that Mexico, too, is undergoing a 'polarization reversal' whereby rapid growth of intermediate-size cities begins to redress the balance of polarization of growth away from one particularly dominant city, leading to a more balanced urban structure (Townroe and Keen 1984; cf. Gwynne 1985; Gilbert 1996). The latest Mexican version of urban development policy in Mexico, published in 1996, is developed against the background of growing deregulation and insertion into the global economy discussed in the preceding chapter, as well as the concerted efforts to reinforce federalist structures through decentralization focusing upon the 100 Cities Programme (Mexico SEDESOL 1996).

The years after the Revolution saw a sharp rise in the City's population as stability began to draw back many of those who had fled the strife and as camp-followers joined the principal protagonists of those vying for power. Between 1921 and 1930 the population of the central city grew from 615 000 to over 1 million (Negrete Salas and Salazar 1987; Sánchez Almanza 1993). Once the traumas of the Revolution were over the city grew steadily and the pace quickened, with industrialization from the 1930s onwards. The population of the 'urban area of Mexico City' grew by 4 per cent per annum during the 1930s, and this rose to over 6 per cent between 1940 and 1950; until the early 1970s or so it appeared to be continuing to grow at 5.5 per cent per annum.

The 1980 census indicated a significant slowing in this trend, but even so that census is widely regarded as being seriously flawed and as having overestimated the Metropolitan Area's population by almost one million, and CONAPO officials have since adjusted the estimates to a 1980 level of 13.7 million (see also Camposortega Cruz 1992; Salas Paéz 1992; Garza and Rivera 1995; Monnet 1995). It appears that between 1970 and 1990 the rate of increase declined to an average of 2.3 per cent (Table 2.2), giving a 1990 total population of 14.7 million. Analysts offer different figures from the official census showing a range from 14.7 to 15.8, although these higher figures may include population from the metropolitan zone and not just the metropolitan (built-up) area (see for example Camposortega Cruz 1992.) Since 1990 the growth rate is argued to be around 1.5 per cent (CONAPO 1996: 1; Rowland and Gordon 1996). This means that all of the projections for Mexico City's population in the year 2000 and beyond must be drastically revised. Scenarios of 26–30 million which seemed not unrealistic some 10 years ago are now gross overestimations (see for example Delgado 1988 and my own estimates in the first edition). If we take the baseline

TABLE 2.2 Mexico City's population growth 1940–90 for different 'rings' of expansion

	Total population (millions) and decennial growth rates (%)								
	1940		1950		1960		1970		1990
Metropolitan Area	1.64	6.7	3.14	5.6	5.4	5.5	9.2	2.3	14.7
Percentage in DF	107[a]		103[a]		96		80		56
Central city area	1.44	4.5	2.2	2.3	2.8	0.6	2.7	−2.1	2.7
First 'ring' areas[b]	0.18	15.8	0.8	10.2	2.2	8.3	4.9	1.9	7.6
Second 'ring' areas[c]	0.01	–	0.05	–	0.4	14.2	1.3	6.3	3.3
Third 'ring' areas[d]	–	–	–	–	–		0.01	22.3	0.8

Source: Adapted from Negrete Salas and Salazar 1987: 128; and from Rowland and Gordon 1996: 179. 1980 data excluded because of misleading growth rate information.

[a] 1940 and 1950 figures exceed 100% because some population centres within the Federal District were located outside the built-up area of Mexico City.

[b] Includes the following *delegaciones/municipios*: Alvaro Obregón, Azcapotzalco, Coyoacán, Gustavo Madero, Iztacalco, Ixtapalapa, Cuajimalpa, Naucalpan, Netzahualcóyotl.

[c] Includes the following *delegaciones/municipios*: Magdalena Contreras, Tlalpan, Xochimilco, Tlahuac, Tlalnepantla, Chimalhuacán, Ecatepec, Atizapán, Coacalco, Huixquilucan, La Paz, Tultitlán, Atenco, Cuautitlán Izcalli.

[d] Includes the following *delegaciones/municipios*: Milpa Alta, Cuautitlán de Romero Rubio, Chalco, Chiautla, Chicoloapan, Chiconcuac, Ixtapaluca, Nicolás Romero, Tecamac, Texcoco.

figure of 14.7 in 1990 and 15.64 in 1995, then the total population in the year 2000 will be 18 million or thereabouts (CONAPO 1996).

The dynamics of city growth derive from provincial migration and from natural increase. The latter has been most important, and although birth rates were lower in the Metropolitan Area than elsewhere in Mexico, they remained high until the late 1970s, when they began a sharp decline. Crude birth rates for the city have declined from 44.7 per thousand inhabitants (44.7/000) in 1950–60 to 37/000 in 1970–80, and 26/000 in 1990. Death rates have declined from 12.9/000 to 7.3/000 to 4.6/000 during the same period (Partida 1987b; CONAPO 1996). Mortality and morbidity rates for the city appear higher than for many areas of Mexico, but this may reflect more assiduous reporting and the higher level of treatment available in the capital (Fox 1972).

Migration is also an important factor, although its relative weight is often overstated. During the early decades of the City's growth, when the demand from industry for labour was high, migration flows accounted for around 60 per cent of population expansion, with the remainder the result of natural increase (Unikel 1972), but in the absence of a sharp decline in the birth rate achieved nationally or locally until the late 1970s, natural increase quickly took over as the principal component of city growth. The initial in-migration of young adults accentuates those cohorts about to embark upon the family-building stages of their life cycles. For example, at the Metropolitan level, decennial rates of annual natural increase declined from

3.18 per cent to 2.97 per cent between 1950 and 1960 and between 1970 and 1980, respectively, while the proportion attributed to migration fell from 1.66 per cent to 1.09 per cent to 0.1 per cent between 1980 and 1990 (Camposortega Cruz 1992: 8). Indeed, as I will explain later, some downtown areas of the Federal District have been losing population through out-migration to the suburbs (see also Graizbord and Mina 1995). Nevertheless, cityward migration added an estimated 38 per cent to the city's net population between 1950 and 1980 (Partida 1987a), but according to CONAPO it has begun to show a net negative balance as population decentralization overtakes in-migration to the outlying areas of the metropolitan zone (CONAPO 1996: 16; see also Corona Cuapio and Luque González 1992; Graizbord and Mina 1995). In 1978 the Metropolitan Area's growth rate was 4.45 per cent per annum, comprising 2.30 per cent natural increase and 2.15 per cent migration (Stolarski 1982). According to the National Population Council (CONAPO) the aim was to reduce this to 3.51 per cent by 1982 and to 1.64 per cent by the year 2000, with most of the decline relating to natural increase. In fact, if we accept that Mexico City is now experiencing a net migration loss, then the current rate of natural increase of 2.1 per cent puts them more or less on track for the year 2000 (but see below).

Province-to-city migrants do not usually move much further than they have to in order to satisfy the original reasons for their move (Cornelius 1975; Gilbert and Ward 1986). In Mexico City, by far the largest proportion came from adjacent states or from those that were relatively near (Ward 1976a; Stern 1977: 126). During the earlier stages of out-movement from villages and towns there is evidence that migrants are 'positively selected' from among their home population and tend to be slightly better-off, better educated and more venturesome than those who stay (Balán *et al.* 1973; Kemper 1974, 1976). Combined with ready access to work in the expanding industrial base during the 1950s and 1970s, it is not surprising that one observes few economic or housing-improvement differences between city-born people and migrants, even where lower education opportunities in rural areas have led to significantly lower levels of schooling (Gilbert and Ward 1986).

Thus at least until the mid- to late-1970s, when access to job opportunities and land markets began to tighten, migrants to Mexico City do not appear to have been disadvantaged relative to city-born inhabitants. Nor is there a general tradition in Mexico City of migrants from particular regions or villages concentrating themselves spatially and almost exclusively in one or two neighbourhoods, although some anthropological studies of specific groups do give a contrary view (Butterworth 1972; Orellana 1973; Lomnitz 1977). Although kin and *paisanos* (people from the same village) are very important in providing orientation and assistance to newly arrived migrants, the large size of most Mexico City neighbourhoods and the sorting processes associated with selection of permanent residence make unlikely the local dominance of migrants from a single region. However, information flows and antecedent kin contacts do lead to some minor (but not dominant) concentration in particular settlements. Within settlements or tenements some spatial clustering and concentration may be observed.

Spatially this population growth has led to a 'wave' of rapid population expansion moving outwards, first through the Federal District (DF) and then into the surrounding State of Mexico (Table 2.2). Prior to 1940, the central area of the city absorbed most of the population increase until rapid suburbanization processes began to take over during the 1940s. Thereafter, as the population began to soar, many city centre residents began to move out to the intermediate ring *delegaciones* (boroughs), several of which tripled or quadrupled their population between 1940 and 1950 and doubled it further during the 1950s (Figure 2.2). A ban imposed in 1954 upon the authorization of low-incomes sub-divisions in the DF also led to some premature movement into the adjacent State of Mexico municipalities of Netzahualcóyotl and Naucalpan where the law did not apply. This process was accentuated later once the wave spread out further into other munici-palities during the 1960s and 1970s. In addition to those municipalities already mentioned, Tlalnepantla and Ecatepec expanded greatly at this time, as did some southern *delegaciones* of the Federal District. Since the 1980s the wave of growth has run into the more distant municipalities of Cuautitlán, Tecamac and Chalco, today's rapid-growth areas (Hiernaux 1995). For every immigrant that the DF receives, six migrants leave to municipalities in the State of Mexico (Graizbord and Mina 1995: 107). It was predicted that the population of Tecamac will grow from around 156 000 in 1987 to over 1 million by the turn of the century (Delgado 1988). However, this population count was reduced in the 1990 census (to 123 000), and while Tecamac remains one of the few 'hot spots' in Mexico City's contem-porary growth, it is not likely to approach Delgado's earlier predicted figure.

If, as it would appear, migration is to play a relatively minor role in Mexico City's future growth, then the age/sex population pyramids can help us to understand the future principal demographic challenge. Figures 2.3a and b depict the changes underway. In 1970 the pyramid was a classic broad-based shape with a very high dependency ratio of children aged less than 15 years (i.e. not formally in the workforce). Above this dependent group in the pyramid – over 40 per cent of the population – are the new generations of workers, often recent migrants to the city, or first-generation children of migrants who arrived in the 1950s. Many of these younger adults are at the early stages of their family-building and careers, or still have their child-rearing years before them. This means that the population is likely to grow depending upon the now desired number of children, and the capacity of families to effectively curtail further growth once they have achieved their 'optimum size'. The effects of the sharp decline in fertility rates from the 1970s onwards is clearly observed in the population pyramid

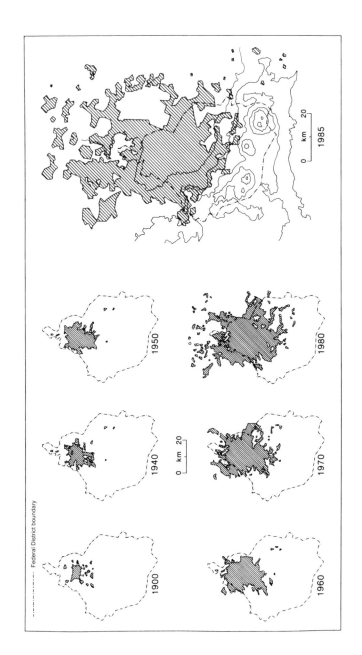

FIGURE 2.2 The physical expansion of the Metropolitan Area 1900–1985

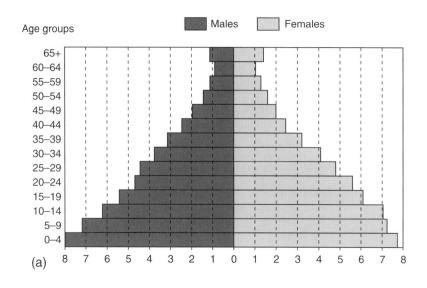

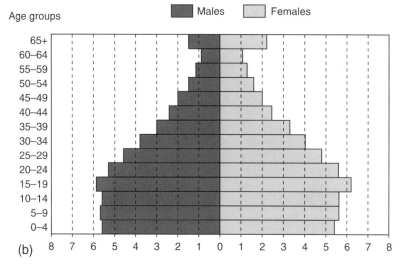

FIGURE 2.3 Population 'pyramids' for Mexico City: a, 1970; b, 1990. Source: XI and XIII *Censo General de Población*, 1970, 1990

for 1990 (Figure 2.3b), but the pyramid remains heavily 'loaded' in the young parent age group (20–35), and while the lower cohorts have become more truncated, they still remain over 30 per cent of the total. Unless a large proportion leave the city or become celibate, these are the next generation of parents – already born. The whole demographic equation, therefore, hinges upon these future parents' decisions regarding family size.

Another element in the demographic equation upon which the pyramids shed light is Mexico's changing social policy needs. All countries that have experienced a baby-boom have had to address the need to contract certain social services (primary school education for example), and to expand new ones. For most developed countries today the increasing size of the dependent population comes from the aged (nominally over 65) and the retired populations. This is creating major new social challenges, particularly where that country – France, for example – has moved into overall negative growth. While Mexico does not face that problem, nor is it likely to for very many years, it is having to shift its attention from a single vision of how to provide a particular service (given its poverty and lack of resources), to a dual vision that includes not only provision, but also *changing* provision needs. Mexico City will have to take the lead here, since it has enjoyed relatively privileged access to resources (i.e. they have, generally, been provided; see Chapter 6), and since it has a fast-changing population structure. In my view, one of the major challenges for Mexico City today, and for the next two decades at least, is how to cater for the social needs of young middle-aged cohorts.

Mexico City's short-term demographic future: the debate

This brings us to the crux of the debate. We probably should accept the revised census figures for 1980, but exercise caution in any analysis of the data. Some analysts ignore it altogether and project the trend using 1970 and 1990 data (Monnet 1995; Rowland and Gordon 1996). I am reluctant to do the same and prefer to keep the 1980 data, but often I, too, will scan the 1970–90 trajectory most closely and be circumspect about exaggerated trends suggested by the 1980 data. Until the next census, however, we will not be able to be definitive about the accuracy of the 1990 base level, and assuming that it is shown to have been accurate, only then may we ditch the 1980 census for good – as an expensive and highly misleading aberration.

Looking beyond the revised predictions of 18 million by the year 2000, and estimating to the year 2010, the figures arrived at depend entirely upon the assumptions made about the dynamics of the two principal variables discussed above: the rate of natural increase, and net migration. At a recent (1996) meeting at which I was privileged to participate as a discussant of CONAPO projections, I took issue with assumptions which, to me, seemed overly optimistic and contained an element of wishful thinking, no matter how sharp the downturn has been over the last 15 years. As observed above, CONAPO's projections estimate a total population of 18 million in the year 2000 and 20 million a decade later in 2010. This halving of the projected decennial increase from 1990 to 2000 and from 2001 to 2010 is predicated upon natural increase declining from 2.1 to 1.1 per cent from

1990 to 2010, and on the average fertility rate of 2.8 children per woman in her fertile years declining very early in the 21st century to 2.1 (i.e. the intergenerational replacement rate), and dropping to a negative replacement rate of 1.9 by 2010. Given the age/sex pyramids discussed earlier and the high potential for growth – notwithstanding the achievement of intergenerational replacement rate – it seems to me inevitable that the population will be considerably higher than that envisaged by CONAPO.

Of course the other side of the coin is net migration, and here, too, CONAPO anticipates an overall net loss for the Metropolitan Area. Although the Commission recognizes that some of the flow outwards from the DF is into the state of Mexico, and that there is also a minor flow from the province to peripheral municipalities, it argues that this is offset by the decentralization of population out of the metropolitan region altogether. They estimate a small net loss of 6 out of every 10 000 inhabitants each year (0.006 per cent). While I agree that the new inflow into the conurbation will be modest, I am less convinced about the extent to which such a large population is actively decanting out of the region through a process of decentralization. There is some decentralization from the DF to surrounding municipalities, but until we have data from the next population census it is probably premature to be too bullish about active out-migration from the region, New Federalism and political decentralization notwithstanding. Having based my last predictions upon the 1980 census and, like almost everyone else, got it so badly wrong, I am loathe to stick my neck out again. However, I suspect that finding the next one per cent decline in natural increase among Mexico City's parent population cohorts (i.e. from the 2.1 per cent in 1990) is going to prove more difficult to achieve. My informed guess is that the population in 2000 will be over 18 million, and that in 2010 it will be considerably closer to 22 million than the 20 million predicted by CONAPO (see also Camposortega Cruz 1992). Whatever and whoever is proved correct, these are nevertheless dramatic reductions on previous forecasts, and Mexico should be congratulated for having achieved a demographic transition in a single generation.

The physical expansion of the built-up area

Until the latter part of the nineteenth century Mexico City was confined to what is often referred to as the First Quarter (*Primer Cuadro*), comprising an area of about 20 km^2 centred around the Zócalo or main *plaza* (Morales 1987). In Chapter 7, I analyse the architectural influences and urban investment interests which shaped the beginnings of the move outwards on the part of the élite, and only brief mention will be made here. Traditionally, the élite lived in and around the city centre in large palaces and residences close to the prestigious main square and its municipal and ecclesiastical buildings (Schnore 1966; Scobie 1974). The poor lived in precarious hovels and tenements well away from these streets, but remained within walking distance of their place of work. Transport to the outlying townships was by private or public carriage, but there was no daily commuting (Vidrio 1987; Rodríguez Kuri 1996).

In Mexico City, as elsewhere in Latin America, the movement of the élite out of the city centre was predicated upon a changing social base in which displays of status through housing and consumption were fast becoming a substitute for status ascribed through birth. A new political élite, economic mobility, and an emerging class of *nouveau riche* and middle classes led to property development in the physically most attractive areas of the (then) periphery. This was to the south and west, down the *Paseo de la Reforma* (the Mexican equivalent of Paris's *Champs Elysées*) which had been designed as a splendid boulevard during the nineteenth century to link the Executive's official residence (Chapultepec Castle) and his workplace at the National Palace in the Zócalo. Congestion in the city centre was becoming problematic, as was the fear of exposure to dangerous diseases. Many wealthy élites already had summer houses in outlying *pueblos* such as Tacubaya, Mixcoac and Coyoacán. During the earlier period only they could afford private horse-drawn transport, but the improved roads facilitated greater and more continued use of these residences.

Animal-drawn trams existed in the late nineteenth century and were gradually replaced by electric trams from 1900 onwards. These new trams, combined with two suburban railway lines to Tacubaya and Villa Guadalupe, allowed the rich and middle classes to move outwards, as well as the expansion north and east of working class *barrio* districts (Vidrio 1987; Rodríguez Kuri 1996). As the rich moved out, so their residences were turned over to alternative land uses, either for commercial purposes or subdivided as tenement accommodation for working class families. If colonial mansions were not available for conversion to single-room accommodation for low-income households, then they were purpose-built (Figures 2.4 and 2.5). Once set in motion, the process whereby properties were evacuated by the wealthy and 'invaded' by the poor intensified, and accelerated further land-use changes, rising densities, greater congestion and insalubrity.

During the 1930s and 1940s expansion took place in all directions but most markedly in ribbon-type development towards the south, some of which began to incorporate the nearest *pueblos* along the newly extended main roads of Insurgentes and Calzada Tlalpan. Subsequently the interstitial areas were also in-filled (see Figure 2.2). From the 1940s all social classes were engaged in land acquisition processes, usually in different directions. The appropriation of space and the segregation between social groups intensified. Broadly speaking, the better-off groups moved west and south, while the poor moved east and north. During the 1950s large tracts of urban land began to be privatized for conversion to residential subdivisions. Later

FIGURE 2.4 Classic *vecindad*

chapters of this book will take up the rationale for these processes, but this privatization of space was often achieved illegally through the improper disestablishment of *ejidal* land (held under use-rights and in common by specified residents of agrarian communities), which was subsequently converted to élite and upper-income estates. Alternatively, *ejidatarios* sold off parcels of land to low-income households (Varley 1987). At the other extreme, real-estate developers privatized government lands which were ceded for agricultural improvement purposes, only to convert and sell these areas as unserviced plots to the poor. Private landlords in the east of the city also saw the opportunity to capitalize on poor-quality land holdings by selling off plots with minimum capital investment. Settlements such as Ramos Millán and Aeropuerto in the east of the DF were laid out (if not occupied) during the early 1950s before the ban was introduced in 1954 prohibiting any further residential subdivisions. Thus the ban, although enforced, was not terribly effective because many large settlements had

FIGURE 2.5 Purpose-built *vecindad*

been established, if not populated, before it was imposed. Elsewhere, landlords struck informal deals with households and, in exchange for some payment, turned a blind eye to the occupation of parcels of their land. However, an important feature of the ban was that it stimulated the supply of plots in the State of Mexico (where the ban did not apply), and by 1960 residential expansion into Naucalpan, Netzahualcóyotl and Ecatepec was well under way (see Figure 2.2). Between 1940 and 1970 the built-up area of the city grew almost seven-fold from 117.5 km^2 (47 square miles) to 746.4 km^2 (298 square miles), and the population increased concomitantly (Delgado 1988).

Since the 1970s the Metropolitan Area has grown rapidly and by 1990 it covered over 1250 km^2 (500 square miles), extending significantly into the

State of Mexico where some 43 per cent of the total population now live. The current 'frontiers' of physical expansion have spread into the south-eastern municipality of Chalco, where *ejidal* lands are being alienated alongside the motorway to Puebla, to the north into Tecamac, and into several municipalities in the north-west and west. In the Federal District opportunities for physical growth are more restricted by the lack of suitable available land and the tight controls exercised by the urban authorities over its alienation. The principal zones of conflict are the southern mountain slopes of the Ajusco and the rich agricultural lands around Xochimilco in the south-east. Further out, the *delegaciones* of Tláhuac and Milpa Alta are beginning to grow appreciably and are expected to double their populations between 1980 and 2000 (Partida 1987b). Elsewhere in the DF much of the population growth is being absorbed through increasing densities on existing plots.

Population densities in Mexico City

Crude population densities are high in Mexico City relative to other world cities, being slightly higher than Tokyo, double that of Metropolitan New York, triple that of Paris, and four times that of London (Connolly 1980: 70). Compared with other major Latin American cities, densities are at least double those of São Paulo and Buenos Aires, and roughly similar to the very topographically constrained Caracas. Only the Asian cities of Bombay, Calcutta and Hong Kong appear to have higher densities (Connolly 1980). Moreover, some areas of the city have extremely high densities (the central area for example) and also some of the older consolidated low-income irregular settlements have densities of over 400 people per hectare, although the average is around 260 per hectare (Connolly 1980; CONAPO 1996: their Table 1). Once all plots are occupied in irregular settlements, densities rise as young households have children, and as other families are accommodated on plots either in formal rental tenements developed by small-scale landlords, or as kinsfolk and/or grown-up children double-up on plots, living independently in a 'compound' type of arrangement (Ward 1976a; Lomnitz 1977; Gilbert and Varley 1990).

Until the early 1950s population densities in Mexico City corresponded with the normal bell-shaped curve distribution usually associated with western developed city structures (Connolly 1980). Densities were high in the city centre (around 800 inhabitants per hectare) and declined outwards, giving an average of 133 in 1940. Significantly, however, these densities and the nature of the curve have changed since that time. First, overall densities declined to 104 in 1960, before rising again to 122 in 1970 and 148 in 1981, then dropping to 114 – a level more consistent with 1970. In particular there has been a sharp difference between the density changes experienced in the DF and the State of Mexico. In the Federal District average densities rose steadily from 127 to 172 between 1960 and 1981. In the State of Mexico, where more recently established settlements led to much lower densities, these, too, have fluctuated. They increased from 23 per hectare in 1960 to 135 by 1975, but have since fallen back to 121 and 112 in 1981 and 1983, respectively (Connolly 1980: 81).

A second major change is that the top of the bell-shaped curve began to cave in as central downtown densities fell from 800 to 550 by 1970. This was a result of the absolute decline in cheap rental accommodation opportunities and low profitability of housing investments in the city centre since the 1940s. These densities may have been overestimations in the first place: certainly today they are nowhere near as high, being on average around 167 persons per hectare in the Centro Histórico area (CONAPO 1996), rising as high as 280 in the *barrio* of Tepito and to over 200 in the neighbouring *barrio* of Guerrero (Monnet 1995: 58). In part these declines were the result of a deterioration of the inner-city area, intensified as a result of the extensive damage caused in the downtown area by the 1985 earthquake, despite the intensive reconstruction and *in situ* housing redevelopment that has taken place (Mexico RHP 1988).

This structure and these fluctuations may be explained primarily by the dynamics of the city area expansion, which are themselves informed by opportunities for finance capital to invest profitably in the built environment, by public policies to facilitate such profit-taking, and by the agents involved in promoting land sales. This is not the moment to analyse these factors in detail, but the overall production of irregular settlement led to the rapid areal expansion of the built-up area as people moved out of renting into illegal 'ownership'. Thus overall densities declined sharply from 134 persons per hectare in 1940 to 104 persons per hectare in 1960, and were especially low (around 50 persons per hectare) in the sparsely populated and newly created sub-divisions of the State of Mexico (Connolly 1980). Since then, as noted above, densities have increased owing to a slow-down in the rate at which new land is being alienated illegally for 'ownership' at the periphery, and the greater difficulty that families who rent are experiencing in gaining access to a plot of land in a convenient location and at a price they can afford (Ward 1986). Densities have also fluctuated according to the effectiveness of state efforts to control irregular settlement expansion on either side of the Federal District boundary, and as a result of pressures from petroleum boom-induced finance capital searching for suitable investment outlets in urban development and redevelopment (Ward 1986; Connolly 1980). More recently, too, massive new urban development projects such as the mall and office development complex on the western hillsides of Santa Fé has led to some evictions of working class communities in what were narrow valley gravel pits and mines.

HOUSING MARKETS AND INTRA-URBAN MOBILITY

Housing production in Mexico City

City expansion and the dynamics of housing markets are closely linked, but the relationship between the two remains poorly understood. Much of the following analysis seeks to identify the processes and the functioning of the (largely) low-income housing system and the considerations that intervene to determine people's moves. For Mexico City there is a lot written about the mechanisms of land development for housing, the agents engaged in the process, the housing needs and strategies of different groups, and the appropriateness and effectiveness of public policies. We know a considerable amount about the nature of some of the interventions within the housing production, circulation and distribution processes depicted in Figure 2.6, but we know precious little about how and *why* the whole processes operate over time (Drakakis-Smith 1981; Burgess 1982, 1990; Ward and Macoloo 1992). In Mexico City, at least, little work has successfully explained the dynamics of housing production and the rationale underpinning investment behaviour in the built environment for production and consumption. Some authors have analysed certain aspects which impinge upon housing production, such as the construction materials industry (Ball and Connolly 1987). Others have tried to relate housing development to broader structural conditions, but have done so in ways which fail to develop the analysis in sufficient detail (COPEVI 1978; Cisneros Sosa 1993), or their interpretations are wedded to a particular ideological position and therefore fail to tackle evidence which is counter-factual (Legorreta 1983; Pradilla 1988).

Indeed, a weakness within my own work has been the tendency to focus upon certain patterns of consumption and distribution that have emerged at different times rather than addressing head-on the dynamics of different types of housing production process and their significance within wider processes of capital accumulation (Gilbert and Ward 1982a; Ward 1986, 1990). Although I have recently begun to address these questions, I have deliberately chosen to do so in cities other than the capital (Ward 1989a; Jones *et al.* 1993; Ward *et al.* 1994). Mexico City is probably too large, too complicated and too fast-changing for these issues to be explored in sufficient depth to afford satisfactory explanations – and certainly to cope with the complexity hinted at in Figure 2.6.

In Mexico City, housing is provided through either the public or the private housing markets. The latter includes both formal and informal systems of supply. Public housing intervention has changed in nature and has increased dramatically in recent years (Garza and Schteingart 1978; Ward 1990). Both qualitatively and quantitatively it has become more responsive to different sets of needs and income groups. Until the Housing

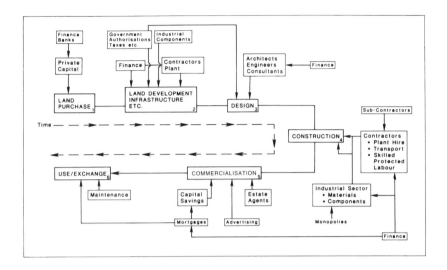

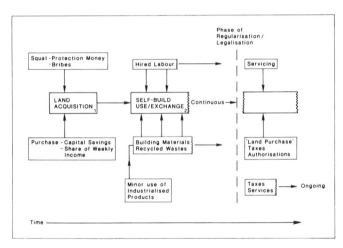

FIGURE 2.6 Modes of housing production: the 'industrialized' mode (above) and the 'petty-commodity' (self-help) mode (below)

Finance Programme (PFV) came on-line in the mid-1960s (financed through Alliance for Progress 'seed' capital), housing production had been built solely for specific social security affiliates, often for rent, and much of it in the Metropolitan Area. Subsequently the PFV generated so-called social interest housing (Figure 2.7) which, in fact, came to house lower-middle-income groups which could afford the mortgage repayments. Alternatively, the same groups 'raided' housing allocated to low-income groups reaccom-modated from squatter areas and tenements elsewhere in the city but which

FIGURE 2.7 'Social interest' housing

could ill afford the transportation and other costs associated with the new housing locations (e.g. Vicente Guerrero, Figure 2.7). Only a few 'minimalist' dwellings which were insufficiently attractive to middle-income groups came to serve exclusively low-income populations, usually relocated from tenement or inner-city shantytown sites (e.g. Ejército de Oriente, Figure 2.8). Recently, the housing funds (FOVI and FOGA) have raised their profile of financing middle-income housing provision in the city and elsewhere.

In the 1970s various housing agencies were deliberately created to raise the national profile of housing production and to ensure that housing policy genuinely met the needs of low-income populations. The creation of INFONAVIT in 1973 for blue-collar workers in formal employment raised production dramatically, so that during its first 3 years the agency generated as many dwellings as the entire state sector had achieved during the previous four decades. Middle-income state employees' needs were met in part by a special fund established for them (FOVISSSTE). Even so, these two funds only met an estimated 11.3 per cent of total annual demand between 1973 and 1980 (González Rubí 1984). Between 1981 and 1983 a large Popular Housing Trust Fund (FONHAPO) was developed to support housing production for those people (then) earning up to or around 2.5 minimum wages and who were not in formal employment or eligible through INFONAVIT. Thus state housing production has become

FIGURE 2.8 Government resettlement housing project

increasingly significant, although it still falls far short of annual total demand (Ward 1990). Moreover, much of the housing production today is orientated towards support for self-help housing processes, especially through FONHAPO. Both INFONAVIT and FOVISSSTE have been especially active in the Metropolitan Area, while FONHAPO has had greater impact outside the city where housing costs are much lower, and where it has been able to produce housing at prices affordable to the poor (Coulomb 1992).

Given the limited extent to which demand has been met through the state sector, housing production in Mexico is largely private. Middle-income and upper-middle-income groups seek housing through formal and (usually) legal supply systems, while the poor acquire land illegally and self-build (Connolly 1982). A large proportion of the population (around 44 per cent nationally in 1980) rent dwellings, yet until recently there has been little research into this important minority, and even less consideration of how public policy should address the rental sector (Coulomb 1989, 1992; Gilbert and Varley 1990; Gilbert 1993). Indeed, during the 1980s, inflation, low profit ratios on investment, and the state-provided opportunities to convert former rented accommodation into condominium ownership, all led to a drastic reduction in the supply of rental housing (Coulomb 1992: 169).

Thus, much of the supply of housing for low-income groups in Mexico City is privately produced and illegal (Ward 1976b; COPEVI 1977). Rental tenements (*vecindades*) may comprise old vacated élite residences in which

FIGURE 2.9 *Ciudad perdida* ('lost city') shantytown

a household occupies a single room and shares toilet and washing facilities which are located in the patio area (see Figure 2.4). A single tenement may house several dozen families. Some large *vecindades* were purpose-built during the first four decades, but the physical arrangement is broadly similar (see Figure 2.5). Located in and around the inner city, many of these tenements had their rents 'frozen' in the 1940s (Eckstein 1990c). This led to a withdrawal of investment in rental housing by landlords and greater population stability among many working-class households in the central city area which continued to enjoy the pre-1940s rent levels. By the 1970s many buildings had become dangerously dilapidated and there was an absolute decline in the downtown rental housing stock as buildings collapsed (COPEVI 1977). To compensate, some landlords developed temporary shackyard accommodation on plots around the city centre – the so-called lost cities (*ciudades perdidas*) – the rents of which were not frozen and, although low, represented a high return on the minimal investment made in provisional shacks with limited or non-existent services (Figure 2.9). The most rapidly expanding rental accommodation, however, is in the new tenements (*vecindades nuevas*) located in the older irregular settlements. Developed by petty landlords, these tenements are much smaller than their

FIGURE 2.10   Purpose-built *vecindad nueva*

precursors and usually house between five and fifteen families (Figure 2.10). Overall these rental housing systems accommodate around 35–40 per cent of the city's population (Turner *et al.* 1972; Ward 1976b).

Irregular settlements in Mexico City comprise squatter settlements where households capture land through well-orchestrated invasions that involve large numbers of families. Although in Mexico City several famous invasion settlements exist in the south of the city, this mode of acquisition tends to be the exception rather than the rule. Illegal subdivision of land for sale – by landlords, real-estate companies or *ejidatarios* and/or their representatives – is a much safer, if more expensive, means to acquire a plot. These subdivisions are illegal because servicing norms are not met, or because authorization of sale and transfer of title is not forthcoming or sought by the developers. Whichever mechanism of land development is adopted, the

FIGURE 2.11   Self-build: early phase of consolidation

outcome is broadly the same: unserviced plots (usually around 200 m^2) upon which households take primary responsibility for dwelling construction and management (Connolly 1982). As we observed earlier, rapid expansion of these neighbourhoods occurred during the 1950s and 1960s, since which time the pace of formation has slowed. An estimated 50–60 per cent of the city's population live in settlements which began through one or other of these land-alienation processes, although *post hoc* legalization and servicing combined with on-site dwelling consolidation and improvement have often dramatically changed the legal and physical status of the neighbourhood (Figures 2.11 and 2.12; see also Chapter 7). Those settlements established in the early period of expansion have long since been engulfed and incorporated to form the spatial intermediate ring of the city, and their densities have increased in the manner described earlier in this chapter.

Intra-city migration patterns in Mexico City: flight to the suburbs?

Explanations about why and how people migrate around Mexico City owe much to the work of John Turner, whose seminal paper in 1968 offered the first general model to explain low-income migration patterns in Latin

FIGURE 2.12   Self-build: later phase

American cities. Residential location was determined essentially by three variables: (1) tenure, specifically the choice between renting and owner-ship; (2) location, i.e. proximity to unskilled employment opportunities mainly located in the central city; (3) shelter, i.e. an individual's priority for modern standard shelter. Recent migrant arrivals ('bridgeheaders') favoured cheap rental accommodation in the central city, from which they could search for work, and had a low preference for ownership or adequate-quality accommodation. However, gradual integration into the employment market, greater urban familiarity, and growing family size would affect these priorities. The established migrant would now be in a position to become a 'consolidator': an (illegal) owner in the urban periphery. Such 'ownership' offered space for expansion and the possibility to extend a dwelling through self-help. The theory suggested, therefore, that most low-income migrants would live first as renters in the inner city and later move as owners to the peripheral low-income settlements.

From his work in Lima and Mexico City, however, Turner recognized that this two-stage (province to city centre to city periphery) model was liable to become distorted in large cities as the opportunities for cheap rental accommodation dried up, and where previously formed irregular settle-ments had become integrated into the urban fabric. Residents in this consolidated intermediate ring were now prepared to rent rooms to 'bridgeheaders' or to help their recently-arrived friends and kin by offering them temporary shared accommodation. In Mexico City this was exacerbated by the rent controls imposed upon many *vecindades*, which slowed down the throughflow of migrants. Thus a breakdown in the classic pattern was proposed, with new migrants arriving to the intermediate ring, or indeed direct into the periphery (Turner 1968a). In turn, these migrants later moved to the expanding current periphery following the same priorities of former 'consolidators' (Brown 1972).

By the end of the 1960s, evidence from numerous Latin American cities had provided support for Turner's hypothesis, and the classic two-stage model had become 'widely accepted' (Morse 1971: 22). However, there are several problems with the theory. First, as with all behavioural models, it tends to emphasize housing preferences of residents and their ability to exercise a *choice* between options, but are the preferences endogenously determined or are they a response to the housing environment? Second, there was growing evidence during the 1970s that challenged the Turneresque pattern (Brown 1972; Vaughn and Feindt 1973; Vernez 1973). Indeed my own survey of mover trajectories into squatter settlements in Mexico City also pointed to a breakdown in Turner's classic two-stage pattern. Although many residents of irregular settlements during the 1940s and 1950s had begun their urban lives in inner-city tenements, a substantial proportion had not, but had moved direct to the periphery (Ward 1976c; Lomnitz 1977). Moreover, residents in newly-formed settlements created during the late 1960s and early 1970s had rarely lived in the inner-city tenements. Rather, they had either rented or shared lots with relatives and friends in the intermediate ring or current periphery (Ward 1976c).

As part of a larger study concerned with government intervention in the housing and land markets in Bogotá, Valencia and Mexico City, the intra-city trajectories of residents in six irregular settlements in Mexico City were analysed (Gilbert and Ward 1982b). Very few migrants to the city moved directly into these settlements. Although most of them received assistance from antecedent kinsfolk and/or friends, only 33 per cent lived with kin for more than one year after arrival; 45 per cent rented accommodation (Gilbert and Ward 1982b). In terms of location of 'bridgehead' residence, there appears to have been a clear shift away from the traditional city centre, initially towards the older working-class areas to the north and east, and subsequently to the more dispersed areas of irregular settlement that emerged during the 1950s and 1960s (Figure 2.13). These data suggest that even in the earlier periods irregular settlement attracted many more migrants than is implicit in the Turner model – a conclusion supported by my data for the Sector Popular settlement founded in 1947, to which a substantial minority of migrants arrived direct without any stopover in the downtown district (Ward 1976c). It is also apparent that some of the old *pueblo* cores that had been absorbed by the city's growth now fulfilled the role of reception centres for incoming migrants. These areas offer many of

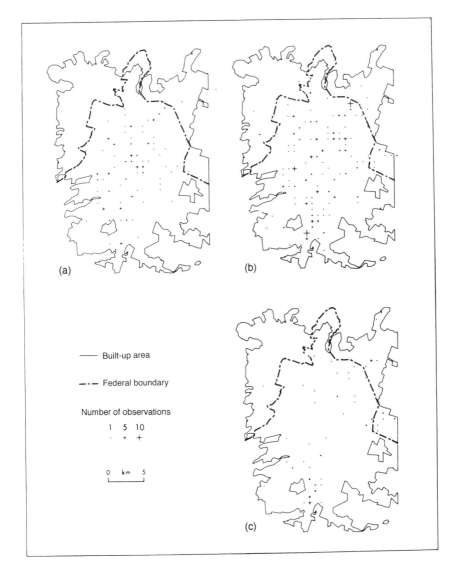

FIGURE 2.13 The changing locations of migrant arrivals to Mexico City: a, 1935–1955; b, 1956–1968; c, 1968–1979

the advantages of the city centre, and suggest the need for a further modification of the original Turner model.

Turning to examine the mobility patterns for all residents (i.e. migrants and city-born), it is apparent in Mexico City that the last settlement of residence before moving to the current home was located relatively nearby (Figure 2.14). This feature is most apparent in the newly-created settlements

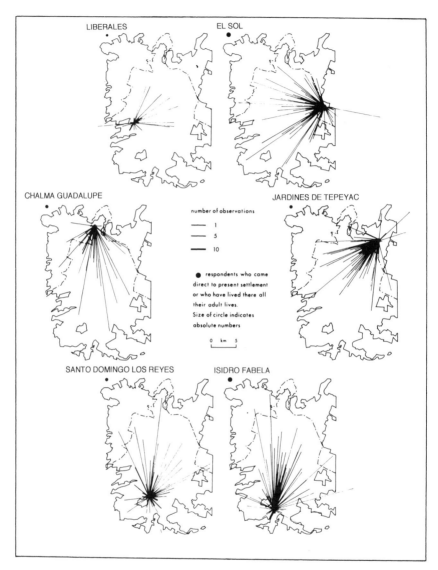

FIGURE 2.14 Location of last place of residence before moving to one of six irregular settlements surveyed in 1978–9

such as Liberales and Santo Domingo. Only in the two oldest settlements (Isidro Fabela and El Sol) did many come from further afield – in part inevitable given the fact that at the time of formation their highly peripheral location was always going to draw residents from further-flung districts. The siphoning-off of residents from nearby arises because most information about housing opportunities comes from family and friends living locally

(Jackson 1973; Gilbert and Ward 1982b). Moreover, in Mexico City the illegal settlement process leaves 'owners' vulnerable if they fail to occupy their plot immediately. There is always the threat that someone else may usurp the plot and this makes for more rapid settlement; it also means that residents living nearby can best maintain surveillance over their plots. In Santo Domingo, for example, a large minority (approximately two-fifths) had been sharing with parents or kin (*arrimados*) in surrounding squatter areas. When the invasion took place they were well placed to join in, always with the proviso that they could return to their kinsfolk if the invasion was repressed. Many, too, could continue living with kin, maintaining a single member of the family on the plot to 'guard' over it and to warn off would-be usurpers (Ward 1976a).

In our comparative analysis of patterns of residential movement in the three Latin American cities, we concluded that such patterns were more a product of constraints imposed by the land and housing markets than the outcome of migrant choice (Gilbert and Ward 1982b). Access to land ownership appears to be critical. Where land is freely available at not especially distant locations (as in Valencia, Venezuela), then 'bridgeheaders' often move direct to the periphery as owners. Why rent when one can just as easily own? In places like Mexico City, where the supply of land is more limited and often risky to capture, migrants and city-born are obliged to rent or to share with kin for long periods. State intervention may also have a critical effect on the housing and land markets. Legalization of plots, service provision, and tougher controls imposed against the formation of new settlements are likely to drive up land prices and reduce the supply of plots. This, in turn, will intensify the pressures of non-ownership and prolong residence, either as renters or sharers. Also, rent controls and a lack of direct state support has suppressed the rental housing market and accentuated the propensity for many households to subdivide and share their plots with kinsfolk. Finally, the physical fabric of the city and its rate of growth are likely to affect residential patterns. The large size of Mexico City now means that people tend to relate to a sector of the city rather than to the overall area. Moreover the existence of subcentres – whose functions resemble the central core – offers opportunities within the urban fabric that will further shape people's mobility patterns.

THE APPROPRIATION OF SPACE IN THE METROPOLITAN AREA

Residential segregation in relation to positive and negative externalities

During its conversion from plaza to suburb to megacity, Mexico City has become spatially more differentiated and more segregated. The city's land-use pattern will be analysed in greater depth in Chapter 4, but a brief glance at Figure 4.1 (p. 136) shows that most of the built-up area comprises residential land use, and that the largest industrial sites are located in the north-east (in the State of Mexico) and north-west (DF and State of Mexico). These locations, together with the unsuitability for urbanization of the eastern ex-lakebed areas, determined that the cheapest end of the land market would be to the east and to the north. Indeed, the first waves of wealthy suburbanites moved west and south towards areas with the greater positive externalities (woodland, fresh water, low (dust) contamination, existing road access and the small extra-urban townships and services these offered). Thus a broad pattern of social differentiation was entrained between south and west (richer) and north and east (poorer).

The 1950s ban on new subdivisions in the Federal District did not greatly disturb these directional trends. Although some new upper-middle-income residential estates were established in Naucalpan, and a large number of low-income subdivisions were created in various municipalities of the State of Mexico, within the Federal District the existing divide remained, even though both rich and poor had to adopt illegal methods of land appropriation (Cisneros Sosa 1993). I will return to discuss these mechanisms later, but it is sufficient to note here that different pretexts were used to disestablish *ejidal* land. The rich used the mechanism of *permuta* (exchange), while the poor invaded or purchased direct from *ejidatarios* (Varley 1985a, 1987; Cymet 1992). The point is that not even the monopoly control of *ejidal* lands by *ejidatarios* disrupted the pattern that had been established. This 'sifting' of the allocation of residential space continued until the early 1970s when political conditions facilitated several large-scale low-income invasions of *ejidal* lands in the south of the Federal District (Cymet 1992).

Some would argue that today the whole of the Metropolitan Area constitutes a negative externality, such is the generalized way in which everyone is affected by the problems associated with living in conditions of high levels of atmospheric contamination, the lack of adequate servicing for many, small amounts of green space, long journeys to work, and so on. The existence of, and factors shaping, these problems will be analysed in the following chapters, but although everyone suffers they do not do so in equal measure. Notwithstanding major servicing improvements in the areas which, traditionally, often had minimal levels of servicing (the east and north), the levels of relative deprivation remain much higher than elsewhere in the city. Levels of overcrowding, dwellings constructed with inadequate or provisional building materials and without proper toilet facilities reiterate the same pattern (Puente 1987). Parkland is at a premium in the city and is preferentially distributed to the west and south. Chapultepec Park may be intensively used by lower-income groups at weekends, but during the week it is the preserve of the better-off who use it for recreation, jogging and as a general exercise work-out area.

Contamination, however, is less respectful of such socially differentiated spatial nuances. Air pollution occurs because of the frequent temperature inversions, a large number and wide distribution of sources of contamination, and the complexities of regional air flows within the Central Valley (Jáuregui 1987: 38). Vehicular emissions generate the largest source of contamination and are concentrated where the traffic is greatest: in the downtown area. Photochemical smog, which may form after several hours on sunny days, affects most severely the south-west of the city, being transported across it by the breezes which usually come from the north-east in the afternoon (Jáuregui 1973). These same winds bring dust and particle-born diseases from the poor eastern suburbs and are distributed throughout the city without regard to the social status of neighbourhoods (Fox 1972). The *tolvaneras* (localized dust storms) which are most common during the hot dry season (March–May) affect mostly those areas where they are generated: the eastern settlements on the ex-lake bed (Jáuregui 1969). Isolines showing the concentrations of sulphur dioxide are highest in the city centre, extending north-westwards across the Vallejo industrial zone into Naucalpan and Tlalnepantla. A second outlier hovers over the north-eastern industrial district of Xalostoc. Thus everyone in the city suffers the effects of air pollution, although the periodicity and source of contamination may vary across social areas.

In recent years city authorities have begun to take systematic action for environmental protection and to control contamination. The Programa Integral contra la Contaminación Atmosférica en la Zona Metropolitana de la Cd. de México (PICCA) was published in 1991 and provides for a series of priority actions designed to reduce contamination levels in the city (Castillo *et al.* 1995). Principally, these focus upon vehicle emissions, and statutory means for reducing them. While problems of effective enforcement remain, there is a more concerted effort by the authorities today, and a greater awareness and public concern. Television and newspapers offer daily reports and advisories on pollution levels, and this is a relatively new feature in Mexico's news media. An ongoing difficulty, however, is that while the PICCA is a metropolitan commission, the adjacent State of Mexico is not subject to the same pressures to apply the programme with similar assiduousness as in the DF. I will return to this problem of administrative jurisdictions in the following two chapters.

Changing patterns of social segregation

Before we contemplate present levels of social segregation and how these might be changing, we should recognize that this is not a new phenomenon. In pre-industrial and pre-revolutionary Mexico City, while the rich and poor resided in close proximity, they did not live cheek by jowl. The poor lived apart in discrete *barrio* areas at the then northern and eastern edges of what came to be the *Primer Cuadro* (Lira 1983; Lombardo 1987; Morales 1987). The principal difference is that suburbanization reproduced social segregation over a much larger area. Now an important question is whether, once entrained, the process has become self-perpetuating, or whether there are other processes of social and spatial integration at work.

The existing pattern of social segregation is readily demonstrated by the distribution of population according to income levels (Figure 2.15). The highest income areas of Jardines de San Angel and Las Lomas (de Chapultepec, de Reforma and de Tecamachalco) are all clearly differentiated, as are the more numerous second category of areas such as Nápoles, Polanco, Satélite, etc. In contrast, the poorest areas are to be found in the eastern and northern peripheries. The mixture of socio-economic groups in the inner city generates lower-to-intermediate areas of income distribution, but there is also evidence that low-income groups living in and around the city centre are significantly better off than their counterparts who live at the periphery (Valencia 1965; Brown 1972; Mexico RHP 1986). This is because in most cases the inner-city population is stable (albeit declining) working class, closely tied into the local economy.

This spatial distribution may be depicted as a series of zones, sectors and nucleii which form the broad pattern of the city's ecology (Figure 2.16). Poorer areas have developed as a series of concentric zones in the east and north. As one moves outwards, the settlements become poorer and more recently established. Hence their level of physical integration is lower (measured in terms of levels of urban infrastructure, residential consolidation, population densities, etc.). Generally speaking, these zones expand through new housing production at the periphery with increasing densities in the inner and intermediate zones. Those groups in the upper-income bands also provide a *leitmotif* for urban expansion, creating new areas of exclusivity in which symbols of wealth and cachet may be displayed. However, the desirability for clearly defined neighbourhoods which may be protected against encroachment from other groups has led to the emergence of wedge-shaped sectors following the contours of the land and using natural barriers as divides (Figure 2.16). Some élite residential development is also occurring through the gentrification and infilling in the more attractive ex-*pueblo* cores such as San Angel and Tlalpan. In the past, some formerly exclusive élite areas have moved slightly downmarket as upper-middle-income groups 'filtered' into residences and plots that were vacated by their would-be peers who have moved out to more recently developed and ever more exclusive areas (Johnston 1973; Ward 1976a).

The spatial locations for residence of middle-income groups are, therefore, determined either by their willingness to filter into these vacated residences or, more usually, through residence in suburban estates developed specifically to meet their needs. Colonia Del Valle in the centre–south

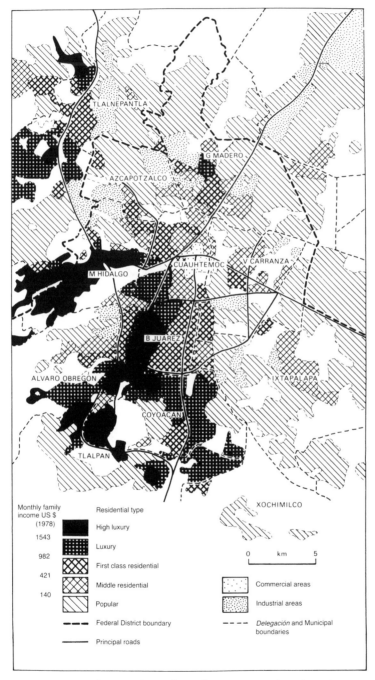

Monthly family
income US $
(1978)

1543

982

421

140

Residential type

High luxury

Luxury

First class residential

Middle residential

Popular

Federal District boundary

Principal roads

XOCHIMILCO

0   km   5

Commercial areas

Industrial areas

Delegación and Municipal
boundaries

FIGURE 2.15   Distribution of population by income and residential type. Source:
Buró de Investigación de Mercados, SA

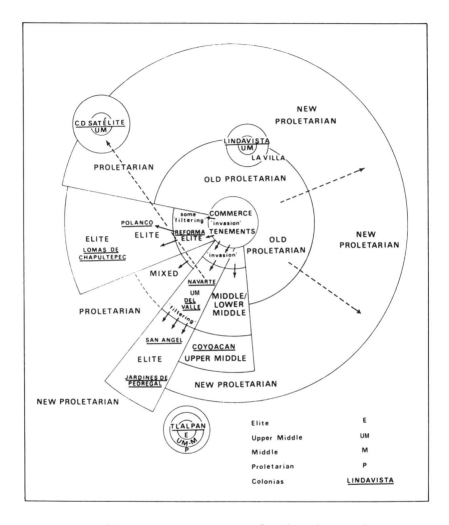

FIGURE 2.16 Diagrammatic representation of 'ecological' areas of Mexico City

of the city, and Satélite and Echegaray in the north-east are good examples. These, too, may be subject to subsequent 'filtering' processes. Parts of Polanco have moved downmarket two categories from élite to middle-income during the past 30 years. Elite areas and upper-income areas developed during the last decade of the century (e.g. Roma Norte) have long since been subject to 'invasion' processes whereby commercial redevelopment pressures have led to changing land uses from single-family residences to shops, offices and multifamily poor or middle-income housing.

However, the largest ecological areas are occupied by the poor. As already noted, these are in eastern zones of the city, but the poor have also occasionally managed to drive a wedge between social classes in the south and west of the city. The ability to capture these areas relates to the specificities of original land tenure and/or the political period in which neighbourhoods were created, but the effect since 1970 has been to insert the poor into some western and southern areas of the city, thereby breaking up the middle-income economic homogeneity of these districts.

A systematic attempt to analyse these processes of social differentiation was made using census data and factor analysis of some 18 variables (subsequently reduced to 7; Rubalcava and Schteingart 1985, 1987). Two broad factors of differentiation emerged: (a) 'urban consolidation' associated with variables such as levels of home ownership, dwellings with water service, and persons per room; (b) 'socio-economic development' associated with the proportion of economically active persons, the proportion with primary education, and the proportion earning more than six times the minimum salary. Between them these two factors explained almost three-quarters of the total variation, with urban consolidation emerging as the most important way of differentiating socio-spatial patterns in the city. Unfortunately, in their analysis the data were aggregated and displayed at the level of *delegación* and municipality, so that the resulting patterns are rather generalized (Rubalcava and Schteingart 1987). The factor 'urban consolidation' shows sharp differentiation between the high levels in the three western downtown *delegaciones* of Miguel Hidalgo, Cuauhtémoc and Benito Juárez, but is lower across a broad west–east divide. Factor 2 (socio-economic development) shows even more clearly the sharp divide between western political entities and those of the north and especially the eastern municipalities. More significant, perhaps, was the finding that until 1970 there was a tendency towards greater polarization between social areas, but that the evolution of the urban area during the 1970s and 1980s has begun to reverse this process. In particular, they note a tendency for the position of middle-income groups to improve between 1970 and 1980 at the expense of the upper-income and lower-income groups. They conclude that there has been 'a decline in the spatial and social differences, despite the fact that extreme disparities remain for important indicators between the zones' (Rubalcava and Schteingart 1987: 114; but cf. Esquivel Hernández 1995).

One of the reasons why social areas are not so sharply polarized as they might have been is the existence of *ejidal* land to which middle-income groups have had limited access (since its development would be illegal), and which has become largely a preserve of low-income housing development. This has allowed the incursions of working class populations into the south, west and north-west, thus balancing, at least modestly, the expansion of irregular settlements to the east. Now that *ejidal* land may be sold legally, it remains to be seen whether this will lead to a greater incursion of better-off groups into that part of the land market (Austin 1994).

Our data for other cities suggest that, thus far at least, there is little evidence of higher income or other sectoral 'raiding' of *ejido* lands (Jones and Ward 1997); nor is the new legislation likely to make a dramatic difference in the Federal District, since it is already substantially urbanized.

Nevertheless, the finding that there has been a decline in spatial and social differences is important because it underlines the fact that conditions in Mexico City may not be deteriorating inevitably and inexorably in the manner often claimed by Marxist theorists (Esquivel Hernández 1995). In making this point I am not seeking to extenuate the existence of the clear disparities that exist, nor am I suggesting that, left to their own devices and market mechanisms, these spatial inequalities will gradually be resolved, but it does underscore the need to take account both of the complexities of the processes involved in the evolution of the Metropolitan Area, and the fact that as the city develops it also makes adjustments that may *raise* people's life chances and reduce the more onerous aspects of city life

THE INNER-CITY 'PROBLEM' IN MEXICO CITY

In the final section of this chapter I want to explore in some depth the nature of Mexico City's inner city, and ask whether Mexico City and cities like it in less-developed countries are experiencing a decline in their inner cities similar to that experienced in the US and in Europe (Smith and Williams 1986; Robson 1988; Frieden and Sagalyn 1990; Halpern 1995; Smith 1996). While there is a wealth of material available on the latter, there are virtually no urban analyses on the downtown areas in less-developed countries (Eckstein 1990a). Most of the attention has focused upon suburbanization at the periphery, much of it illegal as described earlier. Indeed, analysis of the inner city *per se* was omitted in the first edition of this book, so what follows is entirely new.

As will have been observed so far in this chapter, there is much evidence for *convergence* in the urban processes in Mexico City similar to those widely experienced in the study of developed cities. This includes suburbanization, élite and middle-income vacation of the downtown areas, and 'leapfrogging' over existing settlements to new higher-*cachet* areas, as well as a whole range of newly entrained economic processes that demand more 'flexible' production systems and new locational constraints and criteria (see also Garza 1992). Some authors have even sought – not inaccurately – to draw rough equivalence between working class suburbs in the developed cities and the peripheral 'self-help' consolidating settlements in cities such as Mexico (Johnston 1973). So, there ought to be evidence for substantial convergence, but in fact there is not (Ward 1993; see also Home 1982).

Few analysts have sought to look systematically at Latin American inner-city areas. Important exceptions are Hardoy and Dos Santos' early work (1983), and more recently, Scarpaci and Gutman's ongoing inventory and analysis of land uses and building structures in a number of Latin American and Caribbean cities (Scarpaci and Gutman 1995; see also Scarpaci et al. 1997). The latter body of work suggests that while many cities are valued for their inner-city cultural patrimony, and some – like Mexico City – have been designated as UNESCO World Heritage Sites, it is the constellation of intervening variables such as governmental (national and municipal) and private-sector commitment and support for renovation projects that is most important. Those cities that have assiduously sought to renovate (e.g. Cartagena in Colombia) have often been highly successful, whereas those cities where urban revitalization has been largely ignored are terribly run down (e.g. Havana and Trinidad – both in Cuba and both UNESCO Heritage Sites). Nor do Scarpaci and Gutman see mixed commercial and residential functions as incompatible in historic centres; quite the opposite, as such a mixture bodes well for revitalization efforts. Evidence from Quito also suggests that renovated properties are more usually associated with mixed land uses and that the impetus is motivated more by economic than by residential criteria. This is leading to some reduction of the residential opportunities in the historic core – both through declining densities and through change of building functions (Jones and Bromley 1996). In the case of Quito, at least, the key to successful conservation will be persuading private owners to renovate their properties. These same authors also found major inconsistencies and breaches in the application of municipal codes, so that many properties displayed external writing, signs, aerials, brick cladding and colour that was out of keeping with the image sought. However, most of these studies are suggestive of an evolutionary trajectory that is markedly different from West European and North American historic centres (Ward 1993; Scarpaci and Gutman 1995). Scarpaci and Gutman correctly argue that most Latin American central core areas have low skylines and remain anchored to historic plazas (see also Herzog 1995).

Thus, for the most part, while they show many similarities in overall processes of urbanization, Latin American inner cities have not shown the same level of decline and population loss as their European or North American counterparts. Nor have they experienced the same upswing or resurgence of reinvestment and back-to-the-city movement associated with classic 'gentrifiers' (Hamnett 1991; Smith 1996). Although there are important examples of downtown urban clearance schemes in cities like Montevideo and São Paulo (Batley 1982; Benton 1986), the planned-for redevelopment and replacement regeneration rarely happened – largely because macro- and micro-level economic conditions made other forms of investment more profitable. The land clearance schemes of the 1970s and early 1980s did not result in the follow-through of redevelopment.

Part of the reason for these 'stalled' development projects is the relative lack of private sector interest given the large (working class) populations still living in and around the inner city, and partly because the 'rent gap' between existing ground/office rents and those that might accrue after redevelopment are insufficient to stimulate private investment (Ward 1993; Smith 1996). Moreover, despite considerable convergence between middle classes worldwide in aesthetics and consumer tastes, for most élites and middle-income professionals living in the old city centre remains an anathema. These are highly classist and often implicitly racist societies in which location of residence remains an important mechanism whereby status is displayed and through which stratification patterns are reproduced. In fairness, the location of many important services (private schools, shops, leisure activities, etc.) not surprisingly follow those markets, so that unless the move to gentrify the inner city were to become a concerted one by many, major family diseconomies would arise from any move to the downtown area. Nor do younger professionals and bohemians, of which there are many, appear to be eager to move into the inner city, although they are to be found making their homes in other former upper-income areas (in Mexico City this is the case in *colonias* Roma and Condesa, for example).

Nor have we observed a 'revanchism' of public protest and mob reaction in inner cities that some authors have begun to describe, especially in the North American inner cities where local groups have moved to resist evictions of residents and street sleepers as city authorities seek to 'clean up' their downtown areas, and to arrest the downward spiral of decay that is leading to de-gentrification (Bourne 1993; Beauregard 1993; Smith 1996). This is not to say that social movements and anti-urban project protest demonstrations are not a feature of Latin American inner cities; they are. Residents of the inner city in Mexico have a long (and often successful) tradition of local-interest organization that has led to them having major input in housing and land-use development projects such as 'Plan Tepito' in the 1970s, and the spontaneous mobilization in the wake of the 1985 earthquakes that resulted in their participation and being the primary beneficiary in the re-housing programme (see Chapter 7). Subsequently, too, this organization led to the development of the Barrio Assembly, which was very influential for almost a decade (Eckstein 1990b, c; Greene 1993). However, even in the economic climate of 1995–96 there are no large-scale upwellings of urban protest and revengeful and radical activity such as that described by Smith (1996) and others surrounding the Tompkins Square Park closure in New York in 1991. Crime has increased dramatically in Mexico City (see Preface), but it is not attached to the lightning rod of reactionary urban redevelopment projects in the historic core of the city – or in any part of the city for that matter.

It is probably fair, therefore, to characterize Latin American inner cities as being different in kind rather than in degree, certainly when compared with their European counterparts. In addition to some of the class-based ideological differences mentioned above, the demography and the economy are substantially different. While many cities are experiencing some population loss, and that loss often appears to be accelerating, there is not the same 'sacking' of the inner city as occurred in London, for example, where the population declined by 750 000 between 1951 and 1971, and by a further half-million between 1971 and 1977 alone, much of it from inner-city boroughs (Balchin and Bull 1987). Philadelphia, too, lost over 400 000 people between 1950 to 1980, even though the suburbs grew by almost 1.5 million (Beauregard 1989). Invariably these left the inner cities with a very small vestige population comprising a high proportion of the aged and poor working classes, and often ethnic minorities which immigrated into the area because of the lower housing costs brought about by dereliction and planning blight. Economically, too, these areas were the location of older industrial and manufacturing plants which were now anachronisms in the new era of bright-light, cheap and flexible labour needs with minimal traffic and utility diseconomies.

As we observed earlier in this chapter, in Mexico City the four central *delegaciones* began to experience a net loss of population to surrounding areas from 1970 onwards (−2.21 per cent per annum between 1970 and 1990), resulting in a total population decline of one million (approximately one-third of the total, see Table 2.2). This is a substantial loss, but it is not a 'gutting' of the heart and soul of the city, and notwithstanding the damage wrought by the 1985 earthquakes, the central city *delegaciones* are still home to almost two million citizens, the large majority of them working class.

Similarly, the inner area of Mexico City was never the location of new industries established during the 1950s and 1960s. These went instead to the first and second rings, so there was never the same level of job loss associated with industrial dereliction and job relocation to the periphery associated with new, more modern branch plants and factories. In Mexico City these new industries *began* in the (then) periphery. This is not to suggest that there have not been significant job losses, but these have been neither wholesale, nor without some level of compensatory job creation, especially in services, as we observed in the previous chapter.

Commenting upon these processes in a nuanced way is rather difficult given the lack of detailed analyses about Mexico City's inner city, on the one hand, and the lack of good disaggregated data on the other. The data in Table 2.2 and in Table 1.5 provide some insight into what is going on, but each of these four inner-city *delegaciones* has a population of over 400 000 and many processes vary internally in important ways. This is the principal drawback of Garrocho's otherwise comprehensive analysis, complicated further in his case by the comparison between 1980 and 1990 data (Garrocho 1995a). Given the shortcomings of the 1980 census, a 1970/1990 comparison might have been more appropriate. Nevertheless, he shows that for five dimensions of change which embrace population, employment and welfare, all but one of these *delegaciones* (Venustiano Carranza) is experiencing urban decline and decay, and in one of them (Cuauhtémoc) this is especially marked (Garrocho 1995a: 95).

Monnet's (1995) excellent study helps us to overcome some of these data analysis problems, since while he compares 1970 and 1990 census data, he focuses almost exclusively upon the 1990 material. Moreover, these data are disaggregated at a much smaller *AGEB* level (basic geo-statistical areas). However, his inner city is rather overly circumscribed, being limited to approximately two-thirds of two *delegaciones* (Cuauhtémoc and Venustiano Carranza) and focuses especially upon the area traditionally known as the *Primer Cuadro*. The rough boundaries of his study area are the *Eje 3* on the east side, the *Viaducto* to the south, and the *Circuito Interior* to the north and west (although on both the north and south sides the area stops about a kilometre short of both routeways). Data are analysed for 100 sub-areas (*AGEB*) and are complemented by a cross-sectional analysis of business enterprises from east of the Zócalo through to Bucarelli Street. While the study is not comprehensive for the full inner city, nor does it adequately capture *change* given that it almost exclusively draws upon the 1990 data, it is the first of its kind to effectively get a handle on the highly heterogeneous nature of the area.

One feature of Monnet's study is the bi-modal division between the economic and population characteristics of the tourist-orientated Zona Rosa, and the principal centre of the *Primer Cuadro*, which runs between the Zócalo and the Eje Central. Most of these differences are expected, although the much higher than average female residency of the south-west part of the area (Zona Rosa especially), which he ties to single-person families and domestic servants, is quite striking (Monnet 1995: 60). The *delegación* of Venustiano Carranza as a whole has a female-to-male ratio of 115:100, yet many sub-areas in the area identified by Monnet have a ratio of 125:100 or 150:100. In contrast, the areas of Tepito and La Merced have relatively high male ratios, although women still dominate (albeit marginally). In these areas the higher-than-usual proportion of men is tied to the traditional 'reception zone' nature of some parts of the inner city for recent arrivals, although as we saw earlier, this area is generally no longer important in this respect. Densities in the northern part are especially high, embracing the *barrios* of Tepito and Guerrero, with more than 300 people per hectare being commonplace. Likewise, the number of residents per dwelling varies across the inner city, rising from an average of 2.7–3.6 in the west, to 3.7–4.0 in the central area, to 4.01–4.83 in the east and north-east. This accurately tracks the principal *vecindad* areas.

Maps of the economic activity show that this is an area of primarily small establishments (with the exception of the Paseo de la Reforma axis, and the Zona Rosa). Far from being 'marginal', industrial activities are intimately linked into the Centro Histórico. Sewing and dressmaking is especially important, and the city centre employs over 13 000 workers (one-quarter of all industrial workers in the zone), and is almost exclusively concentrated immediately north and south of the Zócalo. Shoemaking is almost exclusively the preserve of Tepito and very small self-employed workshops, which local workers self-name 'the capital of shoemaking'. This is a misnomer, since later in the analysis one observes that, nationally, the DF and Tepito play a relatively insignificant role (Monnet 1995: 124). The centre is also host to a large number of other activities – often highly skilled artisan – tied to the commerce of the area: jewelry, the making of musical instruments, and so on (Mantecón and Reyes Domínguez 1993).

The bi-polar nature of the inner city emerges clearly when one disaggregates the distribution of different services; travel agencies, banks, hotels and car and other mechanical repair shops appear in the east, and insurance companies, offices etc. in the west. Not captured adequately in these or other data are the large number of street peddlers (*ambulantes*). This, too, is a complex and at first sight anarchic universe (Mendoza 1995). Yet it contains a multiplicity of organizational levels ranging from the roving 10-year-old shoeshine boys to regular (and regulated) shoeshine stands. The same spectrum occurs in almost every area of activity: lottery ticket sales, jewelry, foodstuffs, toys, balloons, and so on. Street peddling has become an important political issue and source of tension in the inner city. It is estimated that there are over 149 000 street traders in Mexico City, many of them in the inner-city area (CONCANACO 1993). Local businesses complain increasingly vociferously, since it takes trade away from them and causes disruption in front of their shops (Cámara Nacional 1993). They also resent the unlicensed, untaxed and low-overhead nature of these shop-front competitors. The authorities are under pressure from the shop owners to remove the peddlers from the streets. They are also concerned about the unregulated and often unsanitary nature of the itinerant enterprises, and its ramifications upon tourism (Tejeda 1995).

In recent years, therefore, Mexico City has conducted a series of periodic purges against these *ambulantes* – as have many mayors in cities around the country (Lezema 1991; Jones and Varley 1994). Federal District Mayor Manuel Camacho (1988–93) made it an important priority in his administration, although it was sensitively tied to a programme that sought to concentrate their activities to particular controlled locations and to purpose-built covered markets, of which some 37 were planned (*La Jornada* 28 January 1992). Some 10 000 street traders from a variety of social classes (not just the poor) who operated in some 300 blocks of the inner city were targeted. Between May and December 1993 some 24 markets were built by 16 separate private architect firms working in conjunction with the Public Works office and mandated to develop designs with façades which were in accord with the historic context of the area (Tejeda 1995). After a year's operation it was estimated that only one-half of the markets had been a success, with poor location and design being the reasons that some were not. The best designs were those which facilitated walk-in traffic through the market and which, in effect, most closely replicated the traditional street-vending practice (Tejeda 1995). It appears that some street vendors used their market sites as store areas and continued to ply the streets as traders. The latest recession once again increased the propensity for street trading in Mexico City, and has led to a further crackdown and resistance under the Espinoza administration (1994–97). Most street traders belong to one of over 60 separate organizations, and the majority (76 per cent) belong to three organizations, the leaders of which are very influential and opposed removal to sedentary sites. There were police clearances and some street violence during the summer of 1995. Although the timing was inauspicious, many streets are now free of traders, but this is at the cost of a heavy police presence. However, this is a difficult problem to resolve, especially during periods of economic crisis and austerity. Notwithstanding the 1995 push, most governments tend to be more lenient in such times, and generally only push hard when the economy is expanding and when alternative jobs are available.

Thus, we are slowly beginning to develop a more satisfactory and nuanced socio-economic understanding of the characteristics of Mexico's inner city area. Excluding the western-most tourist area for a moment, this area is associated with a very strong and dynamic popular culture (García Canclini 1993; Tamayo 1995). Just as London's Cockney East End has its language and slang, songs, foodstuffs and, of course, boxers, so too does Tepito (Eckstein 1990a; Mantecón and Reyes Domínguez 1993). Most of Mexico's internationally renowned boxers emanate from or train here. It is also the location for the city's 'thieves' market. In terms of atmosphere it is like a mini-Naples in downtown Mexico City.

Given that there is no inner city 'problem' in the sense that it is understood in the UK, it is perhaps not surprising that there is no great policy-making preoccupation about the inner city either. However, in Mexico and elsewhere, there is major public- and private-sector concern about the physical deterioration of the colonial core of many Latin American cities (Jones and Bromley 1996). This cultural patrimony is often being lost due to failure to maintain the physical fabric of buildings, or due to failure to enforce protection and conservation ordinances. Indeed the historic core of Mexico City is a UNESCO-designated (1985) World Heritage Site (Jones 1994b), and like many other Mexican cities has an enormously rich patrimony of buildings and monuments spanning all eras: colonial, nineteenth century, art nouveau, art deco, modern and now post-modern. Some 1500 buildings and monuments in the 9 km^2 (or 668 blocks) are registered as having historic and architectural value (Tejeda 1995), and two institutions have primary responsibility for these buildings: INAH, the anthropology and history agency whose aegis is over the pre-twentieth-century patrimony, and the Fine Arts Institute (INBA) which monitors and administers the remainder.

While both institutions actively do what they can, they are inhibited by a lack of resources, and many buildings are lost or continue to deteriorate. There is also a problem of perception, since most conservation and preservation organizations in Mexico City – as elsewhere – tend to view cultural patrimony in purely physical terms: as objects rather than as processes (Hallqvist 1994). This ignores, therefore, the rich cultural patrimony embedded in the local population, namely its social patrimony (see also Tamayo 1995). As this discussion has emphasized, in Mexico the inner city continues to have a large resident population, with a strong popular culture (García Canclini 1994). This means that conservation schemes must seek to restore and maintain the physical fabric without displacing the population either directly through evictions, or indirectly through influencing the prevailing ideology of popular culture and the valuing of buildings and built environments such that they will embrace modernization projects and reject historic patrimony – as threatened to occur in Mexico City's inner city (Tamayo 1995). Of course, outright gentrification will lead to displacement. Unfortunately, eviction and displacement have sometimes been the goals of inner city redevelopment, although only a foolish politician would admit it publicly today; hence the attractiveness of displacement-by-stealth through gentrification.

Today's redevelopment of the South Alameda threatens to be just that. This area is bounded by the following streets: Juárez, Artículo 123, Balderas and Eje Lázaro Cárdenas. This largely commercial area was badly affected by the 1985 earthquakes and, given its less important residential functions, it has seen little reconstruction or reconfiguration since then. Dangerous structures have been pulled down; others remain closed. Some streets retain important small-scale industrial and commercial functions. However, since 1993 there has been ongoing interest from a large private-interest group (Reichmann Internacional) in a major office–commerce–banking redevelopment project for the area. They have contracted leading Mexican architect Ricardo Legorreta to develop a Master Plan for the South Alameda. This has brought the plan into conflict with the INAH, which is responsible for the preservation of the many historic monuments and buildings in the area (Prieto Inzunza and Delgado Lamas 1995). If it goes ahead, there is little doubt that it will displace a large number of small businesses and some residences, no matter how respectful the Legorreta plan seeks to be towards the cultural patrimony.

Thus, while there is no significant residential gentrification in Mexico City for reasons outlined earlier, 'commercial gentrification' is a more viable prospect. In Puebla the renovation of the Victoria Market into a series of boutiques and tourist attractions has had an important role in stimulating inner-city regeneration, but it has also displaced many activities and residents (Jones and Varley 1994). In Mexico City and elsewhere, restoration of colonial monuments into public art galleries and museums, public libraries, government buildings, banks, hotels etc., often displays great imagination and architectural sensitivity, but these same buildings are 'dark' at night (see, for example, Hallqvist 1994). Later in this book the reader will have an opportunity to share my admiration for many of Mexico City's buildings, and I find the renovations of some of the inner-city buildings quite breathtaking. Mexico City's historic core is a UNESCO World Heritage Site, but the 14 impressive projects described by Hallqvist (1994) are almost entirely *exclusionary* of the popular classes – comprising museums, art galleries and the Bankers' Club. Two of the buildings comprise a bar and a restaurant, but these are for lunchtime use and for the middle classes. Regrettably, not one of the 25 new covered markets described above made it into this collection. As Hardoy and his collaborators argued, the challenge is to conserve these historic core areas without turning them into museums (Hardoy and Dos Santos 1983; Hardoy and Gutman 1991). Thus, the people – the popular culture – need to be considered as well. Mexico's inner city has rich traditions, yet few understand or care enough about the vibrant and living culture of the *barrios* themselves.

In this chapter we have seen how Mexico City has grown, and examined many aspects of the recent dynamics of that growth. The remaining chapters in this book will examine specifically the ways in which the city is developing, and the impact that these processes may have upon the physical patterns of social inequality depicted above.

3

THE POLITICS OF CITY MANAGEMENT: DEFENDING THE HIGH GROUND OF MEXICO'S FEDERAL DISTRICT

It is not only the economic, demographic and physical space of the city that has undergone profound changes since the 1970s. Perhaps the most profound changes are in the broader national political arena, which in turn has completely altered the political space of Mexico City's government. One of the most significant changes is occurring as I write and as this second edition goes into production – namely the direct election of the Federal District mayor (to be called governor) on 6 July 1997, this being the first time that the mayor has been elected in 70 years. In the 1990 edition, much of this chapter was dedicated to examining the growing demand for direct elections, and the various mechanisms and arguments adopted by the federal government to stave off the fateful day when the mayor of the Federal District would not be of the national president's choosing, but of the electorate. That day has arrived, and this chapter will examine how this breakthrough has been achieved and its implications for the party that will form the city's government.

However, before we turn to look at Mexico City specifically, the reader will need to be briefed on the national political structure and its recent dynamics. This is necessary because, as we have seen already, the economic and demographic importance of the Metropolitan Area in national life is reinforced by the heavy centralization of federal government in the capital. City politics are, to a significant extent, national politics. Moreover, national politics since 1988 have been in a state of flux. Broadly, the party political and governmental structures have progressively drawn apart in recent years, so that the careers and personnel overlap less and less (Rodríguez and Ward 1994a). In particular, the government is manned increasingly by technocrats rather than by 'old style' politicians (Cornelius and Craig 1991; Centeno 1994). Yet despite all of their technocratic sparkle, they have not managed to avoid many of the same pitfalls as their predecessors. While Salinas' political project was to begin an overhaul of the electoral process in Mexico, paving the way for a relatively free and open election in 1994, he also needed to embark upon a modernization of the party and its candidates in order to make it, and them, a credible force in what would be genuine and *competitive* elections. This need to overhaul the party which has evolved over almost 70 years, holding power through-out, accounts for much of what has happened in the political arena since 1989.

Yet Presidents Salinas and Zedillo appear to have adopted very different methods of 'getting there from here' (Coppedge 1993). Salinas found that he could only achieve the reforms of political opening by continuing to exercise firm centralized control, prompting Lorenzo Meyer to comment in 1991: 'Here in Mexico, *perestroika sin glasnost*' (restructuring without true political opening). Therefore, following timeworn traditions, the political reform process was constructed almost by presidential fiat (Rodríguez and Ward 1994b, 1995). This included: attacks on the most powerful unions, destroying their leadership; 'allowing' the recognition of some opposition victories (particularly of the PAN) and resisting others (particularly the PRD), and generally putting elections results up for negotiation; modernizing the institutions responsible for conducting elections and eventually placing them under non-party (citizen counsellor) control; continuing to hand-pick the party's candidates for the most important elected positions (cities and states), thereby ensuring his own maximum political control. Here, too, Salinas had ample opportunity since, in addition to selection of candidates for election, he also strongly influenced the choice of substitute governor in more than half of the states whose governor was obliged to step down – a sort of *dedazo* in reverse (Rodríguez and Ward 1995). Moreover, Salinas had to personally 'tap' two candidates for the presidency after his first choice, Luis Donaldo Colosio, was assassinated while campaigning in Tijuana in March 1994. Whether the party liked it or not, Salinas led from the front and kept firm control.

Zedillo, on the other hand, appears to be seeking to push forward the political reform process in an entirely different way: letting the process take its course with minimal intervention on his part. For Mexicans used to the traditional forceful and interventionist leader, this back-seat approach is difficult to absorb, particularly when the country is faced with an emergency economic crisis. This has created at least an appearance of a power vacuum in Mexico – in so far as leadership from the top is concerned. In the first 2 years, Zedillo insisted on keeping a healthy distance between the PRI and the Executive ('*la sana distancia entre el gobierno y el partido*'), although from late 1996 onwards he appears to have made a decision to become more actively engaged, placing one of his most trusted senior collaborators in an influential position in the party hierarchy. He has also indicated that he does not expect to hand-pick the next PRI presidential candidate in the year 2000. He has stood back from becoming embroiled in the legislature, even when a PRI faction pressed him hard over the decision to raise VAT from 10 to 15 per cent in 1995, and then in November 1996 PRI legislators pulled back from a cross-party agreement mediated by Zedillo on extended electoral reforms, dealing him what was seen to be a personal slap in the face. Nor has Zedillo intervened directly in the states, even though major issues have arisen over illegitimate electoral campaign expenditures in Tabasco, a peasant massacre by state police in Guerrero etc. In the latter cases the governor was removed, and it is difficult to know exactly how much influence Zedillo exercised, but in general he is letting the judicial and legislative branches take responsibility, and not using his 'metaconstitutional' powers to make changes (Garrido 1989). Now, 6 years on from Meyer's remark, one can observe that there have been major political changes in Mexico that are engendering a democratic transition, although it is debatable how genuine and how profound that transition actually is (Garrido 1993; Crespo 1995, 1996; Handelman 1996).

THE NATIONAL POLITICAL STRUCTURE: WHO GOVERNS IN MEXICO?

On paper, the Mexican government closely resembles that of the United States. It is a federation with three autonomous branches of government comprising the Executive, Legislative and Judicial (Cornelius and Craig 1991; Camp 1993; Morris 1995; Handelman 1996). The Federation contains 31 states and a single Federal District. With the exception of the latter, each state, on paper at least, has constitutional autonomy, as do individual municipalities. Elected officials govern at both levels. Despite this federalist structure and the principle of 'municipal freedom' enshrined in the Constitution, in practice autonomy has traditionally been heavily constrained by centralism – both political and governmental. Central government controls the purse-strings, and most developmental activity is undertaken through the ministerial or parastatal agencies. As Fagen and Tuohy (1972) poetically report, from the state governor's perspective, 'the central government screws me; so I screw the municipality'.

The De la Madrid government in 1983 sought to give greater effective power to the municipal level, but this was resisted by state governors who were reluctant to sacrifice any of their power (Rodríguez 1987). Political centralism remained entrenched, so that in practice those allowed to 'run' for local and district elections continued to be hand-picked by higher-ups within the PRI-government apparatus (Cornelius and Craig 1991). However, important shifts towards greater state and local autonomy have been observed in the past 6 years. Salinas' privatization programme dramatically reduced the activities of federal parastatal agencies, transferring greater responsibility to the states themselves. The national social welfare programme Solidarity (PRONASOL), instituted in 1989, targeted poor local communities and not only brought in additional funding directly to municipalities for development projects, but also required greater levels of public participation and prioritization in those projects (Cornelius *et al.* 1994; Cabrero Mendoza 1995, 1996). This strengthening of local government was also supported by major external (largely World Bank) funding (Rodríguez 1997). President Zedillo is addressing this more directly through New Federalism, which seeks to strengthen state and governmental institutions, to improve local government capacity to generate local revenues, and to raise the level of revenue sharing (Foro Nacional 1995; Aguilar Villanueva 1996; Rodríguez *et al.* 1996). While Zedillo has downgraded PRONASOL and substituted it with a 'Programme to Combat Poverty' of his own, the principal federal budget line which served Solidarity (Ramo XXVI) remains in place and 80 per cent is earmarked for local (municipal) expenditure. The education and health sectors are being actively decentralized to the states, which will now administer them. However, despite these significant shifts towards effective decentralization and greater local autonomy, Mexico remains a heavily centralized system. Seventy-eight per cent of the total revenue sharing remains in federal hands, and while more than fifty per cent of that goes to benefit states and municipalities, much of it is discretional and controlled centrally (Rodríguez and Ward *et al.* 1996).

Until very recently, too, all effective governmental power was centralized in a single party, the PRI. Since the 1930s Mexico has been dominated by a single party, which has evolved through several stages from its early origins as the National Revolutionary Party (PNR), to become the Mexican Revolutionary Party (PRM) under President Cárdenas, and finally in 1945 to emerge in its definitive form as the Institutionalized Revolutionary Party (PRI). During the metamorphosis, the Party shed much of the influence of the military that had existed during the post-revolutionary decade (1910–20) and took on board a greater representation of labour, subsequently broadened to include middle-income and 'popular' groups. It has been described as 'a party of consensus, moderation and stability' (Needler 1982: 29). The significance is that since its formation the PRI has always been the governing party. The President is a PRI 'candidate' and at least until the dramatic 1988 July elections, always won an overwhelming proportion of the vote. Nor had the PRI ever conceded the loss of a state governorship until July 1989, when the National Action Party (PAN) took Baja California, adjacent to the north-west border with the US.

Since then, of course, the PRI's dominance has been rapidly eclipsed, especially by the PAN, which is intensifying its challenge for government. By September 1997, the PAN's tally included six governorships (Baja California, which it held onto for a second 6-year term in the 1995 elections, Chihuahua, Guanajuato, Jalisco, Nuevo León and Querétaro), all of the major metropolitan areas (except Mexico City), and many other principal cities and municipalities. The other major party, the Party of the Democratic Revolution (PRD), greatly expanded its influence in the July 1997 elections, adding the Federal District governorship to the large number of smaller cities and rural municipalities, and the adjacent (1.25 million population) municipality of Netzahualcóyotl on Mexico City's east side, which it won in

November 1996. In short, in less than 8 years the government of 50 per cent of the national population had slipped away from the PRI's control.

In the federal congress, until 1997, the erosion of power was dramatic, since the mixed system of direct and proportional representation guarantees an overall majority to the party polling most votes (so long as this is over 42 per cent of the total). However, while PRI senators and deputies have in the past dominated almost all elections for the legislature, this is no longer the case. Although there are signs that between 1995–97 the PRI's national party base and organization had begun to implode in many areas with the closure of many sections, it had nevertheless managed to sustain itself as the majority party in Congress (Lujambio 1995). However, that majority was lost in the dramatic 6 July 1997 elections when the PRI's vote fell to 39 per cent – 3 points below the minimum level required to be eligible to secure an absolute majority. Thus in the new Congress, after the proportional representation seats have been allocated, the PRI holds 239 of the 500 total. The PRD won 125 and the PAN 122, the remainder being distributed among the minor parties. In the Senate the PRI will continue to have a majority. Nevertheless, this means that from now on President Zedillo and the PRI will have to cut deals with the opposition in order to secure the passage of legislation, and that constitutional amendments which require a two-thirds majority to pass will be very difficult to achieve without substantial cross-party support. Taken together with the apparent distancing between party and president, these election results made PRI-control of Congress much less of a 'slam dunk' than of old.

Party politics in Mexico: the growth of genuine opposition?

The pre-1990s Mexican political system was generally considered authoritarian. It displayed a low level of political mobilization and limited pluralism in which the contest for power was restricted to supporters of the regime. The latter possessed a 'mentality' rather than a clear ideology (Smith 1979: 53; Whitehead 1994; see also Needler 1982). Inevitably, in a system such as this, considerable importance was placed upon election results as a source of legitimacy for the governing élite.

Until 1988, when its proportion of the presidential vote fell to fractionally over 50 per cent, the PRI had been accustomed to receiving overwhelming electoral support: almost always more than 75 per cent of the turnout at presidential elections (Smith 1979; Cockcroft 1983). Despite this fact, an ongoing dilemma faced by the PRI was how to retain absolute control and sustain existing levels of support while at the same time stimulate sufficient interest among the opposition in competitive electoral politics. This was resolved, on the one hand, by ensuring support from the grassroots through its tripartite structure (see below) and by rigging the ballot box. On the other hand, although competitive party politics was narrowly circumscribed and controlled, the presence and activity of opposition parties was carefully sustained and sometimes even sponsored by the PRI. Indeed, the greatest threat to the PRI's cultivation of a democratic façade used to be posed by abstentions (González Casanova 1970).

If the PRI is considered to occupy the middle-left ground of the political spectrum in Mexico, then the only concerted opposition, at least until recently, was provided by the right-wing National Action Party (PAN). Established to combat the left-wing tendencies adopted by President Cárdenas (1934–40), the PAN traditionally attracted support from within conservative business circles, provincial and large-city middle classes, and the Catholic Church (Cockcroft 1983: 305; Story 1986). Although it rarely won more than 15 per cent of the national vote, it regularly took at least a few electoral districts and municipalities by majority vote. Very occasionally these included large city municipalities such as Ciudad Juárez and Chihuahua (1983–86) (Rodríguez and Ward 1992; Aziz Nassif 1994). Its strongholds were located primarily in the north of the country, and in Mérida, Yucatán. It was not until 1989 that the PAN was finally allowed to accede to a governorship; previous elections in PANista strongholds were almost certainly rigged in favour of a PRI 'victory'.

However, it was important for Mexico to retain at least the illusion of democracy, and by the late 1960s the need to revitalize the political structure and to restore the legitimacy of the governing élite was widely felt. Political reforms were initiated in 1973 and extended further in 1977. Two important changes were introduced. First, the reforms provided for the registration of a host of new parties, most of which were left-wing. The most important among these were the Mexican Communist Party (PCM), the Socialist Workers' Party (PST) and the Mexican Workers' Party (PMT). On the right, and far more populist than the PAN, was the Mexican Democratic Party (PDM) with a regional stronghold in Guanajuato. Second, the size of Congress was increased, and one-quarter of the (then) 400 seats was given to opposition parties to be allocated on the basis of proportional representation of the votes received.

These initiatives had an important effect upon the political process. In 1982 for example, 50 of the congressional seats went to the PAN, while the remainder were shared between the PDM (12), PST (11), PPS (10) and PSUM (a PCM-led coalition of several left-wing parties) (17). While the PRI's preeminence was assured and a clear majority in the Congress guaranteed, there was now a greater incentive for opposition parties to participate in elections. Their representation in the Chamber of Deputies sharpened the level of debate and criticism of government policy. Although still a carefully controlled minority, they provided an important channel for registering political dissent. Whether this ultimately made any appreciable difference to the position of working class Mexicans is open to question. However, the *apertura democrática* initiated by President Echeverría, and extended by López Portillo, represented a significant step in opening the political franchise and freedom of expression in Mexico. However, we should recognize that its purpose at that time was not one of reducing the authority and role of the PRI, but rather to enhance and sustain it.

This arrangement changed as a result of the 1988 elections, and the necessity for Salinas to undertake political reforms that would enhance and give credibility to his neoliberal economic project. Here is not the place for a full chronology of events leading up to the 1988 elections, but the bare 'facts' begin with the failure of the PRI in 1986 to resolve and manage the democratic current that had emerged within the Party led by certain senior members (Garrido 1993). Several of these individuals had held high office in the government, came from the political left, and were disillusioned with the inability of the Party to respond adequately to contemporary pressures and social needs. They were also alarmed at the apparent shift that the federal government was taking towards the political right, evident in the negotiations to join GATT in 1986, as well as in the moves towards strengthening Mexico's competitive base abroad: tearing down tariff barriers, etc. More specifically, it seemed likely that De la Madrid's choice for the next presidential candidate would go to someone who would intensify this process – as indeed proved to be the case once Salinas was tapped.

Ordinarily, one would have expected the PRI to 'accommodate' this position within its ranks. However, after much debate and acrimony, several key figures in the *corriente* withdrew from the Party late in 1987, and Cuauhtémoc Cárdenas (son of the former President and himself recently a State Governor) launched himself as candidate for the presidency. Supported by the majority of the opposition parties of the left, his Democratic Front ran a close second to Salinas. In 1989 Cárdenas formally created a new party – the Party of the Democratic Revolution, the PRD – and was elected its first president

The 1988 election results were a huge embarrassment for the PRI, in part because they did so badly, and in part because of the fraud and the doubts that surrounded the way in which the results were published. The alleged computer 'crash' and delay (of almost 1 week) before full results were announced fuelled rumours that the PRI had actually lost the election. The results, when they came, declared that Salinas (PRI) had gained 50.36 per cent of the vote, Cárdenas (Democratic Front) 31.12 per cent, and Clouthier (PAN) 17.07 per cent. There seems little doubt that the bare 50 per cent majority over the opposition was contrived (Barberán *et al.* 1988). In Congress, however, the failure to put up single opposition candidates meant that the PRI swept the board by 249 to 51 of the 300 seats allocated by absolute majority. However, as was noted above, a large number of seats are also allocated according to proportional representation, and this meant that the PRI only had an overall majority of 15 or 16 seats in the Legislature. Opposition (*Frente*) senators won in one of the 31 states and in the Federal District.

The PRI was alarmed that it no longer had sufficient seats to undertake constitutional amendments (requiring as they do a two-thirds majority), so in 1989 it legislated a 'governability' clause that would grant the majority party fractionally less than 66 per cent of seats, but ensuring more than that proportion once the small number of 'para'-PRI opposition minority parties were included. In any event, the PRI did very well in the 1991 national mid-term elections, taking 290 of the 300 direct-election seats; including the 31 proportional representation seats to which it was eligible, it had 321 seats in the (now) 500 seat house (Camp 1993; Colosio 1993). It no longer felt sufficiently threatened to require the protection that the 'governability' clause provided; nor was it easy to justify publicly, so it was dropped in 1993. Indeed, so large was the PRI majority that Salinas was concerned that the legitimacy of major pieces of legislation, particularly the Electoral Codes' Reform of 1993, would be questionable if it were driven through by the PRI alone. Extensive negotiations with the PAN and PRD took place, and eventually the PAN signed off on it along with the PRI, allowing Salinas to insist that it was passed with cross-party support.

If Salinas' own election was seriously flawed by alleged fraud, his (then) popularity was such that he won the 1994 election on behalf of Ernesto Zedillo. That election was regarded as clean but not fair, given the enormous advantage that the PRI had in terms of campaign finance and media access, and a very clever campaign to harness the 'fear' vote of those alarmed by the Chiapas insurrection and apparent upsurge of political violence (see Ward *et al.* 1994). The electoral reforms had gone a long way in permitting free elections, but the playing field remained far from level (Handelman 1996). Zedillo won 53 per cent of the vote, his PAN rival (Diego Fernández de Cevallos) took 28.6 per cent, and Cuauhtémoc Cárdenas (PRD) 18 per cent. In the elections for deputies, the PRI won 50.3 per cent (down 11.4 from 1991), but with their proportional representation seats the PRI held 60 per cent of all the seats, the PAN 24 per cent, and the PRD 14 per cent (Handelman 1996: 76). As we have observed already, that dominance of Congress was seriously eroded in the July 1997 elections, when the PRI lost absolute control for the first time ever and the balance of parties became much more of a three-way split.

The parties: who's hot and who's not in 1997

The PRI   After almost 70 years of being the only 'hot' party in Mexico, the past 2 years have been major doldrums for the PRI. Traditionally, the Party has been built around three sectors: the National Confederation of Farm-workers (CNC), a labour sector (CTM), and a socially heterogeneous

Confederation of Popular Organizations (CNOP) comprising middle class professions such as teachers as well as local organizations representing low-income settlements, trade unions etc. This latter sector has changed its name and organizational status since the 1980s becoming the UNE and latterly the Movimiento Territorial (Craske 1994, 1996). Each of these sectors represented solid grassroots support organized on a strictly hierarchical basis, with minimal horizontal linkages between either sectors or individual federations. Thus all party or federation bosses looked upwards for their orders and often competed openly against those on a similar level to themselves (Schers 1972; Eckstein 1977).

Although they were all within the same umbrella organization (the PRI), this hierarchical structure offered enormous scope for political manipulation from above. Up-and-coming party militants could be set against one another; those who showed particular promise could be promoted and lifted into a bigger pond; those who became too powerful could be frozen out and isolated (Schers 1972; Smith 1979). It was an excellent proving ground for party politicians. However, these corporatist sectors are much weaker in the 1990s than in recent decades. The CTM, while still headed by Fidel Velázquez (now in his 90s) has become far less of a force. Unions have become more internally democratic and wrested of their corrupt leadership (Middlebrook 1995: 300; Cook, 1996). Privatization, market opening, export promotion and NAFTA were especially favourable to large manufacturers and to the interests of financiers who became the principal base of political support for the Salinas administration. These groups were favoured at the expense of organized labour (Middlebrook 1995). The strong corporatist model of the three sectors was displaced by more personalistic and direct dealings with unions as well as with states and communities (for example Salinas' frequent forays into Valle de Chalco in the east of Mexico City).

Despite the mass base of grassroots support for the governing party, these sectors have never functioned to funnel working class interests upwards through the appropriate executive committee to the PRI executive, and thence to shape government policy directly in a manner resembling an 'aggregate interest model' (Scott 1964; Huntington 1968). In fact the Party has minimal power over decision making, and only limited access to resources (Padgett 1966; Hansen 1974; Eckstein 1977; Smith 1979). Even the illusion of party/government overlap is beginning to fade. The PRI's role has principally been to provide a career structure for up-and-coming politicians, to conciliate the negotiation of jobs (i.e. patronage) given the high turnover of electoral posts every 3 and 6 years, and to ensure the legitimacy of the government by mobilizing support at the polls. This latter function has, of course, become much more difficult to achieve now that the government no longer controls the electoral institutions, appears to be wedded to the idea of open elections, and from the PRI's perspective is caving in to opposition demands for equity in campaign financing and media access. Faced with these new conditions, the PRI is beginning to recognize the necessity of being able to select its own candidates locally, and of ensuring that these candidates have local credibility and, if elected, that their performance in government reflects well on the party (Rodríguez and Ward 1996). This runs counter to the tradition whereby candidates for senior elective positions (governors in particular) have been chosen centrally by the national president and by senior party and governmental leaders (Yescas Martínez 1994).

Nevertheless, the PRI still has considerable advantages over the other parties. First, it remains the party in government, and while this has counted against its candidates in the most recent elections (since the 1995 crisis) if the Zedillo administration proves capable of achieving some level of growth by 1998–9, then this may be expected to carry over into electoral support for the PRI. Second, the PRI is the only party with a truly *national* party base structure, and if it can successfully define a convincing message, then it has the wherewithal to get that message out. For electoral purposes the PRI is organized at four levels into sectional, municipal, state and national committees, and notwithstanding some erosion in the sections and the unpopularity evident in 1997, in my view it is still too early to write-off the PRI's prospects for the year 2000.

The increasing pressures associated with electoral competition have begun to translate into increasing pressure from within the PRI's internal party bases to assert themselves – insisting upon a greater say in the selection of candidates, and introducing a new clause at the 17th Party Assembly in 1996 which requires that in future all candidates for governor and president must have held an elected representative position beforehand. (None of the past four presidents would have qualified.) It is also beginning to call for definition of a more precise party ideology that goes beyond the broad-brush catch-all of 'revolutionary nationalism' of the past, or of 'social liberalism' (which it now firmly rejects as being too closely associated with Salinas). At the same Assembly the Party voted against the proposed opening-up of the petrochemical industry to private investors. Then PRI legislators reneged on the political reform arrangement supported by Zedillo. To publicly spurn the Executive, and to begin to seek to transpose ideological positions into government policy, while it is the stuff of governing parties in the US and the UK, is without precedent in contemporary Mexican politics. For President Zedillo and other senior PRIístas and powerful groups within the PRI, it appeared that the reforms may have been going too fast and that they were insufficiently controlled or 'guided' by the then Party president, Santiago Oñate – so much so that he was forced to resign in December 1996, and the PRI's majority leader in Congress took over the leadership barely 8 months before the crucial elections of 1997.

The PAN The PAN was established in 1939 by disaffected businessmen, professionals and Catholic intellectuals who opposed Lázaro Cárdenas' nationalization of the petroleum industry and his revolutionary agenda. While it has retained strong religious (Catholic) underpinnings, during its evolution it has included within its ranks progressive Christian Democrats and other democratic reformers (Sigg 1993). The common thread that bound these various groups together was their overarching concern that the Mexican state had become too powerful and too interventionist. The PRI and the government's control of the ballot box forestalled their electoral challenge, but the PAN continued to campaign for free elections and achieved a core of support of around 15 per cent in presidential elections (although it boycotted the 1976 election and did not put up a candidate).

Events such as the nationalization of the banks in 1982 galvanized that opposition and moved it further to the right. Moreover, it also promoted the entry into politics of businessmen and entrepreneurs, particularly in the northern states of Chihuahua and Nuevo León (Mizrahi 1994, 1995). Businessmen such as Francisco Barrio in Chihuahua and Ernesto Ruffo in Baja California won city mayorships in 1983 and 1986, respectively. Given the limited local party base and the lack of experience in power, these new victors brought other local businessmen into government (Mizrahi 1994; Camp 1995). Their business backgrounds brought a new *modus operandi* to local government – one of greater transparency and more effective accounting and efficiency, i.e. it was very much the business enterprise model of government (see Rodríguez and Ward 1992, 1994b, 1995; Cabrero Mendoza 1996). Their apparent openness and relative efficiency appear to have won considerable local confidence, and although the PAN lost the two principal cities that it held in Chihuahua between 1983 and 1986 as well as the state gubernatorial election which mayor Barrio contested in 1986, there is little doubt that the PRI won through fraud (Rodríguez and Ward 1992; Aziz Nassif 1994). Several years later, with Salinas' greater willingness to tolerate opposition victories, one began to observe the PAN winning back-to-back elections in a number of large cities (Tijuana, León, Cd. Juárez, etc.), as well as the state of Baja California in 1995 (having first won it in 1989). So successful has the PAN been in local elections, that by 1996 it governed over one-third of the population.

These victories have led to the emergence of several different groups in the PAN. On the one hand are the pragmatists – those who have experience in local and state government, and who tend to be less identified with the tenets of PANista ideology. On the other are the more traditional militant party membership who have tended to dominate in party headquarters as well as in legislative positions. In the early 1990s the PAN's president was long-time militant Luis H. Alvarez, who managed to straddle both camps, having been mayor of Chihuahua City (1983–86), as well as being a militant PANista with impeccable party credentials. It was he who began to foster a more pragmatic stance of dealing and negotiating with Salinas, although this led to considerable disquiet among a dissident group within the party who were alarmed by the way in which the PRI (which was itself moving to the right) appeared to be stealing the PAN's political and economic agendas. They wanted an uncompromising non-cooperation stance towards the Salinas government. Ultimately the members of this dissident group left the party in 1992 (Reynoso 1994; Vicencio 1996).

Luis H. Alvarez was elected senator in 1994. Since he stepped down as party president in 1993, the party has had two leaders, Carlos Castillo Peraza (1993–96) and Felipe Calderón Hinojosa. Both are party militants with extensive experience in the centre – within party headquarters and within the legislature – but neither has held an elected executive position (mayor or governor). Indeed, former governor Ruffo was Calderón's principal rival for the presidency. Another leading figure in the PAN is Diego Fernández de Cervallos, a close ally of Alvarez and PAN candidate in the 1994 presidential elections. Although Zedillo and the PRI won easily, the PAN emerged (then) as the clear second in Mexican party politics, with Fernández de Cevallos polling almost 29 per cent of the vote.

In less than 10 years the PAN has emerged as a major force in politics and in government in Mexico: so much so that since 1994 the previously unthinkable has become thinkable, that the PRI might lose the presidency in 2000. Whether it does or not will depend largely upon how the Zedillo administration fares in its economic policy, and whether the PRI manages to reorganize successfully. The PAN still lacks an effective national party structure capable of mobilizing the vote and extending its level of support beyond the one-third level it now has. Until it develops such a structure it is not likely to be master of its own fate, but will depend for its success upon the failures of the PRI. In 1997 it had high hopes for success in the congressional and Federal District elections, but in the event these were eclipsed somewhat by the strong showing of the PRD, especially in Mexico City.

The PRD   As described above, the PRD was formed in 1989 after Cárdenas had challenged Salinas for the presidency. Built around disaffected PRIístas such as Cárdenas himself, Porfirio Muñoz Ledo, Ifigenia Martínez and others, the party occupied the centre-left that had, until 1982 at least, always formed part of the PRI's revolutionary ideology – in rhetoric if not in practice. The PRI's shift to the right under President De la Madrid, intensi-fied by Salinas, encroached sharply upon the ideological high ground of the PAN, and left a large space that the PRD could slip into virtually unchal-lenged, particularly after Salinas' alliance with major economic interest groups and his destruction of some leading union figures had weakened and uncoupled the labour movement's capacity to resist (Middlebrook 1995).

Not only did the PRD provide a home for disaffected PRI leftists, but it also became a catch-all for many of the parties and coalitions on the left.

This tendency towards accretion of camp followers of former parties and different ideologies has become a problem for the PRD, and has resulted in it not becoming the force expected when it was formed. The urgency to develop a viable party capable of contesting the 1991 and 1994 elections has meant that it has much less of a national party base than even the PAN. It has therefore been obliged to adopt a large number of local candidates who have considerable local following and credibility, but are often themselves disaffected for one reason or another. In some cases this has led to 'good' government by locally respected leaders (see, for example, Cabrero Mendoza 1996: 159–192), but it has not produced party coherence and militancy. Under Mexico's requirement that all candidates be adopted by a party, the PRD has often served as a flag of convenience, and while many have been elected into office, the PRD has taken on the appearance of a rather motley collection of political actors and leaders. Nor have Cárdenas and the subsequent president Muñoz Ledo proved capable of melding these camp-followers under a clear party and ideological banner. This will be the principal challenge of recently elected party president Andrés Manuel López Obrador (himself also a disaffected former member of the PRI and former state secretary for Tabasco).

Another reason for the less dynamic performance as an opposition party (compared with the PAN) was the violence and oppression visited upon it by the Salinas government. The enmity between Cárdenas and Salinas was deeply personal and intense, Salinas blaming the former presidential challenger for having sullied his own election victory and legitimacy to be president (which Cárdenas never accepted). Nor would Cárdenas 'deal' with Salinas in order to secure recognition of PRD electoral victories – in Michoacán (Cárdenas' stronghold) in 1992, for example. Where the PRD won control of cities, as in Morelia, the state capital of Michoacán, there is clear evidence of attempts by state and federal officials to punish the city and to make life difficult for the municipal government (Bruhn and Yanner 1995). Such vindictiveness and blatant partisanship does not seem to have been shown towards the PAN, nor even towards the PRD in other states such as Oaxaca (Bailón 1995; Rodríguez and Ward 1995). Nor was this repression merely administrative; the Salinas administration had a poor record of human rights abuses towards the PRD and its militants, over 200 of whom died as a result of political violence (Cornelius 1994; Morris 1995).

Tensions eased somewhat once Zedillo took office and, as outlined earlier in this chapter, there is now greater respect for legitimate electoral victories of non-PRI parties and fewer systematic attempts to undermine PRD local governments. Nevertheless, with the exception of the Federal District which is a special entity, the PRD has still not been successful at the gubernatorial level, although it came close in Tabasco in late 1995. Although the PRI appears to have won by a relatively close margin, subsequent allegations that it grossly exceeded the limits of campaign spending appear to be well founded. These accusations were fuelled by the losing candidate's (López Obrador) ambitions to become the PRD's national president, which he ultimately succeeded in doing in 1996. So far the PRI governor, Carlos Madrazo, has hung on, and the pressure appears to have declined now that López Obrador has shifted his attention to PRD party headquarters and centre stage, but this is a good example of a situation where Salinas would almost certainly have intervened to force Madrazo's replacement. Zedillo has held back and argued that it is a matter for the other branches of government (legislature and judiciary) to resolve constitutionally.

Within the party Cárdenas remains an important *eminence*; so much so that he successfully pressed his case to be candidate for the governorship of the DF elections in July 1997. Had he not won that election, it would have been difficult to imagine how he might figure in the future, given two failed runs at the national presidency and his poor showing in the 1994 election campaign. Also, he failed to meld the party as its president. But his stunning success, coming almost from nowhere to win 48 per cent of the vote in the Federal District governorship (almost double that of his nearest rival, PRI candidate Alfredo del Mazo), places him in a very strong position to mount a third attempt on the presidency in 2000. Much will depend, of course, on how he performs in managing Mexico City's Federal District over the next 3 years, but politically speaking he has raised himself from the dead.

The previous PRD president, Porfirio Muñoz Ledo, may also be expected to remain a force given his renowned political ability and prodigious capacity at debating. For party president López Obrador the main challenge is to create an effective party structure which builds upon a coherent ideology and is not seen to be the sum of parts being made up of disaffected militants from elsewhere. He, too, was formerly a leading PRI figure in Tabasco, but his strong links to the labour sector in that state might provide a basis for forging some party unity, particularly if the PRI does not recover its influence over the labour sector and if the government continues to seek to weaken its influence.

The government and the executive

If the PRI has relatively little influence over national policy, we may ask how policy is determined. To evaluate this question we must look briefly, first, at the structure of government and, second, at the way in which different groups articulate their interests and the factors that determine their success.

In Mexico the President holds office for a non-renewable 6-year term and appoints cabinet members and many other high-level officials according to a wide range of criteria. People are selected for their personal loyalty and past support. The President must also aim to reconcile a wide range of interest groups and seek to ensure that all are included in his cabinet

(Needler 1982). However, to balance this and to keep a cross-check on the actions of ministers, he will often appoint his own people to sub-ministerial posts. Until restrictions were imposed in 1983, nepotism and sinecures for relatives and friends were widespread. Increasingly, though, appointees must be professionally competent. Important jobs require sensitive handling, and banana skins must be carefully avoided.

As we have seen, differences in ideology do not usually form the basis that determines the constitution of different 'groups' in Mexican politics (although they may be tied to specific vested interests). Rather, groups are organized into 'leader–follower' alliances, sometimes called *camarillas* (Grindle 1977; Cornelius and Craig 1991; Camp 1993). These may be best envisaged as teams which form around a particular person, and as that individual moves between different posts in government so, too, does his team. This explains why the same people may appear in such unlikely consecutive positions as the Subsistence Foods Enterprise (CONASUPO), the Ministry of Health and Welfare, and the State of Mexico Government (Grindle 1977). Each *camarilla* actually comprises a series of layers with 'leaders' and sub-teams at each level. Ultimately, however, they lead to the same top politician. Occasionally, *camarillas* overlap, leading upwards to two influential leaders. In such cases a close alliance would usually exist between the two, and the sharing out of jobs and placement of personnel may be done by agreement. Here working for one boss after previously working for the other is acceptable. Otherwise, transfer across groups is not tolerated, and among the 'rules' of behaviour the greatest breach is disloyalty (Grindle 1977; Smith 1979). One feature of political 'nous' in Mexico is the ability to recognize and predict the implications of any single action upon competing *camarillas*.

Over the past three decades an important shift has taken place in the type of person who gains top public office. Gone are the old-style politicians from provincial and often military backgrounds (Needler 1982). While the ruling élite continues to be drawn from among wealthy well-known families, they are increasingly likely to be from the central regions of the country, and from the Federal District in particular. Increasingly, too, they are 'technocrats', although clearly if they are to advance significantly they must also show political acumen (Centeno 1994). For the most part these groups are formed at university. For politicians in the 1960s and 1970s the National University (UNAM) was the principal starting point, but more recently it has been the private schools (Iberomericana, ITAM etc.) that have become more frequent sources of *camarilla* formation for the PRI, and the ITESM for the PAN and for northern PRIísta families (Colosio for example). In addition, the high flyers are taking postgraduate degrees abroad – a sort of technical finishing school to hone one's skills and to develop one's English. Both Salinas and Zedillo have doctorates from Ivy League universities, as have many of their closest collaborators.

Until the 1980s the Mexican bureaucracy was vast and had expanded considerably since 1970. In 1975 it comprised 18 ministries, 123 decentralized agencies, 292 public enterprises, 187 official commissions and 160 development trusts (Grindle 1977: 3), but at that time a distended bureaucracy was functional for the state. By providing jobs it facilitated the circulation of patronage. It created opportunities for manipulation by the Executive: personnel posing a threat could be 'frozen-out' or their authority undermined by the creation of a duplicate agency; support could be bestowed upon certain agencies and subtly withdrawn from others. Also, an intricate bureaucracy with ample red tape slowed down the outflow of resources while at the same time creating an appearance of being 'busy' and overworked. Such distended bureaucracy is now a thing of the past. As we saw in Chapter 1, almost 1000 state and parastatal enterprises, trusts etc., have been privatized or wound up since the beginning of the Salinas administration.

In Mexico, back-to-back re-election is not allowed under the Constitution. Nor are legislators expected or encouraged to develop a constituency role for the districts they represent. These features are deliberate, and reflect Mexico's concern to avoid one individual dominating the same stage in perpetuity, as well as the PRI's concern that it, alone, should control individual political careers, and that no-one should be allowed to build an independent constituency powerbase of their own.

This 'no re-election' clause also makes for a *sexenio* dynamic: the first year to 18 months comprise the coordination of teams, establishing new policies which will usually disassociate the approach of the new team from that of its predecessors, and securing adequate finance to carry through the programmes (Grindle 1977). During years three, four and five these programmes are introduced, after which people begin to look around and get close to those who are likely to figure prominently in the forthcoming administration. Once one of the existing cabinet has been named as the new candidate (in effect President elect), then all bets are off. Those overly associated with the losers are said to be 'burned' (*quemado*), and know that they will not figure significantly in the next government. Although it would be incorrect to suggest that during the last year the President is a lame duck, within government agencies and ministries few new actions are undertaken and most work concentrates on completing projects already underway. One of the unusual features of the Salinas administration was the fact that he sustained programmes and control over government right until the last days. Moreover, he did not 'take the hit' and clean the decks for his successor.

Policy making: who rules?

We have observed that public policy in Mexico does not emerge from within the ranks of the official party, nor from the Legislature. Neither is it the product of a clear ideological stance. Mexico watchers tend to have their own particular analogy that best describes the nature of the political process. Some see it as a card game in which different interests participate, occasionally winning a little, sometimes losing, but never destroying everything by kicking over the table (Needler 1982). Others see it as a 'marriage', governed and delimited by certain rules yet actually worked out on a day-to-day basis of negotiation (Purcell and Purcell 1980). In fact it is very difficult to say precisely how policy is formulated, since discussions take place behind closed doors 'beyond the purview of the general public and the rank-and-file adherents of the official party' (Grindle 1977).

Nor do non-PRI governments appear to be much different. The governor or municipal president develops policy out of his or her own 'kitchen' cabinets with little direction coming from party headquarters or from local party militants. PAN local governments are sometimes described as business enterprise models, with the municipal president acting like a CEO (Cabrero Mendoza 1995). While they may be more open and transparent, and in some respects more participatory in their dissemination of information, the executive still exercises firm control, and where there are exceptions – such as the PRD mayor in Atoyac de Alvarez in Guerrero state – these serve to prove the rule (Cabrero Mendoza 1995). More generally, however, it does appear that the quickening of interest in local governance and the emerging civic and political culture in Mexico will lead to more democratic and participatory government at all levels. In particular, the legislative branch is beginning to take a more proactive role, as are local party organizations, in selecting candidates and shaping local political agendas.

In the past, however, the political system was usually envisaged as a delicate balancing act involving all élite interests incorporated into a 'political bargain' which was constantly renewed in day-to-day action (Purcell and Purcell 1980). It was 'inclusionary' in so far as all groups or interests were represented, although inevitably any sharp change in policy advanced certain interests at the expense of others. The adverse effects of such action were usually minimized, and a tacitly agreed aim was to avoid the existence of outright 'winners' and 'losers'. However, every administration created certain imbalances, and the expectancy was that these would be redressed in the following administration. This helps explain the tendency demonstrated in Figure 3.1 for a pendulum-type shift back-and-forth between 'activist' and 'consolidatory' presidents (Purcell and Purcell 1980: 222; Cornelius and Craig 1991). The critical task of the President within this arrangement was to strike and maintain that balance within his administration (Smith 1979). That preoccupation – to counter the imbalances of the previous administration – appears to have been sacrificed since 1982. While Colosio (Salinas' original choice) would have represented a move back to the political centre, Zedillo is very much in the technocratic and neo-liberal mould. It was precisely this breaking of the equilibrium-seeking

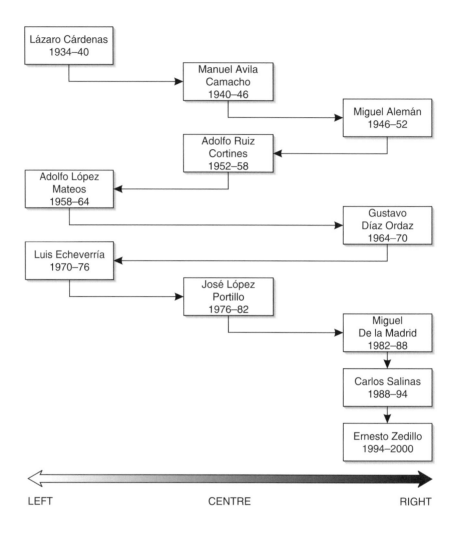

FIGURE 3.1 'Pendulum politics' in Mexico: swings between 'activist' and 'consolidatory' presidents, 1934–2000. Source: adapted from Skidmore and Smith 1989, p. 243

tradition of the past that drove the PRIísta leftists to leave the party. It has also intensified opposition from those national economic groups who are excluded, and has fuelled their willingness to look to the PAN; they no longer 'hedge their bets' by offering lukewarm support for both parties.

Key groups incorporated into the governing élite were the leaders of the CTM, CNC and the popular sector, but while they were likely to be accorded significance they did not predominate, especially not under De la Madrid and Salinas (Morris 1995). Also closely involved is the private sector.

Opinions differ about the degree to which it actually forms part of the governing bloc, and most analysts see a clear separation between government and business interests (Smith 1979: 214; Needler 1982; Story 1986; but cf. Cockcroft 1983: 210). However, there are several state/corporatist entities such as the Confederation of Chambers of Industry (CONCAMIN) and of Commerce (CONCANACO) which are designed to directly inform government decisions. Equally there are numerous other independent 'voices', such as the Employers' Confederation (COPARMEX) and that of manufacturing industries (CANACINTRA). Undoubtedly soundings are taken from these groups, but policy is essentially decided within the Executive: the President, his private office, and others whom he sees fit to involve (Teichman 1988). While decisions may be taken that hurt certain interests, the 'bargain' demands acquiescence on the understanding that imbalances will eventually be redressed. That bargain has been broken, and Salinas in particular appears to have moved away from a broad-based sectoral alliance (including wider business groups), and instead favoured a small coterie of large-scale national economic groups and individuals who benefited preferentially from his privatization and economic development policies, but who in return gave him their political support.

GOVERNMENT WITHOUT DEMOCRACY IN MEXICO CITY: DEFENDING THE HIGH GROUND

The structure of government in the Metropolitan Area

The Federal District (DF) has existed as a special political entity within the Federation since August 1928, when it lost its status as a state and series of municipalities. It then became a special political entity divided into a central department comprising a number of quarters (*cuarteles*) and 13 *delegaciones*. There were two principal reasons for the change. First, the municipalities were in major financial difficulty and incapable of delivering essential services. Second, intense political in-fighting among fledgling political parties during the Carranza period was being played out through the local *ayuntamientos*, even where these parties all supported the President. These troubles continued through the 1920s until Obregón, as part of his presidential election campaign, embraced the proposal to create a special district. In a single move he sought to marginalize the (then) Labour Party's strength in the municipalities and to create a less anarchic structure capable of improved city management (Meyer 1987; Cisneros Sosa 1993; Davis 1994). In 1970 the *cuarteles* were reconstituted as *delegaciones* to make a total of 16 that still exist today. However, the original reconfiguration was more political than spatial; a special district, as the seat of federal powers, belonged to the nation as a whole. Instead of locally elected representatives running City Hall, the Mayor (*Regente*) was a Presidential appointee, as were the 16 local mayors (*Delegados*), although in practice many were nominated by the *Regente* for confirmation by the Executive.

The argument has always been that the national President is, in effect, also elected as Governor of the Federal District. Given his other duties, he delegates these responsibilities to the *Regente* and to the local mayors. The administrative and political structures of the Federal District are shown in Figure 3.2. The National Congress is charged with legislative functions both for the nation and for the Federal District. An additional 'tier' was created in 1988 (the Federal District *Asamblea de Representantes*), comprising elected party-political representatives. Its functions at the outset were vague, but in practice during the first two assemblies (1988–91; 1991–94) it appears to have acted as an important 'watchdog' assembly on City Hall expenditure and policy. Increasingly, however, it has developed functions akin to a local congress (Bassols and Corona Martínez 1993; Incháustegui 1994). Much earlier, in 1977, the DF had also created a hierarchically ordered neighbourhood consultative structure on civic matters organized at the levels of *delegación* (the *Juntas de Vecinos*) and Federal District (the Consultative Council).

Once appointed, the Mayor brought in his own staff to key posts within City Hall (the Federal District Department, DDF). He held a high-ranking cabinet office and his influence grew as a result of the economic predominance of the Federal District within the national economy, its role as the political centre, and its spotlighted position on the national, and sometimes international, centre-stage. The large population, too, had to be kept sweet, for this is the President's backyard and he could ill afford to be embarrassed by it. Therefore the city received a disproportionate share of national resources and its citizens had preferential access to housing, urban services, subsidized transportation, and so on. Traditionally, therefore, Mexico City governments bought 'social peace' and well-being and passed on the costs to the nation at large. In addition, the President was likely to appoint to the Mayor's Office either a political heavyweight (since 1954 good examples are Mayors Uruchurtu, Corona del Rosal and Hank González) who can be relied upon not to 'screw-up' (Figure 3.3). Alternatively, he would appoint a malleable but close ally from his own political group whom he trusted implicitly and through whom he could intervene directly if required (e.g. Mayors Sentíes, Aguirre and Camacho).

Past mayors: rulers from elsewhere

Until Manuel Camacho took office in 1988, no previously appointed mayor was a native of the Federal District: all came from the provinces. Since the 1950s only one person has held the office of Mayor across *sexenios* –

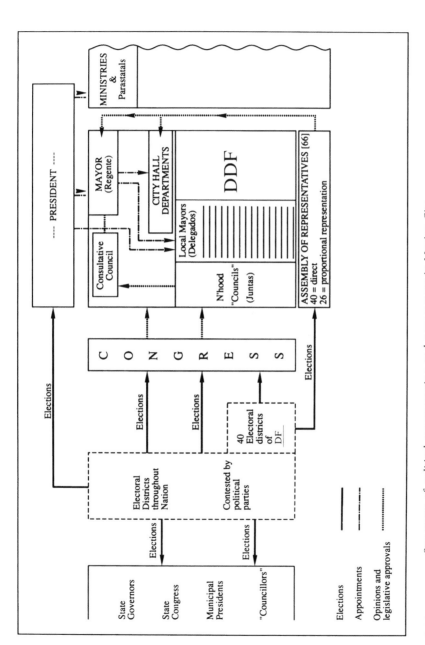

FIGURE 3.2 Structures of political representation and government in Mexico City

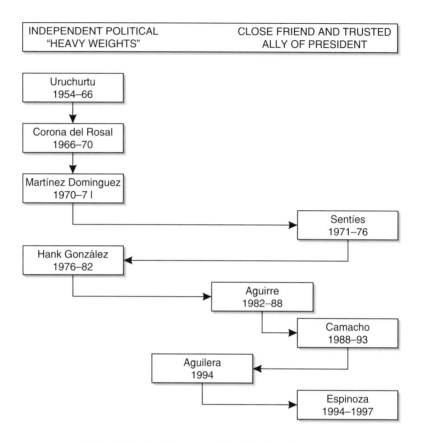

FIGURE 3.3 Federal District Mayors and their basis of appointment

Ernesto Uruchurtu – who held office consecutively under three different Presidents (cf. Figures 3.1 and 3.3), largely because his firm control over city affairs and administration won him the confidence of successive executives. However, rapid city growth, the increasing complexity of city affairs, and his eventual loss of control over illegal settlement developments in the south of the city, demonstrated that his policies had outgrown their usefulness and he was forced to resign in 1966 (see also Davis 1994). Alfonso Corona del Rosal, who succeeded him, had close links with the National Confederation of Popular Organizations (CNOP) and mobilized cliente list links with local groups in order to win support and head-off social unrest (Cornelius 1975).

The maintenance of social peace in the city is the primary political task of the mayor. When street rioting broke out in 1971, for example, Mayor Martínez Domínguez was held responsible and was sacked. In his place Echeverría appointed a close personal friend, Octavio Sentíes, and, more than any other President, he intervened directly in city affairs, often over the head of the *Regente* (Ward 1981a). This pattern changed when Carlos Hank González was appointed Mayor by López Portillo in 1976 (Figure 3.3). Hank González had a considerable power base of his own, but was ultimately ineligible for the presidency because his parents were not born in Mexico. A political heavyweight, he was also perceived to have done a good job in the sphere of urban development while Governor of the State of Mexico (1969–75), which surrounds the Federal District. He knew the problems of the low-income areas of the city intimately, and knew how to handle them. His specific interests, however, focused upon major urban development projects which would push contracts and resources towards his political backers. In large part because of this, and because Hank González left the Federal District Department bankrupt and heavily in debt, Ramón Aguirre (an accountant) was charged with stabilizing city finances by his close friend President De la Madrid. He lacked the clarity of political purpose of his predecessor, but muddled through and was one of the six 'pre-candidates' identified by De la Madrid in 1986–7 for possible adoption as Party presidential nominee.

Manuel Camacho (1988–93) was also a trusted friend of Salinas, for whom he had worked for many years. A former academic and technocrat, he was considered highly capable and was widely respected. The losses sustained by the PRI in the Federal District in the presidential and con-gressional elections would have been important considerations in his appointment to that particular job. Camacho performed well as *Regente,* and while the position has never been considered a good springboard to the presidency, Camacho emerged as a principal contender for the candidacy in 1994 and was Colosio's chief rival. Politically, though, he shot himself in the foot – not by making a mistake in the Mayor's office, but by breaking party discipline the moment Colosio was 'tapped' (Whitehead 1994). Instead of hiding his disappointment and showing solidarity with the candidate, he let his bitterness show, and subsequently sought to undermine the Colosio campaign. He resigned as Mayor and was, for a brief period, Mexico's Foreign Minister, before being appointed by Salinas as a high-profile lead negotiator in the Chiapas conflict. Camacho kept his hopes alive by stealing the limelight from Colosio and by being 'eligible' were Salinas to have a change of heart and pull his first choice, or if he (Camacho) decided to run as an independent. (Under the Constitution, cabinet members are excluded from being a candidate for several months prior to the actual election, but Camacho was no longer a minister.) After various political moves and ambiguous statements by Camacho, Salinas forced him to renounce any presidential intentions and to endorse Colosio. This he finally did, but just 1 week later Colosio was assassinated. The Colosio camp and senior PRIístas had become so embittered by Camacho's lack of loyalty and party discipline that he was considered beyond the pale as a possible substitute, and his political career in the party was over. His ambivalence towards the party and his dalliance with the PRD continued until eventually the PRI threw him out late in 1995.

Outside of the PRI Camacho remains a potential force, and he will probably seek to create a minor party of his own or will join another party – perhaps the PRD. However, he represents something of a poison chalice for the PRD, since his seniority would require a leading role and since he, too, is a PRI cast-away. His joining the party would compound many of the image difficulties that the PRD currently faces. A new small party is the most likely prospect.

When Camacho moved to the Foreign Ministry, his number two, Manuel Aguilera (the DF Government Secretary), was appointed *Regente* and successfully saw out the term. Zedillo's choice for *Regente* was one of the few surprises in the cabinet, since little was known about Espinosa Villarreal, but it was considered to be of little importance since recent constitutional changes had meant that the basis of selection to the mayorship was to change in 1997: therefore Espinoza's appointment was clearly seen as a 3-year term. I will return at length to this issue of the basis of mayoral appointments.

Outside the Federal District, in the surrounding State of Mexico, the local populace elects its Governor and Municipal Presidents who thereafter exercise executive authority for 6 and 3 years, respectively. However, as we have seen, the actual candidates are usually selected by the President, Governor (for municipal presidents), organized (compliant) labour groups, and the PRI itself. The PRI orchestrates the election on behalf of candidates who emerge from this non-democratic process which takes place behind closed doors (Cornelius and Craig 1991). Nonetheless the electorate can demonstrate their dissatisfaction with the proffered candidates by abstaining or by voting for the opposition. There are also local elections for the state legislature and for the equivalent of councillors in the municipality (although the latter are on the same slate as the municipal president; councillors are not elected directly in their own right). At the settlement level there is the opportunity to vote on two tickets, although this is patchy in its operation. The first ticket is for settlement representatives on neighbourhood development issues; the other is for a handful of local residents to act with the authority of the Municipal President and to see that law and order are effected and represented within the settlement. Although this arrangement embodies the principles of municipal autonomy, these principles are seriously undermined by centralized or state control exercised over scarce resources (Fagen and Tuohy 1972; Rodríguez 1997).

Apart from Mayor Hank González, there has been no tradition of movement of executive officers from the State of Mexico to the Federal District. By and large, *camarillas*, career trajectories and unwillingness to concede political power have conspired to accentuate the split between the two political entities – a point to which I return later.

Políticos and técnicos

Earlier in this chapter I argued that administrations in recent years have become increasingly technocratic, but individual bureaucracies differ in the extent to which they are guided by 'technical' or 'partisan political' rationality (Gilbert and Ward 1985). This spectrum of rationality embodies parameters of bureaucratic autonomy covering day-to-day partisan political interference, the stability of personnel and budgets, accountability of performance, and 'objectivity' of decision making according to established criteria and procedures. Generally speaking, the more critical an area of sectoral activity is to economic production or to strategically important activities, then the more likely it is to be towards the 'technical' end of the spectrum. By and large, ministries and federal agencies will be less subject to partisan political pressures than those whose responsibilities are explicitly spatial in character (Governors, Municipal Presidents, state agencies and local decentralized branch offices of national ministries).

But which type of rationality applies in the Metropolitan Area? The short answer is both. Officers whose brief is to manage and maintain social peace in spatial entities such as *delegaciones* and municipalities are more likely to make decisions based upon political criteria (i.e. who might benefit or suffer given a particular action). Generally, however, their control over resources is limited and they must approach centralized departments for assistance. Other officers in charge of sectoral programmes are more likely to be orientated towards establishing norms and criteria of management that can be implemented as widely as resources will allow.

The Mayor and State Governor set out the policies to be followed. Each also exercises an overall watching brief through control over extra-budgetary or centralized resources and can respond discretionally to competing demands. Hence the Mayor and State Governor, ultimately, must respond more to political influences than to technical ones, no matter what their personal background. Not only do these pressures vary in space, but also in time. Changing economic conditions, social unrest and class struggle, the political orientations of those in authority, and one's own predilection will shape the nature of the decision-making environment. Also, in the past 6 years the political imperatives of the ballot box have greatly reduced the margins for error of 'bad' or ineffectual government. Thus, starting often with opposition parties, local city governments are exercising greater autonomy from their traditional overlords (the state governors), and are raising their administrative capacities to respond to local population needs and demands (Rodríguez and Ward 1995, 1996). Some cities, PANista and PRIísta alike, are becoming highly technocratic in their government styles – within the Metropolitan Area both Naucalpan and Tlalnepantla (1993–96) provide prime examples of the excesses of technocratic administration (the PRI in this case; see Conde Bonfil 1996; Ward 1998).

From central government's viewpoint, good city management in the Metropolitan Area requires that social unrest be contained and appeased. This may be achieved through political mediation as well as through successful and efficient systems of delivery of public goods (Ward 1986). Depending upon individual career tracks, if party-political and personal ambitions can be advanced at the same time, so much the better, but this is secondary. Although future advancement is always uncertain, loss of political control and weak management ability will almost certainly lead to removal. Nevertheless, several areas of the Federal District Department structure are more overtly political than others. The post of Government Secretary 'A' is an especially critical one – in effect the Mayor's right hand. Note in Figure 3.4 that the *delegados* (i.e. the decentralized political officers) are under this individual, as are other key organs of state control (judiciary, social welfare, land and commercial registries). Public security and the police are controlled directly by the Mayor, while big-spending technical departments are coordinated under a single Secretary of Public Works.

Mexico City's fiscal structure: rich DF uncle, poor state cousins

Within the budgets accorded to different departments, certain technical agencies stand out (Table 3.1). These are invariably those public enterprises engaged in large-scale 'lumpy' activities such as power and water supply systems. These are big-spending departments, essential to both production and consumption. Always likely to be important, their budgetary priority will vary according to the particular policy emphasis of different adminis- trations: sometimes deep drainage (early 1970s); sometimes urban highways (1979–81); at other times Metro extensions (1981–3). One study found that of the 19 per cent of the federal budget allocated to regional development, the DF received more than half (Rodríguez 1993). Although the rate and order of introduction of local services such as domestic water and electricity to specified communities may be prone to some political interference by *delegados*, the procurement of water and power, together with the con- struction of drainage works, are usually governed by relatively technical procedures. For these major projects, special financial appropriation is almost always required.

The financial basis of the Federal District and that of the State of Mexico are quite different, and as we saw in Chapter 1, the Federal District has tended to receive a disproportionate share of national income and invest- ment expenditure, intensifying resentment against the *chilango* population. Throughout Mexico City revenue comes from two sources. First, revenue sharing from the federation, the most important of which are called *partici- paciones*. These shared funds go to the states, which are obliged to share at least one-fifth with their municipalities. Given that traditionally only around

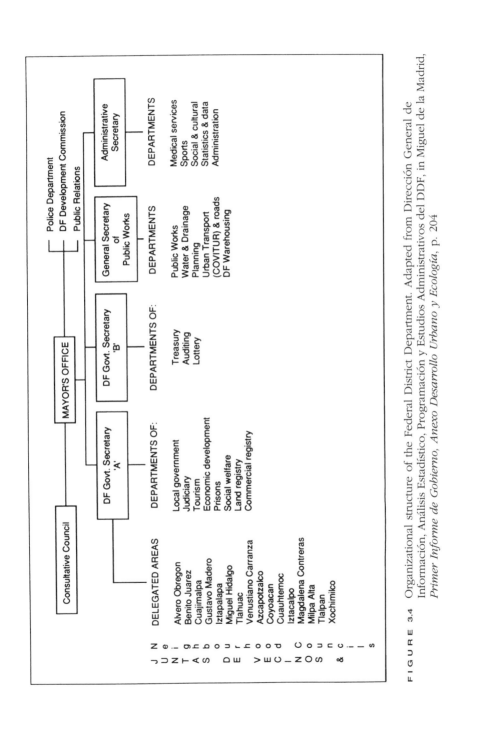

FIGURE 3.4 Organizational structure of the Federal District Department. Adapted from Dirección General de Información, Análisis Estadístico, Programación y Estudios Administrativos del DDF, in Miguel de la Madrid, *Primer Informe de Gobierno, Anexo Desarrollo Urbano y Ecología*, p. 204

TABLE 3.1 Total *DDF* expenditure and proportional allocation to certain specified areas

Year	DDF expenditure (billion *pesos*)[a]		Public debt (%)	Public works (%)	Water and drainage (%)	COVITUR (%)	*Delegaciones* (%)	Planning department (%)
	Actual	Constant 1978						
1971	4.4	13.1	12.3	9.7	20.0	ND	ND	1.7
1973	11.7	29.2	8.3	8.1	17.2	ND	5.2	3.3
1975	15.4	26.9	21.9	8	7.6	ND	6.0	1.1
1977	20.6	24.2	9.1 (24)[b]	4	5.0	ND	11.0	1.1
1979	50.4	42.7	15.3	17.9	9.6	10.3	9.9	1.1
1981	108.4	56.5	14.7 (23)	13	7.2	29.2	9.1	0.8
1982	222.6	73.9	32.8	4.6	3.7	22.2	7.6	0.2
1983	274.6	44.8	12.2 (48)	4.8	6.0	25.3	12.1	0.8
1984	498.6	49.2	12.2 (21)	6.4	7.7	13.3	15.9	0.3
1986	1086.2	36.5	10.2 (31)	4.7	9.1	13.1	17.9	0.9

Source: *Cuenta Pública del DDF*, 1970–87.

[a] Billion = 1 thousand million (old *pesos*).
[b] Figures in parentheses indicate debt budget allocations in specified years – probably a more realistic indication of its actual importance and size in any one year.
ND, no data available.

19 per cent of the total was returned to the states in the first place, municipalities received around 4 per cent of the total through the revenue-sharing formula – considerably lower than in most countries. (There has been a recent increase in the total amount transferred to the states, which now receive almost 24 per cent; García del Castillo in Rodriguez and Ward *et al.* 1996.) There are clear formulae about the designation of these funds to the states which take account of population, level of poverty and revenue contribution to the federation. By 1996 approximately half the states had developed a corresponding state formula. The second source is locally derived income – from fees, user charges and local property taxes (Cabrero Mendoza 1995; Rodríguez 1995, 1997). (In addition to these two sources are direct-line federal investment income for major public works and development projects, but these are discretionary, not of right.)

As municipalities began to assert their autonomy after the municipal reform in 1983 (especially PANista cities), so cities began to explore the local revenue creation prospects in order not to have to depend so heavily upon revenues which came down the pipe from the federation. Until the late 1980s, most municipalities expected 70–80 per cent of their income to come from *participaciones* (Rodríguez 1997). By pursuing more aggressive local fiscal policy, cities were able to increase their locally derived incomes dramatically without any decline (in real terms) in their *participaciones*. They were, in effect, doing more with more (Ward 1995), and to the extent that their programmes were more efficient and better accounted for, they were enhancing their use of the budget. Since 1988–9, nationally, there has been a sharp rise in the proportion of locally derived revenues, achieved mainly by charging the real consumption cost of services (e.g. water), by raising property taxes, and by regular revision of the cadaster upon which these are levied to ensure that they are not eroded in real terms (Rodríguez 1997).

Returning to the municipalities of the Metropolitan Area, in 1981 approximately 62 per cent of revenues came from *participaciones*, but by 1989 this was down to 29 per cent, the lion's share now being generated locally (Pichardo Pagaza 1990). In Naucalpan, for example, it declined from 86 to 33 per cent during the same period, rising again slightly to 38 per cent in 1994 (Conde Bonfil 1996: 354). The increase came primarily from taxes, although user charges were also significant.

Despite its anomalous administrative status and it not being a state, the Federal District also receives *participaciones*. In 1989 22.4 per cent of the national total went to the DF, while the State of Mexico received 9.3 per cent (Blancas Neria 1993: 284). In the late 1980s revenue sharing contributed around 51 per cent of the DF revenues, compared with 37 per cent in the conurbated municipalities (Rowland and Gordon 1996). User charges appear as a particularly important item within locally generated income sources in the DF (around one-quarter of the total revenues), but these were grossly insufficient to cover the real costs of providing the services and federal

FIGURE 3.5 President Salinas' revenge on the Chilangos, 1989, says 'That'll teach those *Chilangos* who didn't vote for me'

subsidies made up the difference (Bassols Ricárdez and Corona Martínez 1993). Salinas instructed Camacho to raise local-revenue generation dramatically by raising user charges, taxes, fees, and so on, so that by 1990 the *Regente* was able to report to the Representative Assembly that the city was no longer 'subsidized by the provinces' and generated locally more than 90 per cent of its annual budget (Bassols Ricárdez and Corona Martínez 1993: 353). Certainly there were complaints about the dramatic rise in these charges, but in large part these reflected the past practice of subsidy and the failure of previous governments to revise taxes and charges in line with inflation. Some depict this as Salinas' vindictiveness against the city population which had largely voted for Cárdenas less than 2 years earlier (Figure 3.5).

Local democracy in Mexico City: lost and found?

An important feature arising from the special status of the Federal District is the structure of political representation of Mexico City's citizens – or, stated more accurately, the lack of representation. Few places in the democratic world have less local democracy than Mexico City. This is the 'high ground' that City Hall authorities have sought to defend for so long and which finally, on 6 July 1997, was breached when the Federal District elected its Governor directly (to take office in December).

Between 1928 when the Federal District lost its municipal structure and 1997 when it made a significant step towards rediscovering it, citizens of the Federal District have been ruled by the President through delegated authority. Thus huge city resources are disbursed by unelected nominees and officials, of whom few people will have heard before their appointment. This situation has not passed uncontested. For many years opposition parties as well as the PRI have demanded greater democracy in the Federal District on two fronts. First, demands for an elected local congress with powers and responsibilities for the Federal District had virtually won all-party support by the end of De la Madrid's *Consulta Popular* in 1984. A second demand, with no overall consensus, was the call for direct elections for the *Regente* and *delegados*. Generally, members of the PRI were circumspect, knowing that their masters had some misgivings, while opposition parties were more openly in favour. But even the PRI wanted more direct and preferential access to policy making and resource allocation through its local district secretaries and through local corporatist channels. For many years the PRI had looked askance at the unwillingness of many City Hall officials to provide their representatives with privileged access to services, land entitlement and so on (Ward 1981a). These were sought in order to reinforce the legitimacy and influence of local PRIísta leaders, and as sources of patronage in order to secure the vote on behalf of PRI candidates at elections. During the 1970s and 1980s opposition parties (especially on the left) were also acutely aware that, in most cases, the majority of their support came from residents in the Metropolitan Area, and were frustrated in their efforts to exercise any power on behalf of their would-be constituents.

'Adequate representative structures already exist' For as long as possible the government has resisted calls to democratize the Federal District and reinstitute its municipal status, instead creating alternative structures which embodied locally elected representatives although they enjoy no executive authority. As the saying goes: *'El PRI quiere cambiar todo para que nada cambie'* (the PRI wants to change everything so that nothing actually changes). Since 1929 the Federal District has had 'Consultative Councils' comprising representatives from local enterprises, interest groups, lobbies, residents' associations and so on. Regular (weekly) meetings, chaired by the Mayor or his appointee, would allow the Consultative Councils to express an opinion over servicing needs and public works.

In 1970 a new Organic Law of the Federal District retained the Council but extended it through local *juntas de vecinos* made up of representatives from different neighbourhoods. The *delegación* president sat on the Federal District Consultative Council. Although it was in place from 1970, the structure was not activated until considerably later. Instead, President Luis Echeverría (for it bore his *imprimata* more than that of Mayor Sentíes) used traditional patterns of patron–client relations in order to achieve social and electoral control over low-income neighbourhoods (Cornelius 1975; Ward 1981a).

It was Mayor Hank González who began to use the *juntas de vecinos* structures, partly because he recognized that they provided a mechanism for deflecting responsibility (and *bronca*) away from himself onto his local *delegados*, but more importantly as a means of meeting criticism that the Federal District was fundamentally undemocratic and unrepresentative. What better than direct civic elections for block, neighbourhood, *delegación* and city-wide representatives? Although the first 'round' of *junta* representatives was largely drummed up by local *delegados* in 1977–8, Mayor Hank González expended an inordinate amount of effort to ensure that elections in 1980 were highly publicized, that there was a large turnout, and subsequently that the *juntas* should be made to work (Ward 1981a; see also Jiménez 1988). This was not because Hank González believed in local democracy and elected officials: it was precisely because he didn't. The aim was that citizens would be satisfied with the opportunities for local representation that were now in place (Cisneros Sosa 1983; Ramírez Saíz 1983). Or so he hoped.

However, the creation of the *juntas* structure neither produced greater local democracy nor allayed demands for an elected local congress and for elected officials and chief administrators. Although there are signs that the *juntas* played some role in determining the prioritization of settlement servicing programmes (Ward 1981a; but cf. Jiménez 1988), there is little evidence that this continued once Hank González left office. From 1983 onward their role diminished to that of an instrument of local control exercised by *delegados*. Increasingly, too, they were hijacked by middle-class representatives, the individual fortunes of whom were closely tied to patronage received from the *delegado* (Jiménez 1989; see also Aguilar Martínez 1988). Demands for an elected congress arose once again during the 1982 federal elections (*Proceso* 14 May 1982). The nationwide *Consulta Popular* initiated by President Miguel De la Madrid in 1983 also fuelled similar demands from opposition parties as well as from the PRI (*El Día* June 1984). Mayor Aguirre's response was that these proposals would be studied carefully by the Federal District Department, and recommendations would be put to the plenary sessions of the *Consulta*.

This led subsequently to another arrangement purporting to extend democracy and representation to the local populace. This was a compromise arrangement announced by the DDF Government Secretary for a local assembly with responsibilities for creating *bandos*, setting up local regulations, monitoring local authorities and so on (*Gaceta Oficial* 25 February 1988). Created through the elections on 6 July 1988, the Representative Assembly of the DF was, in my view, the latest in a long line of government initiatives to head off demands for a full democratization of the Federal District and its administrative structure.

Salinas hoped that demands for an elected mayor and local authorities had been circumvented – for the time being at least. Yet as many of us sought to point out, there were few cities in the world in which residents had so little say over who governs them, and over local urban policies and expenditure. Other special districts – for example, Washington DC and the Capital District of Bogotá – embody greater local democracy and enjoy direct elections of local urban authorities. I argue that this is not a historical accident; it was an outcome of the fear among the revolutionary élite that the city would fall apart without discretionary controls exercised by the President and delegated through the *Regente*. They were also worried by the possible destabilizing political effects of two powerful figures who had both been elected – with differing views and policies. The backyard was too big, too important, and too close to home to be entrusted to the opposition or to other factions within the same party (Ward 1989c).

Direct elections for DDF officials: the arguments for and against   One argument in favour of an elected Mayor is that the failure to have elected officials would appear increasingly anomalous and unsustainable in the face of Salinas' drive to democratize the Party, the unions, and the nation as a whole. In particular, the argument that the President is elected by Federal District residents as the *de facto* Governor no longer held up, since President Salinas lost the Federal District by a very large margin to Cárdenas. Second, it was quite clear that the level of subsidization for the Federal District was unsustainable, and there was growing recognition that it was probably impossible to govern the city successfully and that the PRI and government might, in fact, have little to lose. If the problems of Mexico City are insoluble, then in a no-win situation, why not let in the opposition to make a hash of things? The government of Mexico City was not necessarily a 'zero sum game' for the PRI (at least not as long as it controlled the overall purse strings through Congress). The checks-and-balances system, although it had never really been used in the past, could quite easily tie the hands of opposition local government officials. In the United Kingdom the Conservative Thatcher government demonstrated that by withholding central funding it could squeeze Labour-controlled councils whose spending policies it did not like.

A third factor in support of a locally elected congress and officials was that Camacho's people had looked seriously at the experiences of other large metropolitan cities (London, Paris, Rome and São Paulo (where the Workers' Party (PT) had just won the elections)). These cities had elected opposition parties without posing an unacceptable threat. Mexico was also beginning to have some greater experience of 'opposition governments' (Merida, San Luis Potosí, Chihuahua, Cd. Juárez, Hermosillo, etc.), and with the exception of Juchitán (a left-controlled municipality in Oaxaca), most experiences had not been intensely problematic from the federal government's point of view. Moreover, the existence of opposition local mayors in the backyard need not pose an insuperable problem for reasons that I have just pointed out (federal and/or local congressional supervision), and because the large slice of city line funding remained federally controlled. Finally, a growing proportion (around 40 per cent) of the population already lived outside the DF boundaries where they exercised their constitutional rights, apparently without posing an unacceptable threat. As long as there was no single politico-administrative entity for the Metropolitan Area, this overall political control would not be threatened.

Viewed from these perspectives it is perhaps difficult to understand why the opposition was so eager to assert the principles of local representation and to demand that top officials be elected to City Hall – and also to understand why the government should contrive so hard to resist such moves. But there were strong reasons. First, there are technical arguments relating to the location of federal buildings and institutions which have a national role and belong, therefore, to the nation rather than to a single entity. However, although this argument was invariably rehearsed by officials, it had begun to sound lame and unconvincing. The technical constraints were not insuperable. Second, there was always the possibility that the Federal District was a zero sum game and advancement for the opposition would be at a concomitant loss to the PRI. No-one could be sure. Third, was the possibility that the danger was not the opposition at all, but the PRI itself. If the President and the *Regente* were elected by popular national and local vote, respectively, it would be extremely difficult for the former to constrain the latter through budgetary controls in Congress. In this situation one would have two very powerful elected political heavyweights operating in the same entity. This could cause political imbalance and the potential for conflict. As a diluted example one need only look at the situation which already applies in the State of Mexico, where the PRI candidate for governor is tapped by the outgoing Executive a full year before the new President takes office. As a result, relations between the State of Mexico Governor and the incoming President have often been uneasy, and coordination between the two entities has traditionally been poor. The political instability would be magnified were the *Regente* to have a popularly elected mandate independent of the President's. Indeed, it would be very difficult for him to be controlled and, ultimately, dismissed.

Fourth, it would be a major symbolic victory for the opposition, heralding or accelerating the ultimate loss of the PRI – the presidency itself. Domino effect, slippery slope, thin end of the wedge: none of these metaphors does justice to the insecurity that the governing party would feel if it lost executive control of the Federal District. As we observed earlier, in November 1996 PRI congressmen reneged on a previous electoral agreement that was before Congress, after elections a week before had suggested major losses in 1997. A fifth reason was undoubtedly the personal ambition of the then incumbent. Camacho knew that while he had to respond to these demands, any presidential ambitions he might entertain would probably be killed if he took constitutional steps that might end up delivering executive authority for the Federal District – or some parts of it – into the hands of the opposition parties.

At the time of writing the first edition of this volume (1989) it seemed to me that the issues of the creation of a local congress and that of a locally elected executive need not stand or fall together. They could easily be separated, and this could prove a politically prudent and expedient option. It seemed especially likely that if the Representative Assembly could be seen to work without significantly interrupting city management, then resistance to an elected local congress would probably decline, as has indeed been the case. In the first assembly the opposition parties had an overall majority and were seen by many to have added an important forum for developing multi-party demands for more representative and partici-patory democracy in the DF (Incháustegui 1994; Bassols and Corona 1993).

In the end Camacho dealt with the Gordian knot of an elected mayor quite brilliantly. The matter was put to a plebiscite – itself an innovation – in March 1993 and three questions were asked: (1) Whether to create a 32nd state?; (2) Whether to have direct elections of city authorities?; (3) Whether to create a local legislature? The response was overwhelming in favour of change and greater representational democracy. Over 84 per cent answered positively to the second two questions, while a smaller number (67 per cent) were in favour of creating a new state. While the results were clear-cut, they largely confirmed what Camacho had expected (*El Financiero*, Informe Especial, 15 May 1993). Controversy surrounded not so much the results but the turnout, with opposite spins being placed upon the significance of a total vote of 330 000. While this was a small proportion of the electoral register (less than 6 per cent), many argued that it was a large number, especially given the campaign of most parties against the plebiscite. Small or large, it was interpreted as being a clear mandate to Camacho to move forward.

The new proposal, which was passed by Congress in 1993, really addressed the two highest yes votes: for direct elections and for a local legislature. The Representative Assembly would become a legislature (and therefore have a policy-defining role) from 1994 onwards, and from 1997 (i.e. when the following Assembly was installed), the mayor would be chosen by the President from among one of the elected *Asambleístas* in whichever party held the majority. This was the brilliant element in Camacho's proposal, since the Mayor would be directly elected (to the Assembly), but the actual selection rested with the President to choose someone with whom he felt he could work. The Assembly would have to ratify the selection, but in the case of an impasse after two votes on two consecutive candidates presented by the President, the Senate would make the appointment. In essence it combined a parliamentary type of selection procedure with the existing *dedazo* arrangement, but ensured that structurally it would be what is known in the US as a 'weak mayor–council relationship' and quite different from the 'strong mayor' (albeit beholden to the President) system that had existed in the past (Ward 1996). However, it did place the DDF firmly under congressional control (rather than under presidential control).

In the event, although this reform had been passed by Congress, Zedillo acted to simplify matters (either because he felt that it was unnecessarily convoluted, or because he distrusted Camacho). Whichever, what had formerly been unthinkable became fact: the mayor would be directly elected. In another reform in the summer of 1996 it was proposed that the DF should have a legislative assembly and a *directly elected Mayor*, although the DF would continue to have a special status. The reform stops short of creating a 32nd state, and also contains no proposals regarding the elections of local mayors. Doubtless the latter will come later. Also, the first Mayor would serve for 3 years only in order to bring the elections back into synchronization with presidential elections in 2000. Thereafter it will be a 6-year term. As a rider, Congress has legislated to prevent any former mayor from being a candidate in 1997 – targeted primarily at stifling any ambitions that Camacho or his recent predecessors (Aguilera or Aguirre) might have of running for election. (Not that Aguilera was ever likely to break ranks with the PRI since he continues to be a leading force within the party in Mexico City. Indeed, he has just entered the Representative Assembly at the top of the PRI's *plurinominal* list, and his former experience as DF Senator, *Regente*, and director of the earthquake reconstruction programme will make him a major force to be reckoned with, particularly when it comes to negotiating with many of the relatively inexperienced local neighbourhood and social movement leaders who won election to the Assembly for the PRD.)

Mexico City: into the hands of the opposition With the exception of the 1988 elections, the PRI stands out as the majority party in the Metropolitan Area when taken overall, although it is well below its national average. Generally the PRI does less well in urban than in rural districts, averaging 49 per cent versus 76 per cent of the vote respectively between 1979 and 1988 (Cornelius and Craig 1991: 70). In the Federal District, during that period, it averaged even less (41.2 per cent), and has received only a slightly higher proportion than that in recent elections (Table 3.2). However, given the fact that the non-PRI vote is shared between the other two parties, and the winner-take-all nature of the direct elections, to date the opposition

T A B L E   3.2   Per cent vote for parties and presidential candidates 1988–94, for the whole of the Metropolitan Area

Year and type of election	PAN (%)	PRI (%)	PRD (%)	
1988, President	Clouthier 23	Salinas 27	Cárdenas 49	
1988, Federal Deputies	22.6	27.7	14.51[a]	16.6[b]
1991, Federal Deputies	19.3	48.0	11.6	
1994, Federal Deputies	27.0	41.5	20.3	
1994, President	Fernández 27.1	Zedillo 44.0	Cárdenas 11.6	

Source: Calculations by the author.

[a] PRD not in existence in 1988, = FDN (*Frente Democrático Nacional*).
[b] PPS, *Partido Popular Socialista*.

parties have had to rely almost exclusively upon the proportional representation votes for its participation in the 40 DF district seats in the national Congress and the 66 seats in the Representative Assembly (although here, in 1988, in the direct elections districts the PRI took 24 seats, the PAN 13 and the *Frente* 3). In 1988 and 1991 none of the opposition parties won a direct election seat, with the exception of the Muñoz Ledo's DF Senatorship victory for the *Frente* (shortly to become the PRD). The PAN did win seats outside the DF, and took three direct election (deputy) districts in the DF in 1994.

Therefore, looking towards the 1997 first elections for Governor, it appeared that it was going to be a hotly contested race led by three 'heavyweight' contenders, one from each party: Carlos Castillo Peraza (PAN), Alfredo del Mazo (PRI) and Cuauhtémoc Cárdenas (PRD); that is, two former party presidents, and a former governor of the State of Mexico (Del Mazo). The data portrayed in Table 3.2 showing a past PRI majority were always going to be somewhat deceptive of what could be expected in 1997, given the poor showing of the PRI nationally in elections held between 1995 and 1996. Also, in November 1996, municipal elections in the State of Mexico resulted in gains for the PAN and PRD in key Metropolitan Area municipalities, all at the expense of the PRI, which formerly held them. Another important consideration is that unlike nationally, where the opposition parties have not yet built a comprehensive party base, they are well organized in the Metropolitan Area of Mexico City.

Nevertheless, no-one quite expected the PRI's vote to fall away quite so dramatically as it did. But by examining the pre-1997 results spatially for the Metropolitan Area, we are able to get a more nuanced understanding both of the (then pre-election) prospects of the parties in the 1997 elections, and also of the likely areal power bases that each might expect to develop if and when the *delegaciones* are also permitted to directly elect their mayors. In order to depict the areas where each party has particular strength, I plotted each party's results around its own metropolitan area average; the heavier the shading the better that party did in that area. While there are distortions because the larger the party's share of the total vote the more numerous will be the areas in which it appears as 'strong', this method does, nevertheless, offer insights about respective areal strengths and weaknesses. Data were plotted for three sets of federal elections since 1988 and for the presidential elections in 1988 and 1994 (the former were in the first edition of this book, and are not reproduced here). Setting aside the 1988 results (interesting though they were at the time), the 1991 and 1994 deputy elections and 1994 presidential elections show remarkable consistency about where the parties do well, and where they do less well. That being the case, I shall not reproduce all figures here, but simply portray the results for the three presidential candidates in 1994. This seems appropriate since voters were electing an individual for a party, and the same would apply in 1997 for the DF elections for governor.

Figure 3.6 (b–d) shows the performance by district (Fig. 3.6a) of each party's candidate around his own average for the whole of the Metropolitan Area. All three parties traditionally appeared to do moderately well in the Federal District, and have carved out 'niche' strengths in different parts: the PAN in the hard-core middle-income areas of the centre–south and in the north; the PRI in central areas and in the high-income western districts; while the PRD dominates in the more homogenous working class districts of the south-east and in the *colonias* east of the National University. The PAN performs better than its average in 12 of the 40 districts compared with six each for the PRI and PRD, and of the three, the PRI performs less well in many more districts than either of the other parties. This suggested that the PAN was developing its spatial strength at the expense of the PRI, whose spatial bastions were declining. When the PRI had a substantial overall majority (as it did in 1994), this decline was not a problem, since while its vote appeared to be dipping, it was still likely to win most of the district battles. However, if the overall vote between the three parties were to narrow such that the PAN and the PRD began to get closer to the PRI, then the data in Figure 3.6 suggested that it would probably be the PAN that could expect to do especially well in the Federal District and, indeed, might have a good chance of taking it. Given the much narrower distribution of the PRD's areal strength, it seemed unlikely that it would win overall victory.

In the surrounding state of Mexico the 1994 data suggested that the PAN had its dominance in the west and north-west in districts in the municipalities of Naucalpan, Tlalnepantla, Atizapán, Cuautitlán Izcalli and Tepozotlán, and was nowhere in the east. Here the PRD had a relative stronghold in Netzahualcóyotl, La Paz and Chimalhuacán. The PRI's eastern strength was in Chalco (which is hardly surprising given the enormous solidarity expenditure it received during the Salinas period) but other than Huixquilucan in the west, Nicolás Romero in the north-east and the municipalities in the northern XXI district (Tultepec, San Martín de las Pirámides etc.), it had few dominant 'hot' spots, although it did not appear

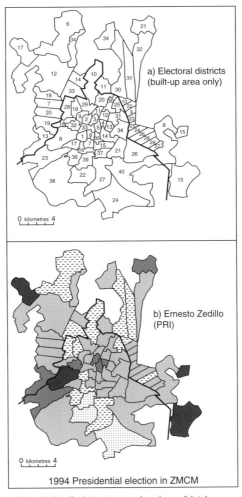

a) Electoral districts
(built-up area only)

b) Ernesto Zedillo
(PRI)

1994 Presidential election in ZMCM

Percentage variation in the district vote around each candidate's
portion of the total vote in the zmcm

■ More than 4% above candidate's portion in zmcm   —— Federal
District

▨ Between 2.0–3.9% above candidate's portion in zmcm

▢ Within 1.9% either side of candidate's portion in zmcm   —— Electoral
District

▨ Between 2.0–3.9% below candidate's portion in zmcm   (built-up

▢ More than 4.0% below candidate's portion in zmcm   area only)

FIGURE 3.6 Electoral districts and voting patterns in the August 1994 presidential
elections, by candidate for the Metropolitan Area

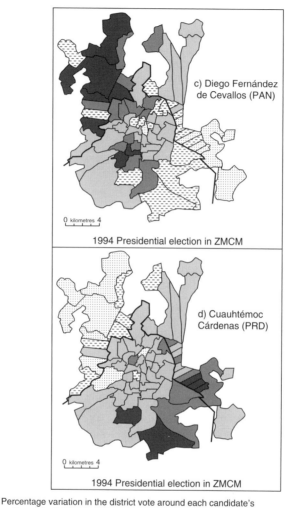

c) Diego Fernández de Cevallos (PAN)

0 kilometres 4

1994 Presidential election in ZMCM

d) Cuauhtémoc Cárdenas (PRD)

0 kilometres 4

1994 Presidential election in ZMCM

Percentage variation in the district vote around each candidate's portion of the total vote in the zmcm

▮ More than 4% above candidate's portion in zmcm

▨ Between 2.0–3.9% above candidate's portion in zmcm

☐ Within 1.9% either side of candidate's portion in zmcm

▨ Between 2.0–3.9% below candidate's portion in zmcm

☐ More than 4.0% below candidate's portion in zmcm

—— Federal District

—— Electoral District (built-up area only)

FIGURE 3.6 *(continued)*

TABLE 3.3   Number of districts in which candidates did better or worse than their overall average for the Metropolitan Area

	Fernández (PAN)		Zedillo (PRI)		Cárdenas (PRD)	
Area of districts: DF or Edo. de Mexico	DF	Edo de M	DF	Edo de M	DF	Edo de M
No. of districts with vote significantly higher than average	12	8	6	5	6	7
No. of districts with vote significantly lower than average	6	14	10	5	3	10

Source: Calculations from Figure 3.6.

to underperform in many areas either (Table 3.3). These 1994 showings were put to the test in the November 1996 municipal elections when the PAN won Nuacalpan, Tlalnepantla, Atizapán, Cuautitlán, Cuautitlán Izcalli and Tepozotlán, but also, somewhat unexpectedly, took Nicolás Romero and San Martín de las Pirámides, where the PRI had formerly appeared to be strong. The PRD took Netzahualcóyotl, Texcoco, Los Reyes and Chimalhuacán (both in District VIII). The saving grace for the PRI was that it held Chalco-Solidaridad, Ecatepec and Huixquilucan. Thus, between 1994 and 1996, the parties tended to *intensify their strengths* to a level at which they won the municipal presidency.

In the final analysis, of course, these previous voting patterns appear to have counted for little – at least when it came to the July 1997 Federal District elections. The results, while not a surprise in the light of the multiple polls conducted prior to the election, were at odds with the foregoing depiction of past voting patterns. In the event it seems that a combination of 'punishment' votes against the PRI, together with a vibrant and determined campaign by Cárdenas on behalf of the PRD, acted to set aside traditional voting trends and earned him a surprise but landslide victory. The final outcome was Cárdenas 48 per cent; Del Mazo (PRI) 25.6 per cent, and Castillo Peraza (PAN) 16 per cent. It appears that almost the entire 'floating' vote as well as some former PRI supporters moved across to Cárdenas and to the PRD. Unlike other elections and in other parts of the country, in the Federal District the PAN did not capture those 'floating' or anti-PRI 'punishment' votes; rather it stuck at the level (16–17 per cent) of its traditional hard core support. The same is true in the Representative Assembly, where the PRD won 38 of the 40 direct election districts (the PAN won the other 2), and in the federal deputy elections for the Federal District and Metropolitan Area where, again, the PRD swept the board (although the PAN retained the district embracing the largely middle class part of Naucalpan which it has held continuously for 18 years). Nor did the PAN manage to convert its local (middle class) district strengths into a broader working class support.

Clearly, during the campaign the personal attacks launched by Castillo Peraza against Cárdenas backfired badly, and the latter as 'underdog', effectively milked his anti-corruption and anti-Salinas policies for all they were worth. For his part, Del Mazo, try all he could, was simply unable to overcome the general public's lack of confidence in the capacity of the PRI and the federal government to respond adequately to the city's problems. The DF was about to embrace an entirely new political structure, and most citizens clearly felt that it should do so without the baggage of the past.

While I am not yet able to map definitively the overall proportions and distribution of votes cast in the Metropolitan Area in 1997, my analysis of the preliminary returns suggests that these resemble remarkably closely those depicted in the first edition of this volume (1990: 83) of the 1988 presidential elections which Cárdenas also won by a landslide. Ironically, I chose to exclude those results from this second edition believing that those data were from too long ago, and related to a one-off election experience!

However, I believe that neither the extent of his victory nor the manner in which it jibes with previous voting patterns makes the data depicted in Figure 3.6 wholly redundant. The patterns display general trends over two or three elections and are suggestive of discrete spatial strengths that may become important if and when local elections take place for 'mayors' in the delegaciones. The PAN's core areas are especially clearly defined and are likely to remain more or less intact. Much more crucial will be the extent to which the PRD can consolidate its 1997 triumph by converting it into local party organizations capable of carrying it to victory in future elections, and of resisting what will inevitably be an attempted PRI fight-back. Ultimately it is the working class vote that will win the day in future elections, and on this occasion it was Cárdenas' party that managed to make the most convincing case that it should be charged with the Federal District government.

In seeking to rise to that challenge Cárdenas faces three major constraints. First, he has only three years to demonstrate any appreciable difference in governance. (Only in the year 2000 will the governorship convert to become a six-year term.) Second, much of the detailed responsibilities pertaining to the new governor and their delineation from those of the President were never worked out. These will need to be negotiated with President Zedillo and with the incoming Congress. For example, the DF security chief and attorney general are traditionally presidential appointments as are a large number of the delegados. Zedillo may be magnanimous and leave these appointments to Cárdenas, but if he is not (as the PRI will urge) then the new PRD administration may get embroiled in wrangling about turf jurisdictions to the detriment of implementing new programmes. A third major constraint that Cárdenas will face is the fact that the Federal District budget will continue to be appropriated annually by Congress, and to the extent that the PRI is able to exercise the upper hand in both chambers, Cárdenas will have to fight to ensure that his administration is not prejudiced financially. Moreover, not being a member of Zedillo's cabinet, he will not have privileged access to additional resources. These constraints aside, however, Cárdenas' personal reputation has been greatly enhanced by this election victory, and unless he fails badly as governor he is almost certainly assured first refusal on the PRD candidacy for president in 2000. More importantly for the future governance of the Federal District is the fact that urban policy creation and implementation are now firmly wedded to *party politics* and to an electoral mandate. At the very least, this should provide some incentive for parties to ensure more effective and accountable governance.

CONCLUSION: CHANGE TO EFFECT NO CHANGE

In this chapter, I have identified the political rationale underpinning city management, particularly that of the Federal District Department. I have expressed the view that the content of the political projects of recent governments has not fundamentally been one of democratization, nor of improved social justice, nor of decentralization and the reduction of centre–province imbalances. Rather, the project is one of sustained social control and a halt to further deterioration in living conditions (Ward 1986). In Mexico City the power structure that has evolved is one of control, not one of development. Notwithstanding the strengthening of the legislative functions of the Representative Assembly and the decision for direct election of the Mayor, there is a continuing reluctance in Mexico to tie executive urban development agendas to political parties.

The latest 'change to effect no change' in this respect is the DF Citizen Participation Law passed in June 1995, which was an initiative of the Representative Assembly. This basically provides for direct elections of citizen counsellors at the *delegación* level with largely non-executive consultative functions only (Martínez Assad 1996). Remembering my earlier discussion about Consultative Councils, *Juntas de Vecinos*, etc., there is a distinct sense of *déjà vu* about this new law (Arreola Ayala 1995). Most interesting of all is the stipulation that political parties may not put forward candidates as citizen counsellors. These are seen as civic, not party-political, organs of representation (Martínez Assad 1996). Once again, party politics is being excised from the discourse of urban development in the Federal District. Probably because of this there was a very low turnout in the November 1995 elections. Most Mexico City voters saw it for what it is – another tier of consultation, for which it was not worth troubling themselves.

In my view a development-orientated power structure would have to implement two fundamental changes. First, the city (or at the very least, certain strategic functions) would have to be conceived and managed as a *single entity* (albeit subdivided into appropriate administrative areas and not, as at present, divided in two). This is important not simply in order to achieve coordination between spatial entities, although this would help, but in order to allow the city to confront crucial issues and implement key policy initiatives, such as whether and where to grow, who pays (local citizens or the nation and in what proportion), and what priority to accord various urban development goals?

To tackle these questions, a second fundamental change is required: *empowerment* through democracy and *full representation*. Only a city administration elected on a political programme and charged with carrying it through has any possibility of approaching a development-based strategy. In order to tackle Mexico City's problems, strong political will is required built around a firm agenda of action, and ultimately only elected politicians have the mandate to carry through policies upon which they are placed in office. If those policies are not implemented or prove inadequate, then at the next opportunity the electorate in a pluralist society may judge that administration accordingly.

Existing government structures are fundamentally structures of non-empowerment. Until 1997, in the Federal District at least, they were anti-democratic and orientated towards sustaining social control in the hope that technical solutions, more efficient management and occasional political compromise would allow the city to muddle through – as in effect it did. Those who imagined that the city was about to fall apart, the doom-watchers, the revolutionaries and the bleeding-heart liberals, have all been disappointed. Mexico City has survived thus far despite intense pressure and entrenched social inequality. It will survive for a lot longer, but it will not thrive. Improvements may be achieved through more progressive systems of local taxation and consumption charges, through administrative reorganization, and through reducing losses from corruption, task duplication, and so on.

In order for existing levels of services to be maintained, let alone developed, Mexico City will have to intensify its local revenue generation and maintain its consumption charges in real terms. The costs of favoured status and heavy subsidies in the past were the inability to elect one's Mayor and for administration to be delegated by the President. That is about to change, and no matter how progressive these systems of taxation, all of Mexico City's population will end up paying more. The often forgotten bottom line is that fuller representation and democracy will be at substantial costs to city residents in terms of the taxes and local rating payments that they are obliged to pay. In clamouring for full representation, citizens must also recognize that they must be prepared to pay the price of local democracy.

I have identified some of the pressures for democratization in the Federal District over the past 20 years, but the level at which these debates were conducted and the content of the debate itself (elected congress and/or elected officials), although important, are a far cry from what democratization is all about. It is about popular participation in political and civic affairs.

It is about experimenting with new opportunities for organization and expression. It is about exploring new forms of leadership and representation. Ultimately it is about different power structures which are less hierarchical and less vertical. Of course, this is precisely what has made it so difficult for the PRI to accept. In many important ways these new civic structures are being experienced and forged in municipalities away from the centre and often away from the PRI (Cabrero Mendoza 1995, 1996).

Nor have social movements in Mexico City contributed, in Castells' (1977: 263) terms, to achieve a 'qualitatively new effect in power relations'. Most organizations have been successfully managed by government and by the PRI through time-worn mechanisms of clientelism, co-option, divide-and-rule and repression. On the very few occasions where horizontal solidarity has been forged and large numbers of people have been mobilized, the government has been quick to strike a deal.

The changes that I have identified do chart some movement towards better city management. Moreover, the current period is one of further important potential changes and opportunities. However, it seems likely that these will be too slow, too narrow, and too carefully moderated and constrained by the state. As such, one cannot be optimistic about significant progress to overcome spatial and social inequality in Mexico City. For that to happen the philosophy and politics of City administration have to change much more radically. Cárdenas' election for the PRD may provide just the momentum required in order to move that process forward.

4

URBAN LAND USE AND TRANSPORTATION

URBAN LAND USE AND ACCESS TO 'SATISFIERS'

There is probably not a large city in the world where residents do not complain about a traffic problem. In the United Kingdom, weather forecasters and transport planners must vie with each other for the position of the professional most often cursed by the general public. Weather forecasting does not really figure in a Mexican's daily life. Given the season, the weather is fairly predictable. More of a problem, perhaps, is the fact that at least until the late 1980s transport planners did not count for much either, and while their role has become more prominent in recent years, the private interests embodied in non-public transportation modes remains a major structural impediment to concerted action (Navarro Benítez 1993; Castillo *et al.* 1995). Moreover, in Mexico City the roots of the problem relate to the fact that transportation policy has been subject to sharp breaks in continuity associated with presidential cycles, has overly favoured the better-off economic groups who use private transport, and has wavered in its commitment towards what is considered the most appropriate form of public transport (García Canclini *et al.* 1996).

Overall, though, I believe that the 'problem' in so far as Mexico City is concerned is frequently overstated and exaggerated. Yes, the city does have major traffic problems and can be particularly vexatious if one expects to drive solo across its extent during peak times of the day, particularly if it is raining, but this represents a distance of over 40–50 kilometres and most people are more circumspect in their needs and daily mobility – or at least they have become so in the past two decades as the city has grown.

This chapter analyses the structure and nature of transportation systems in Mexico City, their evolution and politics. It is about the way in which people gain physical access to what I will broadly term urban 'satisfiers': work, markets, friends, entertainment centres, schools and other social service facilities. In a later chapter, I analyse how in Mexico 'access' is often stratified socially and economically, and I show how this can actively reproduce existing patterns of inequality within society. Here, however, my concern is to identify how people's physical access to urban satisfiers is changing over time, at what cost, and whether the daily journeys that people undertake are becoming easier or more difficult. An answer to these questions requires that we look first at the city's land-use structure and how people relate to it. Only then can we begin to evaluate the efficacy of the changing nature of transport provision and the service it offers.

LAND USE AND ACCESS IN MEXICO CITY

In Chapter 2, I described the physical and population dynamics of growth throughout the Metropolitan Area. I also identified the continuing spatial segregation among economic groups which in large part relates to the expansion and production of different housing opportunities within the city. In terms of proximity to positive externalities, the rich and better-off economic groups bid for serviced land with pleasant views, near to would-be peers and socially 'chic' service and commercial centres, and they avoid negative externalities such as heavily polluted areas, noxious industrial plants and areas lacking social *cachet*. The converse applies to the poor who, with the exception of occasional privileged (illegal) access to some *ejidal* lands, are usually obliged to seek residence in poorly serviced lands with high negative externalities that are undesirable to everyone else.

However, there is also the argument that the poor do exercise real choice about where they live. They make important locational trade-offs at different 'stages' of their urban and residential experience in order to maximize their proximity to certain crucial 'satisfiers': cheap markets, sources of unskilled employment, and low-cost rental (tenement) accommodation (Turner 1968a). For a recently arrived migrant creating a 'bridgehead' in the city, it is the city centre that offers optimum access to these opportunities. In Chapter 2, I challenged several of these assumptions and showed how patterns had never fully conformed to the Turner model, and I suggested that even where there was some resemblance in the past, these patterns have changed significantly in recent decades. One important reason has been the gradual absorption of many formerly outlying towns into the built-up area. For example, in order of absorption from the 1920s onwards: Tacuba, Azcaptotzalco, Tacubaya, Tlalnepantla, Tepeyac/La Villa, Mixcoac, Ixtapalapa, Coyoacán, San Angel, Ecatepec, Contreras and Tlalpan. Today, too, urban expansion at the periphery of the Metropolitan Area is often incorporating well-established *pueblo* cores (moving clockwise and starting in the north: Tepozotlán, Coacalco, Chiconcuac, Texcoco, Chimalhuacán, Chalco and Milpa Alta; see Figure 1.1). These old town centres are important because they offer a large number of land-use and service functions that were, until they were absorbed, exclusively found in the old historic core of the city. Cheap retail markets are an integral element in these centres, as are many unskilled employment opportunities, services such as public baths, schools, shops, parks and entertainments, and often political/administrative functions as well (*delegación* or municipal offices for example). Although some of the large homes in and around such centres have been 'gentrified' (especially those in the south), they may also offer low-income *vecindad* or *'ciudad perdida'*-type accommodation for renters.

The important point to recognize here is that, as the city has expanded in size and areal extent, its functions have evolved to create a variety of spatially decentralized areas within the Metropolitan Area. Therefore, the majority of the population no longer relate to the old historic core of Mexico City for their day-to-day services and needs. Instead, they go to the nearest local sub-centre. The functionality of these 'cities-within-the-city' was recognized by planners by the late 1970s, and several existing *pueblo* cores were scheduled for 'consolidation' as 'Metropolitan Urban Centres' within the Urban Development Plan (see Figure 4.1 and Chapter 5). Where no such centre existed (e.g. Pantitlán and Netzahualcóyotl), then a new one was created. Land-use planners in other Latin American 'megacities' have begun to argue that this polycentric arrangement is an effective mechanism for reducing the focus upon a central city area, cutting daily travel times, and developing greater social equity by meeting people's needs locally and with greater effectiveness (Riofrío 1996: 170).

Although small pockets of industrial development are spread throughout most of the Metropolitan Area, a few of the major industrial districts may be identified here. First, before the 1950s industry developed in two principal sites: north of the rail heads in Cuauhtémoc and into Azcapotzalco, and down the western edge of the (then) city limits focusing upon gravel and sand extraction and latterly cement and other mineral works. Second, since the 1950s there has been some new expansion of light industries in the east of the Federal District in Ixtapalapa, but the major industrial area of note remains Azcapotzalco.

A rather disingenuous attempt was made during the late 1950s to encourage industrial development elsewhere in the national territory, thereby reducing the excessive concentration in the capital. It was disingenuous because no attempt was made to include the surrounding municipalities as part of the industrial exclusion zone (Lavell 1973; Unikel and Lavell 1979). Third, therefore, faced with controls imposed inside the Federal District, industry (like new residential development banned by then DF mayor Uruchurtu), established itself on the other side of the DF boundary in Naucalpan, Tlalnepantla and Ecatepec, and more recently still in Tultitlán and Cuautitlán.

As we observed in Chapter 1, the Metropolitan Area retains a disproportionately high share of the nation's industrial product and employment, and while this proportion has declined significantly since 1975, it remains important. It has also shifted its location somewhat. There are two key sectors of industrial land use running outwards from the centre towards the north-east and north-west respectively (Figure 4.1). Between 1960 and 1980 there has been an overall movement of industrial establishments from the

FIGURE 4.1 Principal land uses and urban 'centres' in the Metropolitan Area

centre to the periphery, with the central *delegaciones* losing relative importance to Azcapotzalco (up to 1970), and to Tlalnepantla, Naucalpan and Ecatepec (up to 1975), and since that time outwards still further to Cuautitlán Izcalli and Cuautitlán de Romero Rubio (Garza 1978: 102–7). The central city area today predominates in activities which require less space (foodstuffs, drinks, shoes, printing), while the first 'ring' (see Table 1.5) concentrates upon capital and intermediate goods and consumer durables, where greater space is required (Villegas 1988; Rowland and Gordon 1996). Between 1975 and 1985 the second 'ring' was the most dynamic, and covered a diverse range of production of industrial goods. However, as we observed in Chapter 1, it was hardest hit by the recession during the late 1980s.

TABLE 4.1 Types of daily journeys undertaken in the Metropolitan Area of Mexico City, 1983

Means of transport	Total number of journeys	Percentage of vehicular journeys
Metro[a]	6 515 616	29.08
On foot[b]	6 104 626	–
City bus[c]	6 821 759	25.98
Private car	4 267 815	19.04
Suburban bus	3 147 929	14.04
Collective taxi	1 838 715	8.20
Trolley-bus	280 614	1.25
School bus	191 612	0.85
Ordinary taxi	154 802	0.69
Bicycle	90 929	0.41
Tram	59 035	0.26
Lorry	29 158	0.13
Motorcycle	15 498	0.07
TOTAL	28 518 208	100.00

Source: Adapted from Lizt Mendoza (1988: 226).

[a] Includes changing lines within the system.
[b] Journeys of more than 500 metres or of 5 minutes' duration.
[c] Includes routes operated by the State of Mexico Transport Commission (COTREM).

This spatial distribution of service and industrial functions thus sets the pattern of over 30 million daily journeys, of which journey to work is the single most important, comprising just over 50 per cent of all daily journeys undertaken. Next come journeys to school (around 35 per cent, which is particularly high in Mexico given the youthful age structure of the population). Shopping and recreational trips cover around 8 per cent each (Lizt Mendoza 1988: 228).

The means whereby people make these journeys are shown in Table 4.1. City and suburban bus services taken together have always been most important, but the Metro has become increasingly important in recent years, as have the collective taxis (UNDIESA 1991; Navarro Benítez 1993). The latter have changed their nature from shared cars carrying up to six passengers in the early 1970s, to converted combis taking 11–12 passengers by the later 1970s/early 1980s, to micro-buses (20+ passengers) from the mid/late 1980s onwards. Correspondingly, the importance of *colectivos* and the network operated has greatly increased, as has the power and influence of that lobby in transport policy matters. Navarro Benítez explains this upsurge as a product of the economic crisis in 1985 onwards, but it is also due to the strengthening of this interest-group's influence. Private cars account for around one-quarter of person-trips per day (Rowland and Gordon 1996).

Low-capacity vehicles (taxis, collectives and private cars) have risen from 10 per cent of 'ridership' in 1966 to 29 per cent by 1985 and to almost 50 per cent in 1990 (Navarro Benítez 1993: 181). 'High'-capacity transport (Metro, Ruta-100 buses, trolley-buses and trams) which were once the principal means of transport for most people (66 per cent in 1972) are down to just over one-half of the daily journeys in 1990. Given the poor standard of driving, the widespread existence of potholes and the occasional uncovered manhole, few people risk riding on two wheels. The easy theft of bicycles and motor-cycles is also a factor restricting their use. Bikes are almost non-existent except for a few three-wheelers used occasionally by sales and delivery people.

The industrial areas are well served by proximate working class districts, many of which were irregular settlements established during the 1950s and 1960s to accommodate the workforce that fuelled Mexico's economic 'miracle'. For those living nearby, transport was not a major problem. However, for the 600 000 plus people who lived in Netzahualcóyotl in the east in 1970, travel to work for many meant a 1–2 hour one-way journey to the factories in the north. Those working in services had a slightly shorter, but no less exhausting, journey to the city centre.

The problem was that Netzahualcóyotl at that time had very few urban 'satisfiers' of its own and enjoyed limited infrastructure, with streets that were often impassable during the rainy season. Thus many people had a long walk through muddy streets to reach a paved street, long queues and an extremely uncomfortable journey by bus to the Federal District boundary where a second leg of the journey by Metro and/or another bus(es) was undertaken (Navarro Benítez 1988a). Although transportation costs were subsidized and fares were often charged at a flat rate, outside the Federal District they were higher. The flat-rate system led companies to run shorter routes, thereby making frequent changes obligatory. For those coming in from far afield during the 1960s and early 1970s, transport costs could be significant, although I doubt if these costs came near to 25 per cent of the basic minimum salary as some authors suggest (Navarro Benítez 1988b).

My own data, collected in 1979, suggest that working class populations spent less than 10 per cent of the daily minimum wage on transport and most workers earned considerably more than the minimum (Table 4.2). Thus public transport costs in Mexico City are financially affordable to the majority of users. It is the social and emotional costs of daily travel which are more burdensome, together with the time lost from other activities and the lengthening of the working day. Nevertheless, although travel conditions have improved markedly in the past decade, for those living at the distant periphery on the high roads to Puebla, Pachuca or Querétaro daily travel into town remains onerous. For people living further out many journeys are centripetal towards the DF; 63 per cent of the journeys

T A B L E 4.2 Journey-to-work time and costs experienced by heads of households in peripheral irregular settlements of Mexico City, 1979

	Isidro Favela (%)	El Sol (%)	Santo Domingo (%)	Jardines de Tepeyac (%)	Liberales (%)	Chalma (%)	Total (%)	Total number
Principal mode of transport								
On foot	15	5	13	12	13	4	11	(50)
Bus	44	51	42	65	25	79	51	(235)
Pesero and bus[a]	13	4	12	1	4	2	7	(31)
Metro and other[b]	3	25	14	5	36	7	13	(62)
Other[c]	25	15	18	17	23	9	18	(84)
Total number	(100)	(78)	(90)	(83)	(53)	(58)		(462)
Time taken in return journey								
1 hour or less	52	19	50	33	51	33	40	(178)
61–120 min	29	32	29	36	39	45	34	(151)
Over 121 min	19	49	21	31	10	22	26	(116)
Total number	(94)	(79)	(88)	(75)	(51)	(58)		(445)
Average time of return journey (min)	86	141	93	116	78	108	104	
Average cost of return journey (US cents)[d]	53	44	53	44	48	40	48	

Source: Settlement survey, PIHLU study; see Gilbert and Ward (1985).

[a] Includes a small number who only took peseros (collective taxis). This proportion will have increased somewhat during the last decade as the pesero network has expanded into micro-buses, and has become better organized and more integrated to complement Metro routes.

[b] Metro, or a combination of Metro and other modes of transportation. (Liberales is near to Observatorio Metro station.)

[c] Includes private car and other unidentified combinations.

[d] The average daily minimum wage in Mexico City early in 1979 was US$6. Most heads of households earned a little more: around 15 per cent above the minimum on average (Gilbert and Ward 1985: 106–7).

originating in the valley axis Cuautitlán–Texcoco are destined for the DF and 98 per cent of the bus concessions in the metropolitan municipalities have an arrival terminus at a Federal District Metro station (Castillo *et al.* 1995: 78). This generates serious problems and difficulties for the effective integration between DF and metropolitan transport networks. To the extent that an estimated 75 per cent of users of the collective transport system are male, these costs fall disproportionately on their shoulders, but some 46 per cent of observed mobility is also around the home, and these 'costs' fall more heavily upon women and children. There is, therefore, a gender division of transportation in Mexico City that has yet to be studied.

Although users of private cars do not suffer the same physical discomforts, their journey, too, can be onerous. Distances are considerable from the more remote residential districts in the south and north-west, and at peak periods or after a storm, traffic moves slowly even on the orbital and interior urban freeways. Isochrone diagrams suggest around 30 minutes' driving time from the western Federal District boundary to the city centre (Domínguez 1987). In addition to the service functions provided by the old *pueblo* cores and other urban 'centres', large hypermarket shopping malls have been established alongside the *periférico* on its northern, southern and most recently western sections. Access is designed almost exclusively for private transport, and these developments cater primarily for the middle class and upper-income groups.

Later in this chapter I will analyse in detail the nature and evolution of the transportation system. Here I want to suggest that average journey times for most Mexico City residents have not increased greatly in recent years. This is likely to prove a contentious point, as most people believe otherwise, but it is important to recognize that the extent and efficiency of the transportation system have improved notably. Also important is the emergence of multicentred land-use functions alluded to earlier. Most people's daily needs are met within the broad sector in which they live. Their search for employment and accommodation tends to revolve around existing social networks and most people relate to one broad zone, or more usually to a single sector of the city (Jackson 1973). Education, shopping and other needs are also met locally – often through the cities-within-the-city structure outlined earlier. Moreover, since 1975 there has also been a notable improvement in the spatial distribution of industrial activities in the Metropolitan Area (Villegas 1988). The industrial structure has become more diversified over time, has generated a growing number of jobs in absolute terms, while spatially the locations of employment have moved outwards, with the most rapid growth in the second 'ring'. The importance of this decentralization of 'satisfiers' through the changing nature of land uses should not be underestimated.

In a major study conducted in 1983 which examined the journeys of a very large sample of people for the Metropolitan Area, it was found that the average journey was 52 minutes (Lizt Mendoza 1988). This includes 21 per cent of journeys undertaken on foot (see Table 4.1). The data correspond very closely to my own. In a 1979 survey of households in six peripheral irregular settlements of Mexico City where travel times could be expected to be much higher, I found that the average round-trip journey to work for household heads was 104 minutes: identical to Lizt Mendoza's findings. Moreover, in three different-sized cities in three countries in which we conducted the survey, size of city and journey time to work did not appear to increase in a broadly linear fashion. Rather, for those travelling the longest distances, travel times tended to level off at around the 60–80 minute threshold (Gilbert and Ward 1982b; see also Table 4.2). In smaller cities, people might well travel right across town or to the city centre, but in large metropolitan areas they keep to one broad area or sector. Less than one-quarter of workers from the surveyed irregular settlements in Mexico City spent more than 2 hours travelling to and from their workplace (Table 4.2). Inevitably, longer journeys were suffered by those living in the most peripheral and isolated settlements, for example El Sol and Jardines, but communications with these settlements have improved considerably since the survey was undertaken. Note, also, the way in which flat-rate, sub-sidized-rate and subsidized fares override any significant time (distance)/cost relationship (Table 4.2).

Despite Mexico City's enormous population it does not sprawl to anything like the same extent as many other modern world cities. Population densities are high and a relatively small proportion of the city comprises green spaces in the form of parks and gardens. In 1978 the Federal District had only 2.3 m^2 of green space per inhabitant (5.2 m^2 in the Metropolitan Area as a whole), compared with the 16 m^2 norm established by the World Health Organization and 9 m^2 recommended by international standards (Guevara and Moreno 1987). Despite these already high densities, con-siderable opportunities were identified for further increases on 'inefficiently' used space within the city, an estimated 19 per cent of all plots being estimated as 'vacant'. Planning policy since the early 1980s has sought to encourage the conversion of vacant plots into active use.

Within the Federal District, land available for future development is almost entirely located in the south. However, a growing ecological aware-ness among state and society at large has identified this region as one which must be preserved for agricultural and conservation areas. Their importance is highlighted both in the need for reoxygenation of the highly polluted atmosphere, and as one of the principal areas for replenishment of the city's natural groundwater acquifers. Some 70 per cent of the city's water supply comes from Central Valley groundwater sources, and without adequate replenishment the problems of depletion, lowering water table, and drying out of the anhydrous clays of the old lake-bed area will lead to further problems of building subsidence.

Changing patterns of land use and capital
accumulation in Mexico City

The changing pattern of economic activity in Mexico City was discussed in Chapter 1. Specifically, I noted the shift towards a more tertiary-based urban economy, especially in the Federal District. There has been a decline in the role of the central city area as an industrial centre, and those functions which remain are orientated towards non-durable consumer goods such as shoes and clothes, printing and, lately, some textiles. The first and second 'rings' are more orientated towards capital and intermediate goods and consumer durables (Villegas 1988; Table 1.5). Nevertheless, the central city area retains considerable importance as an area of industrial production, although the 1985 earthquakes accentuated the decline, and some estimates suggest that as much as 18 per cent of all establishments in the *delegación* Cuauhtemoc suffered extensive damage, especially the small and middle-sized clothing workshops (Garza 1986).

Other factors also intervene to change the pattern of land uses. While the earthquakes threatened to redefine much of the central city, the early decision to rehouse low-income families on the same sites as their collapsed or demolished tenements meant that the land use has remained the same, even though the buildings themselves have changed. Elsewhere in the downtown area, however, land has often been converted to open space or remains vacant – usually where there were once public buildings or private hotels and shops. On prime sites throughout the city one might also expect strong redevelopment pressures from commerce to clear away dilapidated residential properties and to initiate changes to more 'efficient' and profitable activities. In the early 1970s South Insurgentes Avenue, between Colonia Nápoles and San Angel, comprised large residential homes built during the 1940s and early 1950s. Today almost all these residences have been demolished and adjacent plots merged in order to construct new offices and shops. Indeed, for Mexico City's Planning Department one of the most politically sensitive areas and questions is in Polanco – a formerly exclusive high- and low-rise residential district – in which there are strong pressures for commercial redevelopment of land to which residents are strongly opposed. They fear an erosion of the area's residential functions and a decline in residential land values.

Research elsewhere has also begun to emphasize the existence of these redevelopment pressures from large-scale commerce. Inner-city shanty-towns have been identified as especially vulnerable in Rio de Janeiro and Bangkok, to name but two cities (Perlman 1976; Boonyabancha 1983). Indeed, 1980s World Bank philosophy explicitly sought to 'assist selectively in subdivision of new land, particularly for the benefit of poor urban households displaced from central city locations by expansions in commercial uses of land' (Linn 1983: 182). The logic of capital accumulation processes demand the penetration and commodification of formerly illegal or informal land-use functions and their displacement to make way for more profitable investment opportunities.

Thus a particularly important question relates to the fate of the population who have traditionally lived in the inner city. To what extent are residential areas in Mexico City being turned over to more commercial activities? Are the poorest groups most vulnerable to these pressures and, if so, to what extent is there a selective displacement of these groups from the city centre? Certainly displacement of these groups is frequently argued to be a consequence of redevelopment. One study drew attention to the rising pressure upon classic tenements (the *vecindades*):

> (the) continued existence of the central low-priced rented stock is threatened by the substitution of original proprietors by more dynamic property capital (which is) acquiring *vecindades* and vacant lots, sometimes without developing these locations immediately, and in other cases constructing middle-price range condominiums. (COPEVI 1977: 43–4)

There is further evidence to support these arguments of displacement, although it usually relates to large-scale one-off redevelopment projects (Suárez Pareyón 1978; Batley 1982). For example, in São Paulo an extension to the Metro led to a total redevelopment of a working class neighbourhood and to the expulsion of low-income families and traditional economic activities from the area:

> redevelopment shifts gains from tenants and small owners back to creditors, to the recipients of large scale reorganized land and to those who are able to meet conditions of the extended credit based land, housing and consumer goods markets. Expulsion is thus related to accumulation. (Batley 1982: 261)

Although this proposition invites agreement, there are signs that these processes are far from inevitable. The extension of the Metro into working class areas of Bras in São Paulo undoubtedly displaced large numbers of the local population, yet the 70-metre swathe of vacant land cleared either side of the actual railway has only lately been redeveloped or commercialized (1990s onward), and then not aggressively so, comprising mostly lower-middle income and working class apartments. This is probably due to sharp reductions in the investment opportunities for finance and other capital during the recent economic crisis, and to a 'switch' to alternative and more profitable forms of investment elsewhere (see also Benton (1986) on Montevideo). A similar feature may be observed around the old wholesale market area of Mexico City, the surrounding blocks of which are not being 'gentrified' as might have been anticipated (see Chapter 2). However, there seems little doubt that during those periods when large-scale investment in urban redevelopment is profitable, this leads to population displacement similar to that experienced at Covent Garden and elsewhere (Burgess 1978). Such displacement occurred as a prerequisite to the massive new commercial and office development in Santa Fé on the western hill flanks of the city. A similar situation would evolve if the (Reischmann) South Alameda project goes ahead, although this time, in my view, most of the displacement would primarily be small-scale commercial development since the area has relatively low residential occupancy (Herzog 1995; Navarro Alvarez Tostado 1997).

Nor were inner-city rental shackyards systematically turned over to private commercial development during the 1970s – despite their having been scheduled by the government for removal. These *ciudades perdidas* (lost cities) were prime sites for commercial redevelopment given their location in and around the city centre of Mexico City. Detailed information was gathered about these sites in the early 1970s (Ward 1976b). In 1982 all but one of those locations with an original area of 0.5–1.0 hectares (or 50–99 families) – i.e. of a suitable size for redevelopment – were revisited and detailed land-use maps were drawn. This provided a sample of 75 separate sites. Ten of the 75 sites were listed in 1973 as having been eradicated, yet in our 1982 survey 6 of the 10 still had shanties upon them (Ward and Melligan 1985). The widespread presence of dwellings on the majority of sites suggested that removal and redevelopment had had little impact. Only 13 sites had little or no residential function, and here we may assume that major clearance has occurred. A further 21 sites had between 15 per cent and 65 per cent of their area inhabited, and these were defined as of 'mixed' land use. In our assessment, 11 of these appeared to have been partially affected by a programme of removal, but no less than 41 sites still remained as low-income housing. At the very outside, less than one-half of all the settlements studied had been significantly affected by the rehousing programme. Moreover, the evidence suggested that where redevelopment had occurred it had not been informed by pressures from commercial capital. Rather the changes came about through public-sector initiatives: mainly the construction of schools and roads, or road-widening schemes. At that time, at least, there was no clear evidence of changes to commercial usage as a widespread or generalized speculatory process (Ward and Melligan 1985).

Thus if 'switching' of capital investment is occurring in Mexico City, then it is not taking place systematically and certainly not in a way that is leading to significant changes to existing residential and commercial areas. It is clearly visible in land development processes at the periphery, whereby land is converted from agricultural to commercial use, but it appears to have exercised far less importance in gentrifying downtown areas than I, for one, had initially anticipated. In part this is due to the social 'construction' of consumer demand through the built environment, which I consider in Chapter 7. In part, also, it is an outcome of access and the evolution of the transportation system, which I consider below.

MEXICO CITY'S TRANSPORTATION SYSTEM

Favouring the better-off: private companies and private cars

The physical expansion of the city and, in particular, the establishment of major industrial centres in a northern arc of the Metropolitan Area required the emergence of a transportation system that would get workers from the peripheral *colonias populares* to the factories. Yet it was not until the creation of the Metro in 1968 and, more importantly, its expansion from 1977 onwards that direct state intervention in favour of collective systems of mass public transport really emerged. Even now the philosophy remains firmly one of a mixed public/private system, with little evidence that the government is seriously contemplating any move against the use of private cars, nor against the sharp rise in micro bus (*colectivos*) concessions. While there have been positive developments in transportation planning in recent years, the state continues to treat the private sector extremely favourably. Below I look first at the responsibilities and role of the private sector.

Forty-five per cent of the nation's vehicles are registered in the Metropolitan Area and 71 per cent of those vehicles are private cars (Lizt Mendoza 1988: Comisión Metropolitana 1996). As Table 4.3 indicates, 'low-capacity' vehicles – defined as private cars, taxis and collective taxis (today largely microbuses) – carry just under one-half of total daily journeys (up 20 per cent according to Navarro Benítez' calculations (1993)). A not unreasonable proportion one might imagine, but it must be remembered that we are dealing here with a poor population in which the large majority cannot afford these means of transport – in effect they are largely excluded. Moreover, the significance of these 'low-capacity' means of transport is far greater than the one-half of the population carried. Over three-quarters of air pollution emanates from transportation functions, almost one-half of which comes from private cars (see Table 4.5 below; see also Castillejos 1988: 302; Legoretta 1988: 286). Indeed, the source of certain elements are almost exclusively vehicular: 100 per cent of lead emissions, and 82 per cent of carbon monoxide (Navarro Benítez, 1993: 186). Seventy-six per cent of pollution comes from vehicles – of which almost half is generated by private cars. Thus, 50 per cent of daily journeys (around 15 million) are provided by transport systems which generate more than 50 per cent of the total air pollution. Compare this with the other half of all journeys which are provided by only 16 000 units of 'high-capacity' means of transport, most of

TABLE 4.3 Evolution of means of transportation for low- versus high-carrying-capacity vehicles

Capacity	Percentage of total journeys undertaken					
	1966	1972	1979	1983	1985	1990
Low-capacity vehicles (taxis, colectivos and private cars)[a]	10.7	31.5	32.2	32.1	29.2	50.0
High-capacity transport (Metro, buses, trolley-buses and trams)[b]	89.3	66.6	65.5	67.2	54.0	51.1
Others[c]		1.9	2.3	0.7	17.0	na.

Source: Adapted from Navarro Benítez (1993: 180).

[a] Includes colectivos on fixed routes.
[b] Only Ruta 100 buses and other state-run enterprises.
[c] Includes casual pick-up taxis without a fixed itinerary and suburban buses operated by the private sector.

which are buses, and which generate barely 3 per cent of all emissions. It is easy to see that private cars are the principal villains of the piece.

Moreover, other social costs need to be included in the equation. The congestion caused by private vehicles slows down the movement on roads to 16 km per hour at peak times, and this also affects high-capacity transport systems (Lizt Mendoza 1988). Capital investment in road construction and improvements, relatively low fuel costs, low repair and service costs, and non-punitive costs on car tax and circulation licences all encourage private car ownership and usage. Indeed, in Mexico City the only relatively high-cost item is insurance (which not everyone carries). These low costs represent hidden subsidies to private-car users in particular. Private-car usage as a proportion of total daily journeys increased from around one-fifth to one-quarter in the decade from 1975 through to 1985, and the General Transport Coordination aimed to reduce this to 18 per cent by the turn of the century (Table 4.4). However, this is unlikely to occur without the withdrawal of some of the implicit subsidies identified above.

Air pollution in Mexico City is accentuated by its geography. First, its height above sea level (2240 metres) requires the use of higher than normal octane fuel, which has a higher lead content. Second, its upland basin means that under stable, high-pressure air mass conditions (usually winter), thermal inversions trap the air in lower levels of the atmosphere, generating photochemical smog (Guerra 1995). Sunshine at Mexico City's latitude accentuates the process by having a 60 per cent greater efficiency rate of producing smog than is the case in Los Angeles (Rowland and Gordon 1996). Back-of-the-envelope estimates of environmental damage costs associated with living in Mexico City add up to $US830 million a year just for workdays lost through illness and premature death as a result of pollution emissions (UNCHS 1996: 407). Care should be exercised in interpreting

T A B L E 4.4 Journeys per day for different types of transportation

	Number (thousands) and percentage of total journeys undertaken										
	1971	(%)	1975	(%)	1980	(%)	1986	(%)	2000 (estimates)	%
Buses[a]	6209	53.6	7414	50.5	8749	49.2	9300	42.3	16800	47.3
Metro	901	7.7	1510	10.3	2098	11.8	6515	29.0	7120	20.0
Electric service (trolley and trams)	547	4.7	665	4.5	607	3.4	700	3.1	2700	7.6
Collective taxis	371	3.0	438	3.0	2392	12.6	2300	10.5[c]	2500	7.1[c]
Private taxis	1061	9.0	1261	9.0						
Private cars	2206	19.0	2880	19.6	3532	19.8	5500	25.0[b]	6400	18.0[b]
Other means	300	2.6	360	2.5	423	2.4	–	–	–	–

Source: Adapted from Navarro Benítez (1988b: 46; 1989: 34).

[a] Buses include urban and 'suburban'.

[b] Includes taxis and colectivos in the State of Mexico municipalities; also 'others' from 1986 onwards.

[c] In light of the post-1985 expansion of microbus colectivos, these estimates are almost certainly around half of the actual total (see Navarro Benítez 1993).

TABLE 4.5 Sources and toxicity of air pollution in Mexico City

Sector and source	% of total emissions	% weighted by toxicity of emission
Transportation	76.6	42.4
Private cars	34.9	
Gasoline trucks	19.9	
Combis and microbuses	10.5	
Taxis	7.9	
Diesel trucks	1.6	
State of Mexico buses	1.1	
Ruta 100 (DF buses)	0.5	
Others (trains/planes)	0.2	
Industry and trade	4.4	16.9
Industry	3.7	
Trade	0.7	
Energy	4.0	10.8
PEMEX	2.4	
Thermo-electric plants	1.6	
Ecological factors	14.9	29.9
Eroded areas	9.6	
Fires and other processes	5.3	
Total	100	100

Source: Lacy 1993.

these data since they are based upon rather crude calculations, and give no idea of whether conditions have deteriorated or improved in recent years; nor do they offer comparable data with other cities.

Government intervention in pollution abatement has increased significantly in the 1990s. In 1992, President Salinas created a Federal Attorney General's Office for Environmental Protection (PROFEPA), and President Zedillo later placed this office under the aegis of a new (and much more influential) Secretariat for Environment, Natural Resources and Fisheries (SEMARNAP) which is headed by Julia Carabias, the former head of the Instituto de Ecología. Several major measures have been introduced in the last decade to address the problems of pollution in the Metropolitan Area. While low-capacity vehicles and users are to blame for much of the pollution, the toxicity ratio of these emissions is less severe compared with industry and energy production, as can be seen in Table 4.5. In order to address this problem, in 1991 the government closed the 18 de Marzo PEMEX refinery. Also the two new thermo-electric power plants serving Mexico City have been converted to natural gas, and are instructed to suspend operations during thermal air inversions (Rowland and Gordon 1996). The PROFEPA has accelerated its monitoring and interventions in the metropolitan area since 1995. Its brief is to focus largely upon industries operating in the area, and it carried out almost 20 000 inspections between 1992 and 1995, enforced over 700 partial closures and 43 total closures, and imposed fines of over 26 million *pesos* (approximately 3.5 million in 1997 dollars, and considerably more in real terms at the time of closure or fine imposition). Some 12 700 enterprises were found to have modest levels of non-compliance with norms, and half that number were in total compliance. Compliance rates have improved by 25 per cent per year since 1993 (Comisión Metropolitana 1996).

Under the new laws, within the Federal District and State of Mexico responsibility for control over trade and services facilities, as well as all vehicles, lies with the respective governments. Since 1990 The Federal District Department has enforced a *Hoy no circula* programme which prevents users from using their car one day a week (which day depends upon the registration number). This began as a short-term winter experiment when pollution levels reached unacceptable levels, and was retained throughout the year. Occasionally, as an emergency measure when conditions deteriorate even further, a 2-day ban is enforced, and other measures (school closures) are also taken in order to minimize risk. This ban was the first time that the government had taken action against private-car usage in the city and has generally been regarded as a success. However, for those that could afford it the answer was to have more than one car, so that car sales increased significantly as a result. In 1997 most middle-income families have at least two vehicles, and parents adjust their schedules and car use in order to compensate for the day on which one car is off the road. Ecology and transportation are two key areas where the new PRD Cárdenas administration proposes to concentrate its energies, and policies towards private car usage may become more punitive in an effort to encourage greater public transportation usage and lower levels of pollution from car emissions.

The *DDF* is improving its anti-contamination controls on the 3500 buses of the Ruta 100 Bus System which, in the early 1980s when it had almost double the number of vehicles, was a notorious source of pollution. The *DDF* has also phased in the need for mandatory anti-contamination catalytic converters to be fitted on all new cars from 1992, with older cars to be converted by 1997. New (unleaded) petrol and low-sulphur diesel have also been introduced, and there is a compulsory vehicle inspection programme. These catalytic converters are also being installed in taxis as well as in *combis* and microbuses. The situation was so bad that in 1988 only 5 per cent of vehicles in operation were estimated to be operating at optimum levels in terms of air/gasoline mixture (Legoretta 1988).

A paradox revealed by Table 4.3 is that, although the state took concerted action to intervene in stimulating high-capacity transportation systems from the 1970s onwards, its failure to control rising car ownership and usage, together with the dramatic expansion of collective taxis, has meant that the relative importance of low-capacity vehicles rose from 11 per cent to 32 per cent, and most recently to 50 per cent (see Table 4.3). This is due almost exclusively to the reorganization of collective taxis. Not only has the number increased, but the traditional pattern of large saloon cars carrying a maximum of six passengers along a few set routes has been overtaken by the widespread use of green and white combis carrying 10 or 11 people. More recently still, larger microbuses have begun to appear on many routes. The routes themselves are highly organized, criss-cross the city, and are much more tightly integrated with other transport systems than they were a decade ago (Sutherland 1985). As we have observed, they have increased dramatically since 1995, but although there seems little doubt that the service they provide is much improved, they are often subject to many of the previous criticisms about private cars (Navarro Benítez 1988a). It is my view, however, that provided they are well maintained they are far less the villains of the piece than are private cars – given their much higher occupancy ratio. Today, given their micro bus status, it is perhaps even a misnomer to view them as low-capacity vehicles.

The criticisms of high social costs apply particularly to low-capacity vehicles, but until the State seriously undertook to intervene in mass collective transport, the effect of government policy was systematically to favour the private sector. Before the late 1960s, Mexico City's transportation system evolved in a rather *ad hoc* fashion in response to private vested interests at different times. It was basically a privately operated system which began with a (foreign-owned) tram-based service before the Revolution, and developed subsequently (1917–46) into a myriad collection of privately operated bus routes (Navarro Benítez 1988b). State intervention did not seek to cut across these interests in any way. Quite the opposite: bus operators were rewarded for their participation in, and support for, the post-revolutionary State apparatus, and they were encouraged to expand and to displace the foreign-owned trams. It was not until 1946 that the State intervened formally in transportation matters, first to expropriate the trams, and second to create a trolley-bus network to complement the buses. However, the State's role in stimulating collective systems of mass transportation remained extremely limited until it began to develop the Metro in 1968 (Davis 1994).

Until that time, State intervention was focused upon the development of the road network, and particularly that which most favoured the private car: rapid no-stop highways such as the *Viaducto*, the *Circuito Interior* and the suburban *anillo periférico* (Figure 4.2). Other major roads were also widened and lengthened throughout the 1950s and 1960s, serving both private cars and bus routes (e.g. Insurgentes North and South, Calzada Tlalpan, etc.).

Many of these developments quite deliberately not only favoured private transport, but opened up new areas of urban land development and

FIGURE 4.2 The orbital motorway

speculation, especially in the south of the city. For example, an important motive for the creation of the 'Camino al Ajusco' in the mid-1970s was to facilitate the proliferation of real-estate development on the pedregal south of the *periférico*. It also provided more direct access to a State Secretary's *rancho*. Those with prior knowledge were able to acquire large land holdings and to make killings from the subsequent land valorization windfalls that the new road generated. Of course, not all new road routes were motivated by private gain. Occasionally they avoided the land of powerful politicians or private-interest groups where State expropriation would have been an embarrassment (Davis 1994). This accounts for some of the twists and turns in the *periférico* route in the west. Large-scale construction firms such as ICA had also been pressing the government to raise investment in transportation systems, most notably the Metro, but Mayor Uruchurtu held out against them for as long as he could. His political demise occurred in part as opposition rose among powerful business interests whose real-estate and construction proposals were being blocked in the Federal District.

Nor did investment in road construction on behalf of the private sector decline once greater public commitment to collective transportation systems had emerged. Sixteen *ejes viales* were constructed in 1978–9 comprising 3–5 lane one-way highways equipped with integrated traffic signalling. Although built at enormous expense and not without considerable public outcry over

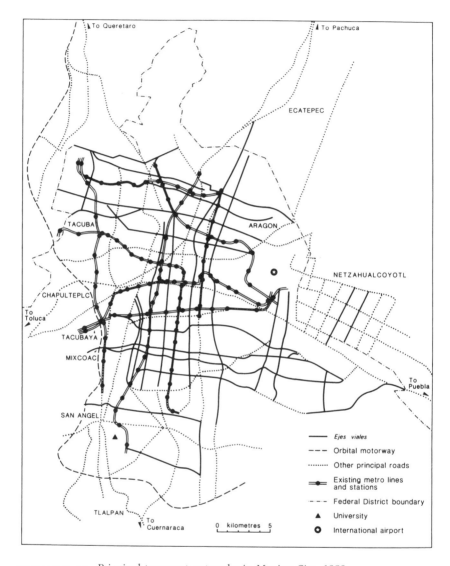

FIGURE 4.3 Principal transport networks in Mexico City, 1989

the way in which they were constructed, the *ejes* have done much to facilitate rapid traffic flow around the city (Figures 4.3 and 4.4). Although many of the *ejes* have an exclusive contra-flow trolley lane (to avoid it being used by other vehicles), these *ejes* by and large are not heavily used by public transportation systems. Once again private cars, *colectivos* and taxis are the principal beneficiaries.

FIGURE 4.4 *Eje vial* with Metro running overhead

Public transport policy

At the outset the Metro was designed to confront two problems: first, to ease the congestion in the inner-city area; second, to help 'dignify' and rehabilitate the Historic Centre (Navarro Benítez 1988a). Despite its inauguration in the late 1960s, the Metro did not really begin to develop its true role until the early 1980s. The original network comprised only three lines which, although modern and fast, inadequately covered the central city and intermediate ring areas along a total network length which was only 40 km. The system did not extend to the heart of the industrial area in the north, nor to any of the main *colonia popular* areas. Thus at best it served as a complementary system to those users coming to the DF by suburban bus and wishing to go downtown, and then perhaps to get another bus northbound to the factory areas. During rush hours congestion on the system was intense, particularly at nodal points like Pino Suárez Station. Conditions became so bad that police have to segregate men into separate areas of the platform from women and children and into specified carriages. On the positive side, the system was clean, quiet, fast, extremely cheap and heavily subsidized. In 1978 the one-*peso* flat-rate fare cost the equivalent of US5 cents, and although it was increased to 20 (old) *pesos* in the early 1980s, and to 100 (old) *pesos* in 1986, and the level of subsidy has been reduced, the Metro remains the cheapest form of transportation that is genuinely available to everyone. In real terms it continues to cost around US15 cents, and still carries a heavy subsidy. A multiple ticket usable on other integrated transport networks is now also available.

Expansion of the system began in earnest in 1979–80 with extensions and new lines over the next 10 years which, for the first time, reached towards the working class heartlands and into the industrial areas of Azcapotzalco and Vallejo in the north-west (Figure 4.3). Particularly important were the lines constructed in the 1980s which run east to north and avoid the city centre, and the extensions south to the University City and down the city's west side – both potentially middle-income-user oriented. The total network length has almost quadrupled in 10 years, and the recent opening of a new line gives Mexico City today 160 km (100 miles) of metro network, making it the largest and most heavily used in Latin America (Figueroa 1996). No other system in Latin America has as large a proportion of daily journeys carried by the Metro: São Paulo, Buenos Aires and Rio de Janeiro have considerably less than 10 per cent of total journeys on their systems (Figueroa 1996). The latest line is not marked on Figure 4.3, but comprises 19 stations running from a terminus just north of the centre at Garibaldi, and then south and then east into Ixtapalapa. Several further extensions and new lines are planned (see Table 4.4).

Moreover, around 70 per cent of the equipment is now produced nationally (rather than in France, which developed the prototypes and most of the earlier rolling stock), so that increased investment no longer accentuates the loss of valuable foreign exchange (Domínguez 1987). However, the Metro remains a Federal District Department enterprise, and with a single exception at 'Cuatro Caminos' Station, which barely makes it into Naucalpan, the Metro has not developed beyond the DF boundary, nor does an integrated and complementary network exist in the State of Mexico, although a light railway now runs east from Pantitlán to La Paz.

For those living outside the Federal District, and also for many city residents, buses provide the main form of transport – often in conjunction with the Metro. Outside the DF these are run by private companies, in contrast with the Ruta 100 system operated exclusively in the DF since the private concessions were expropriated by mayor Hank González in 1981. Prior to the construction of the Metro and the expansion of private cars and micro buses, buses were always the primary means of high-capacity transport (see Tables 4.1 and 4.3), and while their relative importance has declined somewhat, they remain a crucially important component within all daily journeys.

There are indications of a sharp drop in the bus service in the 1980s, and severe criticisms were voiced by President Salinas during his 1988 presidential campaign that the Ruta 100 was not fulfilling its obligations adequately. Although part of the criticism was politically motivated and directed at the intransigent union leadership, the problem was compounded by insufficient buses in operation, and by the fact that the service was too irregular and inefficient (Navarro Benítez 1989). Although they are better equipped than their counterparts of 15 years ago and produce far less contamination, one gets the impression today of a far lower intensity of bus traffic on the streets in the Federal District. Moreover, the price differential between bus and *colectivo* fares has narrowed in recent years as the latter have increased their scale of operations and the regularity of their routes (Navarro Benítez 1988b; cf. Sutherland 1985).

In order to reinforce state intervention in mass transportation systems, there are attempts to develop electric trams and trolley-buses. The 'light train' system links up with the Metro at Tasqueña and extends the service to Huipulco, 5 km further south. An important element in future policy proposals is to expand the role of trolley-buses (see Table 4.4).

COVITUR was created as a DF enterprise in 1978 to coordinate and develop the Metro operations. However, in the State of Mexico no counterpart exists, although COTREM was created in 1982 in order to tackle transportation problems and to liaise with COVITUR and the *DDF* (Flores Moreno 1988; Lizt Mendoza 1988). Several of COVITUR's original functions (e.g. acquisition of equipment and planning) were later handed over to other institutions (Castillo *et al.* 1995: 81). In particular, the Coordinación General de Transporte now undertakes the planning role, and has developed an Integrated Transport Programme which has prioritized developments which serve working class neighbourhoods, primarily to win back political support for the PRI, it is argued (Navarro Benítez 1993: 188). It is also criticized for continuing to be overly centralized, and for failing to take adequate account of other transportation developments in the area, particularly the expansion of *colectivos* (Navarro Benítez 1993; Castillo *et al.* 1995).

The most recent development is the creation of a Metropolitan Area Transport Council embracing federal, DF and state authorities. While they applaud this initiative, Castillo *et al.* (1995) call for a number of options to be considered that would create mixed public and private institutions that would integrate the various transportation providers and users. This would involve a Metropolitan Transport Corporation – a holding company of private and public transport providers – and a Metropolitan Transport Authority that would provide the normative and planning direction. This proposal, also, is heavily centralized as they point out, and would benefit from some level of decentralization to the local *delegación* level. Nevertheless, it would provide for two key advances: the integration of all transport-provider interests under a single umbrella, and for a genuinely *metropolitan* spatial level of organization to be achieved.

Although the government has begun to develop a coherent commitment to mass transportation, this has not led to a fundamental policy change nor to a political willingness to reduce indirect subsidy and supports for the private sector, nor to penalize low-capacity vehicles. Perhaps growing awareness and public preoccupation about contamination will strengthen local government resolve to adopt a more aggressive stance towards private-car owners in particular, and to encourage a switch to greater middle class usage of the Metro or other forms of public transport. Whether or not the Metro could tolerate the increased use – particularly on certain routes and at peak times – is an open question. For many, myself included, the principal disincentive to using the Metro remains the high level of discomfort associated with the overcrowding at peak times, and I have long felt that a two-tier first- and second-class carriage system, strictly enforced, may be the only solution – no matter how much it represents an anathema to the PRI. Only a combination of secure parking lots where vehicles can be left at peripheral Metro stations, combined with guaranteed seats in first-class compartments, is likely to persuade Mexico's middle classes to use the system more extensively. However, so long as the current policies continue, these will crystallize the inequalities that already exist within the system rather than lead to progressive changes. Despite important overall improvements, the transportation structure continues to reproduce social inequality in the city.

The politics of transport policy

The creation of a transport system does not occur in a vacuum. It responds to the economic, investment and political imperatives of the day. Public protest and class struggle generated around means of transportation are also likely to influence state responses. Yet by and large Mexico City has avoided large-scale protest movements developed around such issues – certainly compared with other Latin American cities such as Bogotá and São Paulo. The high levels of public subsidy and the relatively low fares derived from low fuel prices are probably the key reasons. Considerations of low comfort levels and high social costs associated with travel on public systems have not led to protest.

Yet investment in transportation has not been immune from political considerations. The 'Bus Owners Alliance' (*Alianza de Camioneros*) was closely associated with the government during the 1920s–1940s, and offered government a wedge to drive between foreign investment in the tram system before it expropriated the service in 1946. The close government–*Alianza* cooperation continued subsequently during the 1960s and early 1970s despite a deterioration in the quality of bus transport during the period. Keeping the bus companies sweet was important for government in order to get workers to their places of work at low cost, and also to ensure that buses were available to the CNOP in order to transport *colonos* and popular groups to public meetings in support of the PRI and government functionaries. For these reasons, President Echeverría, in particular, could ill afford to alienate the bus-owning and bus-operating sector. There were other reasons too: his wife's family had strong business interests in private urban bus companies. This helps explain the total freeze on further Metro development during his *sexenio*, combined with the fact that the initial Metro development was closely associated with his predecessor (Díaz Ordaz), so that there was little public kudos to be had for Echeverría in making further extensions.

Politics and vested interests also help explain mayor Hank González' transportation policy. He identified the traffic chaos as the 'capital sin' of the DF (Navarro Benítez 1988a: 154). In the late 1970s the Vallejo Industrialists' Association complained that they were losing 224 000 worker hours a day due to the long distances and journeys to work of the 120 000 workers engaged in their 900 firms (Rodríguez 1985; cited in Navarro Benítez 1988b: 42). More important was Hank González' intention to undertake major public building and construction programmes in order to distribute patronage and largesse among his own political supporters. It was no accident that he alighted upon the *ejes viales* and the Metro expansion, both of which suited his spending programmes, particularly once oil revenues came on line (Navarro Benítez 1988a; Teichman 1988). In the following chapter I will explain how the adoption of a formal planning system suited Hank González' political project. Suffice to mention here that the *ejes* programme generated a sharp threat to the Mayor when public protest developed around the disruption caused by construction works, and from residents whose tree-lined streets were being bulldozed and their properties compulsorily purchased. Although many injunctions were sought, only one *eje* was incomplete when the system was inaugurated in 1979.

Unlike the protection offered to the *Camioneros* by Echeverría, there was little love lost between Hank González and the *Alianza*, who he criticized for the inefficiency of their operation and whose share of the market he proposed to reduce from 42 per cent to 19 per cent between 1978 and 1982 (Navarro Benítez 1988b). Eventually, in 1981, under his instructions, the privately run bus service in the DF (which he described as an 'octopus') was expropriated to form the basis of the state-run Ruta 100 in conjunction with the 118 new trolley-buses inaugurated in 1977 (Navarro Benítez 1988a: 157). In 1988–9 the Ruta 100 was itself the focus of politically motivated attack by President Salinas' determination to purge unions of their corrupt and intransigent leadership. As we have observed above, the number of buses operated by Ruta 100 has declined by half, and all have been modernized in order to reduce contamination.

Thus political regimes have in the past had an important impact upon transportation policy in Mexico City, although there are indications that today there is far greater continuity of policy between *sexenios*. The lack of continuity across the DF–State of Mexico border remains a major problem, however, and one that will steadily increase as a growing proportion of the

Metropolitan Area population live in the surrounding municipalities. Questions about a coordinated transportation policy between the two entities, about who should pay the costs of providing public and private services (particularly where passengers pay taxes in the State of Mexico but commute into the DF for work) and so on, demand first a coherent political philosophy of urban development, and second, a unified metropolitan planning system – perhaps along the lines proposed by Castillo and his colleagues, as discussed above. However, we saw in Chapter 3 why divisions between the Federal District and the State of Mexico remain entrenched. In the following chapter I propose to examine the potential for the creation of a unified planning system. But don't hold your breath.

5

PLANNING IN MEXICO CITY: DECORATIVE OR INDICATIVE?

Previous chapters have demonstrated a clear need for some sort of planning authority to monitor, regulate and control land-use development city-wide. In this book I have sought to identify many of the problems associated with rapid urban growth, namely: increased private car ownership, long journeys to work on inefficient transport systems, heavy pollution levels, irreversible damage to the city's ecological system, inadequate levels of servicing and public utility provision to the majority of residential districts, and so on. In Chapter 3, I concluded that these problems can only begin to be resolved by a political commitment to improved life chances and living conditions for the majority. Urban planning by itself will not overcome problems that are structurally derived. No matter how efficient, imaginative or politically supported planners are, their efforts will comprise 'technical tinkering'. Whether planners and planning groups are the instruments of reactionary politicians, overworked mollifiers doing the best they can in a liberal tradition, or the advocates of the people acting as evangelistic bureaucrats will depend fundamentally upon the political conjuncture in which they operate and the political space offered them by their masters.

In Mexico the key problem was that until the late 1970s urban planners occupied no political space whatsoever. Unlike the United Kingdom, where the 'crisis in planning' arose because planners had got it wrong, in Mexico, the crisis arose because planners didn't exist as such. Until that time there had never been any systematic implementation of urban development plans anywhere. Within the Metropolitan Area, any restrictions placed upon urban growth or proposed land uses were the result of particularistic decision making by politicians or officials; they were not based upon legislated norms and regulations. This situation has not been resolved, as I will show in this chapter. Plans are still not being implemented systematically. Within the planning process the opportunities for public participation are extremely limited, especially for proactive involvement. There remains too low a level of coordination between planning agencies in the Federal District and those of the surrounding State of Mexico. However, despite these caveats, I will argue that there is some cause for optimism that a genuine urban planning process is gradually emerging, and that, taken overall, this will lead to progressive rather than regressive outcomes for the majority of the City's population.

Traditionally in Mexico, 'planning' has usually meant economic planning, and until the late 1970s or so relatively little concern was expressed about physical or urban planning. The emphasis lay upon the allocation of financial resources, fiscal controls, industrial development incentives, monetary and exchange policy and so on, usually through the Treasury Ministry (SHCP) and, until its demise in 1988, the Programming and Budgeting Secretariat (SPP). Subject to the overall guidance of the Presidency, these budgeting and treasury agencies in effect controlled the planning processes. Other lesser departments acted in a rather maverick fashion, aiming always to win Presidential approval for their actions and not to be seen to lose advantage to other sectors of the public bureaucracy – in the manner outlined in Chapter 3. Generally each of these departments would have its own so-called planning office. Within this highly competitive mould, the desire for individual sectors to coordinate their actions within a single overall physical plan was unknown.

Since the 1970s, however, the position has begun to change for several important reasons. First, there is a growing consensus that planning is desirable. Urban development in a country the size of Mexico, and in any large city, is a complex business. One cannot expect individual sectors to take into account all needs, nor to take responsibility for evaluating and coordinating all of them equally. Whether this coordination role is a function for planning departments to fulfil is an open question. In Mexico it has usually remained the preserve of the Executive, the State Governor, the Mayor or the Municipal President acting through whatever intergovernmental structure exists at that time (Unique Development Agreements (CUDs later CDSs), and State Development Plan Agreements (COPLADES) and, most recently, State/Municipal Development Plan Agreements (the COLPADEMUN)).

Second, physical planning is likely to become increasingly significant if only as an ideological tool to enhance state control rather than as a regulatory framework for urban development. Formally approved plans can serve to justify political actions. Sometimes, too, they are a prerequisite for acquiring credit from international lending agencies (Gilbert 1976a). Although political considerations remain paramount, the influence of technocrats has risen in recent years. This does not mean that the influence of urban planners will expand incrementally. Indeed, their role and influence will continue to wax and wane with different administrations. Over the past five governments the urban planning star rose with President Echeverría (1970–6), reached its height under López Portillo, but then slipped back when a confirmed economic planner (De la Madrid) took office (1982–8). Although President Salinas' position *vis-à-vis* urban planners was much the same as that of his predecessor, he embraced urban planning more aggressively in so far as this involved public and private sector groups working together to enhance greater economic efficiency and competitiveness in regional development, while the highly targeted social development programme (PRONASOL) sought to alleviate poverty.

Third, new federalism promises to transfer greater responsibility to the state and local levels. Moreover, innovations among 'opposition' party states and municipalities are giving a greater role to planning institutions (often quasi-public institutions in the case of the PAN's Planning Institutes). Similarly, President Zedillo's administration recently released its Urban Development Programme for 1995–2000 which seeks to give greater hands-on responsibility for planning to the states and municipalities and to foster efficiency and equity with more active public participation (Mexico, SEDESOL 1996). However, at a normative level the national social development secretariat SEDESOL retains considerable influence. Given the political 'weight' accorded to SEDESOL since its creation late in 1991, it has become a much more significant agency for 'planning' than either of its predecessor counterparts SAHOP or SEDUE.

In this chapter I first want to ask how and why urban planning has evolved in Mexico. Is it related to the growing complexity of the urban environment, to changing external economic and political pressures, to internal pressure from social groups, to the whims of leading government personalities, or what? Second, what is the nature of planning activity in Mexico City? What are the main constraints acting upon planning and how effective were recent initiatives? Here I propose to examine in particular detail an earlier period (1978–82) during which planning gained considerably in importance and in which I had a personal hand and have, therefore, a modicum of inside knowledge.[1] Specifically I propose to examine the fate of the 1980 Federal District Urban Development Plan. Third, I ask what all this means for the general public. How far do they participate, and what is the likelihood of their ever becoming truly involved in planning decisions? Finally, in the conclusion, I ask whose interests are served by planning. Has it led to an improvement for the poor, or does it provide yet a further means for suppressing their actions? I hope an answer to some of these questions will allow us to make an informed assessment about the rationale for planning in Mexico.

THE STRUCTURAL IMPEDIMENTS TO PHYSICAL PLANNING

In Mexico, as elsewhere in Latin America, urban planning is a relatively recent phenomenon. Although national planning systems existed during the 1950s in a few countries such as Colombia (1953), Nicaragua (1952) and Ecuador (1954), and while some regional or special projects also had significant planning structures, urban planning, if it was considered at all, was relegated to becoming a sub-set of these broader projects – such as that responsible for planning the new city of Ciudad Guayana (Rodwin et al. 1969). Investment programmes in social welfare, agrarian reform initiatives and so on evolved during the 1960s in part because of the support received through the Alliance for Progress, and were important because they to 'some degree legitimized the use of planning as a means of promoting development' (Mattos 1979: 78). But the emergence of planning structures at this time was tightly restricted to aspects which dovetailed with the interests of national economic élites (Wynia 1972).

Planning has also suffered from several structural weaknesses. In part planners were to blame, for they saw themselves as, somehow, above the institutional political system (Cibotti et al. 1974: 40). They were overly concerned with technical criteria and regulations, and often ignored the reality of the ways in which decision making occurs throughout Latin America. In their excessive dependence upon foreign techniques such as linear planning models, input–output analysis, growth poles and urban structure plans, they failed to identify the role of dominant groups in determining development processes (Kaplan 1972: 28; Moore 1978; Gilbert 1984b; Angiotti 1993). For example, planning invariably threatens important interest groups. Proposals such as redistributive tax reforms, controls on land speculation, compulsory purchase, and development restrictions in certain areas are likely to engender conflict with those interests. As Angiotti (1993: 165) puts it: 'the world does not spin on the axis of the architect, the planner or the urban designer'.

Planning also posed a threat to the traditional forms of political mediation exercised through patronage. As Wynia states (1972: 84), 'planning is an orderly process, traditional mediation of political conflict is not'. For politicians the priority is political control, not the efficiency of development (Gilbert 1981). Politicians need to be able to exercise discretionary control over the allocation of resources and to act in a personalistic way. In Mexico, the precarious 'balancing act' referred to in Chapter 3 whereby competing economic and political alliances must be accommodated between successive administrations evokes little sympathy from politicians for a decision-making framework influenced by planners.

A further constraint has been the fear of many politicians that they would become overdependent upon técnicos. Invariably in the past the latter have not formed part of a President's personal trusted team, and an Executive is unlikely to view favourably a growing dependence upon a body of technicians whose data processing and information handling becomes indispensable. Put simply, the Presidential calculus may be firmly invested against formal incorporation of the planning process (Wynia 1972; Gilbert and Ward 1985).

Finally, there was the fear that plans inevitably lead to a greater dissemination of information to the public. In societies such as Mexico, where decisions are often made behind closed doors according to highly particularistic criteria, the last thing that decision makers want is informed criticism. Theoretically, too, planning requires the active participation of the population at large. It should be open, democratic and participative. It would be naive to suggest that these epithets apply fully to planning processes in the UK or the United States, but they are certainly an anathema in most Latin American countries today. Perhaps we should not expect too much, too quickly, from societies such as Mexico which have fundamentally different traditions of decision making and planning.

The emergence of planning in Mexico

Before 1970 national planning in Mexico referred to economic planning and comprised a process of 'mutual adjustment' led by a 'central guidance cluster' of four major institutions: the Presidency, the Ministry of Finance, the Central Bank, and Nacional Financiera (Schafer 1966). A single, centralized planning agency to fulfil this purpose had been shunned earlier by President Cárdenas (1934–40) and was never again taken up. Nor had any integrated regional planning framework ever been established. Rather, initiatives were partial and in addition to the three Metropolitan Areas three other broad investment and development areas had emerged: the Gulf Coast, the *Bajío* (central–north-west), and the northern Frontier Zone.

State promotion of regional development was weak and unintegrated and comprised mostly one-off programmes such as the river-basin projects of 1947 and 1961, the elimination of fiscal advantages for industries locating in the Federal District in 1954, the creation of small industrial parks in a handful of cities, and regional development plans for the states of Yucatán and Oaxaca, both of which were prepared by the Ministry of the Presidency after its creation in 1959. These actions had limited impact, not because they lacked technical expertise, but largely due to the absence of any group within the urban-industrialist or rural sectors that would commit itself to a modern agrarian industry or would take up the question of regional inequalities (Unikel and Lavell 1979).

As part of his strategy of 'shared development', President Echeverría (1970–6) developed planning activities through the creation of various rural development agencies (Goulet 1983). More specifically as far as Mexico City was concerned, he adopted measures designed to promote the decentralization of industry and the stimulation of development 'poles' outside the city. Incentives were provided for industry which discriminated against locations in the large metropolitan zones. Funds were established to promote industrial development, and commissions (the COPRODES) were created in each state to encourage collaboration between private and public sectors to stimulate socio-economic development. From 1973 onwards the Executive gave increasing weight to urban-industrial policies, culminating in a Human Settlements' Law passed in 1976: probably the most important single piece of legislation in the field of urban planning in Mexico.[2] This

Law created the basis for the state to intervene in a consistent and integrated way in the planning of human settlements, and it identified the levels of responsibility for policy making: national (i.e. federal), state, conurbation and municipality.

López Portillo consolidated planning activity within a Ministry of Human Settlements and Public Works (SAHOP). Within a year a National Urban Development Plan was published which aimed to confront the huge disparities in the distribution of national population. The Plan established policies for territorial organization of population taking the Population Commission's (CONAPO) projections of a reduction of population increase from 3.6 per cent in 1977 to 2.5 per cent in 1982 and to 1 per cent by the year 2000. The aim was to restrict the growth of the three largest metropolitan areas (Mexico City, Guadalajara and Monterrey) and to generate an urban hierarchy with 11 centres of a million people each, 17 centres with between 500 000 and 1 million, and 74 centres of over 100 000 (Mexico SAHOP 1978: 42–4).

Indeed, throughout the past two decades the formulation of national urban development plans has been predicated upon variations of growth poles planning theory. Little has changed except the emphasis upon which population centres are to be targeted for growth, and the sectorial strategies adopted to pursue territorial planning (urban investment, housing, industry and economic services etc.). The same basic premise has underpinned the National Urban Development Plan (1988–92), the National Development Plan (1983–88), the Industry and Commerce Promotion Programme (PRONAFICE), the National Urban Development Programme (1990–94), and ultimately the National Urban Development Programme (1995–2000).

Under the first National Urban Development Plan a national framework of 11 integrated urban zones was established with programmes designed to shape efficient urban systems within each. Population centres were subject to policies of either (a) stimulus, (b) consolidation, or (c) ordering and regulation. Mexico City, needless to say, fell within the latter category. The function of the Human Settlements Ministry was to coordinate execution of the plan at the national, state, conurbation and municipal levels, but it fell to another ministry (Programming and Budgeting SPP) to promote it. This dependence upon the goodwill and support of another sector was a major stumbling block. Moreover, the National Urban Development Plan was further dependent upon the goodwill of other sectors if it was to be operative. Particularly important was the attitude adopted by the then Ministry for the Promotion of Industry (SEPAFIN), whose National Industrial Development Plan, although ostensibly congruent with the National Urban Development Plan, in fact added a further 16 priority areas to the 11 zones already established, and in effect rendered SAHOP's initiative virtually inoperable (see also Aguilar Barajas 1992: 112). Despite its apparent activity, planning remained passive in so far as it followed the pattern established by the so-called 'efficient' sectors of economic growth. It therefore validated the economic imperatives of the day (Unikel and Lavell 1979).

After 1983 the traditional dominance of economic planning was reasserted by President De la Madrid whose background was in economics, and during his period as Minister of Programming and Budgeting (SPP) he had engaged in intense bureaucratic infighting with the physical planning axis of SAHOP and with those (such as Hank González) in the Department of the Federal District (*DDF*). The latter, in particular, was more closely associated with the expansionist philosophy supporting increased oil production levels led by Petróleos Mexicanos (PEMEX) and its boss, Díaz Serrano (Teichman 1988). The result was a sharp downgrading of physical planning between 1983 and 1988. SAHOP was emasculated: the large slice of its resources represented by public works was removed, and it was renamed the Ministry of Urban Development and Ecology (SEDUE). From 1983 there was only one 'Plan' (the President's National Development Plan, 1983–88). All others were 'programmes', and in 1984 SEDUE published a National Urban Development and Housing Programme which was little more than a watered-down and less-ambitious version of the previous Urban Development Plan. This 'new' programme identified 168 urban centres, the three largest of which were subject to policies of control and consolidation. A further 59 centres were deemed 'middle-sized', to be the focus of development according to local conditions. Some were scheduled for industrial growth, while others were designated to offer support to agriculture and tourism (Aguilar Barajas 1992). Their selection appeared to be rather unsystematic, based in part upon existing economic processes and in part upon a political need to ensure that all states were included (Campbell and Wilk 1986). If Unikel and Lavell's (1979) criticisms (mentioned above) of the shortcomings of the previous period of planning were a little harsh, they would certainly apply to initiatives in 1983–85.

When Camacho took over at SEDUE in 1986 there was too little time remaining in the *sexenio* to turn things around. However, responsibility for earthquake reconstruction largely fell to him, and his competent and efficient disbursement of these large-scale resources, and his politically sensitive handling of what had threatened to become a major political problem in the downtown area won him considerable respect. However, the option for major decentralization offered by the earthquakes in 1985 was resisted, exposing the lack of underlying political will to make a dramatic commitment towards urban reordering at the expense of the capital city (Aguilar Barajas 1992).

Under Salinas there was a quickening in attempts at the territorial distribution of population, but this owed more to economic restructuring and to a relatively buoyant economy than to a strategic implantation of a new territorial policy. Growth areas were the northern cities and those urban areas geared to take advantage of Mexico's export market orientation.

Sectoral policies focused especially upon those areas most favoured for export-orientated growth (the north, the gulf coast, and the western coast, see Aguilar Barajas 1992; González García de Alba *et al.* 1992). Territorially speaking, the Salinas urban development plan fine-tuned the earlier 100 cities plan, adding the Torreón–Gómez Palacio–Lerdo conurbation corridor to the three principal metropolitan areas as zones for 'regulated control', and identifying a further 20 cities for 'consolidation' and 52 cities for intensified development (*impulso*). In addition, some 70 medium-sized cities were identified for strengthening etc. In short, the plan was yet another iteration which followed, *post hoc*, the economic imperatives of the market place, with the state acting largely as the market's handmaiden.

Nor is the latest urban development programme much different (Mexico, SEDESOL 1996). It also adopts the time-worn strategies: 100 cities, consolidation of metropolitan areas, territorial planning and promotion of urban development and, as an innovation, a strategic programme to promote public participation in the urban development process. In addition to this last point, the latest plan/programme is also suggestive of being substantively better than its predecessors in so far as it is vested in a relatively powerful secretariat which, through some astute footwork in recent years, has managed to manoeuvre itself into a position of dominance over other sectors and land-use 'dinosaur' secretariats such as *Reforma Agraria* (Jones and Ward 1997). Moreover, as part of the decentralization and new federalism project, it is seeking to strengthen state and municipal capacity to undertake local and regional urban development planning that is sustainable both ecologically and politically. Indeed, the programme is quite bullish in these respects.

Thus the last two decades have seen an important growth in Mexico's commitment to planning, although its fortunes have fluctuated markedly. Although a decade ago I remained sceptical that urban development planning would ever weigh heavily within the panoply of Mexican public policy, the recent trends towards decentralization, combined with a greater plurality of political parties and governments willing to experiment, offer some cause for optimism.

There have also been some important changes at the regional and metropolitan level, but the capacity to work effectively across jurisdictions remains woefully inadequate. In Mexico City this has been an ongoing problem. In 1978 a potentially important planning initiative was developed in order to coordinate public policy development and implementation across the metropolitan area. The creation of the Conurbation Commission for the Centre of the Country covered the Metropolitan Area and large areas of the surrounding states of Mexico, Hidalgo, Puebla, Tlaxcala and Morelos, and included each of these state capitals. The Commission's 'Programme for the Territorial Planning of the Central Region and the Metropolitan Area of Mexico City' focused primarily upon population and economic growth of urban centres lying some way beyond the existing built-up area. These centres, such as Huehuetoca, Teotihuacán, Chalco and Amecameca (see Figure 1.1), were to be linked by a major orbital highway (the *libramiento*) and in some segments by a railway as well. The plan offered a strategy and an overall view of regional development, but lacked any specific mechanisms to ensure its implementation. Moreover, it lacked executive authority and it had no budget to speak of (Campbell and Wilk 1986; Castillo *et al.* 1995). As such, it fell pretty much at the first hurdle. Supposedly a forum for all of the key executive officers of all spatial entities, between 1978 and 1988 the Commission hardly ever met and in 1989 it was wound up to make way for a Standing Council for the Metropolitan Area. However, just before its demise a final report was produced, a key proposal of which was the need for a directing agency (*organismo rector*) comprising the principal authorities for all three levels of government in order to agree on the principal planning development imperatives: land-use, services and infrastructure. It also proposed that agencies which provided the primary transport and water service lines should be combined into a single organization under this directing agency. In short, it proposed a *cross-jurisdictional authority with executive control of certain strategic planning functions*.

However, the Standing Metropolitan Council did not fare much better. This Council developed out of a PRI Think Tank document prepared for the '1988–1994 Programme for Government'. It proposed that the Council combine three agency activities at the metropolitan level: water, transport and security (primarily policing). It emerged from the fact that Manuel Camacho, the former head of SEDUE, had been tipped to be the next *Regente*, and relations were good between Camacho and the recently elected governor of the State of Mexico, Ramón Beteta. The proposal for the Metropolitan Council was that it should unite the various government levels around a series of agreements forged within specific (sub)commissions for urban development, housing and land use, water and drainage, transportation, ecology and environment, agro-industries and forestry, and social development/welfare. A series of firm proposals were put forward by these commissions in 1989 and several of them had an assigned preliminary budget, usually derived from the collaborating institutions. However, notwithstanding the major advance towards the creation of a structure capable of developing and implementing a strategy at the metropolitan level, the functions of the Council were never consolidated, and the initiative and commitment were stillborn (Castillo *et al.* 1995: 40). Whether this was simply a campaign proposal to be dropped after election, or whether it was a genuine attempt at strategic planning collaboration which fell short for political reasons is not clear. Certainly it was dealt a blow once Ramón Beteta was forced to resign from the State of Mexico governorship (he was punished for the bad showing of the PRI in that state in the 1988 elections). Also it seems likely that once Camacho had been confirmed as *Regente* he may have had a change of heart about being subject to a meta-authority that he did not directly control. Whatever, the debate demonstrated quite clearly that there existed both the understanding and the appreciation of the need for a metropolitan council, but that the power of the separate political jurisdictions and political reality made commitment to such a strategic council unacceptable.

In effect, therefore, throughout this period planning continued to be undertaken within jurisdictions. This occurred through the Planning Committees of the States and the DF (COPLADES), which had been in existence since 1981. Each COPLADE signs an annual 'Single Development Agreement' (CUD) with the federal government which serves as the primary mechanism whereby major development programmes are approved and financed (primarily from central government). Thus they are the lifeblood of regional development investment programmes, but they are also the outcome of political deals struck by the governor and the federation with some input and lobbying from local groups. By their very nature they are *internally* derived rather than being an outcome of cross-jurisdictional collaboration. As such they sit much more comfortably within the strongly hierarchical structure of the Mexican political system. The CUDs continue, although their name has changed to that of Social Development Agreements, and under President Zedillo's new federalism initiatives some states are seeking to develop state planning committees with municipalities (COPLADEMUN) as a basis for assigning investment programmes state-wide. To the extent that the urban development secretariat in SEDUE has greater influence today, it is able to seek some level of compatability between investment programmes and planning in adjacent jurisdictions, but this continues to fall far short of integrated metropolitan planning authorities.

PLANNING INITIATIVES IN THE METROPOLITAN AREA

The effect of physical planning has always been more important in Mexico City than elsewhere in the country. The period of activity in national planning during the late 1970s and early 1980s described in the preceding section was also marked by the most dynamic phase of urban planning that the capital has undertaken. Therefore, it is useful to analyse Mexico City's planning experience in detail in order to evaluate its rationale, its potential and the impact that it has had upon the lives of its inhabitants.

From 'decorative' to 'indicative' planning

Since 1928 when the city lost its municipal status and became a special entity, legislation for city planning has fallen into three broad phases (Table 5.1). First, the period between 1928 and 1952, when several important pieces of legislation were enacted, the most significant of which was the

TABLE 5.1   The nature of different planning legislation passed for various periods since 1928

	Period					
	1928–52		1953–70	1971–84		
Category of planning legislation	(28–41)	(41–52)	(52–70)	(71–76)	(77–82)	(82–84)
A. Formulation of substantive planning and zoning legislation (includes 'Organic' laws)	7 (5)	(2)	1	(5)	13 (6)	(2)
B. Allocation of responsibilities and creation of bodies concerned with planning	4 (1)	(3)	0	(2)	6 (1)	(3)
C. Legislation concerning specific planning problems or land use (housing, roads, industrial sites)	5 (1)	(4)	6		1 (1)	
D. Changes, annulments, clarifications and administrative procedures	10 (0)	(10)	2	(5)	6 (0)	(1)
Total	26		9	26		

Source: *Diario Oficial.*
Data indicate individual pieces of planning legislation.

1936 Planning and Zoning Law and its precursors which, with minor modifications, remained the basis for planning until 1970.[3] A Planning Commission was established, which in conjunction with the Directorate of Public Works was to create a regulatory plan which would be the key instrument in 'regulating the ordered development of the Federal District' (*Diario Oficial*, 17 January 1933, Article 2). In addition, Federal District Consultative Councils and their local *delegación* equivalents were established as channels through which the public were invited to express opinions about servicing needs and public works. Throughout, the key organs of planning remained under the firm control of the Mayor. The 1940s saw the consolidation of these arrangements. Few new substantive pieces of legislation were passed, but the existing structure appears to have been strengthened and specific problems were dealt with through sectoral plans for industrial zoning, rent controls, and so on.

In contrast the second period, 1953–70, is marked by an almost total absence of any new planning legislation or initiative. This is explained by the influence exercised by Mayor Uruchurtu, who held office throughout most of the period and for whom 'planning was alien to the spirit and methods of . . . operation, which stressed secrecy, flexible interpretation of laws and regulations, rapidity, and spectacular short-term results' (Fried 1972: 680).

The third period (1970–88) covers the three of the administrations analysed in this chapter. Without doubt this is the most significant period in urban planning, both nationally and in Mexico City (Table 5.1). The Echeverría *sexenio* provided the groundwork for a fully fledged planning system that emerged between 1980 and 1988. The Federal District Organic Law was overhauled and initiated a slow process of decentralization of many functions to the *delegaciones*. It renewed the existence of Consultative Councils, although as was argued in an earlier chapter, these were not in fact activated fully until the following administration. For the first time an independent Planning Directorate was created, responsible to the DF Secretariat of Public Works (Figure 5.1). It was charged with developing the Master Plan, and with planning and zoning. Before that date an office charged with responsibility for the Master Plan (*Oficina del Plano Regulador*) existed as a sub-department in the Department of Public Works.

In the State of Mexico planning functions were charged to AURIS (Urban Action and Social Integration) between 1969 and 1982, after which the State General Directorate of Urban Development and Housing took primary responsibility (Figure 5.1). In 1976 the Federal District Urban Development Law was passed which made mandatory the existence of a City Plan, and sub-plans to cover each *delegación*. In addition, the urban area was to have a proper zoning system. Despite these initiatives no planning system was made operational until the end of the decade, when Mayor Hank González adopted a new Master Plan (1980), sub-plans and a Zoning Law (both passed in 1982).

Planning in Mexico City   The new Master Plan applied only to the Federal District and referred to the Metropolitan Area in so far as it identified a total population target not in excess of 21.3 million by the year 2000, 14 million of whom were to be accommodated within the Federal District (Mexico *DDF* 1980). The plan's principal objective was to improve access by the population to centres of economic activity and to the 'benefits of urban development' such as land, housing, infrastructure, services and utilities. The strategy proposed four major actions in urban areas, and two in the non-urban districts to the south (Figure 5.2). In the urban area it aimed to create or consolidate nine centres to provide the locus of commercial and

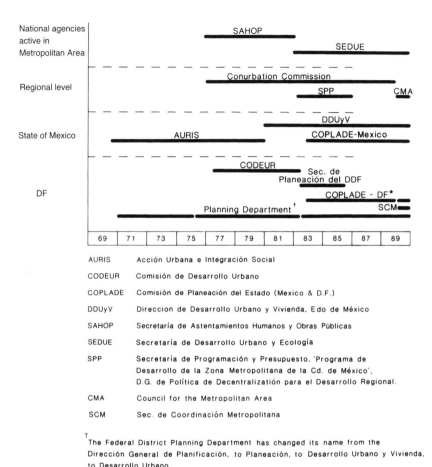

AURIS   Acción Urbana e Integración Social

CODEUR   Comisión de Desarrollo Urbano

COPLADE   Comisión de Planeación del Estado (Mexico & D.F.)

DDUyV   Direccion de Desarrollo Urbano y Vivienda, Edo de México

SAHOP   Secretaría de Astentamientos Humanos y Obras Públicas

SEDUE   Secretaría de Desarrollo Urbano y Ecología

SPP   Secretaría de Programación y Presupuesto, 'Programa de
            Desarrollo de la Zona Metropolitana de la Cd. de México',
            D.G. de Política de Decentralizatión para el Desarrollo Regional.

CMA   Council for the Metropolitan Area

SCM   Sec. de Coordinación Metropolitana

†
The Federal District Planning Department has changed its name from the
Dirección General de Planificación, to Planeación, to Desarrollo Urbano y Vivienda,
to Desarrollo Urbano

*Continues but no longer has planning functions in DF

F I G U R E   5.1   Departments and agencies with responsibilities for urban planning
in Mexico City, 1970–89

industrial activity and, to a lesser extent, housing. Each centre was to be
complemented by sub-centres and barrio centres. Collective transport
systems were to continue being developed, as were the ring motorway and
the urban highways (*ejes viales*). The important routeways were to be
consolidated as 'urban corridors', and finally, a land-use zoning system was
to be implemented. In many respects these measures validated existing
processes and land uses. However, their identification and scheduling for
reinforcement was positive in that it concentrated resources in selective
locations that were already important in people's daily lives. As has been

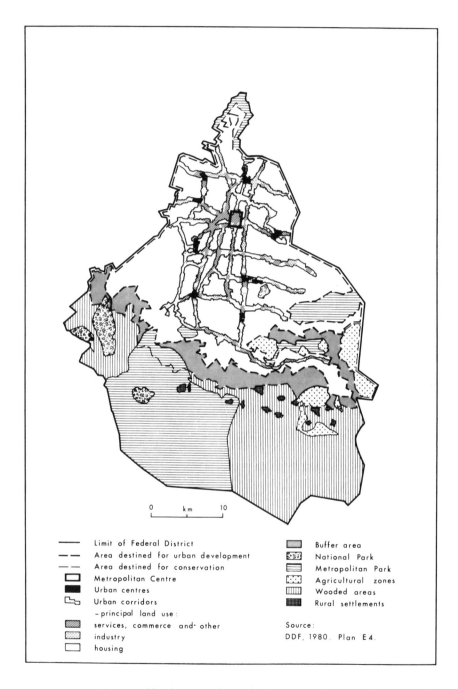

0   km   10

——	Limit of Federal District	▨ Buffer area
— —	Area destined for urban development	▨ National Park
— —	Area destined for conservation	▤ Metropolitan Park
▢	Metropolitan Centre	▨ Agricultural zones
■	Urban centres	▦ Wooded areas
⌐	Urban corridors	▦ Rural settlements

- principal land use:

▨ services, commerce and· other

▥ industry

▢ housing

Source:
DDF, 1980. Plan E 4.

FIGURE 5.2 Proposed land uses in the Federal District Urban Development Plan

shown in preceding chapters, increasingly these sub-centres are the loci of 'satisfiers' in spheres such as housing, markets and work.

In the non-urban areas the plan hinged around strict controls to prohibit development in the conservation area and temporary land-use developments such as sports fields and picnic sites in a so-called buffer zone. The aim was also to reduce the amount of newly incorporated land from 12 km^2 per year between 1978 and 1982, to 8 km^2 between 1982 and 1988, and to 4 km^2 during the period 1988–2000. Densities throughout the DF were to be increased, especially through measures that were designed to oblige owners of vacant plots to utilize their land productively. Some 18 per cent of plots were estimated to be unused (*baldío*).

The plan was passed in 1980, and a year later a whole series of sub-plans (the *planes parciales*) were approved, one for each *delegación* and another for the Conservation Buffer Area (Mexico *DDF* 1980). In turn, each partial plan incorporated *barrio* (neighbourhood) plans which identified permitted land uses in each area (Mexico *DDF* 1982). Formal zoning regulations were introduced in mid-1982, but these measures are meaningless without effective implementation. The planning office simplified the process whereby planning permissions could be obtained, obliging applicants to go to a single 'window' at their local *delgación* office. Thereafter the application was dispatched to appropriate offices for consideration, but this obviated the need for the individual applicant to go from office to office. The chief planner also, to a certain extent, forced the hand of *delegados* by closing selected unauthorized enterprises or building works. Inevitably this invited conflict between the importance of technical or political criteria in decision-taking and was only sustainable so long as it was supported by the Mayor (which was usually the case). (Both the planning chief and the Mayor came in for intense and embarrassing public criticism over allegedly underhand (i.e. discretionary) residential building development which was allowed in Bosques de Chapultepec, an élite residential district in parkland to the west of the downtown area.)

The 1980 plan contained several intrinsic problems, including its failure to address economic or social development issues so that economic, marketing and employment structures were excluded. Nor did the plan address the problem of complementarity with planning initiatives for the built-up area beyond the Federal District boundary. Nevertheless, it was realistic in so far as it attempted to harness existing processes. Most of the new centres already existed informally, and the proposal was to consolidate and integrate them. Also the 'buffer' zone aimed to restrict growth to that area in which expansion seemed inevitable, and thereby increased the possibility of preserving the conservation area beyond, which otherwise would have been quickly eroded. However, relatively few people engaged at the time in capturing land or undertaking construction in this buffer zone had heard about the Plan – a not unimportant consideration when evaluating its success (Aguilar Martínez 1987, 1988). In Tlalpan (a southern *delegación* spanning a crucial part of the buffer zone), some 313 hectares of land were developed between 1980 and 1984, and more than three-quarters of the individual developments were by lower-income or middle-income groups on plots much smaller than the regulations permitted. Thus they were illegal. Nor did many people living in the buffer zone know about the DF Urban Development Plan and its regulations. Most of the 10 per cent who did were from higher-income groups (Aguilar Martínez 1987).

Although patently they were not working terribly well, many of these initiatives lost impetus or were quashed between 1983 and 1988, even though for the first 2 years of the new administration the previous planning chief was kept on. Paralleling the shift away from physical back to economic planning at the national level, Mexico City's incipient urban planning process had been placed on the back burner. Although a new DF Secretariat for Planning was created, with strong political backing from (then) Mayor Aguirre, this had little to do with physical planning. Rather its focus was upon the Federal District's contribution to the National (economic) Development Plan. Physical planning remained the responsibility of a politically weak DF General Directorate of Urban Development and Ecology. While the personnel in this department remained broadly stable, it suffered from a lack of funds (see Table 3.1) and from a lack of credibility. Between 1983 and 1989 its name changed several times, a sure sign of political weakness, insecurity and lack of clarity of function.

Nowhere is this lack of clarity more evident than in the fate of the Programme for Urban Reorganization and Ecological Protection (PRUPE) which appeared from the planning office in late 1984. In its original form the proposal was to expropriate 77 000 hectares in the south of the city as a conservation zone, with the implication that many settlements already established in the region would be subject to removal (Schteingart 1987). Predictably this created a huge row from virtually all sides of the population, and after a series of consultations in the following 10 months the PRUPE was gradually watered down. By August 1985 it comprised a declared area in which further urbanization would be prohibited, the ecological zone defined, and the 37 villages and settlements in the south clearly demarcated (*La Jornada* and other newspapers 24 August 1985). Effective controls or legislation which threatened local interests had been dropped, and the measure was totally emasculated.

This rather absurd initiative ran alongside the regular revisions to the DF Urban Development Plan undertaken in 1984 and 1987–8 (*Diario Oficial* 16 July 1987). The principal difference between these revisions and the earlier 1980 plan related to what was proposed in the conservation zone in the south of the city. The pragmatic concept of a buffer zone beyond which conservation would be enforced was abandoned in favour of the PRUPE. Thus, to the extent that the concept of PRUPE was eroded, so too was the credibility of the plan (now called the Director Programme for the Urban Development of the Federal District). The operation and enforcement of planning permissions initiated 1980–3 appears to have been more lax thereafter, but greater attention was directed to the partial plans, which were elaborated in great detail. These were produced as pamphlets in which each *delegación*'s proposed zoning was mapped out and a detailed table of codes relating permitted and non-permitted uses was displayed. Provided that one could read a map and make sense of clear, but rather complex tables, the material was excellent. However, as a basis for popular consultation about the proposed planning law applied to an adult population, many of whom have not completed primary education, it was not terribly realistic.

As I will argue later, the authority for urban planning has been dissipated by the existence of a multiplicity of agencies with overlapping and/or competing responsibilities within the Metropolitan Area. In the surrounding State of Mexico there have been some recent attempts to develop corresponding plans at the municipal level. These have been prepared through the State Urban Development and Housing Department in conjunction with the respective municipal authorities and to some extent with the DF planning teams. However, in terms of a planning process which embodies legislated plans, zoning and regulations for the implementation of a plan, the process is nowhere near as advanced in the State of Mexico. Detailed land-use maps have been prepared for surrounding municipalities (Garza 1987), and some attempt has been made to ensure broad consistency of land uses in adjacent neighbourhoods on either side of the DF/State boundary, but categories of land use are not the same, and the lack of regulations means that they portray the outcome of unregulated processes, rather than serving as prescriptive guides to control future development. They are what they say they are: land-use maps, but to the extent that the DF Director Programme and partial plans lack 'teeth' and also fail to guide processes, one might argue, not unreasonably, that the distinction between plans and land-use maps matters little.

Nevertheless for a brief period during the late 1970s and early 1980s the planning department functioned much more systematically and effectively than ever before. Since then planning has continued, albeit in a diluted form. In my early 1990 interviews with the current planning chief it became apparent that Mayor Camacho was not greatly interested in developing the role of physical planning – probably for the reasons described above. Rather, one-off troubleshooting was the order of the day, combined with lightweight, relatively inexpensive but highly visible mini-projects (*mini-urbanismo*). In my view this approach is little more than a 'bread and festivals' strategy of social appeasement. Physical planning seemed as far from the minds of the planning team as was the case under Mayor Sentíes during Echeverría's administration.

THE STATUS AND AUTHORITY OF MEXICO CITY'S
PLANNING DEPARTMENT, 1970-1990

It is one thing to identify the 1970s and 1980s as an important period in the history of planning but, as I have already suggested, it is quite another to argue that a process of city planning has been implemented. In this section I argue that the authority enjoyed by planning is constrained in two ways: first by its institutional structure, and second by its low budget.

In Figure 5.1, I have identified those offices or agencies which, during the 1970s and 1980s, had a significant interest and role in planning within the city. It is not exhaustive, and excludes several of the big-spending departments such as the transport commission and the water agency, which also have their own 'planning' offices. While there have been some important changes since 1989, most notably the emergence of SEDESOL as the federal agency to replace SEDUE, and the disappearance of the Metropolitan Council and the Metropolitan Coordination secretariat, neither of which had any impact, the picture remains much as it then was. It demonstrates the difficulty that any single agency has in exercising authority over the planning process. There is a clear multiplicity of offices with responsibility for planning. In part this may be explained by the existence of two federal entities across which the city sprawls, but it also reflects the political tradition for incoming administrations to create new departments to compete with, or to take over, some of the duties of those already in existence. This enhances the opportunities for patronage by providing jobs within the bureaucracy. It also allows the Executive and Mayor to manipulate and play-off one political faction against another – part of the balancing act to which I referred earlier (see Chapter 3). Despite the fact that more recent administrations have set great store by administrative efficiency, it is apparent that there has been a proliferation of the bureaucracy with responsibilities for planning in Mexico City.

As we have observed earlier in this chapter, the government has never seriously sought to create a *city-wide* executive planning authority. The Conurbation Commission did not fulfil this role, but was an advisory body at a much larger scale which covered five central states and the Federal District. Nor did the 'Programme for the Metropolitan Region', which was established in 1984 with a technical committee in Programming and Budgeting (SPP) which was pitched at a regional scale and comprised a broad normative document with no executive status. Its thrust was less physical planning and more the coordination of resource allocation to municipalities.[4] The COPLADES, too, are committees with a broad representative base designed to stimulate local participation of the public and private sectors in economic development, rather than being an executive body for physical planning. Finally the Metropolitan Area Council failed to fulfil its promise and did not lead to greater effective liaison between respective planning bodies.

Thus for city planning to be effective under existing conditions requires close collaboration between the principal planning agencies on either side of the Federal District boundary. Cooperation of this nature was always unlikely given that the personnel invariably form part of different groups built around major political figures (*camarillas*), and that competition between these bureaucratic factions is the hallmark of the Mexican governmental system. A classic example was the SPP's Metropolitan Programme which was elaborated without serious consultation and input from SEDUE, the Conurbation Commission, or the Urban Development Departments in the State of Mexico and the Federal District.[5]

Another constraint on planning is that it is poorly funded. Since its elevation to become a separate directorate in 1971, the planning department has had one of the smallest budgets of the Federal District Department. Although in real terms expenditure on planning doubled between 1971 and the end of the decade, relative to other departments it declined from between 2 and 4 per cent of the total to around 1 per cent. However, low relative cost does not guarantee continued existence or immunity from savage expenditure cuts. During the 1982 crisis, when the Directorate had recently and successfully implemented its Master Plan, it suffered higher proportional cuts than many other departments. Its authorized budget was cut from an initial 1300 million (old) *pesos* to 700 million *pesos* early in the year, and then further to around 280 million old *pesos* in August. Planning, for all that it is a relatively low-cost exercise, is no less liable to cuts than any other department.

The politics of plan implementation

An important feature of plan implementation is the way in which it may serve a useful political purpose for the City's Mayor. Hank González, for example, had little sympathy or interest in planning when he took office. Rather, as demonstrated in Chapter 4, his primary concern was to engage in major construction works that offered opportunities for disbursing patronage and for self-enrichment. Yet he realized that a Master Plan offered several advantages. First, it complied with the Law which demanded the existence and regular review of a Master Plan. By itself this is an inadequate explanation: it would have been quite easy to produce a flimsy plan or a suitable revision of a version of the Master Plan presented, but not implemented, in 1976. Indeed for the first 18 months the Mayor kept the earlier plan 'on ice' and showed little inclination to revise or implement it.

A second reason was that it provided justification and backing in the Mayor's fight for extra resources to carry out the building programme already underway. Considerations of this nature certainly prompted his desire to update the Master Plan. During 1978–9 there was an enormous increase in expenditure undertaken on the building of new rapid highways with integrated computerized traffic signals (the *ejes viales*). Opposition to these building programmes was encountered among his cabinet colleagues as well as on the streets, where protest had erupted against the destruction of tree-lined avenues and the eviction of residents due to street widening associated with the construction of the highways. The Mayor needed to be able to demonstrate that this programme (and others that were in the pipeline) were properly thought-through and integrated within a Master Plan. Thus the plan required speedy elaboration, but for political reasons it was entrusted to SAHOP rather than being drawn up in house within the *DDF*.[6]

Third, planning was implemented around this time because the traditional forms of mediation were no longer adequate. Patron–client links which had predominated between high-ranking government officials and local communities were replaced from 1977 onwards by a more formal arrangement of state–community relations embodied within the neighbourhood councils' structure (*juntas de vecinos* structure (see Ward 1981a)), and as greater decentralization of responsibilities to *delegados* was achieved. As part of this change, the planning system began to be used to provide ongoing political legitimacy. This became imperative once the level of debate over urban issues had begun to be more informed. Increasingly through the 1970s interest in urbanism was no longer a preserve of élitist and relatively conservative groups such as the Architects' and Engineers' Professional Societies, and nor was it an academic backwater; it had entered the mainstream of politics. For several years a radical school of architecture (*Autogobierno*) at the National University had trained graduates with a very different perspective about urban development, which challenged conventional approaches. Moreover, several other professional courses had emerged, such as the Human Settlements Degree at the Metropolitan University. More significantly, perhaps, was the concerted and informed criticism that had begun to appear regularly in the press, many columnists of which were teachers on those courses. Others were advisers to left-wing political parties which were beginning to flex their muscles after the political reforms of 1973 and 1977. Information and critical argument entered party manifestos and even into Congress through minority-party representatives. The Coordinated Popular Urban Movements' Organization (CONAMUP) had successfully united a large number of low-income settlements into a single force, and by 1980 was beginning to assert itself both nationally and locally. It was particularly active within the capital (Ramírez Saíz 1983). There was, therefore, a growing sophistication of argument about urban development which demanded sound technical answers that could only be provided by a competent planning team. An ongoing planning system now became an important tool for political mediation.

However, the adoption of a formal planning system in the late 1970s also required certain compromises and trade-offs that some sectors of government and the PRI would be reluctant to make. Inevitably the publication of plans would add further to the dissemination of information about Mexico City's urban development. It would also require some curtailment of particularistic decisions by *delegados*, such as issuing their friends with planning permissions for developments that were not authorized by the Plan, or the condoning of actions of certain groups in exchange for political support. These were threatened once run-of-the-mill decisions were much more likely to be decided upon technical criteria rather than political ones. However, for the government, these were relatively small concessions to make, and in any case they were probably inevitable once the level of public debate had risen.

Clearly the apparent reduction in the importance accorded to physical planning since 1983 might appear to contradict my argument about the inevitability that Planning Departments should play an increasing role in political management. In some of my later (1989–90) interviews with high-ranking functionaries I attempted to explore this point. Some officials expressed surprise that an urban planning department had survived *at all*. Given the backgrounds of President De la Madrid and Mayor Aguirre, whose emphasis was upon economic planning and administrative efficiency, together with the President's antipathy towards many of the leading figures associated with physical planning under the previous administration, it was suggested that the continued existence of an 'urban development' department was unexpected. Yet it survived in a very weakened state, and its previous chief was confirmed in his post. The only explanations are either administrative ineptitude or, more likely, that some form of physical planning structure remained politically useful. It avoided formally changing the Law to revoke the Master Plan, with all the political embarrassment that would cause. It provided an important cushion for politicians to meet public criticism when urban infrastructure fails – as, for example, when there was intense flooding during the 1984 rainy season. A planning programme also gave the illusion of activity. Even the PRUPE, for example, while it backfired and did not win the support and approbation that the Mayor had expected, nevertheless engendered a long and wide-ranging debate which could be turned to good effect by the *DDF* authorities. It demonstrated that they were concerned and serious about the rising current of public debate on ecological issues, and it cost virtually nothing! Also planning may be used to head-off social unrest. In Mayor Aguirre's own words when presenting the revised plan in 1984: 'the Government of the Federal District cannot allow things to continue their present course, and cannot allow such an important problem for the maintenance of social stability to get out of hand . . .' (*Ovaciones* 24 August 1984). Although physical planning remained very low priority, its survival in vestige form was politically useful. This usefulness grew still further after the establishment of the Representative Assembly of the Federal District in 1988, and particularly once it began to intensify its scrutiny of the *DDF* and urban development policy from 1991 onwards. In the future there seems little doubt that the planning department will remain an important cushion between the legislative body and the elected mayor.

Public participation in planning

In many respects public participation is the acid test of whether or not a true process of planning exists. In the early 1980s several high-level planning officials in Mexico singled it out as the most important criterion in any definition of planning. They saw it as a means of ensuring that planning policy was carried out. By incorporating the public into the process and making them aware of the issues at stake, and of public authorities' obligation to install and maintain essential services, planners sought to establish a dynamic whereby proposals contained within the Master Plan would be implemented. Similarly, a raised level of public consciousness might help sustain policies across *sexenios* and provide a degree of continuity previously lacking in the Mexican political system. It would also make the planning office more accountable. However, planners' statements suggest a greater concern for information dissemination than public *participation* in decision making or in the effective ordering of local priorities. In my conversations with those planning officials most sympathetic to the idea of public participation, even they demonstrated little understanding about how the public might actively be involved in a proactive way (see also Gil Elizondo 1990). In fairness, however, this is also a lacunae in planning theory in Europe and in the Americas, where early initiatives at advocacy planning and at more pluralist involvement of local groups in the planning process were never fulfilled (Davidoff 1965).

Public participation was built into the preparation of the Master Plan primarily at the level of the *delegación* sub-plans and the neighbourhood *barrio* plans. The latter were the brainchild of Mayor Hank González himself, and the Planning Department incorporated them without enthusiasm. They felt that *barrio* plans made sense in small towns and villages, but were unworkable in large cities. It was simply not feasible to build a pyramidal structure in which a plan was compiled from the bottom up. Mistakenly perhaps, the vehicle selected for the process of consultation and participation were the then recently elected neighbourhood councils. Over 30 000 questionnaire schedules were distributed through the *delegaciones*. Some 200 were returned. The circulation was ignored by almost all of the local mayors (*delegados*), and in retrospect the planning office realized that they should have made direct contact with the neighbourhood councils. One *delegación* insisted that they draw up their own sub-plan, which they did with considerable success. However, most of their proposals were ignored, largely because they were submitted too late, but also because they did not dovetail adequately with the Master Plan

(*Unomásuno* 3 July 1982). Because of external political pressure the plans had to be completed within three-and-a-half months, so it was impossible for the central planning office to delegate responsibility. Neighbourhood plans and sub-plans were prepared by consultants closely supervised by the Planning Directorate. Public participation was purely nominal, and while the planning chiefs argued that they would seek to ensure greater involvement in subsequent revisions, they appeared to be unclear about how it could be achieved. Moreover, as I pointed out earlier in this chapter, the majority of the population did not know about the existence of an Urban Development Plan (Aguilar Martínez 1987).

Other opportunities for participation in urban development were through the 'popular initiative' and through the holding of a Referendum (Ramírez Sáiz 1983; *Unomásuno* 21 January 1985; Aguilar Martínez 1987). However, from the point of view of the government both presented a major threat and constraint to executive action. The regulations for the calling of a referendum were never elaborated satisfactorily, and this was a frequent demand made by political parties during the DF Popular Consultation of 1984. As it then stood, the initiation of a referendum lay with the Executive or with Congress (and subsequently with the DF Representative Assembly). In order to proceed, the referendum issue must also affect all DF citizens in areas related to social needs, and would not apply in matters of public finance and fiscal affairs. Little wonder that no referendum had never been held. However, as we saw in Chapter 3, a plebiscite was called in 1993 on the issue of elected officials and citizen representation in the DF.

The important point is that public opinion and involvement was not sought in any of the major urban projects that were undertaken between 1978 and 1982. In neither the *ejes viales* highway system nor in the New Wholesale Market project was there any public participation or consultation. However, both generated fierce debate. In the case of the *ejes viales*, public protest was the most intense ever experienced on an urban development project. Largely middle class in origin, local resident groups and defence committees arose in an attempt to prevent the land clearance necessary to create the grid of the proposed 16 muti-lane highways. The groups that were formed enjoyed only minor success. One of the 16 roads was shelved when injunctions served against the Federal District were upheld. Mostly, however, these failed or were sought too late, when the bulldozers were already tearing down houses. A second success was the announcement that 'betterment' taxes to recoup some of the enhanced land values from property owners who benefited from the project were to be waived by the authorities (*El Día*, 1 June 1979). Those who protested against the environmental loss due to the removal of trees were expected to be appeased by promises to transplant them elsewhere. Apart from these rather trivial concessions, little was achieved. The protest groups remained isolated, and failed to organize a united front against the authorities. Once defeated, they rapidly disbanded. The only urban development projects where 'popular' participation has been actively encouraged are minor public works associated with *barrio* servicing, but in these cases the primary aim has been one of reducing overall costs through the use of community labour.

It might be argued that participation in planning has been achieved through the neighbourhood associations and through the Consultative Council of the Federal District. Monthly meetings between top Federal District officials and the *juntas de vecinos* served to reinforce this structure of neighbourhood participation, and occasionally groups had their demands met after participating in *junta* meetings (Ward 1981a). During 1982, protests from well-organized middle-income residents' associations used the platform provided by the monthly *juntas* to denounce certain local mayors and developers for contravening zoning regulations established in the Master Plan, but senior DF officials (other than the local *delegado*) did not regularly attend such meetings after 1983. Nor did the *juntas* appear to lead to direct positive outcomes for local neighbourhoods (Jiménez 1988).

After 1983 the term participation was widely emphasized by President De la Madrid. First a series of popular consultations was established to feed in ideas and opinions to inform government policy. Although these meetings have generated substantial involvement from a wide range of interest groups, there is little evidence that proposals have been taken on board. Secondly, in May 1983 a National Democratic Planning System was established under the aegis of SPP. Its functions covered the organization of popular consultations and specific forums such as municipal reform; to make proposals for the implementation of state-wide planning systems; to create regional plans; to assist the implementation of the National Development Plan; to coordinate the President's State of the Nation Report, and so on (Mexico 1983: xviv). There was little in either of the two structures to suggest genuine participation: at best they were consultative, and at worst they became channels for the dissemination of information on behalf of government.

One instance where the public were more actively involved was in the earthquake reconstruction programme (Gamboa de Buen 1990). In order to achieve agreement over the nature and beneficiaries of the rehousing programme, some 70 groups were asked to become signatories to a *concertación*, and from their temporary shelter adjacent to the lots on which their new homes were being built, they were able to monitor and check up on the progress of the contractors. A few groups insisted on being allowed to develop their own designs in conjunction with local NGOs, and were allowed to do so within the overall cost and modular norms governing the reconstruction project (see Chapter 7). In part, however, this participation was born of the important role that local groups had played in the earthquake rescue process, and by the high level of internal organization and mobilization that the prospects of reconstruction had come to generate (Eckstein 1990b; Tamayo 1995).

Therefore public participation in the planning process in Mexico is more nominal than real. In many ways the failure to incorporate a far higher level of active and real public involvement constitutes the most important single caveat to the argument that a planning system has been introduced in Mexico City. Moreover, as I argued in Chapter 3, it is difficult to envisage greater devolution of decision-making powers to local groups occurring in the immediate or medium-term future. Planning may persist, and structures designed to facilitate community–state interaction and popular participation may continue to evolve, but their raison d'être will be one of maintaining the status quo. Genuine innovations to empower local organizations and opposition parties will require fundamental societal and political changes.

CONCLUSION: PLANNING FOR WHOSE INTEREST?

In 1979 a principal planner at the Human Settlements Ministry said during an interview that, in his opinion, planning in Mexico was 'still in the dark ages'. This was at a time when urban planning was at its most active, but only a few of the plans prepared by SAHOP were actually implemented. Even in the Federal district, where the experience had been much more positive, planning was implemented primarily for political reasons. Moreover, neither fundamental changes in the rationale governing urban decision making nor genuine public participation within the planning process had been broached. Nevertheless it is worth while asking, by way of a conclusion, in whose interest planning has operated in contemporary Mexico. Has the position of the urban poor in Mexico City been helped or hindered by the existence of the 1980 Master Plan and associated zoning regulations?

The Plan would appear to have had little impact in preventing illegal physical expansion in the south of the city and encroachment upon the conservation area (Aguilar Martínez 1987). The cushion that the buffer zone represented was removed from subsequent versions of the Plan. One of the original functions of the PRUPE was to justify and legitimize evictions of settlement in the area. However, the furore surrounding the publication of the PRUPE, and its substantial revisions as a consequence, meant that the programme that was implemented lacked teeth. In the absence of effective land-use planning controls, *delegados* have taken a hard line against encroachment by settlers. This involves boundary fences, guard posts, mounted police patrols and summary evictions of any new irregular settlements (Pezzoli 1989). If planning *per se* has proved ineffective within the DF then the situation is even more acute at the rapidly expanding urban periphery in the State of Mexico.

Planning initiatives will lead to different advantages for various social groups. As we have observed, government planning has been used primarily to legitimize decisions. The principal motive for revising the Master Plan was to incorporate the new urban highway system and the extensions to the Metro, both of which had been decided upon behind closed doors by the Mayor and his advisors without consultation with the planning department or the public. The Plan provides further legitimacy to justify decisions to evict squatters and other groups from newly formed irregular settlements. Elsewhere it may justify decisions not to extend services. Ideologically, too, the planning department strengthens the ability of the government to meet criticisms about its handling of urban development problems. Yet the adoption of planning also implies certain disadvantages for government. It reduces flexibility of decision making. This does not mean that particularistic decisions and authorizations are no longer made; I have evidence that they are, but they are probably less widespread than in the past. Another disadvantage for government is the increased dissemination of information which makes informed criticism from opposition groups and from middle-income residents' associations much more of a problem than in the past.

Land developers and speculators may be affected negatively in so far as they no longer have such a free hand to develop what they want where they want. They will be obliged to comply with the more rigorous regulations that now exist. If they do not, then their developments may be closed down. However, they also benefit in so far as the Plan offers an amnesty and effectively condones previous illegal transactions that they may have made. Moreover, the incorporation into the Plan of land and land uses that were previously excluded, and which they own, is likely to raise land values to their advantage.

For the general public, outcomes are mixed. Middle-income groups are more likely to adhere to zoning regulations and to seek formal planning permissions as they have neither the resources nor the political weight to overcome planning regulations. However, they may be expected to gain in so far as they are able to press more strongly for the exclusion of any undesirable land use from their neighbourhood. Low-income housebuilders are unlikely to seek full planning permissions, but they may benefit where their previously unrecognized settlement is included on the Plan and in the zoning. This enhances their security of tenure and may strengthen their claim for service provision. It may also work the opposite way and isolate settlements beyond the servicing grid. One group of *colonos* who approached the planning chief about the possibility of services being installed to their settlement were informed that according to the Plan they were beyond the servicing network. Their only recourse, he said, was to participate in the next revision of the sub-plans to ensure that the servicing net was extended to cover their area (*Unomásuno* 8 April 1983). For those seeking to enter the irregular land market for the first time, the existence of the Plan may justify their eviction. However, the existence of the 1980 Plan cannot be blamed for settlement eradications, which also occurred widely before it was implemented. In the past planning *per se* has not usually been a cause of evictions, although it may be used to justify them.

To the extent that implementation of the Master Plan will lead to a more rational land use, to improved access to place of employment, markets, public services and recreational areas, and to the conservation and preservation of the natural environment, then everyone will benefit. Yet, as I have argued, progress towards a fully-fledged planning system in Mexico is both slow and ephemeral. The changes that have occurred over the four *sexenios* are significant, but superficial. The emergence of planning forms part of an accretional response of the state in Mexico to maintain the underlying structure. Certain concessions have been made, but they are modest, and overall the benefits that planning generates for the state in terms of enhanced legitimacy, greater social control and access to financial resources suggest that the continued existence of some form of physical planning structure is assured. For these reasons alone its relevance for the state is likely to grow. For those officials who believe that planning may assist in the improvement of conditions for the poorest sectors of society, my conclusion is not totally negative. Although the scope for improving conditions for the least advantaged groups is constrained, it does exist. Sometimes societal inequalities may be reduced slightly by curbing the excesses of the more powerful. Sometimes, too, the demands of the poor can be strengthened by identifying the obligations of public authorities to comply with the Plan. There are indications that some headway in this direction has been made within the Federal District.

If planning as an open, democratic and largely technical process is ever to exist in Mexico, then the key is almost certainly one of public participation. Only by actively involving the public in decision making is continuity across *sexenios* a possibility. This does not mean that aspects of the plan would not be expected to change as governments change. It is perfectly reasonable to expect that different administrations should have different development priorities. It is also reasonable for politicians to continue to expect to be able to appoint top personnel of their own persuasion to head the planning department or ministry, but the institutional apparatus for planning should be clearly defined and remain fundamentally unchanged, as should the bulk of the staff and channels of public participation. Once established, plans should be implemented according to technical criteria and be open to public scrutiny. Any major shifts in content would have to be approved by the public.

A view of the possible future of planning in Mexico is provided in a recent planning blueprint 'The Democractic Recovery of Mexico's Territory and Environment' drawn up by the '*Grupo Democracia y Territorio*' (Pradilla 1995). Despite its rather nationalist and jingoistic title and rhetoric, this document which was drawn up by a highly respected group of planners and architects, seeks to set down the blueprint for a more democratic and equitable national planning framework in an increasingly pluralist society. *Inter alia* it calls for a range of affirmative actions to ensure: (1) a greater plurality of economic and social groups to be embraced by territorial planning; (2) greater democratic involvement and accountability in the three levels of governmental planning activity (adding, also, a fourth metropolitan level); (3) greater strategic and technical competence of planning agencies and institutions and their juridical strengthening; (4) greater social equity in planning measures to redress inequality and to assert the public good over private gain; (5) greater environmental protection. Few would quarrel with either the general or the specific proposals in the document, but it remains difficult to envisage how to get 'there' from 'here'. Only an intensification of the democratization process, and a significant change in the underlying political process will pave the way towards a more effective and politically accountable planning system, but here, too, there is evidence of significant headway in recent years. This still may not be 'ripe time' for the blueprint to be adopted, but it is to the group's considerable credit that they have laid down such a clear and detailed vision of planning in the foreseeable future. Moreover, several leading members of the group appear likely to be brought into the Cárdenas administration to take leading positions in planning and urban development. Perhaps, after all, this may be ripe time.

6

THE REPRODUCTION OF SOCIAL INEQUALITY: ACCESS TO LAND, SERVICES AND HEALTH CARE IN MEXICO CITY

Compared with elsewhere in the country, residents of Mexico City have traditionally enjoyed privileged access to social expenditure. Indicators for various dimensions of social welfare reflect this spatial inequality (Mexico COPLAMAR 1982; CONAPO 1990, 1996). This does not mean, however, that within the city access to those resources is not spatially or socially differentiated. Moreover, the means whereby these resources are provided, 'filtered' or fought over are also the principal mechanisms through which social differentiation is replicated and, in some cases, intensified. This constitutes the main argument of this chapter. I want to examine four key issues. First, how does the changing environment of social welfare provision in Mexico City offer opportunities for political mediation by the state? By social welfare I mean a wide range of areas of provision including social security, social services, health care, education, urban planning and community development, and infrastructural services such as water and electricity (Ward 1986). This can be analysed by examining both the content of programmes as well as the way in which these are managed by the bureaucracy. Second, what is the effect of the stratification of delivery systems upon patterns of social inequality? Here it is necessary to examine the multiplex nature of provision and its impact upon the take-up of benefits, and the disposition of different social groups to press for improvements. Third, how far does negotiation and demand-making between the state and the community replicate or dissipate existing social divisions? Fourth, how far has the improved technical content of social welfare policy (greater efficiency, more appropriate and low-'tech' solutions, expanding distribution, reduced subsidies and greater programme replicability, and so on) led to a reduction in levels of inequality in Mexico City?

Space does not allow me to address these questions systematically in the context of each and every dimension of social welfare provision. Therefore, in each case, I propose to bring to the foreground a different aspect of provision as an example for analysis. I acknowledge that not all dimensions of social welfare provision considered highlight to the same extent answers to these questions. Thus I have been selective, but I would argue that the general principles identified for one particular area will probably also apply to a greater or lesser extent elsewhere, and that in all cases the outcomes lead in a similar direction. My purpose is to shed light on the nature, rationale and effects of social welfare provision in the city.

THE HOUSING AND SERVICE PROVISION BUREAUCRACY IN MEXICO CITY

The growth of state intervention

An important question about public intervention to emerge in recent years is why the state takes responsibility for providing certain services and not others. Numerous writers have attempted to explain the growth of state intervention (O'Connor 1973; O'Donnell 1974; Collier 1979; Harvey 1985). In particular, Castells' work (1977, 1979) has attracted attention. In the case of advanced capitalist societies he argues that growing state intervention is an inevitable outcome of the falling rate of profit in the capitalist economy. In order to maintain the rate of capital accumulation, the state undertakes responsibility for providing services that are 'collectively consumed'. Generally speaking these services are those which offer low profit to the private sector but for which there is rising demand from organized working classes:

> . . . the intervention of the state becomes necessary in order to take charge of the sectors and services which are less profitable (from the point of view of capital) but necessary for the functioning of economic activity and/or appeasement of social conflicts. (Castells 1979: 18)

However, as President Salinas emphasized in his first State of the Nation address, public intervention does not necessarily mean public ownership. The private sector may be heavily subsidized rather than being nationalized. In Mexico City until 1981, bus services were exclusively run by private companies with large state subsidies on fuel prices, a structure which continues to apply outside the Federal District. The state only tends to become the sole provider of a service when the size, complexity and inherently monopolistic nature of the product has created problems: as when the private electricity company was incorporated into the public sector during the 1960s as the demand for power increased. During the 1980s in Mexico there has been growing interest in the privatization of services and utilities, taking a lead from the World Bank and experiences such as those of the United Kingdom (Roth 1987). Airlines, hotel chains and telephones have been transferred from public to private hands. In Naucalpan, rubbish collection was privatized only to be re-municipalized 2 years later (Conde Bonfil 1996). Yet compared with many of its mega- and large-city counterparts elsewhere in Latin America, Mexico City has not rushed to privatize its public utilities and transportation systems (Ward 1996).

However, the city has followed the general trend towards reducing and/or removing subsidies on most goods and services. Moreover, the city authorities have adopted more efficient systems of recovery of the real costs of service provision and consumption, together with more effective tax and rates collection.

Whether or not one accepts Castells' argument, certain services and activities appear more likely to fall under the wing of the state, and some will be accorded higher priority than others. The ranking will relate to both growth and legitimacy reasons. Connolly (1981) argues that every activity falls along a continuum which runs from directly productive (and therefore beneficial to capital) to unproductive. A related continuum runs from activities with high social content (i.e. they both contain and integrate the population) to those with little social content. I would argue that in Mexico City concerted state intervention occurs primarily in those areas necessary to the acceleration of economic growth rather than in those vital to the welfare of the poor. When the poor benefit and receive water or electricity, it is after the needs of key productive enterprise and better-off social groups have been met. Social services such as education, housing, public health, refuse collection and market facilities, which have little direct interest for the corporate sector, receive much lower priority and may even be neglected. The affluent can satisfy these needs through the private sector. Other groups are likely to benefit only in so far as they are able to exercise influence over the state. Inevitably, therefore, labour that is well organized or which occupies strategic industries such as power, railways and petroleum is most likely to have its particular social needs met; the remainder will be less fortunate.

Responsibility for housing and servicing in Mexico City

A matrix was constructed to provide an overview of the differential involvement of public and private sectors in a range of activities in Mexico City (Figure 6.1).[1] This shows the main responsibilities of the private and public sectors with respect to low-income and higher-income populations at a variety of levels (local, regional and national). The influence exercised by international agencies is also indicated. The rows in the matrix show the major functions which affect low-income populations in their housing and settlement situations. Each row is subdivided to differentiate between those living in the conventional, legalized market ('U') and those living in the irregular low-income market ('B'). Clearly this is not intended as a watertight distinction, but it is not misleading at the level of generalization that I wish to portray. The aim is to depict the different roles of public and private sectors with respect to richer and poorer groups, and the different ways in which poorer and richer groups in Mexico City are housed and serviced.

		PUBLIC				PRIVATE		
		INTERNATIONAL	NATIONAL	REGIONAL	LOCAL	CORPORATE	COMMUNITY	INDIVIDUAL
Land	U		$\square^2$	$\square^4$ $\blacksquare^5$ $\square^6$		$\blacksquare^8$	$\blacksquare^{10}$ $\blacksquare^{11}$	
	B		$\blacksquare^1$ $\square^3$	$\square^4$ $\square^7$		$\blacksquare^9$	$\blacksquare^{10}$ $\blacksquare^{12}$	
Building materials	U		$\blacksquare^1$ $\square^2$			$\blacksquare^4$	$\blacksquare^5$	
	B		$\square^2$	$\blacksquare^3$		$\blacksquare^5$	$\blacksquare^6$	
Housing	U	$\square^1$	$\blacksquare^3$ $\square^5$	$\blacksquare^7$ $\square^9$		$\blacksquare^{11}$	$\blacksquare^{12}$	
	B	$\square^2$	$\blacksquare^4$ $\square^6$	$\blacksquare^8$ $\square^{10}$			$\blacksquare^{13}$	
Water/drainage DF	U	$\square^1$	$\blacksquare^3$	$\blacksquare^4$	$\blacksquare^6$	$\square^8$		
	B	$\square^2$	$\blacksquare^3$	$\blacksquare^4$	$\blacksquare^6$		$\blacksquare^9$	
State of Mexico	U	$\square^1$	$\blacksquare^3$	$\blacksquare^5$	$\blacksquare^7$	$\square^8$		
	B	$\blacksquare^2$	$\blacksquare^3$	$\blacksquare^5$	$\blacksquare^7$		$\blacksquare^9$	
Electricity (domestic)	U		$\blacksquare^1$	$\blacksquare^2$		$\square^3$		
	B		$\blacksquare^1$	$\blacksquare^2$			$\blacksquare^4$	
Health	U	$\square^1$	$\blacksquare^2$			$\blacksquare^6$	$\blacksquare^8$	
	B	$\square^1$	$\blacksquare^{2,3,4}$ $\square^4$	$\blacksquare^5$		$\blacksquare^7$	$\blacksquare^9$	
Public transport	U	$\square^1$	$\square^2$	$\blacksquare^{3,4,5,6}$		$\blacksquare^{7,8}$	$\blacksquare^{10}$	
	B	$\square^1$	$\square^2$	$\blacksquare^{3,4,5}$		$\blacksquare^{8,9}$		
Rubbish	U				$\blacksquare^1$ $\square^2$	$\blacksquare^3$		
	B				$\blacksquare^1$ $\square^2$		$\blacksquare^4$	

F I G U R E 6.1 Matrix of responsibility for housing and servicing in Mexico City

Notes

Land

1. Lands provided by the state for *barrio* overspill developments, site and service schemes, etc. Agencies involved: BANOBRAS 1960–70; INDECO 1976–81; INFONAVIT 1977–83; FONHAPO 1981 to present day.
2. National housing and economic policies, tax legislation on real estate, etc. all affect the supply of land.
3. National policy towards illegal land development affects willingness of developers to promote low-income settlement.
4. Conurbation Commission (1976–83) provides normative plans which affect future land uses and the supply of land for residential purposes.
5. Agencies provide land for urbanization (usually lower-middle-income housing). BANOBRAS 1960s–1983; AURIS 1969–83; INDECO, 1973–6; CODEUR 1977–83.
6. Local zoning policies or tax laws affect the supply of land.
7. Local policy towards invasion and illegal land occupancy and willingness to regularize and service affect propensity to supply land.
8. Real-estate companies' speculatory developments (usually legal).
9. Real-estate companies' speculative developments usually illegal, 1950s and 1960s.
10. *Ejidal* lands are alienated illegally by the *ejido*. Results mostly in low-income settlements, but some notable middle-income residential developments have occurred.
11. Small-scale landowners also provide land for subdivisions.
12. Invasions and small-scale purchases of land by groups of residents.

Building materials

1. National enterprises produce steel and other goods used in the building industry.
2. Price controls and restrictive practices affect total output.

3. Cheap supply centres provide materials for self-help. Sponsored by INDECO 1973–82; AURIS 1970–5.
4. Industrialized large-company and monopolies sector.
5. Building materials produced by middle-sized enterprises.
6. Middle-sized enterprises, artisans, petty-commodity production, recycled throw-aways, etc.

Housing
1. International assistance for 'social-interest' housing and international conventional wisdom affect national housing policies. Specifically, the Alliance for Progress provided seed capital for PFV 1964.
2. International agencies' espousal of self-help affects national housing policy.
3. Social-interest housing projects provide housing. Specifically: BANOBRAS 1960s; INVI 1964–70; INDECO 1973–6; INFONAVIT 1973–83; FONHAPO 1981 to the present day; State Housing Institutes.
4. Supply of site and service housing opportunities.
5. National housing policies, provision of credit, tax incentives, etc.
6. National housing policies towards self-help-type solutions.
7. Housing projects produced by Habitación Popular, 1972–6; AURIS, 1970–5.
8. Development of self-help projects (Habitación Popular, 1972–6; AURIS 1970–5; INDECO 1977–82; FIDEURBE 1973–6; FONHAPO 1981 to present day).
9. Local policies towards social-interest housing and urbanization.
10. Local policies toward self-help and towards illegal settlements.
11. Corporate provision of private housing.
12. Individual provision via private architects' offices, etc.
13. Individual self-help.

Water and drainage
1. International finance for water procurement and regional drainage schemes.
2. International finance and pressure to provide service to low-income communities; pressure from WHO, etc., to reduce mortality and morbidity levels.
3. National procurement and supply to regional authorities. SARH before 1977; SAHOP 1977–83.
4. CAVM supplies 20 per cent of the DF's requirements. Sells to the DF in bulk.
5. CAVM sells water to CEAS which supplies households in the State of Mexico.
6. Procurement and supply within the DF. Water is obtained from wells and a proportion of the DF needs are brought from CAVM. Before 1977, responsibility of Dirección General de Operación Hidráulica and the Dirección General de Aguas y Saneamiento. Since that date merged into single Dirección General de Operación Hidráulica. The DCGOH provides primary and secondary networks, while domestic supply is the responsibility of the *Delegación*.
7. Secondary supplies of water procured and supplied by municipal authorities in the State of Mexico.
8. Provision of network by urbanizer.
9. Self-help drainage, pit latrines, etc.

Electricity
1. CFE provides national grid.
2. Compañía de Luz y Fuerza del Valle de México provides domestic supply.
3. Provision of domestic network by urbanizer.
4. Illegal wire taps supply households.

continues overleaf

Health
1. Pressure from international health organizations to improve health standards and provision.
2. Social security affiliates. IMSS, ISSSTE and those created for certain groups of workers in railways, the military, petrochemicals.
3. State sector (SS).
4. National policy regarding treatment of low-income groups.
5. *DDF* Dirección General de Servicios Médicos provides some medical services, blood for transfusions, etc.
6. Private clinics and hospitals.
7. Charities, Red Cross, etc.
8. Private doctors.
9. Private doctors, chemists, *curanderos*, etc.

Public transport
1. Tied aid from France for the Metro.
2. National government policy towards fuel prices, subsidies and public transport.
3. Metro, trams and buses within the DF (since 1981).
4. Trolley-buses (Servicio de Transporte Eléctrico).
5. DF policy towards servicing needs of private transport: car parks, freeways, etc.
6. DF policy towards transport in general (COVITUR).
7. Taxis.
8. Collective taxis.
9. Buses in the State of Mexico. The privately owned bus service that operated in the DF was nationalized in 1981.
10. Private cars.

Rubbish
1. *Delegación* cleansing department, and outside the Federal District in the hands of the municipalities.
2. Incentives for interest groups to invest in recycling materials.
3. Private services, industrial-waste-disposal services, etc.
4. Self-help tips and dumping

F I G U R E 6.1 (*continued*)

For every function, the matrix depicts which of six possible public and private 'agencies' is responsible for provision. The influence of international lending institutions, aid agencies, private lending and commercial organizations is depicted in the first column. There follow three public-sector columns which demonstrate the responsibilities of national, regional and local government institutions. The final two columns deal with the private sector, one with the corporate and large-scale sector (i.e. manufacturing industry, commerce, large landowners, building companies), the other with the small-scale, individual and community sector (one-person businesses, individual home owners, community groups).

Where an institution or a group or set of individuals is deemed to exercise direct influence or responsibility over supply, this is indicated by a shaded square, and the extent of that influence is suggested by the size of square (small or large). Where influence or responsibility is indirect (by controlling prices, prohibiting land invasions, through planning etc.) this is represented by an unshaded square. The numbers accompanying each symbol relate to the notes of explanation.

There are obvious limitations to the matrix. The portrayal is a static one compiled for 1979–80 and changes are only explained in the accompanying notes. I have not further subdivided each vector into the two administrative units of the DF and the State of Mexico, with the exception of the water/drainage row where important differences occur. It fails to identify the relationship between different actors, for example between the government and the corporate sector. Nor does it offer any insight about the efficiency with which a responsibility is dispensed; while the public sector is depicted as being responsible for the poor, this does not signify that it performs this role well.

Looking across the matrix it is clear that the private sector dominates in the area of land provision; a point developed below. The corporate private sector exercises enormous importance in its role as owner and developer of land. Also important are the formerly agrarian *ejidal* communities, which offer land primarily to poor groups. Building materials production and supply are also firmly the preserve of the private sector, and mostly corporate enterprise. The state's direct involvement is limited largely to steel production, although it does exercise indirect influence through pricing and through its role as regulator of the economy. Housing, too, is mainly an activity which is carried out privately, either through large and small-scale construction companies, or through self-building. Increased direct state action has led to greater availability of housing (see also Ward 1990). Overall, therefore, housing generated directly by government initiative is less important than that produced privately.

With respect to public utilities the state is the major supplier. With the exception of itinerant water sellers and the provision of bottled drinking water, it is the public sector which is wholly responsible for water and drainage, although different institutions are involved in procurement and supply. Electricity is much the same. Refuse collection is organized by local DF and municipal authorities, but there are also private corporate cleansing services which operate for some industrial and commercial enterprises. Recent attempts have been made to privatize some municipal rubbish collection (Conde Bonfil 1996). In the more recently established or more distant working-class *colonias* which do not enjoy a regular service, the poor, individually, have to burn, bury or dump their rubbish.

Health and public transport, on the other hand, are the responsibility of both sectors. As I will demonstrate below, the state provides various tiers of health care to different social security affiliates and to the rest of the population through the government Health Ministry, but the private sector is also very important. While most affluent groups and many of the middle classes use private medicine, so too do the poor, usually by visiting their nearest local doctor. Similarly, transport services are shared between public and private enterprise. In Mexico City the Metro and trolley-bus services are run by the Federal District, and so are most of the buses (since 1981). Taxis, *colectivos* and of course private cars all form part of the private sector.

We may now return to the questions posed at the beginning of the chapter and begin to examine the ways in which some of these dimensions of social welfare provision reproduce social inequality. First, access to land for housing development.

REPRODUCING SOCIAL INEQUALITY THROUGH POLITICAL MEDIATION: ACCESS TO LAND FOR ILLEGAL HOUSING DEVELOPMENT IN MEXICO CITY

Methods of land acquisition in Mexico City

Although Mexico City has received the lion's share of resources allocated for government housing provision, the supply has never come close to matching demand. Even during the 1980s under De la Madrid, when public-sponsored housing programmes reached their peak, I estimate that nationally this only met approximately one-fifth of total annual demand (Ward 1990). Therefore the majority of the population have had to seek alternative informal methods of shelter provision – most usually through illegal land acquisition and self-build.

In any society the process of land allocation is highly competitive between groups, and in most capitalist societies it is the market which acts to allocate land (Jones and Ward 1994). Those who can afford to pay more, or according to economic theory are less indifferent to location, acquire the more desirable areas (Gilbert and Ward 1985). In Mexico City the vast majority of the poor are at the bottom end of a single market, and the land that they bid for is cheap because full title is not provided, and because it is unserviced, poorly located and not desired by economically better-off groups. To that extent they may be said to hold a monopoly over the land at the outset, but the process of commercial exchange penetrates this market very soon afterwards (see Chapter 7).

There are innumerable ways in which the poor acquire land, within the broad generalization that they are usually illegal (see Gilbert and Ward 1985 for details). In Mexico City there have been two basic alternatives: the first is to invade land and the second is to purchase land beyond the limits of the conventional legalized housing areas. In Mexico City invasions occurred most frequently during the 1950s and 1960s when there was a formal ban on any new authorizations of low-income subdivisions within the Federal

District. Large-scale invasions were more common after Mayor Uruchurtu lost office (1966) and during the earlier years of the Echeverría administration, when the political climate encouraged popular mobilization. The purchase of land may also take many forms and is common throughout Latin America. In Mexico City it is by far the most important means of acquisition. Land is frequently bought through company-sponsored illegal subdivision (*fraccionamientos clandestinos*) in which some form of title is usually provided, but services are non-existent or severely limited (see Figure 2.12). The enormous scale of some of these developments sets them apart from other Latin American, or indeed from most other Mexican, subdivisions. Settlements comprising several thousand families are common in Netzahualcóyotl and Ecatepec. Alternatively, plots may be purchased on *ejidal* (community) lands, and an estimated 16 per cent of the total city population in 1970 were living on land that was *ejidal* in origin; a proportion that has increased since that date (Varley 1985b; COPEVI 1978; CONAPO 1996; see Figure 6.2). The sale of plots – again without services – takes place either directly by individual *ejidatarios* or by their elected local representatives, the *comisariado ejidal* (Mexico SAHOP 1979; Varley 1985a). Whichever applies, the process is illegal because *ejidatarios* have use-rights only over the land which is, theoretically, inalienable (cf. Cymet 1992). Nor is it only low-income groups that are involved. During the 1960s large tracts of *ejidal* and were privatized for élite housing developments, while in the 1970s rich and poor alike bought plots illegally on *ejidal* lands in the south of the city (Varley 1985a, b). Since the late 1980s the largest single area of active low-income settlement formation is on the far eastern frontier of Mexico City on the *ejido* of Ayotla in the Chalco Valley, which extends over some 2500 hectares. The municipality was renamed Chalco-Solidaridad in 1993 in recognition for its being favoured with PRONASOL funds by President Salinas. Since the reform of Article 27 of the Constitution in 1992, it is now possible for *ejidal* lands to be sold legally (Austin 1994). However, to date, research suggests that deregulation has not unleashed significant legal alienation of *ejidal* land for residential or other purposes in Mexico City or elsewhere, although this might happen in the future (Austin 1994; Jones and Ward 1997).

I now propose to examine how the process of illegal land development in Mexico City has facilitated political mediation and social control by the state, and thereby perpetuated patterns of inequality. By political mediation I mean the ways in which the state attempts to advance the interests of powerful and organized groups which it seeks to placate and, at the same time, manages to maintain social control and to legitimate itself through the securement of political support for the government – although, as I observed in Chapter 3, since the 1988 elections this process has also entered a period of crisis. Faced with austerity programmes during the 1980s, the

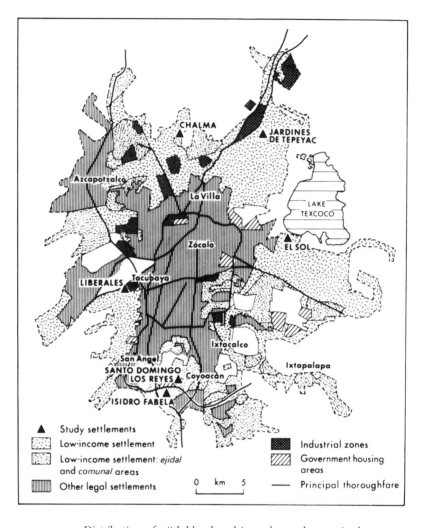

FIGURE 6.2 Distribution of *ejidal* land and irregular settlement in the
Metropolitan Area

government intensified its efforts to maintain social peace and continuing
support from the labour sector (Carr 1986). Land for housing the poor has
always been an important element in Mexican statecraft, and my aim here is
to analyse how successive Mexico City regimes have achieved similar ends
of political control through handling land issues in two ways: first, through
controlling the content of land development policy; second, through the
ways in which the Mexican government has cultivated a bureaucracy to
manage land issues.

Mediation through the content of land
development policies

An analysis of government intervention in the land market must take account of both *action* and *inaction* on the part of the authorities. Failure to act may reflect policy choices, and this has been (and continues to be) an important feature of Mexico's management of low-income land developments. Two types of response are identified. First, those actions that affected the provision of land for low-income settlement, and second, remedial actions such as regularization, as well as recognition and approval to extend services to unregularized areas.

Three broad periods of land development may be identified: a *laissez faire* phase before 1970, when many of the low-income *colonias* were formed against a backcloth of little government intervention. In Mexico City during this time irregular settlements increased from 23 per cent of the built-up area and 14 per cent of the population in 1952, to 40–50 per cent of the built-up area and a slightly higher proportion of the total 8.5 million city population in 1970 (Mexico BNH 1952; Ward 1976a; COPEVI 1977). The period between 1971 and 1977 saw a much more *interventionist* phase in which government created an extensive housing bureaucracy and in particular instigated large-scale remedial actions, although they were largely *ad hoc* in nature. Since 1977, handling of land development has been one of technical management in which interventions in both the sphere of land provision and remedial action have been more efficient and more systematic. In essence I argue that since 1977 governments have sought to achieve social control less by manipulation and more by 'delivering the goods' (Ward 1986). I now propose to analyse the primary mechanisms whereby land policies have sustained political mediation during these three periods.

Government policy towards the provision of land for low-income settlement between 1950 and 1970 differed on either side of the Federal District boundary. In the State of Mexico during the 1950s and 1960s the authorities acted consistently to further the interests of the land developers.[2] So-called 'Improvement Boards' established by the Governor from 1952 onwards, ostensibly to coordinate the installation of services in the region, achieved little beyond the promotion of lot sales on behalf of the companies. Moreover, the State authorities took no action against the common abuse whereby the same plot was sold several times over to different individuals. Despite comprehensive regulations governing the creation of low-income subdivisions (the *Ley de fraccionamientos* of 1958), neither the State nor the Federal Government pressed for sanctions against the developers. Indeed until 1969 authorizations for further developments continued to be given by the authorities even where the offending companies had been denounced by residents for their failure to satisfy the conditions laid down in earlier settlements (Guerrero *et al.* 1974; Connolly 1982).

In the Federal District City Mayor Uruchurtu imposed a ban upon the authorization of new subdivisions, and this led to a proliferation of invasions and illegal subdivisions developed by owners whose land-development plans were frustrated. Uruchurtu's sectoral jurisdiction did not extend to *ejidal* land, and the continuing informal supply of land on the *ejidos* was assisted by government action and inaction throughout this period. Until 1992, the use of *ejidal* land for urban expansion was prohibited under the Agrarian Law (Article 91). However, *ejidal* land could be disestablished 'in the public interest' in one of two ways: by *permuta* (exchange of one area of an *ejido* for equivalent lands elsewhere), and by expropriation. There was widespread abuse of *permutas* during the 1950s and 1960s to secure land for a variety of purposes, not all of which could be justified as having been in the public interest. Large upper-income residential districts such as Jardines de Pedregal and part of Ciudad Satélite came into being in this manner. Low-income irregular settlement usually came about through the manipulation of a legal facility whereby part of an *ejido* could be set aside as an urban centre to house the *ejidatarios* and other community workers. Application would be made to the Agrarian Reform Department for an urban *ejidal* zone, or for the extension of an existing one, but meanwhile lots were sold by the *ejidal* community. The formal procedure to create an urban zone on an *ejido* was a long and complicated one, and often the later stages were never reached because after several years a full settlement had emerged as a *fait accompli*. It then became a matter to be resolved through legalizing 'clouded' land titles – a process called regularization in Mexico (Varley 1985a).

Mediation through land development was also apparent by the removal of specific politicians whose policies were proving too inflexible. A good example is the concerted opposition that built up against Mayor Uruchurtu's policies during the 1960s as a result of his consistent refusal to authorize or to approve servicing to low-income settlements within the Federal District and, perhaps more importantly, once his policies began to threaten the more powerful groups involved in speculative land development in the south of the city (López Díaz 1978). He had also consistently blocked initiatives for the development of a major collective transportation system, which added further opposition – particularly from the large-scale construction sector (Davis 1994). That his policies had become dysfunctional to the state by 1966, when he was forced from office, is also confirmed by the more circumspect and conciliatory approach of his successors and by the rapid development of a Metro system (Cornelius 1975; Alonso *et al.* 1980).

Action to prevent the uncontrolled growth of irregular settlement was not undertaken until it was virtually too late, and even then has only affected the sale of private land by the companies. Significantly, this occurred only when a mass-based organization in the State of Mexico (Movimiento Restaurador de Colonos: the MRC) precipitated a political crisis in 1969 by calling a strike on further payments to the land developers. By this time, however, many company developers had begun to lose interest in the development of irregular settlement and transferred their attention (and gains) to the legal middle-income real estate market. Not until relatively late in the process did the state respond sharply to company-led low-income subdivisions. Several settlements have been 'embargoed' by the State of Mexico government: an option always open to previous administrations but not exercised. The embargo is usually achieved by requiring land developers to comply with servicing norms, and to make immediate payments of massive amounts of backdated taxes and fines relating to improper management of the subdivision. Failure to comply results in the development being sequestrated by the State authorities. However, as we have observed, this initiative came too late to affect land provision significantly.

Although several major land invasions occurred between 1970 and 1973, these are no longer tolerated. During 1977–9 firm action was undertaken by the Federal District authorities to remove squatters from newly occupied land. In one large-scale invasion attempt in the south of the city named after López Portillo's wife, *colonos* were evicted as many times as they reoccupied the land. Their temporary houses were destroyed despite injunctions taken out against the authorities to prevent this from happening. Eventually the squatters gave up, and the land remained vacant. Explicit instructions were given by Mayor Hank González to *delegados* to resist all new occupations and to raise the surveillance of vacant land.

As I described in Chapter 5, even a decade later the south of the Federal District remained a principal zone of conflict between government and would-be squatters. During 1988–9 there were frequent evictions of settlers in a well-established *colonia* of El Seminario in Tlalpan. It fell on the 'wrong' side of the road to Picacho, in an area designated as an ecological reserve: a concept which counted for little until it was adopted by the Government as an integral item on its new and widely publicized ecological agenda.

Given the breakdown in supply through company sales, the *ejidal* sector became the most important means of land acquisition for the poor. Yet here, too, the government failed to take action. No direct attempt was made by either the Federal District or by the State government to use *ejidal* land for low-income housing purposes, despite the clear opportunity that it provided. One author, as early as 1965, noted: 'Land reserves of this kind, under public control, have long been advocated in many metropolitan areas, but few can match the good fortune of Mexico City in having such reserves readily at hand' (Frieden 1965: 86). Good fortune or not, the government failed to act. Although some effort to develop land reserves was made through newly established housing agencies such as INDECO and INFONAVIT, these were very limited in size and potential (Makin 1984). CoRett, another new agency in the early 1970s, offered greater potential scope in this respect. In addition to its main functions of regularization of irregular settlement on *ejidal* land, CoRett was also empowered to develop low-income subdivisions on suitably located *ejidos* (*Diario Oficial* 7 August 1973). The latter function, had it been seriously pursued, would have offered the state a major opportunity of developing land supply for the poor. However, strong opposition from the *ejidal* sector blocked this area of potential responsibility and it was subsequently excised from CoRett's charter (*Diario Oficial* 3 April 1979). Anything that interfered with the process which worked firmly to the advantage of some *ejidatarios* was to be resisted. Indeed, for the state, the process also had certain attractions: the *ejido* sector upon which it depended for considerable political support was mollified; at the same time the supply of low-cost land for the poor was sustained. Although the principal agents of land development might have changed, government passivity towards informal land provision did not.

The combined clamp-down on subdivisions and invasions meant that the only source of land for the poor is provided by the *ejidal* sector. Yet little attempt has been made by successive governments to restrict illegal sales by *ejidatarios*. In 1979 an Inter-Sector Commission was established comprising the Ministries of Agrarian Reform and Human Settlements and CoRett in an attempt to expedite the identification and expropriation of *ejidos* whose land would be affected by future urban growth. Although this potentially offered a major step forward in the acquisition of rural land for long-term urban development, in the absence of additional preventive measures it was unlikely to succeed in controlling land alienation by *ejidatarios* in the short or medium term. Quite the opposite: faced with the danger of government intervention to deny them the possibility of illegally selling land, it stimulated them to sell or to find ways of slowing up the process of hand-over to government. Although firm action against particular *ejidatarios* might appear to represent a responsible undertaking in technical terms, politically it would be regarded as irresponsible, leading to conflict with vested interests in the agrarian sector, and this the Mexican state appears to have been unwilling to do until the early 1990s. By reducing the supply of land to low-income groups it would also have engendered potential conflict with the poor: from the government's point of view, better to leave well alone. This rationale applied particularly in the State of Mexico, where most of the *ejidal* land available for incorporation into the Metropolitan Area is located. Expansion of irregular settlement in Ayotla and in Chalco, together with the PRI's need to retain the *campesino* and popular sector support in order not to lose the 1993 (State) election, made strong intervention to head-off illegal settlement unlikely. Indeed, these areas became the target for massive state (Solidarity) interventions to regularize and service in order to draw political support for the PRI – successfully so in the 1994 elections and, at least in the case of Chalco, in the November 1996 elections as well (see Chapter 3; Varley 1996).

The ongoing battle for control over *ejido* land-use development and regularization that had been going on between the Agrarian Reform secretariat and planning secretariats since the latter's inception in the late 1970s (SAHOP, SEDUE etc.) was not resolved until after 1992. Until that time the Agrarian Reform ministry had pretty much got its own way, and had successfully resisted any serious incursions upon its mandate (Varley 1996). As I argue above, this incapacity of planning agencies to act pro-actively was not accidental, but represented a principal medium of political mediation and statecraft. This changed in 1991–92 when President Salinas took the dramatic (and unexpected) step of deregulating the *ejidal* sector. The motive was primarily one of macro-economic policy and liberalization of the agrarian sector in order, ultimately, to make it more efficient and to open it up to private capital. Deregulation weakened the former strangle-hold of the Agrarian Reform secretariat and opened up a greater role for SEDESOL intervention in the land regularization and privatization/deregulation process (Jones and Ward 1997). Under trade and economic liberalization the traditional corporatist state–society relations became counterproductive, and in order to win electoral support Salinas placed his confidence in economic growth and in more efficient and targeted delivery of social welfare benefits (Dresser 1991; Cornelius *et al.* 1994; Jones 1996). Decentralization to the states also meant that hegemony over *ejidal* land development needed to shift from the Agrarian Reform to the Social and Urban Development secretariat (Mexico SEDESOL 1996; Jones and Ward 1997).

The content of 'Remedial' land policies since the 1960s

Remedial actions on the part of the state were limited before 1970 on both sides of the DF boundary. Within the Federal District, regularization of selected settlements occurred either through persuading the landowner to install services and to give legal title or, more usually, by expropriation and resale to residents. In theory there was an agreement between the Electricity Company and the Federal District Department that the power supply would not be connected until legal title had been obtained; in practice the supply was invariably provided.

The provision of standpipes, regularization, and lightweight one-off campaigns such as the vaccination of children, the removal of rubbish from settlements, etc. were negotiated and provided primarily by the Oficina de Colonias in the Federal District and by the municipal authorities in the State of Mexico. However, serious remedial actions did not emerge until Echeverría took office. In the State of Mexico, as was noted above, the incoming administration faced an immediate political crisis brought about by the payments strike by residents to companies. The government's response is illuminating in that the crisis prompted a much more interventionist approach in the handling of land issues, especially in the area of *remedial action*, which was tackled in several ways (Tello 1978; Ward 1981a).

First, the immediate political problem was solved through a special deal whereby developers were reimbursed less 40 per cent to take account of the services they had failed to install, and residents received a 15 per cent discount on the overall purchase price and full legal title to their lots. Service installation was to begin immediately, also provided by the government, but the costs were to be recovered from residents over a 10-year period. The agreement was accepted by all parties, although it has been strongly criticized for favouring the companies in so far as they were exonerated from responsibility for their illegal transactions, retained a large part of their profits, and escaped the burden of paying for services (Guerrero *et al.* 1974; Martín de la Rosa 1975; Ferras 1978).

Second, political mediation was achieved through remedial actions which identified land regularization as an issue in its own right. Significantly, in no other country does regularization feature with such prominence (Gilbert and Ward 1985), but in Mexico regularization emerged as having critical importance from 1971 onwards, and the creation of a battery of agencies to provide full legal title to *colonos* was an innovation. However, it can be argued that the nature of regularization policies at this time reflected governmental needs more than those of residents, whose main concern was for security of tenure (Ward 1982). The interpretation that this required full legal title was one provided by government rather than by the residents themselves. Full tenure was not required before *colonos* could sell their plots; nor was it necessary for services to be installed, for this requirement had usually been waived since the early 1960s. Security of tenure could easily have been provided by simple recognition of *de facto* occupancy and did not require full legalization through expropriation, indemnization and the drawing-up of property deeds. The point is that there is a social construction to illegality (Mele 1987; Varley 1989). Regularization was seen as a medium of negotiation and social control in so far as it constituted a cheap resource that could be granted or withheld by the authorities.

The regularization of land in existing settlements intensified after 1977, and again after 1989 (Varley 1996: 210). Agencies responsible for regularization became more efficient, and the number of titles issued each year has risen considerably, in part as a response to efforts to simplify the process. However, regularization has also undergone an important qualitative change. Since 1977 it has become a *means to an end* as well as an *end in its own right*. It is now conceived as a mechanism to incorporate the populace into the formal land market, making them subject to greater local authority land-use and planning controls, and equally important, bringing them into the registry for land-tax payments and for service and utility charges. Once included in the property register, the authorities attempt to 'clear' outstanding land-tax debts that the *colono* is deemed to have. These may comprise backdated rates chargeable retrospectively for up to a maximum of 5 years. However, they often also include a range of additional charges. In different settlements I have found multiple examples of valorization taxes relating to motorway construction undertaken several years earlier, charges for building permission and many apparently arbitrary fines. Often failure to have paid these fees and fines previously led to surcharges being incurred. Where residents protested, either through their leaders or *en masse*, the amounts charged became negotiable and, more often than not, a discount was arranged. This demonstrates how the authorities sought both to raise treasury resources and to use the procedure as a dimension of political mediation and control. During 1978 the existence of a deliberate policy link between regularization and taxation was freely admitted by officials in the cadastral office of the Federal District.

As we observed in Chapter 3, locally generated city income has become an increasingly important element in public expenditure, and strengthening municipal administrative capacity has become a watchword of the World Bank's Urban Management Programme as well as of SEDESOL (Jones and Ward 1994; Mexico SEDESOL 1996). There was a dramatic improvement in the effectiveness of expediting and completing the regularization process of *ejidal* land during the Salinas administration (Varley 1996).

Mediation through bureaucratic manipulation

In addition to constructing a changing land policy over time, administrations may achieve social control through the manipulation of the bureaucracy which has responsibility for irregular settlements. For instance, the multiplicity of agencies created by the Echeverría administration with regularization duties within the Metropolitan Area led to numerous overlaps in functions. CoRett's charter gave it responsibility for *ejidal* and *comunal* lands yet, in the State of Mexico, AURIS was also involved in *ejidal* land. Similarly in the Federal District, FIDEURBE was created specifically with the task of regularizing the most conflictive settlements (such as Padierna and Santo Domingo), and many of these were on *ejidal* or *comunal* lands. An added problem was that responsibility for several of these settlements had rested initially with a national agency, INDECO, so there was likely to be an overlap of functions and leader–agency networks brought about by the transfer of responsibility from the first agency to its successor. INDECO was an agency with a broad range of functions, which meant that it operated nationally as a sort of roving troubleshooter and was charged to resolve problems in specific settlements as and when they arose. The *Procuraduría de Colonias Populares* (PCP) had a similarly vague role to fulfil within the Federal District. It was the old CNOP-dominated *Oficina de Colonias*, now reconstituted by Mayor Sentíes to act as a vehicle whereby he could intervene in low-income-settlement affairs. It had some regularization duties, but also distributed free milk, gave out presents to children at Christmas, organized clean-up campaigns, etc. The Director as *Procurador* saw himself, literally, as the 'advocate' or 'attorney' of the poor.

Inter-agency strife is a feature of this type of bureaucratic structure. The informal rules governing inter-departmental behaviour at all hierarchical levels are, broadly, those of either outright conflict and competition, alliance, or tacit agreement not to meddle in each other's affairs. Of these three alternatives, alliance did not figure during this period in relations between the agencies identified above. However, between 1973 and 1976 there is ample evidence from my own early fieldwork and that of others that both FIDEURBE and the PCP suffered from and engendered conflict with each other (Alonso *et al.* 1980: 37–39). CoRett, too, occasionally meddled unnecessarily, such as when it declared that, were it to be in charge of regularization in the settlement of Ajusco, the costs to residents would be much lower than those proposed by FIDEURBE (López Díaz 1978). Coming precisely at a time when the latter agency was trying to secure the cooperation of *colonos*, it is difficult to interpret CoRett's action as anything but deliberate political sabotage.

Furthermore, conflict between agencies was facilitated between 1971 and 1976 by the structure of the patron–client links that agency directors and personnel were expected to form with individual communities, and by the proliferation of different leadership groups within each settlement, particularly the most conflictive (Varley 1993). Each group of residents led, invariably, to a different agency, so that it was common for one group to elicit support from the Procurador, another would seek out the head of FIBEURBE, while others would go to the local *delegado* (Alonso *et al.* 1980). At the same time, when a group felt really threatened they approached President Echeverría himself, who appeared well disposed to receive their delegations and to listen to their case. As a result rumour abounded, contradictory policies were espoused, and orders were countermanded. One agency head bemoaned the frequent practice of calling agency heads to open hearings with the President, which had the effect of undermining their authority without reducing their responsibility. Another described the experience as one of being on a 'constant war footing'.

Whether this bureaucratic structure and functioning were the result of accident or design is a matter for speculation. However, the important point to recognize is its functionality for the Echeverría administration. The existence of several agencies, all apparently active on behalf of the poor, gave the impression that much was being done. Important, also, was the personal contact that Echeverría maintained with grassroots organizations and which he demanded also from his agency directors. The President could appear as arbitrator on behalf of selected groups (Connolly 1982). Also, where one agency threatened to become too powerful, or another too weak, he could shift his support to re-establish the balance. Both land and the bureaucracy itself became the cannon fodder for political mediation by Echeverría.

The structure of the land and urban development bureaucracy and the way in which it behaved changed substantially from 1977 onwards. This was partly a result of the overall streamlining of the various sectors of government activity initiated by López Portillo as part of his Administrative Reform. It was also indicative of the growing technocratization of the bureaucracy in which politicians have been replaced by professionals (*técnicos*; Varley 1993; Centeno 1994). In the Federal District it was part of a conscious effort to change the nature of state–community relations and to make land regularization more efficient and less politicized.

The number of agencies with responsibilities for regularization was reduced (Ward 1989b). More importantly, not only were overlaps avoided, but authority was invested in a specific agency and not between them – as had happened before. Each got on with the job for which it was responsible and kept out of the others' way. The process of streamlining and techno-cratization has continued since 1982. From 1990 onwards, PRONASOL became the primary vehicle for promoting and coordinating CoRett's regularization efforts (Varley 1996), and more recently still, SEDESOL is encouraging the participation of state and municipal authorities in the process (Austin 1994; Jones and Ward 1997).

Several important points emerge from this review of changing government response to irregular settlement. We have seen that land is an important mechanism for political mediation in Mexico City. So far as the provision of land is concerned, the state's response has been passive. In choosing not to act against the real-estate companies or against those responsible for *ejidal* land sales it has favoured certain interests at the expense of the poor, and condoned illegal practices. At the same time the illegal supply of land for low-income groups has been maintained.

In establishing policy towards existing irregular settlement, the covert aims of the state appear to have been paramount. The state has sought to use the land issue as a means of extending its influence over the poor and to maintain their quiescence. The way in which this has been achieved has altered significantly in recent years. Before 1977, control was sought primarily by political manipulation, co-option and patron–client links with the poor. Since that date, while social stability and social passivity remain fundamental goals, the state has developed a more structured framework in which to achieve them. Increasingly, it depends for its legitimacy and support on greater efficiency and delivery of resources desired by *colonos* and less upon traditional forms of mediation such as patron–clientelism and the PRI apparatus. In Mexico, regularization has become an important element in the political calculus. The nature of regularization has evolved to reflect state priorities rather than those of low-income groups. It is not simply a means of extending full property titles to the poor, but increasingly a means of incorporating them into the urban citizenry and into the tax base; a point to which I return in the next chapter.

REPRODUCING SOCIAL INEQUALITY THROUGH STRATIFIED DELIVERY SYSTEMS: HEALTH CARE IN MEXICO CITY

In the Metropolitan Area of Mexico City high mortality and morbidity rates are associated with low-income areas and poor housing conditions. Those living in the eastern suburb irregular settlements of Netzahualcóyotl were especially prone to intestinal infections brought about by the poor sanitary and water-supply conditions that existed in those areas – at least until the early 1970s. Those living in the working class neighbourhoods of Tepito and Guerrero in the heart of the city suffered from especially high rates of respiratory diseases due to cramped housing conditions and high levels of pollution (Fox 1972). Yet despite some shift of focus towards primary health care along lines outlined by the World Health Organization (1978, 1981), the philosophy of health care in Mexico concentrates upon individualized health care and treatment rather than on collective programmes to improve general living conditions.

The stratification of health care in Mexico: who does what?

Public health care and social security provision in Mexico have evolved over more than four decades and, paralleling expansion in other areas of the Mexican bureaucracy, present a pastiche of separate institutions, the individual fortunes of which have fluctuated with administrations.[3] However, as well as the widely documented tendency for organizations to evolve as a response to pressure from the most powerful social groups (Mesa Lago 1978), in Mexico coverage has also been extended to the not so powerful, and specifically to wider sections of the working population that include both blue-collar and white-collar workers. This has come about for various reasons. It is a result of political gestures initiated by the Executive to strengthen the popular ideology that the interests of the poor are being served. It has been used to win popular support for the government; while at other times it provides a means of compensating workers for declining opportunities and for the erosion of real wages.

In Mexico, the principal social security institutions that have been established also organize their own medical service, and here I propose to focus only upon this aspect of their functions. Access to health care for Mexicans falls into three main categories, each of which will be described briefly below.

T A B L E 6.1   Population attended by social security organizations and by private and government sectors

	Metropolitan Area[a]		Nation[b]	
	Per cent	Thousands	Per cent	Thousands
Social security:				
IMSS	43.0	4935.8	29.9	20 000[c]
ISSSTE	15.5	1772.1	7.2	4800
Others	7.2	828.0	2.2	1500
Government: SSA and DDF	17.9	2045.9	15.6	10 500
Private sector	16.5	1884.0	14.9	10 000
Unattended	0	0	30.1	20 100
Total	100.1	11 455.8	100.0	66 900

[a]   Source: *DDF*, Plan Director, Chapter 7, based upon data provided by SSA. Data are for 1976.
[b]   Source: López Acuña (1980: 108), based on data from José López Portillo, II Informe. Data are for 1978.
[c]   Pre-IMSS-COPLAMAR programme.

Social security organizations   First there are the public social security organizations, the largest of which is the IMSS (Instituto Mexicano de Seguro Social) founded in 1944, originally for urban salaried workers. Since then it has been extended to include agricultural salaried workers (from 1954) and, since 1973, coverage has progressively been offered to all people in employment and even for the self-employed. However, these groups are accorded an inferior membership status in which benefits are less comprehensive, are limited to non-specialist medical treatment, and exclude maternity care. In view of these limitations, it is perhaps hardly surprising that people have not rushed to join. Despite attempts to extend coverage to rural areas, membership of IMSS remains overwhelmingly urban: 91 per cent in 1983 (De la Madrid 1984 *Segundo Informe, anexo Sector Salud*).

Next in size is the ISSSTE (Instituto de Seguridad y Servicios Sociales de los Trabajadores al Servicio del Estado). Founded much later (1960) for state employees, it offers the most extensive and generous health and social security package. Affiliation increased five-fold between 1966 and 1976, mirroring the expansion of the state bureaucracy during that period. Expansion was particularly rapid during the early 1970s, although resources per capita have declined steadily since then. Almost all of its affiliates are urban and, as we can observe from Table 6.1, a sizeable proportion live in the Metropolitan Area of Mexico City.

Government sector   The second major level of health provision comes from the public–governmental sector, and most important here is the Ministry of Health (SS, formerly Health and Welfare SSA), which provides the main alternative source of health care for the bulk of the population not covered by any of the social security organizations or private medical insurance. In absolute terms the responsibilities of the Health Ministry have grown. In 1983 the Minister stated that between 15 and 20 million people in rural areas alone were without any access to health care (*Excelsior* 17 April 1983). Of the three institutions it is the worst endowed, yet for many of the poor it is likely to be a crucially important system. Estimates vary, but it seems likely that for between 18 and 20 per cent of the population of the Metropolitan Area the SS system represents the only alternative to private medicine (Table 6.1). Since De la Madrid's presidency, attempts have been made to decentralize the *Sector Salud* responsibilities to the individual states, but the earlier attempts at least fell short of their devolutionary intentions, and actually became an attempt to recentralize power around a different administrative structure (González Block *et al.* 1989; Rodríguez 1997).

Private sector   The third level is the private sector. This includes both a private health care system as well as private charitable institutions such as the Red Cross and the Green Cross. Although limited in number and in the range of services offered, charities are often an important 'bottom line' of health-care provision. Nor should the importance of a private health service in Mexico be underestimated. While the proportion of the total population covered by social security grew from 22 per cent in 1967 to almost 40 per cent in 1980, this left the majority dependent upon the public–government and the private sector. Moreover, as I will demonstrate below, private medicine is not a preserve of the rich: the poor also make extensive use of the private sector, especially for lightweight consultations.

The rise in numbers covered by each of these institutions has had important implications for the manpower and health care resources that each is able to offer. There has been a sharp deterioration in the level of staffing and facilities offered by ISSSTE due in large part to a major increase of affiliates between 1973 and 1978. Per capita ratios of doctors, beds and nurses declined dramatically, and its previous top position was lost to IMSS, which managed to maintain its earlier levels despite an increased membership (Ward 1986). However, in neither case does the level of service drop to anything near the paucity of resources experienced by the Ministry of Health throughout the period. In the 1980s, per capita facilities enjoyed by the social security sector have remained far better than those of the public–government sector. These different levels of benefits offered by the various tiers are an important mechanism whereby inequalities are reproduced.

Policies are not formulated in a vacuum; they emerge within the political economy of a given time. During the early 1970s, under President Echeverría, the emphasis lay firmly on developing large-scale high-technology hospitals and medical centres which López Acuña (1980: 182) described as: 'white elephants which, voraciously, consume scarce resources allocated to health care in Mexico'. Partly as a sop to demands from the rural and urban poor,

Echeverría also espoused more populist programmes which had potentially wide-reaching implications for improving community health care, but which ended up as little more than rhetorical gestures. They included the creation of child-care institutions and general-purpose community development agencies which sponsored lightweight programmes such as the distribution of free breakfasts, education about nutrition, rehabilitation and education of polio victims, and health and immunization campaigns. From the government's point of view these institutions were relatively cheap, offered flexibility to respond to specific crises, and reinforced an ideology that significant action was being undertaken on behalf of the underprivileged. In the previous section we observed parallel actions undertaken in the arena of land policies.

Significant changes in policy date from the beginning of López Portillo's Government (1976–82). Health agencies attempted some reorganization of the structure of medical care that placed more vigorous emphasis upon the need for local communities to have greater access to general services, and to 'soft-pedal' on costly investment programmes in the fields of intensive care and specialist treatment. In the Metropolitan Area the IMSS sought to respond to earlier criticism that it had neglected general medical care in favour of highly specialized treatment, and reorganized its health-care system, establishing a new hierarchy of treatment. Both the IMSS and the Ministry of Health sought to develop the lower tiers of health care: family medical units comprising surgeries to provide out-patient treatment for IMSS affiliates. The Health Ministry developed programmes of education about health problems and preventive work within the *delegaciones*, and a new department was opened to attend marginal areas. However, a lack of funds meant that by 1979 only 59 local health centres had been established out of the 700 required.

Access to health care within the Metropolitan Area of Mexico City

Access to adequate health care facilities is not simply a question of their availability or that they be of the right kind, it is also a matter of their being located at accessible points throughout the city. Large, intensive-care specialist hospitals form an integral part of any hierarchy of provision and can normally be expected to be located near the centre of the city or at a nodal point within the city's transport network. More important, however, is the need to achieve a balance and to ensure an adequate distribution of general treatment facilities (Eyles and Woods 1983; Phillips 1990; Garrocho 1995b).

In Mexico City a broad hierarchy exists, comprising integrated medical centres – general hospitals – clinics and health centres. This is complemented by specialist hospitals and institutes. The latter, together with the multifaceted medical centres, provide a service for the national and regional population. Given the enormous costs of establishing and maintaining these institutions, it is reasonable to locate them in the largest urban centres. However, one may question the desirability of duplicating all levels of the hierarchy for each sector. IMSS, ISSSTE and SS each have large medical centres in Mexico City and, in some cases, more than one.

Here I am not concerned to explain why that situation has come about; rather my wish is to analyse the effectiveness of coverage that exists throughout the Metropolitan Area. If we examine more closely the location of public health services in the city, the glaring inadequacy of coverage becomes apparent. In 1965, when rapid suburbanization of low-income settlement had already been underway for two decades, there was minimal provision of health centres within easy reach of these poor districts. In the east, south-east and north-east there were virtually no public-sector facilities (Figure 6.3). Most medical services were aligned in the shape of a horse-shoe around Chapultepec Park, with an especially large number situated around the city centre. In essence the older, established and richer parts of the city were well served.

Yet despite more than a doubling of population between 1965 and 1980, and the fact that most of the increase had been concentrated in the more suburban *delegaciones* and adjacent municipalities, the pattern established before 1965 has not altered appreciably (Figure 6.4). Although there has been some growth of new facilities in the periphery, they are widely scattered. Both ISSSTE and IMSS have done little more than consolidate their existing network, creating new medical centres and large hospitals but showing little real effort to decentralize coverage in the form of health centres and clinics to poor suburban districts. Granted, ISSSTE's unwilling-ness to shift is partly justifiable on the grounds that only a relatively small proportion of its affiliates live in the low-income settlements, but the same is not true for the IMSS. The Ministry of Health did make some attempt to increase access to their facilities and to shift the locus of services towards poorer areas. Between 1965 and 1971 the SS initiated a reorganization of its facilities and closed several of their outlets downtown while opening others in the poorer districts of the Federal District; a process it extended during the 1970s (Figure 6.5). From 1977 there was a marked expansion of the charity sector. Between them, the SS and the charity sector have taken the major initiatives in extending health-care facilities to poor districts of the city.

Health care for residents of irregular settlements

In 1979, as part of the PIHLU study (see Chapter 2), some 630 households in six low-income irregular settlements on the periphery of the city were

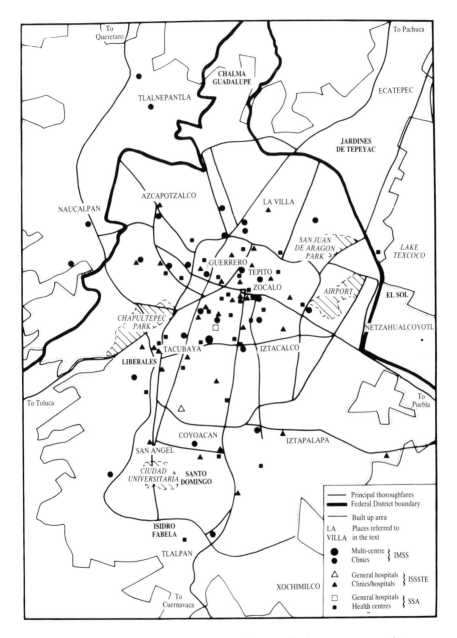

FIGURE 6.3 Location of institutions providing medical treatment in 1965

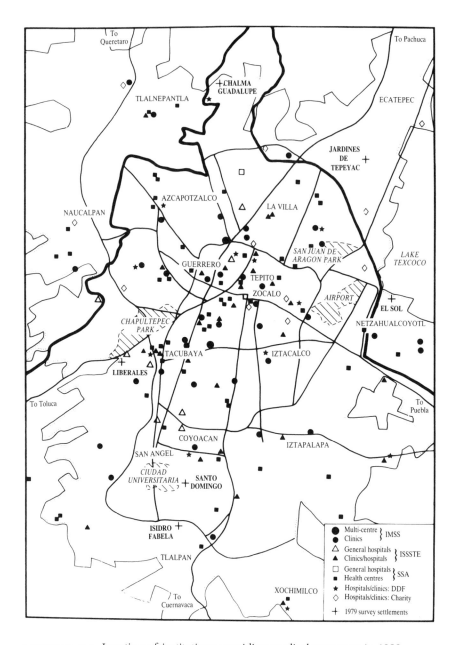

FIGURE 6.4 Location of institutions providing medical treatment in 1982

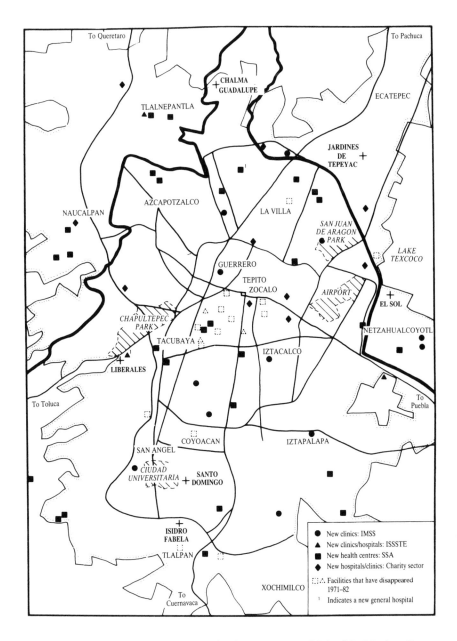

FIGURE 6.5 New locations for medical treatment established in Mexico City between 1971 and 1982

interviewed about matters relating to family health. Specifically, the ques-
tionnaires contained a section about family illnesses suffered during the
preceding 12 months, the treatment received, and opinions relating to
the quality of medical attention. These data are partial in the sense that they
only give an indication of health patterns for low-income residents in the
colonias populares of Mexico City at a single point in time. However, they
provide a basis for independent evaluation of the efficiency of the health-
care system at that time, and several of the findings are interesting in the
context of the preceding discussion.

Of primary interest was the treatment sought both in spatial and sectoral
terms. Inevitably, therefore, this led respondents to identify the more
important illnesses suffered and to under-report minor or short-lived
illnesses (such as colds or intestinal complaints). More than one-half of all
household heads interviewed declared that at least one member of the
immediate family had been ill during the previous 12 months. Mostly the
person specified was either the wife (36 per cent) or a child (42 per cent). It
often proved difficult to identify with any precision the true nature of the
illness, as many were minor ailments that did not fit any easy categorization.
In those cases where the illness was specified, a significant number related
to some sort of natal care or to treatment for 'flu. Intestinal disorders also
figured, but were probably under-reported or form a large part of an
'unspecified' illness category.

The source from which treatment was received appears to relate to two
considerations. First, whether or not the individual was covered by any form
of social security health care. Second, choice intervenes in so far as not
everyone automatically used the cheapest system available to them. In
Mexico City an estimated 66 per cent of the city population is covered by
social security health care, which is broadly similar to the proportion of
heads of household in the sample, most of whom belonged to IMSS (Tables
6.1 and 6.3). Specifically, 60 per cent of those individuals for whom an
illness was reported were covered by one of the social security organizations, although that coverage varied considerably between settlements. Yet
despite the fact that the majority had social security, and that even those not
covered had recourse to the government sector, many respondents opted
for private treatment, usually by consulting a doctor at his surgery (Table
6.2). Indeed, almost two-fifths of all treatment was provided by the private
sector. It appears that the poor often trade-off the use of public sector
facilities in favour of the more conveniently located private service (see
below). This is especially likely where the sickness is relatively minor and
does not require intensive care or hospitalization. For the latter, and for
treatment that is likely to prove expensive, the official and social security
sectors are used almost exclusively. By and large people can afford a one-
off payment to a local doctor, but they cannot contemplate the high costs of
hospitalization or of sustained private treatment. This finding applies to

TABLE 6.2 Type and institutional source of treatment for residents in irregular settlements

	Percentage	Number
Consultations		
In a hospital	2.3	8
By a private doctor	26.9	94
In a health centre (SSA)	6.6	23
In a private clinic	2.3	8
In social security clinic	27.8	97
With a 'healer'	0.6	2
With a nurse	1.7	6
Sub-total	68.2	238
Hospitalization		
Government or charity	7.7	27
Private hospital	6.9	24
Social security	16.9	59
Sub-total	31.5	110

Source: PIHLU settlement survey, 1979.

TABLE 6.3 Sector in which treatment was sought according to whether respondent had social security coverage

Sector in which treated	All (%)	Without social security (%)	With social security (%)
Government and charity	17	32	7
Private	39	62	25
Social security	45	6	68
Total percentage	101	100	100
Total number	349	129	195

Source: PIHLU Settlement survey, 1979.

social security affiliates as well as those not covered, although not equally. Those with social security are more likely to use that service, but 25 per cent of affiliates went private compared with 82 per cent of those without cover, whose only alternative was the official or charity systems (Table 6.3).

Two explanations may be advanced for the extensive use of private medicine by the poor. First, it may indicate dissatisfaction with the public sector brought about by earlier unsatisfactory treatment, long waits or because people feel culturally alienated from using modern medicine. Yet none of these reasons appear plausible given that practically everyone (over 80 per cent) expressed satisfaction with the treatment received regardless of the sector that provided it. This does not necessarily mean that the service offered is satisfactory, but simply that low-income residents expressed few complaints.

A second explanation relates to accessibility. I have shown that there is a marked discrepancy between the location of public health facilities and low-income housing areas. Invariably the latter are poorly served. Most people, therefore, face a long journey on public transport or taxi to a government or social security clinic and, understandably, they prefer to visit the local doctor, often in his consulting room in the same settlement. In most of the survey settlements the majority sought private treatment in the immediate vicinity of their homes. Alternatively, or in cases where specialist treatment was required, they went to the nearest appropriate institution (Figure 6.6). These are indicated by the thicker-line flows on the figure, and one can see that this often means a journey of considerable distance, especially in the most peripheral settlements such as Jardines and Isidro Fabela. The average (crow-flight) round-trip distance to the place of treatment in these two settlements was 12.5 and 10 km, respectively. Even residents in the better-served settlements such as Chalma and Santo Domingo had to travel an average of 6 km. Paradoxically, El Sol, which is one of the most poorly served of all, appears to be not so badly off (8 km), but this is because most residents have little alternative but to use the private local facilities, thereby reducing the average travel distance recorded for that settlement.[4] In this latter settlement, 19 households reported that they had used public facilities to treat the illness identified, and the average round trip (crow-flight) distance was 19 km. This compares adversely with the 5.4 km travelled by those 36 households who took advantage of private (and invariably local) facilities. Many of these people (21) were treated within their own neighbourhood.

The failure of the state to provide an adequate service of primary health care means that many of the poor are obliged to make their own arrangements and to provide for themselves. For the sake of convenience a substantial minority use private facilities, and in the event of a relatively minor ailment most go to a nearby doctor. Although private consultations are relatively inexpensive in these districts, it is a paradox that the poor should make extensive use of this sector given that a comprehensive public system is purported to exist. It emphasizes the need for a wider distribution of local health centres in peripheral areas of the city. In particular, the IMSS and the SS should direct greater investment towards low-cost community health-care facilities given that it is the population dependent upon that sector which uses private doctors with the greatest frequency.

The examination of access to health care in Mexico City demonstrates how various social groups are kept apart through the separate tiers of treatment available to them. Even the attempts to extend coverage of the IMSS to populations that were previously uncovered, although welcome, offered a minimal and inferior service to that received by existing members. This serves to create yet another tier within an already highly stratified system, and existing social inequalities are accentuated further.

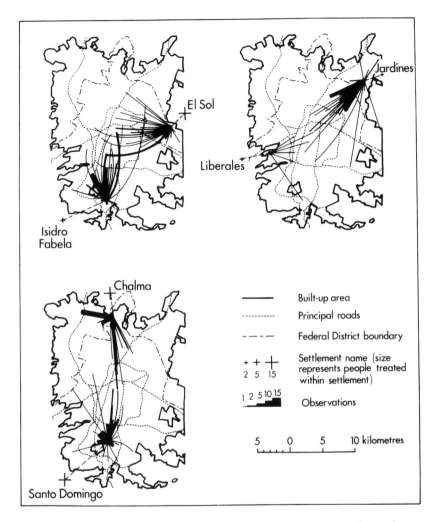

FIGURE 6.6 Place of medical treatment for residents of six irregular settlements in Mexico City

Second, social inequalities are sustained through the sharply differentiated benefits that accrue to each tier and the way in which each is financially regressive (Mesa Lago 1978). Contributions are a proportion of wages, so that although better-off groups pay greater sums, so do the other bipartite or tripartite contributor(s), be they government or employer (Midgley 1984). In the latter case, contributions are usually generated from profits on goods, so the consumer ends up paying. As a result, those organizations which offer cover to better-paid workers and employees are most likely to build up their resources quickly. Clearly this multiplicity of structures is not an historical accident. It is a deliberate outcome of the political system and facilitates the manipulation of one sector or group of the population against another. It also makes the structure highly resistant to change. Few groups will wish to concede the advantage they hold.

This leads to my third general conclusion that a stratified structure has important ideological functions for the state. Covertly, the health and social security systems serve to co-opt the most powerful or organized groups in society. Thus federal workers are catered for through ISSSTE; those in strategic industries enjoy their own health-care facilities, as do the military. These conditions, together with wider benefits provided by each individual social security system, have evolved in response to pressure from these more powerful groups (Mesa Lago 1978). All along they have sought to maintain their relative advantage *vis-à-vis* other groups. IMSS offers the best medical service, but its social security benefits are not as generous as others. The Ministry of Health, which caters for the majority of the population, is no more than a nominal health service. This situation would probably not persist if those people or communities without adequate cover organized more effectively to make demands or displayed a propensity to protest. Currently the state can afford to offer the bare minimum without fear of generating strong protest. In addition, it has created a range of one-off 'trouble-shooting' institutions which appear to make concessions or provide relief where it is required.

REPRODUCING SOCIAL INEQUALITY THROUGH STATE-COMMUNITY INTERACTION

Another means by which social inequality can be sustained is through the arrangements that the state adopts towards engagement and interaction with local communities. As I argued in Chapter 3 in the context of the Federal District, these terms of engagement have changed over time from open-ended patron–client relations to a much more closely structured arrangement comprising the neighbourhood councils (*juntas de vecinos*). Indeed, a general review of channels of community action in three Latin American countries concluded that structures tended to be imposed top-down by the state rather than being an expression of bottom-up mobilization by the most disadvantaged (Gilbert and Ward 1984). The rationale for their existence obeys state needs and criteria more than it reflects the needs of the poor. Of course, there are important exceptions to this highly constrained pattern, but they tend not to be the rule, at least not until the democratization of Latin America began to open the political space for participation in local development (UNCHS 1996: 168). International agencies and many government agencies espouse the virtues of including community action and participation and expect it to figure as an element in the development projects that they sponsor (Skinner and Rodell 1983).

However, if this somewhat cynical view reflects the practice, what about the theory? Surely organized struggle, whether it be class-based in the classic sense or a 'Rainbow Coalition' of interest groups and political parties, offers potential for overcoming social inequality? Some three decades ago there was a strong interest and belief in the possibilities that the *lumpenproletariat* (i.e. the masses in Third World countries who did not conform to a classic proletarian vanguard capable of promoting class struggle) would somehow rise up and destroy the repressive élites (Fanon 1967). Although an idealistic view, and one which failed to identify how a class in itself might become a class for itself, this work encouraged further investigation into the ways in which the poor mobilized themselves and extracted concessions from government (Goldrich *et al.* 1967; Ray 1969; Cornelius 1975). However, these studies pointed not to the radicalism of the poor, but to their conservatism. The privileged access to social and housing benefits offered by large urban centres, compared with what migrants had put up with in the provinces, encouraged support for the system. Moreover, the manner whereby these benefits were won through the exchange of political support also reduced the likelihood of the poor providing the vanguard for successful revolution or for significant social change.

In this context, Castells' work is very important. Indeed his own early thinking was strongly influenced by orthodox theory about class struggle combined with his experience in irregular settlements (*campamentos*) of Santiago, Chile, during the Popular Unity Government (1970–3). However, his contribution was that he was able to offer an attractive theory about the formation of social movements in relation to the growth of state intervention. A brief summary does not do justice to Castells' work, but the existence of other detailed evaluations (Lowe 1986) and the fact that Castells' own ideas about the nature and potential of urban social movements have turned almost full circle between 1971 and 1983, makes this brief treatment a little more justifiable. As I outlined earlier in this chapter, Castells argued that the state's growing obligation to intervene to provide the 'means of collective consumption' in effect provides a point around which conflict can be forged against the dominant class or group who control those 'means' (in this case the state). Given appropriate leadership, and linkage to the advanced working classes (whose struggle around the capital relation – means of production – was paramount), an urban social movement could be forged that would lead to a 'qualitatively new effect' on the dominant structure of relations within that society (Castells 1977).

For several reasons Castells moved away from the strictures of this definition and began to give greater (equivalent) weight to the importance of secondary or displaced class struggle. Linkage to the capital relation through a proletarian vanguard was no longer paramount. Finally, faced with the extremely limited successes wrought by urban social movements during the 1970s, together with the growing internationalization of the economic process, Castells backtracked and argued that social change is only possible when mobilization around an issue of collective consumption is combined with political self-management and with the defence of cultural and territorial identity (Castells 1983: xviii, 328). However, he argues that broadening the issue of mobilization is not enough (p. 329) because urban movements can neither comprehend nor 'recognize the relationship between production, consumption and circulation' – a task that extends beyond the confines of the local community. At best, therefore, local groups are only likely to be effective in their resistance against 'exploitation – alienation oppression that the city represents' (p. 330); therein lies their contemporary role and value.

Others have remained more steadfast in their belief in the possibility of achieving social change under conditions of flexible accumulation, and see the experience of the 'Greens' in West Germany and the 'Rainbow Coalition' in the US as promising in this respect (Harvey 1987; Eckstein 1989; Assies 1992). Harvey (1987: 283) also says that: 'true empowerment for the presently disempowered must be won by struggle from below and not given out of largesse from above'. In Mexico City the problem has been that largesse from above has consistently disempowered any serious movement towards social change. Even the mobilization around post-earthquake housing reconstruction in 1985–86 and the formation of a well-organized Coordinating Committee (CUD) and later the Barrios' Assembly was in effect bought off by the generous terms of the programme itself and by the *Concertacion* (agreement) to which most groups became signatories as a requirement for inclusion (Eckstein 1990b). Although this experience was one of the more positive from the point of view of low-income organizations and heralded more symmetrical relations with local authorities, when push came to shove and mobilization threatened to destabilize social peace in the inner city, then the state responded in its usual way – by cutting a deal. Potential protest by those left out of the initial reconstruction programme was also offset by a second, diluted, programme – Phase II. Also, the internal integrity of the Barrios' Assembly began to implode under leadership struggles and splits (Greene 1993). However, some authors view citizen and social movements more positively, arguing that they represent important means towards greater empowerment and may result in positive outcomes for disadvantaged groups, particularly where there is a convergence of factors such as need, existing social infrastructure, support from better-off supra-local social groups, and an opening of the local political space (Eckstein 1990b). These conditions certainly came together in inner-city reconstruction in Mexico City during the late 1980s. Moreover, the opening of the political space in Mexico nationally since 1989, greater pluralist representation of non-PRI parties on local government, and the deliberate strengthening of local community participation under the Solidarity Programme have undoubtedly fostered me genuine opportunities for more equitable and less constrained citizen involvement in urban development during the past decade (Contreras and Bennett 1994; Haber 1994; Bennett 1995; Venegas 1995). Also, many city governments appear to be responding more openly and positively to local citizen and residential-based groups and eschewing the co-optive and corporatist practices of the yesteryear PRI (Rodríguez and Ward 1994a, 1996; Cabrero Mendoza 1995), suggesting that several of the forms of control described below are becoming a feature of the past. However, considerable evidence also remains to suggest that these changes are far from being complete (Dresser 1991; Varley 1993, 1996). How is this disempowerment achieved in the context of land policy, health care, housing and infrastructure servicing arrangements? Traditionally there have been three main mechanisms: through the structure of linkage and channels to the state; through tactics of divide-and-rule; and through the manipulation of popular ideology.

Control through linkages between the state and the community

The various types of control that may be exercised through different forms of state–community relationship are outlined in Table 6.4. Patron–clientelism involves an informal link between leader/community and a 'patron' in which goods and favours are distributed from the latter, usually in exchange for political support (Grindle 1977). *Co-option* and *incorporation* occurs where the leader/community affiliates with a national organization and thereby becomes subject to its orthodoxy, procedures, rules and so on. This is usually done because the coopted party believes that it will win preferential treatment and benefit as a result of the link. In Mexico, co-option is a classic strategy that the PRI use in giving the impression that it has preferential access to resources. In fact co-option leads to a *reduced* likelihood of winning successful outcomes: what one author appropriately calls the 'irony of organization' (Eckstein 1977). Routinization is a form of integration sought by government agencies when communities are recognized and accommodated by the institution in order for it to fulfil its goals efficiently. Finally, communities may resist external mediation and, through their leaders, reject overtures that might lead to their loss of autonomy. This is done either for reasons of ideological purity, the group being wary of the undermining influence of the state, or it is born of a belief that independence and embarrassment of local authorities will maximize the chances and speed of securing a desired outcome (Montaño 1976).

The ways in which land-development issues and servicing have been managed through state–community relations in Mexico City offers insight into several of these processes. Here, for the sake of brevity, I will deal only

TABLE 6.4 Methods of control exercised by different forms of community–state relationship

Nature of linkage	Way in which external control is exercised
Patron–client	Manipulation
	Ad hoc concessions
Co-option/incorporation	Occasional 'lightweight' concessions
	Compliance with external orthodoxy
'Routinization'	Queuing and concessions
	'Gatekeepers' allocating resources
	'Red tape' in order to delay and obstruct
Autonomy/independence	Concessions made in order to pacify
	Manipulation
	Repression; assassination of leaders, etc.

with land. Until the late 1970s the PRI used clientelism and cooption to good effect – often through the CNOP wing, which was heavily involved as mediator between residents and the government (Cornelius 1975; Eckstein 1977, 1988; Alonso *et al.* 1980). In the Federal District land regularization and service provision assumed importance as a means of ensuring and developing political control and support. Through the Oficina de Colonias, residents were leant on to attend political rallies and to vote for the PRI at elections; in exchange they could expect some form of government recognition for their settlement, and/or the installation of minor services and occasional handouts. This process of negotiation was mediated vertically through settlement leaders who acted as brokers in informal patron–client networks involving the community and top-level politicians and government officials (Cornelius 1975).

Although the Party's direct control over settlement affairs suffered as a result of the creation of new agencies responsible for regularization and housing and with whom it had little direct influence, the proliferation of factions and groups rife in each settlement before 1976 provided ample room in which the PRI could manoeuvre. Different leaders sought legitimacy through the creation of vertical clientelist links created with various 'patrons'. This 'splitting' or hiving-off of several factions within a single settlement was not seriously challenged until 1977, after which routinized relationships between agencies and individuals became the order of the day. In the State of Mexico, the Party's main task during the early 1970s was to penetrate the mass-based urban social movement (the MRC) and its sister organization in the Quinta Zona of Ecatepec. By classic methods of co-option and infiltration, the CNOP successfully undermined the potency of these organizations by 1976 (Cisneros Sosa, no date).

However, radical social mobilization has not always been headed-off by clientelism, co-option and routinization (Montaño 1976; Ramírez Saíz 1983). In such cases government-sponsored repression, either of the community or its leaders, may be adopted in order to overcome opposition. The violence visited upon the 2 de Octubre settlement in Ixtacalco and its leader Pancho de la Cruz during 1974–6 was also a warning to others of the ultimate deterrent.

Control through tactics of 'divide-and-rule'

The second principal mechanism whereby the state exercises control over potentially disruptive or threatening social movements is through dividing one group from another. Any attempt to weld a horizontal movement between different spatial or sectoral constituencies is likely to attract state concern. As I have just explained, the state seeks vertically mediated links to individual leaders or communities. The MRC, the Urban Popular Movements Coordination (CONAMUP) and the Earthquake Refugees' Coordination (CUD) are examples of movements which broke the rules as far as the state is concerned. Government response is illuminating, and various mechanisms have been developed to drive a wedge between one group or faction and another.

One way is to systematically treat settlements differently. Thus deals are struck whereby water or land regularization is provided to one area but not to another. Electricity here, but not there. This opens divisions between different settlement leaders over their settlement priorities for improvements, and was an important way in which settlements in Ecatepec were set against each other during the 1970s (Guerrero *et al.* 1974). Also, as I outlined earlier, links between agencies and local constituencies accentuate these divisions, particularly where inter-agency rivalries exist – as was the case under Echeverría. Sometimes, too, local officials will deal differentially to deny one settlement any benefits while apparently meeting the needs of a similar adjacent area. The aim here is to undermine the settlement leadership considered by the state to be non-compliant, and to encourage incipient factions in that settlement, in order to strip away at the recalcitrant leader's support base. In the 'treatment' of such areas, Machiavelli is alive and well.

Elsewhere it is unneccessary to create divisions between constituencies as these exist already. Renters and owners within irregular settlements will have very different priorities about government intervention. Similarly, the different types of land acquisition processes described earlier will require resolution through different agencies: CoRett for *ejidal* land, other federal and state agencies elsewhere depending upon the jurisdiction. Also, on *ejidal* land the regularization interests often lead in various directions depending upon how land was acquired: by invasion, concession, purchase by an *avecindado*, and so on.

Whether or not the goods are consumed collectively or individually will also shape the opportunities for collaboration. For example, unlike water, electricity, drainage and perhaps regularization, which are collectively consumed (i.e. consistently required by the large majority of the community), health and education are 'consumed' individually and ephemerally. Those who have children of school age send them to school, and demands vary according to the presence or absence of children and according to their ages. Not everyone has an interest in school provision. The same argument applies to health: not everyone has a need for medical treatment. Most tend to trust their luck and to hope that a member of their family will not fall seriously ill. If they do, then that individual seeks appropriate medical attention. Hence settlement leaders identify only those services which they know are likely to evince widespread support as the principal focus of mobilization. Here, too, scale is important. In Mexico the smallest institutional level of health-care service commonly found is that of a clinic or health centre. Usually these are designed to serve several settlements. Therefore, if pressure is to be applied to persuade government to provide a facility, it must be coordinated between several communities at the same time. Several factors militate against this happening. Few settlements are at the same level of 'integration' in terms of service provision. Even in adjacent communities the local leadership will generate a different rank order of priorities for future actions. Moreover, the vertical nature of relations between individual settlements and individual politicians and agencies in Mexico acts, quite deliberately, against communities working together in unison. From a leader's point of view, mobilization around a health-care issue which requires collaboration with neighbouring communities is usually a non-starter.

Control through the ideology of social welfare provision

Another basis for division among people whose class status is similar is to shape popular ideology in a way that is non-threatening to the state. The demand for services or goods may be socially constructed by government. For example, the current content of the ecological debate within the Federal District has largely been appropriated from radical and green groups, thereby upstaging their arguments and hijacking their momentum. Likewise, in this chapter I have demonstrated how full legalization of 'clouded' land title in Mexico has been raised by government as a popular need. The ways in which popular ideology is created and sustained have received inadequate attention in contemporary research in Mexico and elsewhere (Tamayo 1995).

Moreover, in the context of health care in Mexico City one should not underemphasize the ideological role that a stratified social security system exercises in preventing the emergence of social action around health-care issues. The population in irregular settlements in Mexico City is deliberately split several ways: some have full IMSS coverage; others have partial IMSS coverage; a few belong to ISSSTE. Everyone else knows that should they fall ill then the Ministry of Health or a local private doctor will provide appropriate attention. There is not likely to be a single view about the necessity for improved facilities, nor about the type of provision that should be sought. In addition, as we have observed, people do not perceive health-care provision as a problem. Most are satisfied with the treatment that they receive. Although objective criteria suggest that health care in Mexico City is inadequate and unequal, the very existence of several different sources of treatment encourages satisfaction with the status quo. Those who want health-care benefits offered through social security schemes know that the most feasible way to achieve it is by securing a job where it is provided automatically, and not by pressing the state to provide it to the whole population.

Neither are existing pressure groups which have won social security benefits for their members likely to press for changes that would make the system more equitable. They will continue to press only for improvements for their membership and fight to maintain their relative advantage over competing pressure groups. As in the past, any future significant change in the nature of health-care provision for the majority will derive from govern-mental initiative and largesse, rather than as a result of organized trades union or settlement mobilization.

THE PARADOX: IMPROVING OR WORSENING SOCIAL INEQUALITY IN MEXICO CITY?

The improvement of urban living conditions

The academic literature on Mexico and elsewhere is replete with assertions that urban living conditions are deteriorating. The provision of housing and services falls behind demand, densities rise, land prices show a dramatic increase, journey to work lengthens, and people slowly choke to death from pollution and contamination. Throughout this book I have challenged such assertions at least *a priori*. If conditions *are* getting worse in Mexico City and elsewhere, then let us, as academics, show the extent and rate of that deterioration. One area where I believe significant improvements may be observed since the 1960s is that of servicing levels (Table 6.5).

Once land has been acquired, the poor turn their attention towards the introduction of urban services such as water, electricity, public transport, paved roads, street lighting, and other public utilities including schools, covered markets and health centres. Unlike middle-income subdivisions where most of these services are provided from the outset, in irregular settlements they are usually provided only when the area is fully settled, and there may be long delays before an adequate service is obtained – if at all. Whether or not a settlement receives a service, and the time it takes

TABLE 6.5 Changing levels of home ownership and servicing levels in different metropolitan cities of Mexico, 1970–90

	Total number of homes (thousands)			Per cent owner households[a]			Per cent homes w/o electricity			Per cent homes w/o inside water[b]			Per cent homes w/o drainage[c]		
	1970	1980	1990	1970	1980	1990	1970	1980	1990	1970	1980	1990	1970	1980	1990
Total country	8286	12 075	16 035	66	68	78	41	25	12	61	50	50	59	43	35
Mexico City[d]	1477	2528	3041	42	54	69	9	3	1	40	31	36	25	14	9
Tijuana	63	97	161	52	52	65	17	11	14	54	43	43	33	34	34
Ciudad Juárez	39	116	171	51	58	73	18	10	4	49	37	32	33	27	21
Monterrey[d]	204	346	456	50	68	83	14	6	1	37	28	18	29	20	10
Durango	32	55	83	60	68	80	29	12	5	42	27	26	40	30	19
Culiacán	58	97	114	71	79	83	38	16	5	65	52	63	68	60	34
Acapulco	41	81	123	65	70	80	33	20	8	37	57	58	56	47	36
Guadalajara[d]	222	401	557	46	52	67	nd	3	3	28	18	16	16	9	6
San Luis Potosí[d]	41	77	129	57	64	74	18	13	5	32	22	13	23	22	9
Toluca	40	63	93	64	63	75	29	13	5	53	35	38	46	24	20
Veracruz[d]	47	80	111	44	52	70	9	6	7	39	36	38	24	20	16
Tampico	40	57	62	45	55	65	15	12	3	47	50	38	25	25	17
Coatz-Minat[d]	39	66	98	59	62	71	28	29	16	63	68	57	40	35	22
Oaxaca	22	30	44	nd	65	72	31	21	2	63	51	45	50	44	23
Mérida	42	90	122	71	77	84	16	7	4	44	36	31	46	40	26

[a] The classification of tenure altered between 1970 and 1980. In 1970 a two-fold classification was adopted: owners and non-owners (which included accommodation that was rented, loaned or acquired through work). In 1980 the census identifies owners, renters and 'others'. Because of the ambiguity of the census form it is likely that some 'sharers' were included under the owner category.

[b] In 1980 more than 66% of households had access to a piped water supply outside the dwelling – either elsewhere in the building or in the same plot. By 1990, this number was 79%.

[c] In 1970 this was defined as a 'hygienic system' for removing *aguas negras* (waste waters). In 1980 it was defined as those without drainage pipes. (The latter would include connections to mains drainage, a septic tank or, occasionally, a hole in the ground.)

[d] In 1970, the Metropolitan Area of Mexico City included the Federal District, Ecatepec, Naucalpan, Netzahualcoyótl and Tlalnepantla. In 1980, Atizapán, Coacalco, Tultitlán, Cuautitlán-Izcalli, La Paz and Texcoco were added. 1990 additions were Chimalhuacán, Huixquilucan, Chalco, Ixtapaluca, Nicolás Romero and Tecamac. The minimum threshold for inclusion was 100 000. Monterrey includes San Nicolás, Guadalupe, San Pedro Garza García and Santa Catarina. Guadalajara includes Tlaquepaque, Zapopan and Tonalá. San Luis Potosí includes Soledad. Veracruz, in 1980 and 1990, includes Boca del Río. Coatz-Minat is composed of Coatzacoalcos and Minatitlán.

before it is provided, relates to a number of complex factors. Resident priorities, total costs and ease of installation, local leadership attributes, and community adherence to the politiking rules may all be important considerations (Ward 1981a, 1986).

The delivery of public services: electricity and water Industrialization during the 1940s and 1950s required, among other things, provision of an adequate and reliable power supply. For many years federal investment in the Electricity Generating Commission (CFE) was a priority area and, once industrial and commercial needs had been met, there was ample supply to meet domestic needs as well. As a result, most households in Mexico City enjoy a private metered service (Table 6.6). Although Mexico City's population is privileged in this respect, and a much higher proportion of dwellings nationally lacked a formal supply even in 1990, most urban areas throughout the country appeared to be reasonably well provided for. Most places, and the country as a whole, experienced a significant absolute and relative improvement in the distribution of domestic supplies between 1970 and 1990 (Table 6.5).

By and large, supply has managed to keep pace with rapid city growth in both the Federal District and the surrounding municipalities. Moreover, many of those households recorded to be without an electricity supply will in fact receive current through informal illegal hook-ups. This practice is especially common in recently-formed settlements, where groups of residents collaborate to buy cable and splice into a nearby overhead supply.

The provision of water and drainage, both nationally and in Mexico City, is much less widely available than electricity. Overall in 1990 just over one-third of dwellings in the Metropolitan Area lacked an interior water supply, although approximately one-half of these households did have access to a piped supply outside the dwelling – usually in the same plot. The data in Table 6.6 suggest a slight deterioration in water provision coverage since 1980, but this may be misleading and reflect the data imperfections of the 1980 census rather than an actual worsening of conditions. Whatever, it is obvious that the austerity programmes of the 1980s did bite into the state's capacity to significantly improve the relative level of servicing. At a national level, and in most other cities, provision is not as widespread as in the capital. The record for dwellings without a drainage system appears to be better, but this lower figure relates primarily to the broad definition of what constitutes a drainage system under the Mexican Census (a 'hygienic system for the removal of waste waters', see Tables 6.5 and 6.6).

Significantly, too, there is marked spatial variation in the level of service provision. At a national level, rural areas are less well served than urban centres. State capitals appear to be better off than other large urban centres, and cities in the traditionally poorer regions such as Oaxaca, Chiapas and Guerrero are poorly served (see also Ward 1986: 88). Those areas in Mexico

TABLE 6.6 Changing levels of dwelling ownership and service provision in Mexico City, 1970, 1980 and 1990

	Total number of homes (thousands)			Per cent owner households[a]			Per cent homes w/o electricity			Per cent homes w/o inside water[b]			Per cent homes w/o drainage[c]		
	1970	1980	1990	1970	1980	1990	1970	1980	1990	1970	1980	1990	1970	1980	1990
Total country	8286	12 075	16 035	66	68	78	41	25	12	61	50	50	59	43	35
Metropolitan Area	1477	2528	3041	42	54	69	9	3	1	40	31	36	25	14	9
Federal District	1219	1747	1789	38	48	65	5	3	1	36	30	28	22	14	5
Ecatepec	34.5	130.2	238.1	67	69	77	27	4	3	61	36	44	55	11	3
Naucalpan	65.3	134.4	158.1	57	59	68	15	3	1	47	36	43	33	13	3
Netzahualcóyotl	90.3	214.1	238.5	66	63	68	40	4	0	68	40	35	41	2	1
Tlalnepantla	60.4	138.8	144.0	56	63	71	17	3	0	49	32	35	35	15	3
Atizapán*	–	36.2	64.5	–	77	83	–	4	4	–	34	41	–	20	16
Coacalco	–	17.7	31.8	–	79	85	–	2	1	–	12	10	–	8	2
Tultitlán	–	24.0	49.7	–	76	82	–	6	2	–	31	34	–	32	17
Cuautitlán Iz.**	–	31.7	67.6	–	82	83	–	4	2	–	26	23	–	25	8
Nicolás Romero	–	19.4	34.6	–	79	84	–	15	3	–	65	66	–	54	27
La Paz	–	16.9	25.2	–	67	70	–	7	6	–	49	61	–	24	19
Texcoco	–	17.6	25.9	–	66	75	–	8	3	–	36	44	–	42	23
Chimalhuacán	–	–	43.9	–	–	82	–	–	11	–	–	78	–	–	56
Huixquilucan	–	–	25.2	–	–	81	–	–	4	–	–	48	–	–	19
Chalco	–	–	54.0	–	–	86	–	–	5	–	–	86	–	–	75
Ixtapaluca	–	–	26.4	–	–	77	–	–	9	–	–	67	–	–	41
Tecamac	–	–	24.0	–	–	80	–	–	3	–	–	57	–	–	20

* Atizapán = Atizapán de Zaragoza; ** Cuautitlán Iz. = Cuautitlán Izcalli.

[a] The classification of tenure altered between 1970 and 1980. In 1970 a two-fold classification was adopted: owners and non-owners (which included accommodation that was rented, loaned or acquired through work). In 1980 the census identifies owners, renters and 'others'. Because of the ambiguity of the census form, it is likely that some 'sharers' were included under the owner category.

[b] In 1970 and 1980 more than 50% of households had access to a piped water supply outside the dwelling – either elsewhere in the building or in the same plot. By 1990, this was above 90%.

[c] In 1970 drainage was defined as a 'hygienic system' for removing *aguas negras* (waste waters). In 1980 it was defined as those without drainage pipes. (The latter would include connections to mains drainage, a septic tank or, occasionally, a hole in the ground.)

City with extensive irregular settlement experience the highest levels of relative deprivation. However, although adequate drainage and interior water supply is still lacking in many settlements, it would be churlish not to note the significant improvements registered since 1970 (Table 6.6). Nationally and in the Metropolitan Area the number of dwellings with an interior supply of water and a drainage system doubled between 1970 and 1980, a considerable achievement, and while the rate of absolute improvement was not sustained, considerable progress continued to be shown between 1980 and 1990. This contributed to the relative improvement in servicing levels that is apparent in Tables 6.5 and 6.6. Yet it is also important to recognize that despite this investment, in absolute terms the position in 1990 was actually worse than that of one or two decades before. In 1990 there were more dwellings without an interior supply of running water than in 1980 or 1970. The same feature appears in relation to dwellings with a drainage system, with the exception of the Metropolitan Area of Mexico City which had approximately the same number of dwellings unserviced as a decade previously.

These figures also tell us nothing about the quality of the service. Without a purifier, water is not, strictly speaking, drinkable. Most Mexico City residents who can afford it buy purified water in bottles or flaggons. Also, the water supply itself is often irregular. During the dry season a common feature of water provision to some of the survey settlements was the irregularity with which it flowed. In Santo Domingo, for example, residents in the late 1970s complained that the authorities may as well not have bothered to install a domestic supply as water flowed only in the early hours of the morning and was rarely sufficient to fill their tanks. Similarly, in many settlements in Netzahualcóyotl and Ecatepec, where water and drainage networks were installed during the mid-1970s, the drainage system had broken down. Subsequent urbanization works and heavy traffic have ruptured pipes; inadequate maintenance means that many drains are choked; while the lack of water means that the system is not flushed clear.

Given these failings, we must treat the substantial improvements achieved between 1970 and 1980 with a degree of caution. Nevertheless, living conditions recorded for Mexico City do point towards a marked improvement during the 1970s and 1980s, and this improvement continued despite the austerity programmes of the 1980s – albeit at a much slower rate (see also Perló 1988). Since 1990 the Solidarity Programme has prioritized the introduction of drinking water provision to poor communities in urban and rural areas to the extent that some 30 million people were benefited, and 97 per cent of those who had no access in 1990 were provided for (although not necessarily in their homes, Mexico SEDESOL 1994: 100).

In this chapter I have shown that any serious attempt to improve social conditions in Mexico City and to reduce existing patterns of inequality are likely to be constrained by the nature of political mediation and the way in which the bureaucracy is structured; by the stratification of delivery systems in many arenas of social welfare provision; and by the disempowering mechanisms that the state adopts towards social groups that might develop a head of steam directed towards mobilization and social change. Each mechanism has, I argue, an overall regressive effect even though the actual content of policies has usually improved, as have the ways in which agencies are charged to carry out their functions more expeditiously and efficiently. Overall, the Mexican system has emerged to deliver a better service *peso* for *peso* in real terms than it did, say, at the end of the Echeverría term, but this has only negligible effect when viewed against the wider structures and underlying state rationale which act to sustain social inequality in the city.

7

THE REPRODUCTION OF THE URBAN FORM: MODERN, 'VERNACULAR' AND POST-MODERN ENVIRONMENTS IN MEXICO CITY

THE RELATIONSHIP BETWEEN URBAN FORM AND SOCIAL PROCESS

Architecture as the spirit of its time

At the beginning of this book I discussed recent theory about the way in which urban environments are created and reproduced. I also speculated about the impact of the so-called New International Division of Labour and Globalization upon urban environments such as Mexico City. I hope by now the reader will appreciate that economically determinist explanations of the city tell only part of the story. Although a Marxist framework acknowledges the importance of social and political and ideological processes, the economic (capital) relation remains paramount. However, in recent years greater explanatory weight has been given to processes of social production of the built environment and to the role of human agency (Castells 1983; Gregory 1987; Hayden 1994).

In Mexico City I have argued that while economic processes have fuelled the engine of urban growth, the levels of poverty and bases of social differentiation, together with the actual nature of city expansion, owe as much to political and social factors as to purely economic ones. There is nothing new about this argument – as I will demonstrate in a moment. Mexico City, like all cities and urban-based populations, is a product of historical processes. History is *reflected* in the ground plan, collective memory, physical structure, design and monuments of a city. Thus, it reflects the spirit of the time (*zeitgeist*): the nub of Mumford's (1938) argument more than 50 years ago. Other writers such as Glass (1968: 48) have described the 'urban' as 'a mirror . . . of history, class structure and culture', while more recently Simmie (1986) in an introduction to a *Sociology, Politics and Cities* series which he edits, stated that cities 'are the places where the results of past and present economic and political conflicts leave their most obvious marks'. However, it is not just the physical environment that is an outcome of historical processes; the population imbibe that local history and create a new history of the city through their own actions or *praxis*. It is an iterative process. There is, therefore, a collective consciousness of the people in the city or, as Castells (1983: 302) argued when seeking to redefine the 'urban', it is 'the social meaning assigned to a particular spatial form by a . . . historically defined society'. Urban meaning is the synthesis of the historical social form and the specific goal of a society – fashioned through conflict between different groups with different stakes.

Whether there is anything intrinsically urban about these processes compared with processes operating in non-urban environments is a moot, and hotly debated, point. Harvey (1985) reduces the analysis to questions of the built environment and the reproduction of labour power, and underplays the importance of any rural–urban dialectic except in the realm of ideology, where, he says, it remains significant. Saunders (1986) goes further and rejects the notion of the urban as a spatial object. He proposes that the distinctiveness of urban sociology is not a particular concern with space, and still less with the city as a spatial entity. Rather it is concerned with a focus upon one aspect of social organization (the state) inscribed in space. He writes (1986: 287) that 'the work of writers such as Pahl and Castells has been enormously suggestive in terms of substantive focus but has ultimately collapsed in the face of the attempt to tie social processes to spatial form'. I do not agree. In the words of another author, 'space matters' (Massey and Allen 1984) and, as I will show in this chapter, the physical form of the city is another means whereby social inequality is reproduced and sustained. This is not new: Harvey's earlier work in Baltimore demonstrated the same proposition. Fortunately, resolution of these debates is not essential to the argument that I wish to develop here.

Although the importance of seeking to understand the conditioning relationship between economic, social and other processes and resultant urban form is widely recognized, relatively little research has explicitly addressed the ways in which, once produced, the urban structure in turn reproduces social relations in the city. In particular, if we look at a city's architecture we may discover both past philosophies and rationale for urban development, and also the way in which the physical structure of the city cumulatively helps to shape contemporary social patterns and behaviour. The city is both a product of the past and, mediated through its architecture and design, assists in creating the now and the tomorrow. This is not to fall into the trap of architectural or design determinism, even though I believe that both may exercise an important, but not crucial, conditioning of human behaviour (Newman 1972; Lynch 1981; Dicken 1986b). Rather, it is to argue that the physical structure of the city (i.e. its ground plan representing past design philosophy (or absence) as well as its architecture), helps to articulate and to reproduce a wide range of processes.

In an excellent review of the post-modern city, Knox (1987) identifies how architecture can be construed as shaping urban reproduction. First, architecture both expresses and shapes culture in so far as it 'fixes' ideas about ideology and aesthetics in the urban environment, so that it becomes part of us, and we it. Second, architecture expresses the social construction of how things get built in terms of a society's laws, regulations, and so on, but it also articulates strong political themes: of *laissez faire* (irregular settlement for example); of *modernization* (such as Lucio Costa's 'aeroplane' design for Brasilia's ground plan and Oscar Niemeyer's modernist buildings); of *repression* (apartheid cities in South Africa, while in the UK and the US a growing tendency for exclusive and policed zones within residential areas); of *environmentalism*; of *populism* and so on (see also Holston 1989; Ford 1994). There is also a hybridization of politics and culture, such that cities and urban form can take on characteristics of other (dominant) cultures – Mexican architecture and culture bending to the dominant US culture for example (García Canclini 1990, 1994; García Canclini *et al.* 1996; Herzog 1990). In many respects post-modern architecture, discussed later in this chapter, reflects and reinforces contemporary liberal and individualist political philosophies (O'Connor 1984; Harvey 1987, 1989). Third, architecture shapes the process of capital accumulation through its representation of new fashions and the fresh opportunities they offer for investment in the built environment. Harvey (1987: 265) argues that 'spatial practices' are not innocent of capital accumulation processes, and that 'Those who have the power to command and reproduce space possess a vital instrumentality for the reproduction and enhancement of their own power.'

A fourth relationship identified in Knox's paper is the one between architecture, legitimation and social reproduction. Building and urban design shape the ideology of urban citizenry or, as Porphyrios (in Knox 1987: 366–7) has it: 'architecture gives back to reality an imaginary coherence that makes reality appear natural and eternal'. Personally I'm not sure about the eternal aspect, since contemporary modern and post-modern architecture may also reinforce the idea of temporal change, transitoriness and redundancy, but the point about architecture's role in shaping reality as it is perceived is both powerful and important. Buildings carry messages. We need to know much more about the rationality and about the authors of those messages. That is the main purpose of this penultimate chapter. I want to explore the extent to which the architecture of Mexico City carries a message, and what that message means.

In earlier chapters I have argued that social and spatial inequality in Mexico City are an outcome of economic and political processes mediated through a range of sectoral activities: planning, the provision of land, housing and health-care delivery systems, transportation structure, and so on. Now the aim is to identify the currents in Mexico's recent architectural history and to evaluate the influence of architects in shaping the nature of the city. Here, of course, one must examine both informal architecture, embodied in self-help, as well as the more formal elements embodied in urban design. I want to know how far the physical design of the city reinforces existing structures of social inequality. Do they, in Harvey's terms, represent and reproduce the 'violence' enacted against the working classes?

Mexico City: the bases of social stratification and their representation in past city form

The focus of this text has been unambiguously and unapologetically contemporary. However, Mexico City's biography spans a greater range and intensity of history than any other city in the world: from pre-Columbian Aztec glory, to colonial capital for New Spain, through independence and occupation in the nineteenth century, through Social Revolution and upheaval in the first two decades of the twentieth century (Kandell 1988; Burian 1997). All this and much more, before the material considered in this book even begins. Mexico City is a palimpsest of these past struggles and, to a greater or lesser extent, these influences remain embedded in the city today.

Tenochtitlán – the city discovered, conquered and razed by Cortés, formed the centre of Aztec culture and its empire. Emerging as an all powerful force in the fourteenth century, the Aztecs founded their city upon a site on which, as was foretold, they saw an eagle devouring a snake (today symbolized and depicted in the national flag). That it was located in the middle of a network of lakes, some of which were brackish, has meant that from the very first Mexico City's history has been concerned with the procurement of fresh water, and this has remained a key issue in the present day (Perló 1988). Part of the original aqueduct still remains. Food was produced intensively on the 'floating' gardens (in fact man-made islands of silt) of Xochimilco on the southern freshwater perimeters of the lake, but the city was built upon violence and conquest of neighbouring (and distant) territories in order to provide tribute, slaves and male warriors for human sacrifice. The social organization was geared to this project. A king priest was selected from a Council of all the Clans comprising men who had progressed through the ranks of individual clans, or *calpulli* as they were known. Each *calpulli* was spatially separate, occupied a particular neighbourhood, educated its children, dedicated itself to a particular trade or set of functions and, most important of all, operated as a fighting unit: a sort of batallion-cum-guild (Valiant 1972; Offner 1984). Social mobility was achieved through leadership promotion within each *calpulli*.

The cosmology of the Aztecs was clearly reflected in city form. It was a remarkable city: one of great splendour and violence. Pyramids and palaces were covered in stucco and painted predominantly white with fiercely coloured adornments (Figure 7.1). The Aztecs were sun worshippers, and the daily procession of human sacrifices quickened during the instability

FIGURE 7.1 Mural of Tenochtitlán (by Diego Rivera, in the National Palace in Mexico City)

associated with the latter years of the 52-year cycle at the end of which all fire would be extinguished, only to be re-lit if the world did not end (Soustelle 1971). Fortuitously for him, Cortés' arrival coincided with the instability associated with the end of one of these cycles. In pride of place before the main temple were the skull racks of thousands of human sacrifices.

The project of the *conquistadores* and the subsequent colonial admin-istration was the subjugation of the indigenous population, their conversion to Christianity, and exploitation of the agricultural and mineral wealth that Mexico offered. The town was the instrument of this process. Churches were raised on the sites of Aztec temples. The symbolism of defeat and subjugation was reinforced by the massiveness and splendour of these churches, particularly during the later Baroque (Figure 7.2). The city plan conformed with the guidelines of the day and subsequently laid down in the 1573 Ordinances or 'Laws of the Indies'. Streets were laid out on a grid-iron pattern, with the principal administrative and ecclesiastical buildings around a central *plaza*, or *Zócalo* in Mexico. The rich built mansions and palaces adjacent to the central plaza, while the poor lived in hovels and encampments at the periphery.

The social structure was built around an élite administrative cadre of appointees from Spain, the peninsular people (*peninsulares*), who domi-nated both politically and socially, and lived primarily in urban areas. The

FIGURE 7.2 Colonial 'Baroque' architecture

agricultural economy came increasingly to be dominated by a pure-blood Spanish descendent group in Mexico. Conflict developed between this *criolla* population and the *peninsulares*, whose domination and control was increasingly resented and, ultimately, was overthrown by independence in 1821. Below the *criollas* in the social pyramid came *mestizos* (mixed Spanish/Indian), blacks and miscegenated black groups (*mulattos*), and, at the bottom of the pyramid, the Indians – or at least those who had survived the frequent epidemics of illnesses previously unknown to them. However, this was not a rigid caste system; there was some opportunity for social mobility and 'passing' based upon economic wealth (Chance 1975).

The nineteenth century also saw an inflow of other Europeans: some from France during Napoleon III's imposition of Maximilian as 'Emperor';

others from Britain and elsewhere and associated with large-scale infrastructural developments undertaken in Mexico City and throughout the territory during the Díaz dictatorship of the last two decades. As I will demonstrate below, the beginning of the twentieth century was marked by an inflow of European ideas and inspiration in art and architecture. Moreover, the original cultural and phenotype mixing has been further overlain by other population streams of Jews from Eastern Europe, Lebanese, and Spaniards fleeing Franco. During the 1960s and 1970s there was a small inflow of refugees from the southern cone of Latin America. Although in terms of total numbers these twentieth-century immigration streams have been relatively insignificant, most groups have settled into a particular (and often important) niche within Mexican economy and society.

Today the majority of the population is *mestizo*. Pure Spanish descendancy carries slight anti-nationalist overtones and is not highly desired, but Mexicans, while being intensely nationalistic, appear subconsciously to deprecate 'Indianness' and 'blackness' and to reify 'whiteness' and European or North American influences. This is manifest in a variety of ways. The rich are more likely to be fair and phenotypically European than dark and Indian. The converse also applies. In advertising, too, sexist and racist images predominate in a much more pervasive way than, say, in the more politically correct UK or in the USA.

In particular the relationship with the USA is highly ambivalent. Mexicans feel an admiration for North American consumerism and wealth; yet resentment at their own nation's poverty and nineteenth-century losses of territory, as well as at the contemporary cultural and economic dominance posed by the USA. This, together with the intense mixing of earlier cultural traditions, has led to what some have described as a rather 'masked' and contradictory national personality (Paz 1961; Franco 1967). It is also an intensely patriarchal society in which *machismo* (male dominance) remains entrenched, and *marianismo* (motherhood, passivity and a long-suffering 'earth mother' syndrome within the family unit) are esteemed, although understanding of these very general terms is becoming much more nuanced and less stereotypical (see Guttman 1996 on contemporary meanings of being *macho* in Mexico City).

The important point to recognize is that Mexicans have a long history, and one that is racially and culturally very diverse history. It is also one that has been particularly violent. While there is intense national pride at being Mexican, there are also many contradictions. A love/hate relationship towards consumerism and the north; vitality and exuberance combined with fatalism and a sometimes morbid preoccupation with death; male dominance fronting male inferiority and feelings of impotence; national pride yet ambivalence towards the US; passivity and violence. As we shall observe, an appreciation of these attributes and elements of personality is important in any interpretation of Mexico City's built environment.

VERNACULAR ARCHITECTURE RULES OK?

Mexico City's contemporary built form may be examined by looking at formal architecture and its inspiration, as well as informal and traditional building processes. Naturally, given its sequent occupance and a highly diverse culture, it is a city with an especially rich architectural history, but it is rich in another respect: that of popular initiative and vernacular housing traditions. Although irregular settlements are not strictly vernacular environments in the sense of their being indigenous to a particular place or culture, they are sometimes conceived as such. 'Spontaneous settlements . . . are next only to preliterate and traditional vernacular settlements in their supportiveness of culture' (Rapoport 1988: 59). In terms of the processes underpinning their creation and the positive outcome ('product characteristics') that arise for user/inhabitants, the two are, he argues, very similar. He concludes that these self-shaped environments are frequently of higher quality than those of designers working within developed or wealthy societies, and that one can learn a great deal by analysing them (Rapoport 1988: 72–3). My purpose here is to analyse irregular settlement not through such rose-tinted cultural spectacles, but to identify the relationship between social process and spatial form, and to ask how the process of *physical design and development* of self-help settlement in Mexico City reproduces social inequality.

Mobility without moving

In terms of population and the built-up area I have emphasized from the beginning of this book that Mexico City is primarily characterized by poverty and social inequality. Around 50 per cent of the population (i.e. more than 8 million) and 60 per cent of the built-up area of Mexico City occupy settlements that have emerged illegally through one form or another (Chapters 2 and 5). Estimates about the proportion of the city population earning around the minimum wage vary between 45 per cent and 66 per cent (Stolarski 1982: 61). Many households have more than one earner and earn somewhat more, but the previous chapter demonstrated how most low-income city residents are obliged to turn to illegal methods of land acquisition in order to get access to housing. Once a plot of land is secured and households feel a modicum of security that no-one is going to take steps to evict the fledgling community, the settlement is upgraded through mutual aid on the part of residents' cooperative efforts, and through government intervention to install basic services and public utilities, and to guarantee security of tenure.

At the individual plot level, households take responsibility for overseeing the construction of their dwelling, each making individual decisions about matters of design, layout, sequence of room construction, materials used and the level of labour power that will be hired, or applied by themselves through self-help. One observes a process of consolidation over time, so that provided no barriers are put in the way, individual settlements pass through various levels or stages of physical development. Agglomerations of unserviced shacks are replaced by brick-built rooms with laminated roofs, until after 15 or 20 years they comprise consolidated, often two-storey dwellings with all services on line (see Figures 2.11 and 2.12). Given that the people who develop and live in their homes are purported to be one and the same, the process is sometimes viewed as offering social mobility through the medium of upgrading, without having to trade up and move from one neighbourhood to another (Turner 1963, 1968b).

As I will argue below, this portrayal is both simplistic and somewhat disingenuous (see also Eckstein 1990a). It is a portrait which emerged during the late 1960s and early 1970s as a result of research that sought to identify the underlying processes of irregular settlement development and their populations (Abrams 1966; Turner 1968a, b, 1969; Leeds 1969). The research findings were partly a response to the repressive policies of many governments of the day, and probably deliberately overstated the positive aspects of self-help in order to turn governments away from policies of squatter settlement eviction and the construction of relatively expensive project housing that accommodated only a small proportion of the total demand. In quantitative and qualitative terms these policies were inadequate (Gilbert and Ward 1978).

Working specifically in Mexico City, Turner (1976) and his colleagues differentiated between the 'supportive shack' and the 'oppressive house'. The former provide shelter at a cost that the poor could just about afford, in locations that dovetailed with their employment, social interaction patterns and other needs. They argued that instead of evicting squatters and razing such areas, governments should seek to support irregular settlers in doing what they know how to do best: design and manage the construction of their own homes themselves, and volunteer labour and time for local community development initiatives. Governments, for their part, should intervene not through full-blown housing developments, but to provide housing 'elements' that self-builders could not readily provide for themselves: namely 'lumpy' services which require large investment and some degree of monopoly control and coordination, such as water, drainage and electricity. Given that security of tenure was argued to be paramount before residents would invest in permanent building materials, the regularization of 'clouded' land tenure was required to give legal title to *de facto* owners. In Mexico the actual manner through which title transfer is achieved has enjoyed different social constructions over time. Today, the usual practice is to expropriate illegally occupied lands, compensate the original owners, and sell back to individual self-builder occupiers (Varley 1989).

Gradually the arguments of Turner, Abrams and others gained powerful backers, most notably through international agencies seeking to intervene in urban development processes in developing countries (World Bank 1972; UNCHS 1982; Linn 1983). By the mid- to late-1970s two types of self-help supported programmes emerged in Mexico and elsewhere. First, sites-and-services comprised the advanced acquisition of land and installation of basic services before self-builders were allowed to purchase and occupy individual plots. Because of high land values in Mexico City, the existing huge demand and the fear that it might encourage further cityward migration, local authorities have been reluctant to develop sites-and-services in the city to any significant extent. Upgrading is the second type of policy prescription, which in Mexico City was politically much more acceptable and desperately needed given the large number of unserviced settlements, and the high levels of insecurity and conflict that prevailed in those neighbourhoods. As I identified in the previous chapter, Mexico City, like most Mexican cities, experienced significant relative improvements in its level of servicing during the 1970s and to a lesser extent in the 1980s.

However, this positive appraisal of irregular settlement has not gone unquestioned. In the past decade many analysts have questioned the wisdom and analytical utility of this approach from a variety of perspectives. Here, in reviewing the critique, I also want to identify how the physical characteristics of irregular settlement reproduce social inequality.

The limits to self-help: how inequality begets inequality

Through romanticizing reality   As I suggested above, the argument that squatter settlements offered an 'architecture that works' (Turner 1968b) could be excused, at least in part, by the desirability of turning around many of the stereotypical views of self-build processes and low-income populations. But to sustain the argument that it reflects a medium through which self-expression, mobility and dwelling adjustments to suit family size and employment situation could be achieved, is to confuse *choice* with *constraint*. It also belies the enormous social costs that arise from living in irregular settlements. People opt for the insecurity associated with illegal land occupations only because they have to, not because they want to (Harms 1976). Setting up house on land invariably unsuited to urbanization, without services, and with young (often infant) children in tow, is a decision not taken lightly, and one which involves ongoing sacrifice and hardship. One settler described to me how it was to squat on the Pedregal, a lightly vegetated recent volcanic lava flow in the south of the city: 'There were snakes and scorpions. We lived in dwellings open to the skies; there were no roads and no buses. There was nothing at all for us in those early days.' For some of us 'camping out' may be fun for a day or two, but we cannot easily imagine the day-to-day and day-long difficulties associated with raising a family in such an environment. These social costs are better understood today than a generation ago, but invariably the underlying optimism still remains (UNCHS 1996).

Living in irregular settlements invokes enormous social costs, and is one way in which inequality and hardship are sustained and reproduced through the physical environment. Conditions may improve gradually, but the lack of services and failure to provide adequate living environments for workers means that the home is the principal medium through which poverty is experienced and reproduced. These social costs weigh especially upon women who carry out domestic tasks and whose workplace is the dwelling (Chant 1985; Chant and Ward 1987).

As well as a gender differentiation there is also a household division of labour, so that these social costs do not fall only upon women. Children, too, are expected to assist, usually by fetching water from standpipes. Men give up their spare time in order to extend and improve the house, while both men and women may be engaged in the Sunday morning *faenas*, or task groups, organized by the settlement improvement association. Men and women are involved in the often protracted negotiations with local authorities for legal recognition, services and public utilities (Gilbert and Ward 1985). Although men often front these organizations, women tend to predominate and do most of the work (Moser 1989). In the *Asamblea de Barrios* organization for example, created in 1986, 80 per cent of the members are women, yet its leader '*Superbarrio*' (who appears dressed in a Superman-type outfit and mask) is a man. Indeed, even when the leadership split into several factions, each was led by its own version of *superbarrio*, and all were men (Greene 1993). For a short time *superbarrio* was joined by a female leader dressed as 'superwoman', but the general principle was for women to provide the rank-and-file support and to stay in the background.

However, despite this hardship there is an apparent paradox that overall residents seem satisfied with their efforts, and are reluctant to condemn the state or local authorities for failing to provide adequate housing. Viewed in retrospect, all the blood, sweat and tears seem worthwhile, and in my various settlement surveys few respondents have expressed regret at their decision to participate in capturing land, whether through illegal purchase or invasion. Most people state that their principal gains have been a *patrimonio* (inheritance) for their children, and the feeling that they could live more freely (*más tranquilo*) in their plots without the inter-family arguments associated with life in a shared plot and especially in a *vecindad* (tenement). Also, while irregular settlements in Mexico City display especially high intestinal disease and illness levels compared with, say, downtown areas, where respiratory illnesses have a higher occurrence due to the higher densities and contamination (Fox 1972), it is probably true that children enjoy a better living environment than those who live in downtown tenements. They have more space, the streets are safer, and there is a higher level of surveillance over the street by neighbours. Also, many Mexico City citizens living in irregular settlements today arrived as migrants from provincial areas during the 1950s and 1960s. Their move to the city, often from impoverished rural areas, together with the relative concentration of resources in the capital, the opportunities for work, and ultimately the chance of securing a foothold in the land and housing markets, persuade them that they have fared very well. Since the early 1980s the buoyancy of self-help processes has slowed down, and families have had to find alternative ways to adjust to poverty (Tuirán Gutíerrez 1992; González de la Rocha 1994; Chant 1996). Moreover, second-generation migrants and today's young working class families appear to be having fewer opportunities to self-help their way towards residential 'satisfaction' than their parents.

Through the predations of other interest groups A second major area of criticism of self-help as a mechanism for reproducing inequality relates to the failure to recognize the functionality of illegal settlement for a wide variety of other interest groups in addition to some of the urban poor (Connolly 1982). Specifically, it is argued that the relatively cheap 'solution' that self-help settlements provide is an important element in the mechanism in which the state reproduces labour power effectively. New generations of workers are born and bred in these neighbourhoods, providing the labour for the future. These settlements also provide a means whereby labour power may reproduce itself on a daily basis: as an environment in which to live. The low costs of acquiring land illegally, and the practice of investing one's time and money in gradual improvement of the dwelling and environment make it a process that is just about affordable to many, but it is also exploitative in several respects. By cheapening the costs of housing (an important component of labour reproduction costs and therefore wage demands), the internal pressures to raise real wages is eased and alleviated. Also, labour is exploited twice over: in the workplace and then at home as 'spare time' is turned over to dwelling production and improvement. Indeed, for women this often results in a triple exploitation since they also bear primary responsibility for household reproduction activities in addition to extra-home paid labour and house consolidation. Hardship – violence to use Harvey's (1985) term – is exercised both at the place of work and through the home.

In Mexico City the rapid expansion of irregular settlement from the mid-1940s was the mechanism through which the urban labour force was accommodated in the absence of employer or public-sector housing provision (Azuela and Cruz Rodríguez 1989). That it was affordable to workers earning a minimum wage meant that demands for higher wages were not allowed to intensify, especially given union leaderships' highly conciliatory relations with the state. (Nor was it likely that NAFTA would lead to a substantial convergence in wage levels between the US and Mexico, no matter how strongly advocates of the Agreement argued otherwise.) Similarly, middle-income groups benefit in so far as low wages allow them to enjoy cheap services from domestic labour, gardeners, chauffeurs, home decorators etc., most of whom will live in irregular settlements.

In addition to industrial capital, other interest groups have also benefited. The market for construction materials has increased, as have multiplier linkages with local retailers and distributors (Ball and Connolly 1987). Although large-scale construction interests would have been equally served by major public projects, the same does not apply to local suppliers and producers. Irregular settlements also offered a reserve of cheap construction labour that could be hired and fired depending upon major contracts at any one point in time. When the large firms did not need their services, there were opportunities for casual hirings in the self-build sector (Ball and Connolly 1987).

Government officials and politicians may benefit to the extent that irregular settlement offers opportunities for political patronage (through clientelism), empire building, or simply a mechanism whereby pressure from local groups may be mediated and dissipated (Ward 1986; Varley 1993). Only when demands threaten to overload the capability of the system to respond and lead to upwellings of unrest do the costs begin to outweigh the benefits (Gilbert and Gugler 1982). Yet this is rarely allowed to happen. On occasions such as the Movimiento Restaurador de Colonos movement in Netzahualcóyotl and Ecatepec in 1969–70, and the upsurge of protest groups in the downtown area after the 1985 earthquake, the government acted decisively to head off unrest: usually by striking a deal with the protestors, seeking subsequently to deform their movement (Gilbert and Ward 1985).

Exploiting the poor through helping them Irregular settlement development also offers a mechanism whereby capital may penetrate peripheral areas of the urban environment which were previously informal and partially protected from direct capital accumulation processes. This process is referred to as commodification. A key criticism that was levelled at Turner was that he focused upon *use* values of property and ignored the fact that even recently established irregular settlements have an *exchange* value in the market. The process of illegal settlement and self-help, albeit informal, is firmly situated within the sphere of capital accumulation and is subjugated to the logic of the dominant mode. For the squatter, Burgess (1982: 66) argues:

> . . . it is not the absence of a technocratic and bureaucratic system, or the absence of legal housing norms, or the sequence of building operations that have cheapened his house, it is merely *the fact that he*

is operating in a different sphere of circulation of capital – that covered by the petty commodity production of housing. He has not escaped capitalism – he is merely in another part of it. [Emphasis in the original.]

Dualist models of development theory and employment structures have been superseded since the late 1970s in favour of approaches which emphasize the integration and domination of peripheral structures within a wider system (Bromley 1978; Corbridge 1986). Equally, it is erroneous to conceive of housing or land markets in Mexico City as somehow separate from overall land and housing production processes (Jones and Ward 1994). With certain notable exceptions (such as the preferential access to some *ejidal* land), the poor are at the end of the queue for land and bid for those areas in which other groups have little interest (Gilbert and Ward 1985). The point here is to appreciate that access to land for irregular settlement in Mexico City has become increasingly difficult in recent years, and the costs associated with consolidation have risen sharply in real terms. Moreover, the composition of these settlements has changed considerably, with high numbers of non-owner (renter) families within them (Gilbert 1993; see also Eckstein 1990a).

In earlier work I sought to analyse the determinants of successful upgrading in Mexico City and compared three squatter areas at different 'stages' of their physical development trajectory (Ward 1978). I wanted to know whether consolidation was largely a product of years of sweat equity invested in improving one's home, family size and structure, employment type, or what? Through an analysis of indices of dwelling consolidation and the characteristics of individual (owner) households, it became apparent that the ability to create an 'investment surplus' was most closely related to higher levels of dwelling improvement. This directed me to examine more closely the relationship between economic factors and home consolidation: number of household workers, nature of cost-sharing, wage levels, etc. In short, I found that income levels, access to employment (wage type and job stability), and inflation rates relative to wages and the costs of building material were the factors which were most likely to affect consolidation. Thus I concluded that economic structural determinants of poverty at the national and regional level will inhibit the potential success of self-help.

From the early 1970s onwards residents of irregular settlements in Mexico City have found it more difficult to achieve the same rates and levels of successful consolidation than did previous generations between 1950 and 1970. This despite (and in part because of) the more enlightened and efficient government policies adopted since 1971 (discussed in the previous chapter). Recent generations are caught in two jaws of a vice. On the one hand, access to wage employment has tightened and real wages have declined, particularly since 1982. Thus the ability to create an investment surplus has been eroded. On the other hand, the costs of irregular settlement housing production have risen significantly in real terms. Land costs have increased, albeit not as sharply as might have been expected given the growing scarcity of land (Gilbert and Ward 1985; Ward *et al.* 1994). The costs of building materials rose well ahead of inflation during the 1970s (Ward 1978). Moreover, the introduction of government policies to regularize land title, to provide services and public utilities, and *to recover the costs* from beneficiaries has meant that a battery of new costs has appeared as a direct result of enlightened support for self-help. (However, it must be noted that these new costs are often subsidized and may not greatly exceed the informal supply costs to which residents are subject before receiving a formal supply (Ward 1986: 102). This point is one that is frequently conveniently forgotten by critics of government intervention and by those wishing to emphasize the commodification argument (Burgess 1985).) In addition, there are concerted attempts to integrate irregular settlements into the tax base of the city by including them on the cadastral register (Linn 1983; World Bank 1991). In Mexico City under Mayor Hank González there was an active campaign to integrate the legalization programme with property tax assessment and levies. Since the late 1980s the Federal District administration has also resolved not to raise the *rates* of property taxation and service consumption charged, but rather to ensure registration and regular revision of the basis of valuation upon which payments are assessed in order to ensure that the real value of levies is not eroded by inflation. More recently still, as we observed in Chapter 3, the tendency has intensified towards full cost recovery and more extensive and efficient tax collection based around land taxes, user fees and urban development rights (*derechos*). This means that most people are paying more in real terms for land occupancy and for the services they consume.

My inclination, therefore, is broadly to support the commodification thesis of Burgess and others (Angel *et al.* 1983; Burgess 1985; Fiori and Ramírez 1987). Residents of irregular settlements are increasingly exposed to capital penetration processes at the periphery (see Ward and Macoloo, 1992, for a more extensive discussion of the 'articulation' of irregular settlements worldwide). Thus, as well as cheapening the reproduction costs of labour power, low-income groups are more actively exposed to capital accumulation processes from real-estate agents, the construction materials industry, public and private utility industries, and the state itself. Self-help is a response to poverty, but it may also reproduce it.

Reproducing inequality through the ideology of self-help   It is not a new argument that a shift towards widespread ownership in society leads to the adoption of more conservative, status-quo-seeking and *petit bourgeois* values (Bassett and Short 1980). The equity component in householding cultivates a belief in the defence of private property, it secures votes, and it individualizes property relations. The struggle for housing as a collective good which is socially produced is thereby undermined (Burgess 1985).

In Mexico City, housing provision is closely tied to a state project of social control. This is achieved in a variety of ways. First, as we saw in the previous chapter, the stratification of housing provision and land entitlement programmes divides low-income (and other) groups into different interest groups which often have to compete with each other for scarce resources. The issue becomes one not of the size of the overall cake, but of negotiating and competing for a slice of it.

Second, ideological and social control is exercised through PRI manipulation and electoral control mediated through the process of self-help (Eckstein 1977; Azuela and Cruz Rodríguez 1989). Popular struggles for land acquisition, regularization, services, and other urban resources have systematically been penetrated and shaped by clientelist community–state relations, initially through the CNOP and the *Oficina de Colonias*; then more broadly through a variety of political and executive patrons and agency heads (not all of whom were PRI*ísta* affiliates or militants) under President Echeverría; and latterly through more technical and less overtly partisan agencies. Where social peace or popular mobilization have threatened to get out-of-hand or to demonstrate a cross-settlement collective response, then the government has acted sharply to head-off unrest through negotiation and subsequent co-option, using violence and repression as a last resort (Montaño 1976). Although the old-style corporatist mobilizations are much less pervasive today, there are many who argue that political clientelism on behalf of the PRI remains embodied within, and is articulated through, programmes such as PRONASOL (Varley 1993; Dresser 1994; Fox 1994).

Third, the heterogeneity of irregular settlement also undermines collective response by dividing settlements on the basis of mode of land acquisition, the stage of consolidation, the servicing priorities of residents, community leadership structures, social classes, and above all tenure relations (owners v. sharers v. renters: see Coulomb 1989; Eckstein 1990a; Gilbert and Varley 1990). These tenure splits multiply still further the constituencies into which people fall or may be divided. One's ideological perspective is likely to be shaped by one's housing status. Renters, harassed squatters and displaced downtown tenants are likely to be more radical and disposed to anti-government demonstration than are those who have, in effect, been bought off by the government through their inclusion in successive housing policies.

Finally, social relations are reproduced through the physical structure of the dwelling environment. Social interaction patterns vary according to the physical design characteristics, as well as the settlement type and location. For example, because of their locational advantages downtown *vecindades* display considerable population stability. Social interaction patterns are strongly localized *within* the tenement (Lewis 1964; Valencia 1965; Tamayo 1995). Nonetheless, apart from contact with kinsfolk in other tenements or neighbourhoods, much of the day-to-day interaction takes place within the same tenement (especially among women). Solidarity in defence of one's own *vecindad* is high. More recently, established tenements in peripheral or past-peripheral irregular settlements have tended to be smaller, relatively more expensive, and have a higher population turnover (Gilbert and Varley 1991). With the exception of single female-headed households, relations between families in these *vecindades* appear to be more restrained (Chant 1985).

In irregular settlements people come from a wide variety of regional backgrounds, and the relatively large size of most Mexico City settlements makes it unlikely that any one cultural or family group from a single region will dominate. Yet even here, social interaction patterns are constrained to the immediate locality. In three squatter settlements analysed in 1973, social interaction patterns showed a high level of localization, which was particularly marked among the poorest households and between women (Ward 1976a; see also Lomnitz 1977). Men tended to be more outwardly orientated, as did better-off households. Thus the physical environment, be it the squatter settlement or a *vecindad*, has an important effect upon the way in which social relations are articulated and reproduced. However, in this case the social interaction patterns probably serve to reduce intra-group inequalities through mechanisms of sponsorship and exchange (Kemper 1974; Lomnitz 1977). Moreover, Eckstein (1990a: 175–6) notes that both the economic crisis of the 1980s and the greater heterogeneity of irregular settlements has resulted in a sharp decline in internal social solidarity, such that these areas can no longer be viewed positively as 'slums of hope' as they were in the past. She also argues that it is in inner cities that one finds greater stability and organic solidarity among neighbours.

Thus, I have identified four principal mechanisms whereby vernacular architecture acts as an important mechanism for reproducing social and economic relations in Mexico City. It achieves this at an ideological level through romanticizing poverty and by focusing attention upon use rather than exchange values, through the privatization and individualization of housing provision, through generating different and competing constituencies, and through the day-to-day social interaction patterns which emerge in low-income settlements. At an economic level I have shown how vernacular housing intensifies commodification and opens up the low-income settlement process to the predations of capital accumulation. Although the adverse outcomes of this process have probably been overstated and remain to be analysed fully, it seems inevitable that the earlier successes of upgrading and self-build are being actively constrained by conditions of austerity and rising construction costs, and sometimes by cost-recovery and taxation arising from government policy. Low-income settlement production, at costs that are broadly affordable to the poor, facilitates the reproduction of labour power which, in turn, benefits a wide range of other social and economic interest groups. While in Mexico City vernacular architecture 'rules', it is definitely not OK.

THE CREATION OF INEQUALITY THROUGH EARTHQUAKE RECONSTRUCTION

Perhaps the most clear-cut example of how Mexico City's government has acted through physical design to reproduce social inequality and to (inadvertently) create social divisions that did not exist before is provided by the post-earthquake reconstruction programme. This programme was focused largely upon rehousing low-income residents most affected by the earthquake in the downtown area of the City. Many of the old tenements were destroyed or damaged irreparably in the September 1985 earthquakes, and despite its strong public commitment to a decentralization policy the government opted for the politically more acceptable solution of rehousing *in situ*. The basis for inclusion in the programme, carried out by a specialist agency created for the purpose (RHP), was the expropriation decree issued very soon after the disaster (Mexico RHP 1988).

The housing reconstruction programme undertaken by RHP in the Federal District enjoyed huge resources and was financed partly through a World Bank loan and partly from national fiscal resources (in approximately equal amounts). Although not openly admitted, the government did not expect to recover its own real capital investment, while the World Bank only expected a 50 per cent return. In effect this meant that the housing was very heavily subsidized, and the opportunity for developing a capital fund for an ongoing housing programme was eroded.

When it finally came on-line in 1986–7 the housing 'solution' was most impressive. Some 28 000 previous *vecindad* tenant households were rehoused, almost always on their previous sites, but now in owner-occupied two-bedroom accommodation following one of four design prototypes. A further 11 650 dwellings were rehabilitated and 4500 homes were subject to minor repairs (Mexico RHP 1986). Traditional components of Mexican architecture (strong vivid colours, central patios, large common entrance archways (*portón*) and highlighted window surrounds) were incorporated very successfully into these designs. The result, therefore, was a high-standard dwelling, with an exchange value of around (then) 6 million (old) *pesos*, yet each dwelling cost little more than 3 million *pesos*, to be paid over an 8-year period. The fact that most residents identified strongly with a sense of *barrio* that prevails in the area (broadly equivalent to 'Cockney' pride in London), together with their being rehoused *in situ*, and continuing to work in the central area, means that very few have sold out (Connolly *et al.* 1991; Tamayo 1995). Most were eager to stay and to enjoy the windfall that, perversely, the earthquake had provided. So, in what ways did this replicate and intensify social inequality?

It has done so through the arbitrary nature in which the benefits of reconstruction fell among people with an identical class and cultural background. Before the earthquakes everyone rented accommodation, which was often very dilapidated and insalubrious. This was a stable working-class area in which people lived and worked in services, or in the host of small workshops and enterprises which abound. Fate determined where the earthquake did most damage, but it was an inadequate government instrument (the expropriation decree) that determined exactly which families would benefit. Thus, families living cheek by jowl in adjacent *vecindades* found themselves in one of two camps: either included in the group to become owner–occupiers and windfall beneficiaries of underpriced, high-quality housing, or excluded from the RHP programme and at best likely to be included in the less well-financed 'Phase 2' programme designed in part to 'mop up' those who were excluded. What was previously a broadly homogeneous social class was split irrevocably.

From the outset a high level of insecurity emerged among the *damnificado* (refugee) population about who, exactly, would benefit. After several false starts, Manuel Camacho (then an underminister at SPP) moved to head the Urban Development and Ecology Ministry (SEDUE) and brought in a new team to run the RHP. The social unrest and the numerous defence groups that had been spawned in the central area were successfully appeased through a Camacho-inspired 'Democratic Accord' (*Concertación Democrática*) whereby beneficiaries were given guarantees about their inclusion in the programme, the nature of the housing they would receive, its costs, and completion schedule (Mexico RHP 1988). Thus, many groups were in effect bought off, while the minority that were excluded continued to fight on, but now in a severely weakened and badly divided form.

This particular experience also sheds light on how a major government programme can come to shape people's aesthetic tastes in housing. The brightly coloured and generally well-designed apartments are what low-income people throughout Mexico now claimed they wanted: completed housing (rather than self-help) and bold bright colours (*vivienda de colores*). Moreover, they began to deprecate the notions of local history and of collective solidarity embedded in the physical form of a *vecindad* in favour of the commercial individual identity of the condominium (Tamayo 1995). In the next section I will examine the roots and formal architectural traditions of some of these designs.

REPRODUCING THE CITY: MODERN AND POST-MODERN ARCHITECTURE

Although many buildings in the city today are international in style and would not look out of place in London, Frankfurt or Los Angeles, they have usually been developed by Mexican-based architects and practices rather than by transnational or US firms and consortia (Figures 7.3 and 7.4). Indeed, some of the most successful and imaginative Mexican architects have won commissions in the US, and a few have successful practices in both countries. To the extent that MacDonalds, Colonel Sanders, FuddRuckers and others have extended their franchise, logos and exterior and interior designs to the city, this has been done through local firms, but naturally without significantly altering the symbol and design of the franchise. However, it would be quite misleading to understate this Mexican dominance. The following analysis is based in part upon discussions and interviews that I was privileged to enjoy with many contemporary Mexican architects. Specifically, I was interested to discover the architectural and intellectual sources of urban design (past and present) in Mexico City as manifest through its buildings and monuments. I wanted to know how far building design was largely shaped by intellectual currents, or was subject to strong suggestive influence by a state seeking congruence and mutual reinforcement between its development project and the physical structure of the city. That is to say, who creates the ideology of urban form and why? And once created, is it self-sustaining?

Eclecticism and denying the past

Before the beginning of the Revolution in 1910 architectural influences were dominated by European styles – especially from London, Paris and Berlin (Ricalde and Sánchez 1984). Centralization, expansion and European cultural ideas dominated during the *Porfiriato* at the beginning of the century, and this was reflected in large-scale, sumptuous public and private buildings that reproduced among other styles elegant French eighteenth and nineteenth-century designs. Sometimes, too, one observes Art Noveau influences, particularly in window embellishments and in the glass of the windows themselves (Hernández 1981). Congestion in the old First Quarter (*Primer Cuadro*) of the city, electrification of tramways, the emergence of private transport for the rich, and the desire to reflect one's social position through palatial houses and gardens had, by the late nineteenth century, set in train a centrifugal movement to high-income residential subdivisions. Excellent examples of these mansions may still be observed in Colonias Juárez, Cuauhtémoc and Roma Norte, all of which were developed during the first two decades.

Many public buildings also drew upon neo-romantic and neo-gothic inspiration. The Palace of Fine Art (begun in 1904) and the Central Post Office (completed in 1907) were both designed by Adamo Boari and provide excellent examples (Figures 7.5 and 7.6). Classical styles were adopted for public buildings such as the Geology Institute and the Ministry of Communications and Public Works (1902–11), and this is also a feature of monuments erected at the time. For example, one of the most famous

FIGURE 7.3 International logos and international styles

FIGURE 7.4 Modernist architecture and sculpture along Paseo de la Reforma

FIGURE 7.5 The Palace of Fine Art

FIGURE 7.6 The Central Post Office

and most loved monuments – *El Angel* – dates from this time, and is a replica of the original in Berlin. Others such as 'El Caballito' (actually Carlos IV of Spain and erected in 1802), the monument to Benito Juárez (1910) and the one to Christopher Columbus, also drew heavily upon the classical style (Figures 7.7–7.9). Such representations were politically respectable in that their source of inspiration did not portray indigenous origins. Rather, they reflected the grandeur that President Porfirio Díaz wished to project, together with the strong sense of affinity with Europe and a rejection of national roots. Mexico began with Columbus' discovery, and the failure to erect monuments dedicated to Pre-Columbian traditions constituted an attempt to erase from the collective memory the violence of the conquest.

Revolution and modernism

The social tensions entrained during the Revolution are clearly represented in the urban fabric – at least once it was over and the country and the city returned to some level of stability. Also influential was the upsurge of a new middle class during the 1920s, and the inheritance of a large throughflow of provincial population associated with the conflict and with the camp-followers of various leaders who came to the city in order to vie for power and to forge the new Constitution. There was a reaction against the reproduction of European 'Academy' styles, even though these continued to be adopted for some private houses, albeit with less ostentation. Of growing importance, especially for public buildings and monuments, were designs which were inspired by the modern and functionalist movements, but which in Mexico brought with them a strong sense of self, vested in sculpture and modelling. It was through the sculpture and the plastic arts that national bases of inspiration were expressed within functionalist architecture derived from the Bauhaus School in Germany. Art Deco represented an excellent medium for Mexican architects to adapt and model in a nationally unique way (Noelle and Tejeda 1993).

Not only was this a period of social change, but the Revolution and the broadening of Mexico's development base heralded the emergence of a middle class that also needed to display its new-found status through residential segregation and private house design. Colonia Roma, particularly its southern section, was developed at this time, as were the new residential districts of Condesa-Hipódromo begun during the 1920s. Architectural designs which predominated at this time comprised houses which gave straight onto the street, sometimes with interior patios. Façades and sculptured adornments were less grandiose and included narrow 'false' balconies, 'colonial' stucco work, and even occasional pre-Hispanic elements. Now that pre-Hispanic roots were respectable, monuments depicting Aztec heroes were raised, and in emphasizing indigenous images there was a conscious attempt to recast national culture recognizing those origins. The violence of

FIGURE 7.7 'The Angel', Paseo de la Reforma

FIGURE 7.8 Statue to Columbus, Paseo de la Reforma

FIGURE 7.9   Monument to Benito Juárez, Alameda Park

the conquest remained a problem, however, given that most of the population was *mestizo* rather than pure Indian. Cortés went uncelebrated, and it
was left to muralists such as Diego Rivera to blend depictions of the violence
of conquest with the violence of industrial exploitation. In his work in
particular, the struggle for national identity became enmeshed with a
depiction of revolutionary and class struggle.

Modernism of the 1920s, proselytizing as it did the principles of func-
tionalism and of anti-bourgeois sentiment, required an architecture that
would serve the needs of the modern age without adornment. Knox (1987)
describes the emergence of modernism as a rejection of the pitched roofs,
ornate cornices, and so on, which represented the 'crowns' of the old
nobility which the bourgeoisie had imitated. Flat roofs and clean right angles
to sheer façades offered a pure interpretation of the spirit of the age –
exemplified in the Ministry of Health and Social Security Building completed
in 1926 (Figure 7.10) and the Tuberculosis Sanatorium in Tlalpan (then a
small town several miles to the south of the built-up area). In Mexico City
the inspiration for these developments came from the revolutionary and
socialist spirit of the Revolution and from a nationalism that was struggling to
define itself. Artists such as Dr Atl, Diego Rivera, David Siquieros, José
Clemente Orozco, and the generation which surrounded them used their
skills and historical (often indigenous) images to fire that definition. Murals
and modelling on public buildings, sculpture and monuments, all sought to

FIGURE 7.10 Ministry of Health

cement this ideology into national and city culture. In some respects these monuments and art closely resemble Soviet socialist realism, such as the monument to the Revolution itself, and resulted in a classic piece of Mexican nationalist Art Deco architecture/monumentalism. It was initially designed to be the *cupola* (dome) of a new Congress building, but it was restructured into a free-standing monument in 1935–6 when funds ran short (Figure 7.11). Other fine examples include the monument to Alvaro Obregón (1934) in San Angel, and the Open Air Theatre in Hipódromo-Condesa, which was laid out in 1927 in the Parque España (Figure 7.12). Many cinemas, hotels such as The Prado (destroyed in the 1995 earthquake), and the national stadium then located in Orizaba Street, were influenced by modernism but imbued with a heavy nationalist spirit. Sometimes they even recast modernism altogether, as in Diego Rivera's wonderful but all too little visited Anahuacalli Museum, hidden in the south of the city and appropriately described to me by one informant as 'pre-post-modern' (Figure 7.13).

For the élite, new residential areas began to be developed during the 1930s in a leapfrogging pattern of residential estate development that continued until the 1970s. For example, Polanco and Lomas de Chapultepec were developed at this time with further infilling of more modest middle- and upper-middle-income housing in Condesa and Cuauhtémoc. Although Mexican modernism continued to dominate throughout the 1930s and 1940s, it was also accompanied by some degree of eclecticism which adds

FIGURE 7.11   Monument to the Revolution

FIGURE 7.12   Open-air theatre, Parque España

FIGURE 7.13   Pre-post-modernism: Anahuacalli Museum, Coyoacán

FIGURE 7.14   Art Deco residence in Colonia Condesa

to the rich variety of architectural styles observed in these areas today. Art Deco buildings continued to abound (Figure 7.14), and this style was also adopted by Mariscal in his completion of the interior of Boami's Palace of Fine Arts upon which work had been suspended since the *Porfiriato*. 'Functionalist' house designs also incorporated intensely Mexican ideas of texture, movement and above all deep colour, epitomized in Luis Barragan's buildings and gardens and which since the 1970s became such an important inspiration to many contemporary Mexican architects (Figure 7.15, and see Figure 7.25). Once again, however, it is important to underscore that these were highly nationalist representations of the dominant architectural credo of the time, and they were inspired by venacular culture.

It is from the 1940s that architectural fashion developed a quickening dynamic of its own as both the élite and the upper-middle classes tried to outdo their peers through status displays in house design, and through residence in the most 'chic' areas of the day. Thus, there is a sequence of residential developments: Virreyes, extensions to Lomas, Jardines de San Angel during the 1950s and 1960s, Tecamachalco in the 1970s, and more recently the infilling and luxurious house developments in and around the old *pueblo* cores to the south of the city (San Angel Inn), Tlalpan and Coyoacán. House design in each of these areas reflects particular fashions that emerged or were created. During the 1940s, for example, this was a process 'prostituted by the bourgeois aberration of "Colonial Californian"'

FIGURE 7.15   Modernist homes in Parque Melchor Ocampo

FIGURE 7.16 Eclecticism: 'Colonial Californian' style home, Polanco

(Ricalde and Sánchez 1984: 54) design, which was becoming popular, especially among private residences in Polanco and in Lomas de Chapultepec (Figure 7.16). Oddly enough, the popularity of this style was encouraged by a radical in the person of ex-President Cárdenas himself, and this led to his taste in architecture feeling the brunt of Juan O'Gorman's caustic irony. Visiting these areas today the heavy eclecticism of different styles (Californian Ranch, English Tudor, Colonial, French eighteenth century with Mansard Roofs, modern etc.) may be clearly seen – sometimes mixed together in a single house (Figure 7.17).

A parallel sequence emerges for the middle classes. On the one hand, social groups wishing to live close to their would-be peers began to 'filter' into formerly élite housing. This accounts for the densification in Polanco and other areas, as well as a turnover and subdivision of dwellings into apartments in Condesa, Roma Sur and other similar areas from the 1960s onwards. On the other hand, the middle classes began to emulate the élite's move to the suburbs, albeit in a less grandiose manner. Residential areas that developed in this way were Del Valle and Nápoles during the 1950s, Satélite in the 1960s, and a series of subdivisions beyond Satélite in Naucalpan (State of Mexico).

This eclecticism is also to be seen in the monuments of the 1940s, notably in the assertion of national pride through the monument to the Mexican Race ('La Raza' 1940), and the Diana huntress statue which is a modern

FIGURE 7.17 Eclecticism: English mock Tudor, Virreyes

(and rather beautiful) representation of a classical image (Figures 7.18 and 7.19). But although some private houses went overboard to embrace the architectural fetishism during the 1940s and 1950s, most houses, public buildings and monuments of the day represent an intensely nationalist interpretation of modernism. It blended indigenous and vernacular architecture with the wider principles of modernist functional thinking.

The legacy of modernization

Within the public sphere, however, modernism and functionalist orthodoxy prevailed during the period of rapid economic growth and increased state intervention in the modernization process (1945–70). Architecture and city design reflect and reinforce this image, and statism is redolent in the early monuments of the period dedicated to the Petroleum Workers, the Child Heroes and the Roadbuilders (Figures 7.20–7.22). Buildings constructed by the state sector were almost exclusively in the orthodox modernist mould, such as the Social Security Institute on Reforma (1947, Figure 7.23), the Social Sciences building at the National University (1946–52), the Miguel Alemán housing project (1949) and that of Nonoalco Tlatelolco in 1960 (Burian 1997). These were often very large-scale projects comprising high-rise housing developments, multiple-department medical centres (Centro Médico), government buildings (Centro SCOP) and the massive campus of

FIGURE 7.18 'The Diana': Classicism with a modern touch

FIGURE 7.19 Monument to the Mexican Race – 'La Raza'

FIGURE 7.20 Monument to the Petroleum Workers

FIGURE 7.21   Monument to the Child Heroes

FIGURE 7.22   Monument to the Roadbuilders

FIGURE 7.23 Modernism: the Mexican Social Security Institute

FIGURE 7.24 Modernism and Internationalism: the Aztec Stadium

University City. Although orthodox modernist in style, Mexican nationalism once again was not averse to experimentation: for example, while the University City comprised an overall design of Mario Pani and Enrique del Moral, it gave free rein to a large number of architects to design the buildings, resulting in a rich plurality of expressions including, of course, large-scale mosaic murals on building façades (of which Juan O'Gorman's adornment of the old library building at the University City is probably the most famous). To some extent this modernization was accompanied by an era of populism, especially during the administration of President López Mateos (1958–64).

Since the 1960s Mexico City has become part of the international scene. Although as I argued in Chapter 1 it is unhelpful to consider it a World City, it nevertheless moved firmly onto the world centre stage, not least through events such as the Olympic Games (1968) and the World Cup (1970 and 1986, Figure 7.24). Indeed, for the Olympic Games, each participating country was requested to provide a large piece of commemorative sculpture, and these were distributed alongside the southern ringroad. Generally the purpose of monuments constructed since the 1960s appears to be one of ideological reinforcement: of the modern, of the abstract, and of the international. Later in the 1960s and 1970s these came to reflect an even greater international content of geometric sculptures and modern high-tech fountains (Figures 7.4 and 7.24).

Modernism and internationalism

As the international style of glass-tinted and cement buildings began to dominate (Figures 7.3 and 7.4), this threatened to dilute somewhat the strong national essence in design that had existed previously. Architects began to move away from a preoccupation and interest in local materials such as stone and marble, and indigenous representation, towards industrialized materials such as concrete and glass. Of course, this was in part related to the growing influence of the Association (*Cámara*) of the Construction Materials Industry and the role of large national firms within it (COPEVI 1978). The state reinforced the process through standardization of designs for hospitals, IMSS and ISSSTE social security buildings, schools (through CAPFCE), and so on.

Although most bread-and-butter design contracts for private-sector development adopted the international style (albeit through Mexican architectural practices), this was not exclusively the case. The principal Mexican architects of the day adopted the international style, but often in ways which made the outcome distinctively a Mexican adaptation. One architect in particular, Ricardo Legorreta, followed Barragan's work, which has been termed the 'emotional' current of the 1940s and 1950s and which looks to vernacular architecture, sculpture, and art for its inspiration. Following Mexican traditions of strong bright colours (purples, mauves, blues and ochre browns) used on exterior walls in provincial towns, together with the love of large monumental archways, Legorreta has developed an architectural style epitomized by large rough concrete textures, elaborate colour, free-standing walls, interplay of bright light and dark shadow and heavy flowing waterscapes (Figure 7.25). Deservedly, his work is internationally renowned and has inspired his own generation of architects in Mexico and elsewhere. He continues to be active in Mexico, and also runs a successful practice out of Orange County, California. He is lead achitect in the South Alameda redevelopment plan discussed in Chapter 2 and which is creating considerable controversy over the international source of financing for the project, as well as over the possible displacement that it would cause to existing residential and commercial land uses.

In essence, two broad types of architecture feature today. There are the buildings for large-scale national and international firms, banks and so on, which often have a particular 'signature' which they wish to sustain. Internationalist in style, these buildings would not look out of place alongside their counterparts in any other large city of the world. They reinforce the ideas of modernity, functionality, domination (of finance and commerce) and usually a lack of individual humanism. There are also those buildings that, as one architect respondent stated, 'try to make a statement'. These arise from the 'emotional' wellspring, and I have already mentioned the work of Legorreta in this context, but there are several others whose work

FIGURE 7.25   Hotel Camino Real, Mexico City

represents a genuine reworking of modernism incorporating traditional or indigenous elements from the past in a way that avoids being 'kitsch'. Leading contemporary architect González de León explained to me that his principal inspirations were the pyramids of Teotihuacán, and the palpable sense of mass epitomized in churches and monasteries of the sixteenth century which had entered his subconscious from an early age. The use of different levels, ramps, pyramidal form, large free-standing walls, heavy shadow, and so on, are features of recent buildings such as the Military College, the Colegio de México, the INFONAVIT building, the Rufino Tamayo Museum, and many others (Figures 7.26–7.28). Furthermore, as I mentioned earlier in this chapter, rich colours, a range of entrance porches and arches, emboldened surrounds for exterior windows etc. were all traditional features that were embodied in the housing reconstruction programme for low-income groups in the inner city. This not only reinforced local residents' links with the past, it has shaped the future demand for state housing. When the housing was handed over to residents, other low-income groups began to demand not just affordable low-cost housing, but they wanted it to embrace the same heavy colours. As I have also commented, it threatened to cement a particular ideology – one of modern condiminiums and individualism, replacing the social solidarity and the sense of place of Mexico's rich inner-city historical patrimony.

FIGURE 7.26   The Colegio de México building

FIGURE 7.27   INFONAVIT building

FIGURE 7.28 Rufino Tamayo Museum

Eschewing post-modernism

The strong element of vernacular tradition that is characteristic of contemporary Mexican architecture goes some way to explaining why post-modern architecture does not figure significantly in Mexico City. The term post-modernism is rather difficult to define – despite its wide usage (Gregory 1987; Harvey 1987, 1989). Broadly it comprises an intellectual and aesthetic current associated with the condition of late capitalism. It is a reaction against the past philosophy that planning and development should be on a large scale, technologically rational, austere and functionally efficient. In architectural terms it is a response to the crisis of modernism and its impersonality. Instead, post-modernism emphasizes the small-scale, the community level, neo-vernacular styles, and the playful and eclectic use of historical imagery. Pediments, columns, arches, scrolls, lanterns, Venetian colours are in vogue – often in a single collage (Figure 7.29). As Knox (1987: 359) states: 'Post-Modernist architecture is characterized by the self-conscious and ironic use of historical styles and imagery, an emphasis on the scenographic and the decorative (as opposed to the compositional) properties of the built environment, and a rejection of the social objectives and determinist claims of Modernism'.

However, it is more than an architectural or design fetish. It must also be seen as a condition associated with the regime of flexible accumulation that

FIGURE 7.29   Post-modernism international style

has emerged since 1973, and it is an important mechanism whereby capital investment in the built environment may be recycled, thereby conditioning social relations around the renewed processes of accumulation (Dear 1986; Harvey 1989). In the United Kingdom inner-city gentrification is but one expression of post-modernist aesthetics and revitalization of capital accumulation. Harvey describes other more contrived schemes (through 'spatial fixes') of consumption and spectacle (US shopping malls, Baltimore's Harbour, Liverpool's garden festival, and so on). Even the latest trend away from gentrification and the 'revanchist' reaction of homeless and other dispossessed groups in inner-city areas of the United States may be seen as a reaction to post-modernism (Smith 1996).

Nevertheless, Mexico City does not appear to have enjoyed a surplus of capital investment that was unable to find a ready outlet in urban development. Prime redevelopment sites have often become available through buying out large (but now unfashionable) homes along main thoroughfares such as Insurgentes, or by acquiring large areas of former open-cast (gravel) mines (and some rather precarious low-income settlements) in the western mountains. The 1985 earthquake damage in the South Alameda threatens to provoke major redevelopment if adequate financing and local authority support can be found. Generally, though, there are plenty of outlets for commercial capital without the need aggressively to seek to evict people from inner-city sites (Ward and Melligan 1985). Nor did the state-initiated remodelling in the historic core (*Primer Cuadro*), accompanied as it was by the construction of a new wholesale market on the periphery to replace the downtown Merced, lead to a Covent Garden-style gentrification and land-use changes. If this was the intention behind Mayor Hank González' development plans, and if the investment capital was available in the late 1970s, then it quickly evaporated during the crisis and did not resurface until the Reichmann International project for the somewhat different area of the South Alameda. In Mexico there has been no significant gentrification in the downtown area (Ward 1993). Thus, although this is more hypothesis than proven fact, one crucial reason why no strong post-modernist current exists in Mexico City is that the logic and imperatives of capital accumulation do not demand it.

However, on its own this would not explain why contemporary public and private buildings, shopping malls, and so on, have not adopted post-modern 'self-conscious imagery'. I explored this question in my interviews with leading architects during the late 1980s. It would appear that one important reason for its very limited appearance in Mexico is that there is *no aesthetic need*. As I have demonstrated earlier in this chapter, a concern with the vernacular would not be new in Mexico City. Much of the built-up area has developed through self-build. Moreover, middle-income private homes have widely adopted eclectic styles throughout the modernist period. More significantly in the case of industrialized building projects is the fact that Mexican architects have always successfully interpreted modernism using traditional and local imagery. Thus post-modern architectural design would offer little that was either new or significant for Mexico City residents. This is not to suggest that post-modern architecture does not exist in Mexico; it does, but on a rather limited scale. A prime example is the very expensive Marquis Hotel on Reforma, which is pure kitsch. Occasional building pediments echo the Venturi AT&T building, but for the most part architectual post-modernism as we know it in the USA and the UK is absent from the Mexico cityscape. Nor does one miss it. In the introductory notes of a recent contemporary Mexico City architecture guide there is no mention of any post-modern current, and only one building is described which is suggestive of a post-modern inspirational lineage (the Research and Post-graduate Centre of the ITAM; Noelle and Tejeda 1993: 124). Some people might argue that some features of contemporary architecture are post-modern: González de León's steel tubes trim, and the roof gardens on the recently-completed Banco de México building, for example (Figure 7.30), but these features are always integrated into a conception that is Mexican. It is neither pastiche nor kitsch.

Economically, too, post-modern ornateness, ostentation and higher construction costs would not sit comfortably in the climate of austerity that has dominated Mexico City through the 1980s, and again post-1994. Even large-scale private investment projects appeared unwilling to flaunt themselves

FIGURE 7.30   Post-modernism Mexican style

and follow what would have been viewed as the latest imported fad from the United States. While there was greater flirtation with post-modern designs during the Salinas boom years (the Hotel Marquis for example), they remain exceptions which prove the rule.

If Mexican architects have never entirely eschewed overseas architectural influences, neither have they wholeheartedly embraced US orthodoxy. While the international style may still dominate today, it is the fact that it is not unequivocally North American that has made it acceptable for most Mexicans, and the fact that today, as in the past, local architects will bring their own indigenously inspired signatures to such buildings and spaces.

It would seem, therefore, that Mexico City's architecture is a very important medium whereby the reigning philosophy and ideology of development are read and made legible to the general public. However, this reading of buildings is not mindless; nor is it directed by the state authorities. Top architects such as Legorreta and González de Leon profess to listen to their clients about details, but will not be instructed about how their designs should look. If a client has a clear idea of the sort of building to be built, then they seek out the architect whose past work is most likely to reproduce that preconception. Architects, and not the state, determine the design form of the city, although the state may have a great influence when it regularly repeats a particular style or signature: for example the schools built by CAPFCE according to Artigas' original design prototype.

Where the state may be more directly influential is in its commissioning of monuments, which represent a more clear-cut opportunity to create an ideological imprint in people's minds. We have seen how monuments in Mexico City deliberately turned away from indigenous origins before the Revolution, but were warmly embraced thereafter – at least until the influence of modernism and internationalism took over. Monuments are probably a better guide to what the state thinks, and what it wants its citizens to think.

8

MEXICO CITY: A CONCLUSION OR AN EPITAPH?

In this final brief chapter I want to offer an interpretation of the likely direction of Mexico City's future development for the *fin de siècle* as well as for the first decade of the new millennium. The massive changes that I have observed during the many years that I have been acquainted with the city advise caution about the accuracy of any crystal-ball gazing. So, too, does the experience of the collective error made in the first edition of relying upon the national (1980) census to inform demographic predictions. Nevertheless, I hope that in the preceding chapters I have mapped out the directions in which existing problems are likely to lead, as well as demonstrated the ways in which citizens, politicians and urban managers have tended to respond as the city evolves. This ought to provide us with a surface upon which we can obtain sufficient purchase to make some interpretation about the future. I do not propose to repeat or to summarize findings relating to individual chapters. Rather, the intention is to draw those separate conclusions together into a wider interpretation of what the future may hold. It is a personal view, not one taken from other texts. Nor is it one that I have discussed with key contemporary decision-makers in Mexico. As I stated in the (1990) Preface, my intention was always to 'call things as I saw them', and, having come this far, I figure that I'm in as good a position as anyone to do that.

In 1978 I wrote a journalistic article entitled 'Mexico City: the city the world will watch'. Rather a pretentious title you might think, and you are probably right. In some ways, though, I was anticipating Mexico City becoming the largest city in the world. More importantly, given that rapid urban expansion in the future will occur largely in developing nations, I felt sure that Mexico City would be an important test-case of whether large cities could survive in contexts where resources were scarce and where poverty was widespread. In short, if the consequences of megacity growth are dire, they will first come unstuck in Mexico City. Much of the subsequent reporting has, exaggeratedly, focused upon crisis flashpoints and visions of an 'ecological Hiroshima' (*Time*, 2 January 1989; see also the original Preface to this volume). Today (1997) I am no longer so sure that Mexico City is the city that the world will watch. The city's sharp decline in population growth rate, and the revisions downwards of its total population so that it lost its place as the largest city, have both lessened the heat and the scrutiny. Finally, the simple fact that the city has not fallen apart and imploded despite continued growth and boom-to-bust cycles, has further reduced the drama.

Although these crises are real, they are not new. One of the advantages of researching back through government reports, newspaper articles and commentaries, and academic journal articles since the 1950s is that one observes that the crisis is ongoing. During the 1950s, when the city was already large by world standards (then 3.1 million), writers found difficulty in comprehending a metropolitan area with a predicted population of 5 million and 8.5 million by 1960 and 1970, respectively. In the same manner, people gasp at the inevitability of there being over 18 million people living in the Metropolitan Area by the turn of the century, and probably 22 million by the year 2010. I am sure, too, that historians could provide evidence of similar preoccupations in earlier decades, and even previous centuries. Although distant-past crises have not always been associated with issues of growth, the content of debates has invariably focused upon servicing, upon getting water into the city, and getting sewage and wastes out. Echeverría's monument to the deep drainage system situated in Gustavo Madero *delegación* is not only a tribute to the huge investment undertaken during the 1970s. It is a tribute to several centuries of labour and preoccupation about water and drainage issues. Perhaps the only *new* crisis in Mexico City is the one I identified in the Preface to this edition: namely, the lack of security and the rising violence that has occurred over the past decade.

Also, academics are unclear about whether or not cities should be allowed to grow. Some argue that the larger the city, the greater the economies of scale, the higher the productivity of labour, and that infrastructural costs do not increase with city size per capita. Therefore cities should be left to grow (Richardson 1973, 1976). Others urge caution and suggest that there are intervening variables that determine greater productivity (such as better labour supply and infrastructure) which do not relate to large city size and agglomeration economies. Smaller cities are easier to manage and less likely to be dependent upon sophisticated planning devices (Gilbert 1976b). Better, therefore, where possible, to keep them small. Others argue that city growth, left to its own devices, may undergo 'polarization reversal' whereby previous tendencies towards regional disparities are turned around as the growth rates of secondary cities come to exceed those of the metropolitan centre (Townroe and Keen 1984; but cf. Gwynne 1985; Gilbert 1996).

It may be important to resolve these questions in the context of decentralization efforts and contemporary patterns and policies of city growth in developing countries, but in the context of Mexico City they do not matter a jot. The city is already enormous, and as I argued in Chapter 2, it will continue to grow further notwithstanding the significant decline in growth rates that has been achieved since the late 1970s. The crisis is ongoing, but so, too, are citizens' responses and initiatives. So is public policy, and we have observed important advances and reforms that may be expected to impact positively upon future citizens. Therefore, we need to recast the questions. To what extent will future populations of Mexico City be capable of confronting and coping with city growth? And what measures, if any, will improve the chances of success?

In response to the first question, I am cautiously optimistic, despite my criticisms throughout this book about the underlying lack of political commitment demonstrated by successive governments towards *genuine* resolution of city problems and inequality. Nor do I believe in the inevitability of deteriorating living conditions that many contemporary Marxists espouse. I am optimistic for two basic reasons. First, because Mexican citizens are enormously resourceful and have survived rapid and dysfunctional urban growth in the past – albeit at great social costs. Second, because a political commitment appears to be emerging capable of fostering the consolidation of a truly democratic structure in Mexico. It must, and will I am sure, adjust, but not, one hopes, in the direction of repression (although that is always a possibility). Whether it will adjust far enough and quickly enough is the critical question.

In terms of the city's growth and physical expansion, the crisis really turns on what is achieved outside the Federal District. Assuming that there will be no amalgamation of the DF and Estado de México political entities, then success or failure will really depend upon what the State of Mexico government is capable of achieving. In 1984, 64 per cent of the population lived in the DF; the remainder outside. By the year 2000 it will be roughly 50:50. Between 1980 and 2000 most *delegaciones* will have grown slowly, if at all. The large proportion of growth, therefore, is taking place in the State of Mexico – especially in those outer-ring municipalities of the Metropolitan Zone (see Figure 1.1). Thus far, however, I have observed little evidence of any capacity and vision from the State of Mexico authorities to plan for that growth. Most of my focus in this book, as well as that of government and academic analysts, has been towards the past and current weighting of population in the city. We have failed to look adequately at the precise area where the battle over future city growth will be won or lost.

In terms of city structure, my optimism is based upon the evidence that I have identified (largely in Chapter 2) for a reordering of land uses along the lines that have occurred in the past. Despite considerable population loss from the central *delegaciones* since 1970, the inner city retains its vibrancy and popular culture. Elsewhere, sub-centres in the city, often built around old *pueblo* cores, have become the important foci in people's daily lives. This process has been harnessed and stimulated by planning policy throughout the Metropolitan Area during the past 20 years. Mexico City has become firmly multicentred, and people have adjusted to its growth by relating increasingly to a relatively small part. This has been accompanied by important shifts in the appropriate location of industry and other land uses.

Another reason for my optimism relates to the emergence of a planning process in the Federal District, although this has been ephemeral. Exhortation from technicians and academics about the virtues and need for planning will not count for terribly much, but I am confident that politicians will realize that the political advantages outweigh any loss of personalistic and idiosyncratic control. I am not especially impressed by the actions of recent DF planning teams and mayors whose approach has been to respond reflexively by seeking to manage problems as they arise, or as they are constructed from the wider debate (public security, ecology etc.). Initiatives in urban development amounted to superficial 'bread and festival'-type actions (mini-urbanismo) which patently are not good enough. However, this may be expected to change now that the *regencia* has become an elected office of governor of the Federal District. Planners and the planning office will almost certainly play a more prominent part in both proactive and reactive politics of city development.

The second principal consideration central to Mexico City's future relates to changes achieved in its political structure. In Chapter 3 I identified how social mobilization in Mexico has been mediated by the state, first through clientelism and more recently through civic neighbourhood councils. However, neither mechanism proved adequate in circumventing either the emergence of independent urban social movements such as the CONAMUP during the late 1970s and early 1980s, or the CUD and the *Asamblea de Barrios* in the decade after the earthquake. Nor has it offset the electoral swing in favour of the opposition parties. In my view, the originating rationale for the creation of the DF Representative Assembly was to head off demands for a fully elected local congress and for direct elections of City Hall officials along the lines that exist in all other Mexican states. While I expected some movement towards a local congress, I was less sanguine about direct elections for the Mayor and sub-mayors. However, the electoral and political reforms since 1990 have provided sufficient momentum to persuade the national government and the PRI to give up what was, fundamentally, an anti-democratic political structure. The 6 July 1997 elections of a chief executive (Governor) for the Federal District represents a major advance in improving the quality of governance in Mexico City because it takes citizens much closer to what I had identified as two imperatives for Mexico City's urban development.

The first imperative relates to the allocation of responsibility for the built-up area/metropolitan zone. This must take the form of a *single political authority* capable of creating a comprehensive and integrated strategy of metropolitan development. As I mentioned above, events are occurring outside the DF which affect both it and the Metropolitan Area at large, yet the DF is currently powerless to respond. Moreover, some hard decisions about financing overall city development have to be taken, and these can only be confronted by a single executive charged with responsibility for the whole area. Perhaps some sort of Greater London Council (GLC)-type arrangement might serve. This tier of metropolitan government might even leave the municipal structure broadly intact and not require major revision to the political administrative organization of the State of Mexico. However, it would require a new level of executive authority responsible for overall strategy and direction to which municipalities or their borough equivalents would be bound. The fact that the GLC was wound up by the Conservative Government was not because it was ineffective or moribund, but rather that it worked too well! Central government resented its power and the fact that it was able to present strategies and policies that were abhorrent to the Conservatives. For Mexico City it is precisely this sort of metropolitan executive authority and leadership that is required. It is significant that the debates over the need in London for a 'strategic authority' (council) and an elected mayor have come to the fore as part of the Labour Party's programme. While the Labour Party is committed to restoring some level of metropolitan government to Londoners, the arguments for and against an elected mayor bore a remarkable resemblance to those discussed in Chapter 3 in the context of Mexico City. Somewhat to my surprise, from 1997 onwards Mexico *will* have an elected political heavyweight in the President's backyard, but it will still not have a metropolitan tier of government. It seems likely that in London, too, a metropolitan tier of government will soon be restored, with an elected chief executive and a small elected representative assembly – very similar to the arrangement about to be implemented in the DF (HMSO 1997). The principal difference, however, is that in London the new authority will cover the full metropolitan area, not just one-half of it.

Mexico City is unlikely to see the creation of a metropolitan authority in the short term, but it may be that there will be much greater effective coordination and mutual support now that the PRD controls the Federal District, the Representative Assembly, many of the metropolitan congressional districts, and several key contiguous metropolitan municipalities, particularly in the east. Granted, such coordination and collaboration was never a feature when PRI officials were in control, but this was due to intra-party competition between *camarillas*, as I have demonstrated in earlier chapters. If the PRD proves to be less hidebound by similar internal divisions then more active collaboration may be forthcoming, although this will still fall far short of the sort of metropolitan structure that I and others (Castillo *et al.* 1995) are proposing.

The second imperative comprises the relationship between that hypothetical metropolitan executive and citizens. In my view, only a strategy that forms part of an agenda or manifesto of a *political party elected to power* has the ultimate authority and legitimacy to be implemented. If it falls short in its implementation, then people will want to know why. We are talking here of empowerment, of the people, of their elected representatives, and of the *government*. This is why the election of DF governor is such an important step for Mexico, and why the election of 'opposition' (non-PRI) mayors and governors around the country has been so significant. It has brought party politics back into governance (cf. Martínez Assad 1996). New approaches to local government are being adopted, and this has had an important demonstration effect upon the PRI, although whether this is too late for it to remain the dominant party remains to be seen. Allowing some opportunities for incumbent re-election (probably with term limits) would intensify the incentives for more responsible and responsive government, as would a reform of the basis upon which city councils are integrated. These are the probable next steps, although they may not come until after 2000.

Ultimately, though, governing Mexico City is likely to prove far from easy, and there is no assurance of success. An opposition party Governor might easily fall flat on his face. Perhaps the city is ungovernable. This brings me to my third proposition regarding the city's future, and it relates to the content of policies and their implementation. I have argued in this volume and elsewhere that government in Mexico is becoming more technocratic in its approach. Nowhere has this been more obvious than in the Federal District, where politicians, agency heads, and functionaries, have depended far less upon PRI patronage for their jobs. More important is the fact that in most realms of city and sectoral management, policies are much more in tune with people's needs and with a state-of-the-art technical understanding of policy alternatives. There is greater efficiency, tighter budgetary controls, and above all more appropriate policies which affect people's needs. In real terms, *peso* for *peso*, citizens do far better today than during the 1970s.

The improvement in servicing levels, the more sensitive and realistic housing policies, the emergence of a planning structure and process, and the vastly extended and improved transportation system, greater ecological awareness, and so on, have all had a real and positive impact upon the lives and life chances of Mexico City citizens. In none of these cases is there any cause for complacency, but the achievements are real. That they have occurred at all may be explained by the intensifying crisis during the 1970s and 1980s and the need for the state to respond. In so doing, the state was obliged to confront interest groups which earlier it might have protected. Also, as we have seen throughout this book, the state has undertaken action in ways that have sought to improve objective conditions while at the same time pacify, divide and stratify low-income populations.

Whether future Mexico City governments will be able to continue to offset social unrest through efficient management and improved delivery of urban goods I very much doubt. The 1988 and 1997 election results suggest that people are no longer impressed that they can, nor convinced that they will. The city will survive, but unless further reforms and changes along the lines that I have identified are undertaken soon, it will never thrive. My optimism, my admiration for the resourcefulness of Mexican people, and my analysis of Mexico City's recent past suggest that I should not write its epitaph: not yet, and hopefully never.

NOTES

Chapter 5

1. In part the views expressed in this chapter are informed by my own participation within that process. In 1978–9 I was engaged full time as adviser to the department concerned with the elaboration of urban development plans in the then recently established Urban Planning Ministry (SAHOP). I am grateful to Arq Roberto Eibenshutz (then General Director of Population Centres) and to Arq Javier Caraveo, a colleague at that time and subsequently director of the DF Urban Development Plan and its first chief executive as Head of Planning 1980–4. Multiple discussions with both have informed much of the analysis (although responsibility for the opinions expressed is entirely my own).

2. Although it was still a significant piece of legislation, the final version was a substantially diluted version of an earlier draft which contained a wide range of radical proposals aimed at confronting land speculation and the imposition of some form of urban land reform (Saldivar 1981). Passage of the law generated intense conflict between the state and the more powerful oligarchic groups, but this probably emanated more from the latter's hatred of Echeverría and his economic policies than from an intrinsic reaction to the proposals contained in the draft legislation. Whichever, the Executive back-pedalled, and the law that was passed contained a large number of general objectives to regulate and order human settlements into urban systems, to plan for improved access to employment and public utilities, to conserve the environment, to exercise control over the real-estate market, and to encourage public participation in the resolution of urban problems (Mexico SAHOP 1979). The Human Settlements Law was substantially reformed and strengthened in 1993 (under PRD Committee Chairmanship).

3. These data are derived from a content analysis of all legislation about planning published in the *Diario Oficial* since 1928 (see also Gil Elizondo 1987; Castillo *et al.* 1995).

4. The overall director of this programme was Manuel Camacho while he was undersecretary at SPP. His immediate boss was Carlos Salinas, later President.

5. A further reason for low levels of collaboration is that it is unlikely that two planning departments will have roughly equal status at any time. The influence of one group is likely to be waxing or waning with respect to the other. It would be a magnanimous gesture for that department which was on the 'up' to assist its less fortunate counterpart. Therefore, at best one is likely to find little more than active communication between departments; at worst each will attempt to undercut the initiatives of the other. Post-1982 evidence of more active informal collaboration between the Planning Department of the Federal District and the Directorate of Urban Development and Housing in the State of Mexico is the exception that proves the rule. Both 'teams' emerged from the same group of one directorate in SAHOP and were therefore ex-colleagues and often personal friends.

6. At this time I was full-time adviser to the responsible officer at SAHOP, and I am therefore in a position to speculate about the reasons for this rather unprece-

dented request to another ministry to prepare the Federal District Plan. It appears to have been prompted by the continuance in office of the planning chief, whom Mayor Hank González did not trust. In the event she was eventually replaced, yet responsibility for the Plan remained primarily with SAHOP. Undoubtedly an important consideration was the close political alliance between personnel in the *DDF* and in SAHOP. (For a fuller discussion see Ward 1981b: 56–7.) However, by the time that SAHOP officials had submitted estimates and outlines of the new plan, it appears that the Mayor had won his battle within the cabinet and secured the necessary financial appropriations. As for protest on the streets and in the press, the *DDF* made minor concessions: the trees were removed for 'replanting' in Chapultepec Park; residents and tenants were compensated or bribed to leave. The proposal to place the contract with SAHOP was therefore withdrawn, although it was later revived.

Chapter 6

1. The reader is referred to a previous version of this matrix, together with the counterparts for Bogotá and Valencia (Gilbert and Ward 1985).
2. The history of land transfers before they came to be in the hands of the developers is interesting. Briefly, it was originally federal land which was privatized during the 1920s at low cost on the understanding that it would be improved for agricultural purposes (*bonificación*). These improvements were not undertaken and the government sought the restitution of the lands under its ownership. This led to litigation and the Supreme Court found against the Government (Guerrero *et al.* 1974). Thereafter, during the 1940s, the land began to change hands and prices rose.
3. A similar stratification pattern exists for housing provision, and if space permitted a parallel argument could be developed similar to that of health care. See Ward (1990) for details and a figure showing the stratification and levels of housing production by institutions over time.
4. At first sight these distances may appear not unreasonable. However, they are conservative estimates based upon crow-flight distances and make no allowances for inefficient transport networks and transport systems. They are also averages, and include the low distances associated with intra-settlement treatment. Also, one should bear in mind that few people in London would expect to travel more than 2 km to see their local GP, and not a great deal further to a hospital casualty department.

LIST OF ABBREVIATIONS

AURIS	Acción Urbana y de Integración Social
BANOBRAS	Banco Nacional de Obras y Servicios Públicos
BNH	Banco Nacional de Habitacão (Brazil)
BNHUOPSA	Banco Nacional Hipotecario Urbano de Obras Públicas
CANACINTRA	Cámara Nacional de la Industria de Transformación
CAPFCE	Comité Administrador del Programa Federal de Construcción de Escuelas
CAVM	Comisión de Agua del Valle de México
CEAS	Comisión Estatal de Aguas y Saneamiento
CFE	Comisión Federal de Electricidad
CNC	Confederación Nacional Campesina
CNOP	Confederación Nacional de Organizaciones Populares
CODEUR	Comisión de Desarrollo Urbano
CONAMUP	Coordinadora Nacional del Movimiento Urbano Popular
CONAPO	Consejo Nacional de Población
CONASUPO	Companía Nacional de Subsistencias Populares
CONCAMIN	Confederación de Cámaras Industriales de los Estados Unidos Mexicanos
CONCANACO	Confederación de Cámaras Nacionales de Comercio
COPARMEX	Confederación Patronal de la República Mexicana
COPEVI	Centro Operacional de Poblamiento y Vivienda
COPLADE	Comisión para la Planeacioń del Desarrollo del Estado
COPLAMAR	Coordinación General del Plan Nacional de Zonas Deprimidas y Grupos Marginados
CoRett	Comisión para la Regularización de la Tenencia de la Tierra
COTREM	Coordinación del Transporte en el Estado de México
COVITUR	Comisión Técnica de la Vialidad y Transporte
CTM	Confederación de Trabajadores Mexicanos
CUD	Coordinación Unica de Damnificados
DDF	Departamento del Distrito Federal
DF	Distrito Federal
DGAyS	Dirección General de Aguas y Saneamiento (DDF)
DGCP	Dirección General de Centros de Población (SAHOP)
DGCOH	Dirección General de Construcción y Operación Hidráulica (DDF)

DGHP	Dirección General de Habitación Popular (DDF)
ECLA	Economic Commission for Latin America (United Nations)
FIDEURBE	Fideicomiso de Interés Social para el Desarrollo Urbano de la Ciudad de México
FINEZA	Fideicomiso de Netzahualcóyotl
FOGA	Fondo de Garantía de Vivienda
FONHAPO	Fondo Nacional de Habitación Popular
FOVISSSTE	Fondo de la Vivienda ISSSTE
IBRD	International Bank for Reconstruction and Development
IMF	International Monetary Fund
IMSS	Instituto Mexicano del Seguro Social
INDECO	Instituto Nacional de Desarrollo de la Comunidad
INFONAVIT	Instituto Nacional del Fondo de Vivienda para los Trabajadores
INPI	Instituto Nacional de Protección a la Infancia
INVI	Instituto Nacional de Vivienda
ISSSTE	Instituto de Seguridad y Servicios Sociales de los Trabajadores al Servicio del Estado
MRC	Movimiento Restaurador de Colonos
NAFTA	North American Free Trade Agreement
OPEC	Organization of Petroleum-Exporting Countries
PAN	Partido Acción Nacional
PARM	Partido Auténtico de la Revolución Mexicana
PCM	Partido Comunista Mexicano
PCP	Procuraduría de Colonias Populares
PDM	Partido Demócrata Mexicano
PEMEX	Petróleos Mexicanos
PFCRN	Partido Frente Cardenista de Reconstrucción Nacional
PFV	Programa Financiero de Vivienda
PIDER	Programa de Impulso Desarrollo Rural
PICCA	Programa Intergal contra la Contaminación Atmosférica en la Zona Metropolitana de la Cd. de México
PIHLU	Public Intervention, Housing and Land Use in Latin American Cities
PMS	Partido Mexicano Socialista
PMT	Partido Mexicano de los Trabajadores
PNR	Partido Nacional Revolucionario
PPS	Partido Popular Socialista
PRD	Partido de la Revolución Democrática
PRI	Partido Revolucionario Institucional
PRM	Partido de la Revolución Mexicana
PROFEPA	Procuraduría Federal de Protección al Ambiente
PRONAL	Programa Nacional de Alimentación
PRONASOL	Programa Nacional de Solidaridad

PRUPE	Programa de Reorganización Urbana y Protección Ecológica (DDF)
PST	Partido Socialista de los Trabajadores
RHP	Renovación Habitacional Popular
SAM	Sistema Alimentario Mexicano
SAHOP	Secretaría de Asentamientos Humanos y Obras Públicas
SARH	Secretaría de Agricultura y Recursos Hidráulicos
SEDESOL	Secretaría de Desarrollo Social
SEDUE	Secretaría de Desarrollo Urbano y Ecología
SEMARNAP	Secretaría de Medio Ambiente, Recursos Naturales y Pesca
SEPAFIN	Secretaría de Patrimonio y Fomento Industrial
SHCP	Secretaría de Hacienda y Crédito Público
SPP	Secretaría de Programación y Presupuesto
SRA	Secretaría de la Reforma Agraria
SRH	Secretaría de Recursos Hidráulicos
SSA	Secretaría de Salubridad y Asistencia
SUDENE	Superintendency for Development in North-East Brazil
UAM	Universidad Autónoma Metropolitana
UNAM	Universidad Nacional Autónoma de México
WHO	World Health Organization

LIST OF FIGURES

LIST OF TABLES

REFERENCES

Abrams, C. (1966). *Squatter Settlements: the problem and the opportunity*. Department of Housing and Urban Development, Washington, DC.

Aguilar Barajas, I. (1992). 'Descentralización industrial y desarrollo regional en México, 1970–1980', pp. 101–44, in A.G. Aguilar (ed.) *Política regional, ciudades medias y desconcentración urbana*. Instituto de Geografía, número especial, UNAM; Mexico DF.

Aguilar Camín, H. and Meyer, L. (1993). *In the Shadow of the Mexican Revolution*. University of Texas Press, Austin, TX.

Aguilar Martínez, G. (1987). 'Urban planning in the 1980s in Mexico City: operative process or political facade?' *Habitat International*, 11: 23–38. Spanish translation in *Estudios demográficos y urbanos*, 1987, Vol. 5, pp. 273–99.

Aguilar Martínez, G. (1988). 'Community participation in Mexico City: a case study', *Bulletin of Latin American Research*, 7: 22–46.

Aguilar Martínez, G. (1993). 'La ciudad de México y las nuevas dimensiones de la reestructuración metropolitana', pp. 25–51 in L.F. Cabrales-Bajaraes (ed.) *Espacio urbano, cambio social y geografía aplicada*. Universidad de Guadalajara, Guadalajara.

Aguilar Martínez, A. and Graizbord, B. (1992). Las ciudades medias y la política urbano-regional: experiencias recientes en México. *Boletín del Instituto de Geografía*, Instituto de Geografía, Mexico.

Aguilar, A.G., Graizbord, B. and Sánchez Crispín, A. (1996). *Las ciudades intermedias y el desarrollo regional en México*. Consejo Nacional para la Cultura y las Artes, Mexico.

Aguilar Villanueva, L.F. (1996). 'El federalismo mexicano: funcionamiento y tareas pendientes', pp. 109–52 in A. Hernández Chávez (ed.) *Hacia un nuevo federalismo?* El Colegio de México and Fondo de Cultura Económica, Mexico.

Alonso, J. (ed.) (1980). *Lucha urbana y acumulación de capital*. Ediciones de la Casa Chata, Mexico DF.

Amin, S. (1974). *Accumulation on a World Scale: a critique of the theory of underdevelopment*. Monthly Review Press, New York.

Angel, S., Archer, R., Tanphiphat, S. and Wegelin, E. (eds) (1983). *Land for Housing the Poor*. Select Books, Singapore.

Angiotti, T. (1993). *Metropolis 2000: planning, poverty and politics*. Routledge, London.

Arias, P. and Roberts, B. (1985). 'The city in permanent transition', pp. 149–75 in J. Walton (ed.) *Capital and Labour in the Urbanized World*. Sage, London.

Arnold, L. (1988). *Bureaucracy and Bureaucrats in Mexico City, 1742–1835*. Arizona University Press, Tucson, AZ.

Arreola Ayala, A. (1995). 'Ley de participación ciudadana: avance o letra muerta?' *Asamblea*, 1: 30–32.

Arrom, S. (1985). *The Women of Mexico City, 1790–1912*. Stanford University Press, Stanford, CA.

Assies, W. (1992). *To Get Out of the Mud: neighbourhood associativism in Recife, 1964–1988*. CEDLA Latin American Studies Monograph No. 63, Amsterdam.

Austin (1994). 'The Austin memorandum on the Reform of Art.27, and its impact upon the urbanization of the ejido in Mexico', *Bulletin of Latin American Research*, 13: 327–35.

Aziz Nassif, A. (1994). *Chihuahua: historia de una alternativa*. La Jornada Ediciones and CIESAS, Mexico DF.

Azuela, A. and Cruz Rodríguez, M.S. (1989). 'La institucionalización de las colonias populares y la política urbana en la ciudad de México (1940–1946)', *Sociológica*, 4: 111–33.

Badcock, B. (1984). *Unfairly Structured Cities*. Blackwells, Oxford.

Bailón, M.J. (1995). 'Municipios, opposition mayorships and public expenditure in Oaxaca', pp. 205–19 in V. Rodríguez and P. Ward (eds) *Opposition Government in Mexico*. University of New Mexico Press, Albuquerque, NM.

Balán, J. (1982). 'Regional urbanization and agricultural production in Argentina: a comparative analysis', pp. 35–58 in A. Gilbert, J. Hardoy and R. Ramírez (eds) *Urbanization in Contemporary Latin America*. Wiley, Chichester.

Balán, J., Browning, H. and Jelin, E. (1973). *Men in a Developing Society: geographic and social mobility to Monterrey, Mexico*. University of Texas Press, Austin, TX.

Balchin, P. and Bull, G. (1987). *Regional and Urban Economics*. Harper and Row, London.

Ball, M. and Connolly, P. (1987). 'Capital accumulation in the Mexican construction industry 1930–82', *International Journal of Urban and Regional Research*, 11: 153–71.

Barberán, J., Cárdenas, C., López Monjardin, A. and Zavala, J. (1988). *Radiografía del fraude: análisis de los datos oficiales del 6 de julio*. Nuestro Tiempo, Mexico.

Bassett, K. and Short, J. (1980). *Housing and Residential Structure*. Routledge & Kegan Paul, London.

Bassols Ricárdez, M. and Corona Martínez, R. (1993). 'La asamblea de representantes del Distrito Federal: una reforma que nadie quería?' pp. 339–72 in A. Bassols Batalla, G. González Salazar and J. Delgadillo Macías (eds) *Zona metropolitana de la ciudad de México, complejo geográfico, socioecónomico y político: qué fue, qué es y qué pasa*. Instituto de Investigaciones Económicas, Universidad Nacional Autónoma de México, Mexico DF.

Batley, R. (1982). 'Urban renewal and expulsion in São Paulo', pp. 231–62 in A. Gilbert, J. Hardoy and R. Ramírez (eds) *Urbanization in Contemporary Latin America*. Wiley, Chichester.

Bazdresch, C. (1986). 'Los subsidios y la concentración en la ciudad de México', pp. 205–18 in B. Torres (ed.) *Descentralización y democracia en México*. El Colegio de México, Mexico.

Beauregard, R. (1989). 'City profile: Philadelphia', *Cities*, 6: 300–8.

Beauregard, R. (1993). *Voices of Decline: the postwar fate of US cities*. Blackwells, Oxford.

Beltrán, U. and Portilla, S. (1986). 'El proyecto de descentralización del gobierno mexicano (1983–84)', pp. 91–118 in B. Torres (ed.) *Descentralización y democracia en México*. El Colegio de México, Mexico.

Benería, L. (1991). 'Structural adjustment, the labour market, and the household: the case of Mexico', pp. 161–83 in G. Standing and V. Tokman (eds) *Toward Social Adjustment: labor market issues in structural adjustment*. International Labor Office, Geneva.

Benítez Zenteno, R. (1995). 'Distribución de la población y desarrollo urbano', pp.

165–98 in A.G. Aguilar (ed.) *Desarrollo regional y urbano: tendencias y alternativas*, tomo I. Juan Pablos Editor, SA, Mexico, UNAM and U. de Guadalajara.

Bennett, V. (1995). *The Politics of Water: urban protest, gender and power in Monterrey, Mexico*. University of Pittsburgh Press, Pittsburgh, PA.

Benton, L. (1986). 'Reshaping the urban core: the politics of housing in authoritarian Uruguay', *Latin American Research Review*, 21: 33–52.

Birkbeck, C. (1978). 'Self-employed proletarians in an informal factory: the case of Cali's garbage dump', *World Development*, 6: 1173–85.

Blancas Neria, A. (1993). 'Finanzas públicas y gasto social', pp. 276–309 in A. Bassols Batalla, G. González Salazar and J. Delgadillo Macías (eds) *Zona metropolitana de la ciudad de México, complejo geográfico, socioeconómico y político: qué fue, qué es y qué pasa*. Instituto de Investigaciones Económicas, Universidad Nacional Autónoma de México, Mexico DF.

Boonyabancha, S. (1983). 'The causes and effects of slum eviction in Bangkok', pp. 254–83 in S. Angel, R. Archer, S. Tanphiphat and E. Wegelin (eds) *Land for Housing the Poor*. Select Books, Singapore.

Bortz, J. (1983). 'La cuestión salarial actual', *Análisis Económico*, 2: 103–20.

Bourne, L. (1993). 'The demise of gentrification? A commentary and a prospective view', *Urban Geography*, 14: 95–107.

Brambila Paz, C. (1987). Ciudad de México: la urbe más grande del mundo? pp. 146–51 in G. Garza (ed.) *Atlas de la Ciudad de México*. Departamento del Distrito Federal and Colegio de México, Mexico DF.

Brambila, Paz, C. (1992). *Expansión urbana en México*. El Colegio de México, Mexico DF.

Bromley, R. (1978). 'Organization, regulation and exploitation in the so-called "urban informal sector": the street traders of Cali, Colombia', *World Development*, 6: 1161–71.

Brown, J. (1972). *Patterns of intra-urban settlement in Mexico City: an examination of the Turner theory*. Dissertation Series 40, Cornell University Latin American Studies Programme, Ithaca, NY.

Bruhn, K. and Yanner, K. (1995). 'Governing under the enemy: the PRD in Michoacán', pp. 113–31 in V. Rodríguez and P. Ward (eds) *Opposition Government in Mexico*. University of New Mexico Press, Albuquerque, NM.

Burgess, J. (1978). 'Conflict and conservation in Covent Garden', *L'Espace Geographique*, 2: 93–107.

Burgess, R. (1982). 'Self-help housing advocacy: a curious form of radicalism. A critique of the work of John F.C. Turner', pp. 55–97 in P. Ward (ed.) *Self-help Housing: a critique*. Mansell, London.

Burgess, R. (1985). 'The limits to state-aided self-help housing programmes', *Development and Change*, 16: 271–312.

Burgess, R. (1990). *Labor, Shelter and Global Capitalism*. Methuen, London.

Burian, E. (1997). *Modernity and the Architecture of Mexico*. University of Texas Press, Austin, Texas.

Bustamante, J., Reynolds, C. and Hinojosa, R. (eds) (1992). *U.S.–Mexico Relations: labor market interdependence*. Stanford University Press, Stanford, CA.

Butterworth, D. (1972). 'Two small groups: a comparison of migrants and non-migrants in Mexico City', *Urban Anthropology*, 1: 29–50.

Cabrero Mendoza, E. (1995). *La nueva gestión municipal en México. Análisis de experiencias innovadoras en gobiernos locales*. Miguel Angel Porrúa, Mexico DF.

Cabrero Mendoza, E. (ed.) (1996). *Los dilemas de la modernización municipal: estudios sobre la gestión hacendaria en municipios urbanos de México*. Miguel Angel Porrúa, Mexico DF.

Calnek, E. (1975). 'The organization of food supply systems: the case of Tenochtitlán', in J. Hardoy and R. Schaedel (eds) *Las ciudades de América Latina y sus áreas de influencia a través de la historia*. Ediciones SIAP, Buenos Aires.

Calnek, E. (1976). 'The internal structure of Tenochtitlán', in E. Wolf (ed.) *The Valley of Mexico*. University of New Mexico Press, Albuquerque, NM.

Camacho, C. (1987). 'La ciudad de México en la economía nacional', pp. 95–9 in G. Garza (ed.) *Atlas de la Ciudad de México*. Departamento del Distrito Federal and Colegio de México, Mexico DF.

Cámara Nacional (Cámara Nacional de Comercio de la Cd. de México) (1993). 'La economía informal de la ciudad de México', *Economía Metropolitana*, 1: 19–21.

Camp, R. Ai. (1993). *Politics in Mexico* (2nd revised ed, 1996). Oxford University Press, New York.

Camp, R. (1995). 'The PAN's social bases: implications for leadership', pp. 65–80 in V. Rodríguez and P. Ward (eds) *Opposition Government in Mexico*. University of New Mexico Press, Albuquerque, NM.

Campbell, T. and Wilk, D. (1986). 'Plans and plan making in the Valley of Mexico', *Third World Planning Review*, 8: 287–313.

Camposortega Cruz, S. (1992). 'Evolución y tendencias demográficas de la ZMCM', pp. 3–16 in Consejo Nacional de Población. *La zona metropolitana de la ciudad de México: problemática actual y perspectivas demográficas y urbanas*. CONAPO, Mexico DF.

Carr, B. (1986). 'The Mexican left, popular movements, and the politics of austerity', in B. Carr (ed.) *The Mexican Left, Popular Movements, and the Politics of Austerity*. Centre for US–Mexican Studies, University of California, Monograph Series No. 18, San Diego, CA.

Castells, M. (1977). *The Urban Question: a Marxist approach*. Edward Arnold, London.

Castells, M. (1979). *City, Class and Power*. Macmillan, London.

Castells, M. (1983). *The City and the Grassroots*. Edward Arnold, London.

Castillejos, M. (1988). 'Efectos de la contaminación ambiental en la salud de niños escolares en tres zonas del área metropolitana de la ciudad de México' pp. 301–30 in S. Puente and J. Legorreta (eds) *Medio ambiente y calidad de vida*. Plaza y Valdés and Departamento del Distrito Federal, Mexico City.

Castillo, H., Camarena, M. and Ziccadi, A. (1987). 'Basura: procesos de trabajo e impactos en el medio ambiente urbano', *Estudios Demográficos y Urbanos*, 2: 513–43.

Castillo, H., Navarro, B., Perló, M., Plaza, I., Wilk, D. and Ziccardi, A. (1995). *Ciudad de México: retos y propuestas para la coordinación metropolitana*. Universidad Autónoma Metropolitana, Unidad Xochimilco, DF.

Castro Castro, J.L. (1995). 'El programa de 100 ciudades de la Secretaría de Desarrollo Social', pp. 1117–126 in A. Aguilar, L.J. Castro Castro and E. Juárez Aguirre (eds) *El desarrollo urbano de México a fines del siglo XX*. Instituto de Estudios Urbanos de Nuevo León, Mexico, Nuevo León.

Centeno, M.A. (1994). *Democracy Within Reason: technocratic revolution in Mexico*. Penn State University Press, Pennsylvania.

Chance, J. (1975). 'The colonial Latin American city: pre-industrial or capitalist?' *Urban Anthropology*, 4: 211–23.

Chant, S. (1985). 'Family formation and female roles in Querétaro, Mexico', *Bulletin of Latin American Research*, 4: 17–32.

Chant, S. (1991). *Women and Survival in Mexican Cities: perspectives on gender, labour markets and low-income households*. Manchester University Press, Manchester.

Chant, S. (1996). *Gender, Urban Development and Housing*. United Nations Urban Development Programme (UNDP), Publications Series for Habitat II, Vol. 2, New York.

Chant, S. and Ward, P. (1987). 'Family structure and low-income housing policy', *Third World Planning Review*, 9: 5–19.

Chislett, W. (1985). 'The causes of Mexico's financial crisis and the lessons to be learned', pp. 1–14 in G. Philip (ed.) *Politics in Mexico*. Croom Helm, London.

Cibotti, R. *et al*. (1974). 'Evolución y perspectivas de los procesos de planificación en América Latina', in ILEPES, OEA, BID, *Experiencias y problemas de planificación en América Latina*. Siglo Veintiuno Editores, Mexico.

Cisneros Sosa, A. (1983). 'Los ciudadanos del Distrito Federal', *Revista de Ciencias Sociales y Humanidades*, p. 9, UAM, Iztapalapa.

Cisneros Sosa, A. (1993). *La ciudad que construímos: registro de la expansión de la Cd. de México (1920–1976)*. Universidad Autónoma Metropolitana, Iztapalapa, Mexico DF.

Cisneros Sosa, A. (no date). La colonia El Sol. Mimeo, Mexico DF.

Cockcroft, J.D. (1983). *Mexico. Class Formation, Capital Accumulation and the State*. Monthly Review Press, New York.

Collier, D. (ed.) (1979). *The New Authoritarianism in Latin America*. Princeton University Press, Princeton, NJ.

Colosio, L.D. (1993). 'Why the PRI won the 1991 elections', pp. 155–68 in R. Roett (ed.) *Political and Economic Liberalization in Mexico: at a critical juncture?* Lynne Rienner Publishers, Boulder, CO.

Comisión Metropolitana (1996). Comisión metropolitana para la prevención y el control de la contaminación ambiental en el Valle de México. Avances de las acciones para prevenir contingencias atmosféricas, 1995–1996. Agency Publication.

CONAPO (1990). *Indicadores socioecónomicos e índice de marginación municipal 1990*. CONAPO, Mexico DF.

CONAPO (1996). *Escenarios demográficos y urbanos de la zona metropolitana de la Cd. de México, 1999–2010*. Internal document prepared for a meeting in Toluca, April 1996.

CONCANACO (1993). *Estudio nacional sobre comercio informal*. CONCANACO (Confederación de Cámaras Nacionales de Comercio), Mexico DF.

Conde Bonfil, C. (1996). 'El caso de Naucalpan de Juárez, Estado de México', pp. 329–432 in E. Cabero (ed.) *Los dilemas de la modernización municipal: estudios sobre la gestión hacendaria en municipios urbanos de México*. Miguel Angel Porrúa, Mexico DF.

Connolly, P. (1981). Towards an analysis of Mexico City's local state. Mimeo.

Connolly, P. (1982). 'Uncontrolled settlements and self-build: what kind of solution? The Mexico City case', pp. 141–74 in P.M. Ward (ed.) *Self-help Housing: a critique*. Mansell, London.

Connolly, P. (1988). 'Crecimiento urbano, densidad de población y mercado inmobiliario', *Revista A*, 9: 61–85.

Connolly, C., Duhau, E. and Coulomb, R. (1991). *Cambiar de casa pero no de barrio. Estudios sobre la reconstrucción en la Ciudad de México*. CENVI and UAM-Azcapotzalco, Mexico DF.

Contreras, O. and Bennett, V. (1994). 'National Solidarity in northern borderlands: social participation and community leadership', pp. 281–308 in W. Cornelius, A. Craig and J. Fox (eds) *Transforming State–Society Relations in Mexico: the National Solidarity strategy*. Center for US–Mexican Studies, UCSD, La Jolla, San Diego, CA.

Cook, M. (1996). *Organizing Dissent. Unions, the state and the democratic teachers' movement in Mexico.* Penn State University Press, Pennsylvania.

COPEVI (1977). *La producción de vivienda en la zona metropolitana de la ciudad de México.* COPEVI AC, Mexico DF.

COPEVI (1978). Estudio de densidades habitacionales y revisión de la zonificación secundaria. Mimeo, various volumes. COPEVI AC, Mexico DF.

Coppedge, M. (1993). 'Democracy: you can't get there from here', pp. 127–40 in R. Roett (ed.) *Political and Economic Liberalization in Mexico: at a critical juncture?* Lynne Rienner Publishers, Boulder, CO.

Corbridge, S. (1986). *Capitalist World Development: a critique of radical development geography.* Macmillan, Basingstoke.

Cornelius, W. (1975). *Politics and the Migrant Poor in Mexico City.* Stanford University Press, Stanford, CA.

Cornelius, W. (1994). 'Mexico's delayed democratization', *Foreign Policy*, 95: 53–71.

Cornelius, W. and Craig, A. (1991). *The Mexican Political System in Transition.* Centre for US–Mexican Studies, University of California, Monograph Series, No. 35, San Diego, CA.

Cornelius, W., Craig, A. and Fox, J. (eds) (1994). *Transforming State–Society Relations in Mexico: the National Solidarity strategy.* Centre for US–Mexican Studies, UCSD, La Jolla, San Diego, CA.

Cornelius, W. and Myhre, D. (eds) (1997). *The Transformation of Rural Mexico.* Centre for US–Mexican Studies, UCSD, La Jolla, San Diego, CA.

Corona Cuapio, R. and Luque González, R. (1992). 'El perfil de la migración de la zona metropolitana de la Cd. de México', pp. 21–31 in Consejo Nacional de Población. *La zona metropolitana de la ciudad de México: problemática actual y perspectivas demográficas y urbanas.* CONAPO, Mexico DF.

Coulomb, R. (1989). 'Rental housing and the dynamics of urban growth in Mexico City', pp. 39–50 in A. Gilbert (ed.) *Housing and Land in Urban Mexico.* Centre for US–Mexican Studies, University of California, Monograph Series No. 31, San Diego, CA.

Coulomb, R. (1992). El acceso a la vivienda en la Ciudad de México, pp. 179–201 in Consejo Nacional de Población. *La zona metropolitana de la ciudad de México: problemática actual y perspectivas demográficas y urbanas.* CONAPO, Mexico DF.

Cox, K. (ed.) (1997). *Spaces of Globalization: reasserting the power of the local.* The Guilford Press, New York.

Craske, N. (1994). *Corporatism Revisited: Salinas and the reform of the popular sector.* Institute of Latin American Studies, Research Paper 37, London.

Craske, N. (1996). 'Dismantling or retrenchment? Salinas and corporatism', pp. 78–91 in R. Aitken, N. Craske, G. Jones and D. Stansfield (eds) *Dismantling the Mexican State?* Macmillan, London.

Crespo, J.A. (1995). *Urnas de Pandora: partidos políticos y elecciones en el gobierno de Salinas.* Espasa Calpe, Mexico DF.

Crespo, J.A. (1996). *Votar en los estados: análisis comparado de las legislaciones electorales estatales en México.* Fundación Friedrich Naumann, Miguel Angel Porrúa, and CIDE, Mexico DF.

Cymet, D. (1992). *From Ejido to Metropolis: another path.* Peter Lang, New York.

Davidoff, P. (1965). 'Advocacy and pluralism in planning', *Journal of the American Institute of Planners*, 31: 331–8.

Davis, D. (1994). *Urban Leviathan: Mexico City in the twentieth century.* Temple University Press, Philadelphia.

Dear, M. (1986). 'Post-modernism and planning', *Society and Space*, 4: 367–84.

De la Madrid, M. (1984). *Segundo Informe de Gobierno.* Secretaría de la Presidencia, Mexico DF.

de la Rosa, M. (1975). *Netzahualcóyotl: un fenómeno.* Testimonios del Fondo, Mexico DF.

Delgado, J. (1988). 'El patrón ocupacional territorial de la Ciudad de México al año 2000', pp. 101–41 in O. Terrazas and E. Preciat (eds) *Estructura territorial de la Ciudad de México.* Plaza y Valdés and Departamento del Distrito Federal, Mexico City.

Dicken, P. (1986a). *Global Shift: industrial change in a turbulent world.* Harper & Row, London.

Dicken, P. (1986b). 'Review of Utopia on Trial', *International Journal of Urban and Regional Research,* 10: 297–300.

Domínguez, L. (1987). 'Sistema de transporte colectivo: el metro', pp. 198–201 in G. Garza (ed.) *Atlas de la Ciudad de México.* Departamento del Distrito Federal and Colegio de México, Mexico DF.

Dos Santos, I. (1970). 'The structure of dependence', *American Economic Review,* 60: 231–6.

Drakakis-Smith, D. (1981). *Urbanisation, Housing and the Development Process.* Croom Helm, London.

Dresser, D. (1991). *Neopopulist solutions to neoliberal problems: Mexico's National Solidarity Program.* Center for US–Mexican Studies, Current Issue Brief Series, No. 3, La Jolla, San Diego, CA..

Dresser, D. (1994). 'Bringing the poor back in: National Solidarity as a strategy of regime legitimation', pp. 143–66 in W. Cornelius, A. Craig and J. Fox (eds) *Transforming State–Society Relations in Mexico: the National Solidarity strategy.* Center for US–Mexican Studies, UCSD, La Jolla, San Diego, CA..

Durán, D. (1967). *Historia de las Indias de Nueva España.* 2 vols. Editorial Porrúa, Mexico.

Dussel Peters, E. (1996). 'From export-oriented to import-oriented industrialization: changes in Mexico's manufacturing sector, 1988–1994', pp. 63–84 in G. Otero (ed.) *Neoliberalism Revisited: economic restructuring and Mexico's political future.* Westview Press, Boulder, CO.

Eckstein, S. (1977). (Revised edition 1988) *The Poverty of Revolution: the state and the urban poor in Mexico.* Princeton University Press, Princeton, NJ.

Eckstein, S. (ed.) (1989). *Power and Popular Protest: Latin American social movements.* University of California Press, Berkeley, CA.

Eckstein, S. (1990a). 'Urbanisation revisited: inner-city slum of hope and squatter settlement of despair', *World Development,* 18: 165–81.

Eckstein, S. (1990b). 'Poor people versus the state and capital: anatomy of a successful community mobilization for housing in Mexico City', *International Journal for Urban and Regional Research,* 14: 274–96.

Eckstein, S. (1990c). 'Formal versus substantive democracy: poor people's politics in Mexico City', *Mexican Studies/Estudios Mexicanos,* 6: 213–39.

Esquivel Hernández, M.T. (1995). 'Dinámica socioespacial de la zona metropolitana de la Cd. de México y patrones de segregación 1980–1990', *Anuario de Estudios Urbanos,* 2: 297–315.

Eyles, J. and Woods, K. (1983). *The Social Geography of Medicine and Health.* Croom Helm, London.

Fagen, R. and Tuohy, W. (1972). *Politics and Privilege in a Mexican City.* Stanford University Press, Stanford, CA.

Fanon, F. (1967). *The Wretched of the Earth.* Penguin, Harmondsworth.

Ferras, R. (1978.) *Ciudad Netzahualcóyotl: un barrio en vía de absorción por la ciudad de México*. Centro de Estudios Sociológicos, El Colegio de México, Mexico DF.

Figueroa, O. (1996). 'A hundred million journeys a day: the management of transport in Latin America's mega-cities', pp. 110–32 in A. Gilbert (ed.) *The Mega-city in Latin America*. United Nations University Press, New York.

Fiori, J. and Ramírez, R. (1987). Notes for comparative research on self-help housing policies in Latin America. Mimeo.

Flores Moreno, J. (1988). 'El transporte en la zona metropolitana de la Ciudad de México', pp. 265–80 in R. Benítez and J. Benigno (eds) *Grandes problemas de la Ciudad de México*. Dept. del Distrito Federal and Plaza y Valdés, Editores, Mexico DF.

Ford, L. (1994). *Cities and Buildings: skyscrapers, skid rows and suburbs*. Johns Hopkins University Press, Baltimore, MD.

Fox, D. (1972). 'Patterns of morbidity and mortality in Mexico City', *Geographical Review*, 62: 151–86.

Fox, J. (1994). 'Targeting the poorest: the role of the National Indigenous Institute in Mexico's Solidarity Program', pp. 179–216 in W. Cornelius, A. Craig and J. Fox (eds) *Transforming State–Society Relations in Mexico: the National Solidarity strategy*. Center for US–Mexican Studies, UCSD, La Jolla, San Diego, CA.

Franco, J. (1967). *The Modern Culture of Latin America: society and the artist*. Pall Mall Press, London.

Fried, R. (1972). 'Mexico City', pp. 645–88 in W. Robson and D. Regan (eds) *Great Cities of the World* (3rd edn). Sage, Beverly Hills, CA.

Frieden, W. (1965). 'The search for a housing policy in Mexico City', *Town Planning Review*, 36: 75–94.

Friedmann, J. and Wolff, G. (1982). 'World city formation: an agenda for research and action', *International Journal for Urban and Regional Research*, 6: 309–43.

Furtado, C. (1971). *Economic Development of Latin America: a survey from colonial times to the Cuban Revolution*. Cambridge University Press, Cambridge.

Gamboa de Buen, J. (1990). Gestión urbana y participación ciudadana, pp. 431–39 in M. Perló (ed.) *La modernización de las ciudades en México*. Universidad Nacional Autónoma de México, Mexico DF.

Garavito Elías, R. (1983). 'La protección al salario', *Análisis Económico*, 2: 121–50.

García, B., Muñoz, H. and de Oliveira, O. (1982). *Hogares y trabajadores en la Ciudad de México*. El Colegio de México and Instituto de Investigaciones Sociales, UNAM, Mexico DF.

García Canclini, N. (1990). *Culturas híbridas*. Grijalbo, Mexico DF.

García Canclini, N. (1993). *Transforming Modernity: popular culture in Mexico*. University of Texas Press, Austin, TX.

García Canclini, N. (ed.) (1994). *Los nuevos espectadores: cine, televisión y video en México*. Instituto Mexicano de Cinematografía and Consejo Nacional para la Cultura y las Artes, Mexico DF.

García Canclini, N., Castellanos, A. and Mantecón, A. (1996). *La ciudad de los viajeros: travesías e imaginarios urbanos – México, 1940–2000*. UAM, Ixtapalapa and Editorial Grijalbo, Mexico, DF.

Garrido, L.J. (1989). 'The crisis of *presidencialismo*', pp. 417–34 in W. Cornelius, J. Gentleman, and P. Smith (eds) *Mexico's Alternative Political Futures*. Centre for US–Mexican Studies, University of California, Monograph Series, San Diego, CA.

Garrido, L.J. (1993). *La ruptura: la corriente democrática del PRI*. Grijalbo, Mexico DF.

Garrocho, C. (1995a). 'El centro de la zona metropolitana de la ciudad de México: auge o decadencia?' pp. 63–105 in C. Garrocho and J. Sobrino (eds) *Sistemas metropolitanos: nuevos enfoques y prospectiva*. El Colegio Mexiquense and SEDESOL, Mexico.

Garrocho, C. (1995b). *Análisis socioespacial de los servicios de salud: accesibilidad, utilización y calidad*. El Colegio Mexiquense, AC, Mexico.

Garza, G. (1978). *Ciudad de México: dinámica económica y factores locacionales*. Temas de la Ciudad, DDF, Mexico DF.

Garza, G. (1986). 'Ciudad de México: dinámica industrial y perspectivas de descentralización después del terremoto', pp. 219–36 in B. Torres (ed.) *Descentralización y democracia en México*. El Colegio de México, Mexico.

Garza, G. (1987). 'Distribución de la industria en la ciudad de México', pp. 102–7 in G. Garza (ed.) *Atlas de la Ciudad de México*. Departamento del Distrito Federal and Colegio de México, Mexico DF.

Garza, G. (1992). *Desconcentración, tecnología y localización industrial en México*. El Colegio de México, Mexico DF.

Garza, G. and Rivera, S. (1995). 'Desarrollo económico y distribución de la población urbana en México, 1960–1990', pp. 17–53 in A. Aguilar, L.J. Castro Castro and E. Juárez Aguirre (eds) *El desarrollo urbano de México a fines del siglo XX*. Instituto de Estudios Urbanos de Nuevo León, Mexico, Nuevo León.

Garza, G. and Schteingart, M. (1978). *La acción habitacional del estado mexicano*. El Colegio de México, Mexico DF.

Gates, M. (1996). 'The debt crisis and economic restructuring: prospects for Mexican agriculture', pp. 43–62 in G. Otero (ed.) *Neoliberalism Revisited: economic restructuring and Mexico's political future*. Westview Press, Boulder, CO.

Gereffi, G. (1996). 'Mexico's "old" and "new" maquiladora industries: contrasting approaches to north American integration', pp. 85–106 in G. Otero (ed.) *Neoliberalism Revisited: economic restructuring and Mexico's political future*. Westview Press, Boulder, CO.

Gilbert, A. (1976a). *Development Planning and Spatial Structure*. Wiley, Chichester.

Gilbert, A. (1976b). 'The arguments for very large cities reconsidered', *Urban Studies*, 13: 27–34.

Gilbert, A. (1981). 'Bogotá: an analysis of power in an urban setting', pp. 65–93 in M. Pacione (ed.) *Urban Problems and Planning in the Modern World*. Croom Helm, London.

Gilbert, A. (1984). 'Planning, invasions and land speculation: the role of the state in Venezuela', *Third World Planning Review*, 6: 11–22.

Gilbert, A. (1993). *In Search of a Home: rental and shared housing in Latin America*. University of Arizona Press, Tucson, AZ.

Gilbert, A. (1996). 'Land, housing, and infrastructure in Latin America's major cities', pp. 73–109 in A. Gilbert (ed.) *The Mega-city in Latin America*. United Nations University Press, New York.

Gilbert, A. and Gugler, J. (1992). *Cities, Poverty and Development: urbanization in the Third World*. (2nd edn), Oxford University Press, Oxford.

Gilbert, A. and Varley, A. (1991). *Landlord and Tenant: housing the poor in urban Mexico*. Routledge, London.

Gilbert, A. and Ward, P. (1978). 'Housing in Latin American cities', in D. Herbert and R. Johnston (eds) *Geography and the Urban Environment*. Wiley, Chichester.

Gilbert, A. and Ward, P. (1982a). 'The state and low-income housing', pp. 79–128 in A. Gilbert, J. Hardoy and R. Ramírez (eds) *Urbanization in Contemporary Latin America*. Wiley, Chichester.

Gilbert, A. and Ward, P. (1982b). 'Residential movement among the poor: the constraints on housing choice in Latin American cities', *Transactions of the Institute of British Geographers* (New Series), 7: 129–49.

Gilbert, A. and Ward, P. (1984). 'Community action by the urban poor: democratic involvement, community self-help, or a means of social control?' *World Development*, 12: 769–82.

Gilbert, A. and Ward, P. (1985). *Housing, the State and the Poor: policy and practice in three Latin American cities*. Cambridge University Press, Cambridge.

Gilbert, A. and Ward, P. (1986). 'Latin American migrants: a tale of three cities', pp. 24–42 in F. Slater (ed.) *People and Environments*. Collins Educational, London.

Gil Elizondo, J. (1987). 'El futuro de la ciudad de México. Metrópoli controlada', pp. 415–18 in G. Garza (ed.) *Atlas de la Ciudad de México*. Departamento del Distrito Federal and Colegio de México, Mexico DF.

Gil Elizondo, J. (1990). 'Planeación y participación ciudadana', pp. 421–30 in M. Perló (ed.) *La modernización de las ciudades en México*. Universidad Nacional Autónoma de México, Mexico DF.

Glass, R. (1968). 'Urban sociology in Great Britain', pp. 21–46 in R. Pahl (ed.) *Readings in Urban Sociology*. Pergamon, Oxford.

Goldrich, D., Pratt, R. and Schuller, C. (1967). 'The political integration of lower-class urban settlements in Chile and Peru', *Studies in Comparative International Developments*, 3: 1.

González Block, M., Leyva, R., Zapata, O., Loewe, R. and Aragón, J. (1989). 'Health services decentralization in Mexico: formulation, implementation and results of policy', *Health Policy and Planning*, 4: 301–15.

González Casanova, P. (1970). *Democracy in Mexico*. Oxford University Press, New York.

González de la Rocha, M. (1988). 'Economic crisis, domestic reorganisation and women's work in Guadalajara, México', *Bulletin of Latin American Research*, 7: 207–23.

González de la Rocha, M. (1994). *The Resources of Poverty: women and survival in a Mexican city*. Blackwells, Oxford.

González García de Alba, L. *et al.* (1992). 'Distribución territorial en las estrategias sectoriales 1990–1994', pp. 168–88 in A.G. Aguilar (ed.) *Política regional, ciudades medias y desconcentración urbana*. Instituto de Geografía, número especial, UNAM.

González Rubí, R. (1984). 'La vivienda, un desafío atroz', *Comercio Exterior*, 34 (May, July and August issues): 390–96, 592–98, 728–34.

Gottlieb, M. (1976). *Long Swings in Urban Development*. NBER, New York.

Goulet, D. (1983). *Mexico: development strategies for the future*. University of Notre Dame Press, Notre Dame, IN.

Graizbord, B. and Mina, A. (1995). 'La geografía de la descentralización demográfica de la ciudad de México', pp. 101–14 in A. Aguilar, L.J. Castro Castro and E. Juárez Aguirre (eds) *El desarrollo urbano de México a fines del siglo XX*. Instituto de Estudios Urbanos de Nuevo León, Mexico, Nuevo León.

Grayson, G. (1995). 'Pemex to gain currency abroad?' *Petroleum Economist*, 62: 20–22.

Greene, K. (1993). Complexity, cohesion, and longevity in an urban popular movement: the Asamblea de Barrios de la Cd. de México. Mimeo.

Gregory, D. (1987). 'Post-modernism and the politics of social theory', *Society and Space*, 5: 245–8.

Grindle, M. (1977). *Bureaucrats, Politicians and Peasants in Mexico: a case study in public policy*. University of California Press, Berkeley, CA.

Guerra, L.M. (1995). *El aire nuestro de cada día*. Editorial Diana, DF.

Guerrero, Ma.T. *et al.* (1974). La tierra, especulación y fraude en el fraccionamiento de San Agustín. Mimeo, Mexico DF.

Guevara, S. and Moreno, P. (1987). 'Areas verdes de la zona metropolitana de la ciudad de México', pp. 231–6 in G. Garza (ed.) *Atlas de la Ciudad de México*. Departamento del Distrito Federal and Colegio de México, Mexico DF.

Gunder Frank, A. (1967). *Capitalism and Underdevelopment in Latin America*. Monthly Review Press, New York.

Guttman, M. (1996). *The Meanings of Macho: being a man in Mexico City*. University of California Press, Berkeley, CA.

Gwynne, R. (1985). *Industrialisation and Urbanisation in Latin America*. Croom Helm, London.

Haber, P. (1994). 'Political change in Durango: the role of National Solidarity', pp. 255-80 in W. Cornelius, A. Craig and J. Fox (eds) *Transforming State–Society Relations in Mexico: the National Solidarity strategy*. Center for US–Mexican Studies, UCSD, La Jolla, San Diego, CA.

Hallqvist, M. (1994). *Centro histórico de la Ciudad de México: restauración de edificios. 1984–1994*. Cementos Apasco; Colegio de Arquitectos de la Ciudad de México, AC; Sociedad de Arquitectos Mexicanos, AC, Mexico DF.

Hamnett, C. (1991). 'The blind man and the elephant: the explanation of gentrification', *Transactions of the Institute of British Geographers*, 16: 173–89.

Handelman, H. (1996). *Mexican Politics: the dynamics of change*. St Martin's Press, New York.

Hansen, R. (1974). *The Politics of Mexican Development*. (2nd edn) Johns Hopkins University Press, Baltimore, MD.

Hardoy, J. (1967). *Urbanization in Pre-Columbian America*. Studio Vista, London.

Hardoy, J. and Dos Santos, M. (1983). *El centro de Cuzco: introducción al problema de su preservación y desarrollo*. UNESCO.

Hardoy, J. and Gutman, M. (1991). 'The role of municipal government in the protection of historic centers in Latin American cities', *Environment and Urbanization*, 3: 96–108.

Harloe, M. (1977). *Captive Cities*. John Wiley, Chichester.

Harms, H. (1976). 'The limitations of self-help', *Architectural Design*, 46: 231.

Harvey, D. (1973). *Social Justice and the City*. Edward Arnold, London.

Harvey, D. (1985). *The Urbanization of Capital*. Basil Blackwells, Oxford.

Harvey, D. (1987). 'Flexible accumulation through urbanization: reflections on "postmodernism" in the American City', *Antipode*, 19: 260–86.

Harvey, D. (1989). *The Condition of Postmodernity*. Blackwells, Oxford.

Hayden, D. (1994). *The Power of Place: urban landscapes as public history*. MIT Press, Cambridge, MA.

Heath, J. (1985). 'Contradictions in Mexican food policy', in G. Philip (ed.) *Politics in Mexico*. Croom Helm, London.

Henderson, J. (1986). 'The new international division of labour and urban development in the world system', pp. 63–84 in D. Drakakis Smith (ed.) *Urbanisation in the Developing World*. Croom Helm, London.

HMSO (Her Majesty's Stationery Office). (1997). *New Leadership for London: The Government's proposals for a Greater London Authority. A consultation paper*. HMSO, Cmnd. 3724, London.

Hernández, V. (1981). *Arquitectura doméstica de la ciudad de México (1890–1925)*. UNAM, Mexico City.

Hernández Franyuti, R. (ed.) (1994). *La Cd. de México en la primera mitad del siglo XIX*. Instituto Mora, Mexico DF.

Herzog, L. (1990). *Where North meets South: cities, space and politics on the United States–Mexico border*. University of Texas Press, Austin, TX.

Herzog, L. (1995). Rethinking public space in Mexico City's historic core. Paper presented at the International Research Workshop 'The cultural patrimony of Mexican inner-cities: towards equitable conservation policies and practices'. The Mexican Center, University of Texas at Austin, 8–9 December 1995.

Hiernaux, D. (1995). *Nueva periferia, vieja metrópolis: el Valle de Chalco, Ciudad de México*. UAM–Xochimilco, Mexico DF.

Holston, J. (1989). *The Modernist City*. Chicago University Press, Chicago, IL.

Home, R. (1982). *Inner City Regeneration*. E. & F.N. Spon, London.

Huerta García, R. (1993). 'Aspectos monográficos de la industria manufacturera', pp. 154–74 in A. Bassols Batalla, G. González Salazar and J. Delgadillo Macías (eds) *Zona metropolitana de la ciudad de México, complejo geográfico, socio-económico y político: qué fue, qué es y qué pasa*. Instituto de Investigaciones Económicas, Universidad Nacional Autónoma de México, Mexico DF.

Huntington, S. (1968). *Political Order in Changing Societies*. Yale University Press, New Haven, CT.

Incháustegui, T. (1994). *La ciudad de México ante el cambio en el modelo económico y ante la reforma política*. UNAM, Facultad de Ciencias Políticas y Sociales, Mexico DF.

Jackson, H. (1973). Intra-urban migration of Mexico City's poor. Unpublished PhD dissertation, University of Colorado.

Jáuregui, E. (1969). 'Aspectos meteorológicos de la contaminación del aire en la ciudad de México', *Ingeniería Hidráulica en México*, 23: 1.

Jáuregui, E. (1973). 'The urban climate of Mexico City', *Erdkunde*, 27: 298–307.

Jáuregui, E. (1987). 'Climas', pp. 370 in G. Garza (ed.) *Atlas de la Ciudad de México*. Departamento del Distrito Federal and Colegio de México, Mexico DF.

Jeannetti Dávila, E. (1986). 'Descentralización de los servicios de salud', pp. 91–118 in B. Torres (ed.) *Descentralización y democracia en México*. El Colegio de México, Mexico.

Jiménez, E. (1988). 'New forms of community participation in Mexico City: success or failure?' *Bulletin of Latin American Research*, 7: 17–31.

Jiménez, E. (1989). 'A new form of government control over *colonos* in Mexico City', pp. 157–72 in A. Gilbert (ed.) *Housing and Land in Urban Mexico*. Center for US–Mexican Studies, University of California, Monograph Series No. 31, San Diego, CA.

Jiménez, J.H. (1993). *La traza del poder*. CODEX, Mexico DF.

Johnston, R. (1973). 'Towards a general model of intra-urban residential patterns. Some cross-cultural observations', *Progress in Geography*, 4: 81–124.

Johnston, R. (1980). *City and Society: an outline for urban geography*. Penguin, Harmondsworth.

Jones, G. (1994). 'World Heritage Sites', in T. Unwin (ed.) *Atlas of World Development*. Belhaven, London.

Jones, G. (1996). 'Dismantling the *ejido*: a lesson in controlled pluralism', pp. 188–203 in R. Aitken, N. Craske, G. Jones and D. Stansfield (eds) *Dismantling the Mexican State?* Macmillan, London.

Jones, G. and Bromley, R. (1996). 'The relationship between urban conservation programmes and property renovation: evidence from Quito, Ecuador', *Cities*, 13: 373–5.

Jones, G. and Varley, A. (1994). 'The contest for the city centre: street traders versus buildings', *Bulletin of Latin American Research*, 13: 27–44.

Jones, G. and Ward, P. (eds) (1994). *Methodology for Land and Housing Market Analysis*. University College London Press, London.

Jones, G. and Ward, P. (1997). 'The privatization of the commons: reforming the ejido and urban development in Mexico', *International Journal of Urban and Regional Research*, in press.

Jones, G., Jiménez, E. and Ward, P. (1993). 'The land market under Salinas: a real estate boom revisited?' *Environment and Planning A*, 25: 627–51.

Jusidman, C. (1988). 'Empleo y mercados de trabajo en el area metropolitana de la ciudad de México 1975–88', pp. 225–50 in S. Puente and J. Legorreta (eds) *Medio ambiente y calidad de vida*. Plaza y Valdés and Departamento del Distrito Federal, Mexico City.

Kandell, J. (1988). *La Capital: the Biography of Mexico City*. Random House, New York.

Kaplan, M. (1972). *Aspectos políticos de la planificación en América Latina*. Biblioteca Científica, Montevideo.

Kemper, R. (1974). 'Family and household organization among Tzintzuntzán migrants in Mexico City: a proposal and a case study', pp. 23–46 in W. Cornelius and F. Trueblood (eds) *Latin American Urban Research*. Vol. 4. Sage, Beverley Hills, CA.

Kemper, R. (1976). *Campesinos en la Cd. de México: gente de Tzintzuntzán*. Sepsetentas, Mexico DF.

Knox, P. (1987). 'The social production of the built environment: architects, architecture and the post-modern city', *Progress in Human Geography*, 11: 35–77.

Knox, P. and Taylor, P. (eds) (1995). *World Cities in a World System*. Cambridge University Press, Cambridge.

Lacy, R. (ed.) (1993). *La calidad del aire en el valle de México*. El Colegio de México, Mexico DF.

Lamarche, F. (1976). 'Property development and the economic foundations of the urban question', in C. Pickvance (ed.) *Urban Sociology: critical essays*. Tavistock, London.

Lavell, A. (1973). 'Capital investment and regional development in Mexico', *Area*, 5: 1.

Lear, J. (1993). Workers, vecinos and citizens: the revolution in Mexico City, 1909–1917. Unpublished PhD dissertation, Department of History, University of California, Berkeley.

Leeds, A. (1969). 'The significant variables determining the character of squatter settlements', *América Latina*, 12: 44–86.

Legorreta, J. (1983). *El proceso de urbanización en ciudades petroleras*. Centro de Ecodesarrollo, Mexico City.

Legorreta, J. (1988). 'El transporte público automotor en la ciudad de México y sus efectos en la contaminación atmosférica', pp. 262–300 in S. Puente and J. Legoretta (eds) *Medio ambiente y calidad de vida*. Plaza y Valdés and Departamento del Distrito Federal, Mexico City.

Lehmann, D. (1990). *Democracy and Development in Latin America: economics, politics and religion in the postwar period*. Polity Press, Cambridge.

Lewis, O. (1964). *The Children of Sánchez: autobiography of a Mexican family*. Penguin, Harmondsworth.

Lezema, J.L. (1991). 'Ciudad y conflicto: usos de suelo y comercio ambulante en la Cd. de Mexico', pp. 121–35 in M. Schteingart (ed.) *Espacio y vivienda en la Ciudad de México*. El Colegio de México, Mexico DF.

Linn, J.F. (1983). *Cities in the Developing World: policies for their equitable and efficient growth*. Oxford University Press, Oxford.

Lira, A. (1983). *Comunidades indígenas frente a la ciudad de México. Tenochtitlán y Tlatelolco, sus pueblos y barrios, 1812–1919*. El Colegio de México, Mexico DF.

Lizt Mendoza, S. (1988). 'Respuestas del transporte urbano en las zonas marginadas', pp. 21–52 in R. Benítez Zenteno and J. Benigno Morelos (eds) *Grandes problemas de la Ciudad de México*. Plaza y Valdés and Departamento del Distrito Federal, Mexico DF.

Lojkine, J. (1976). 'Contribution to a Marxist theory of capitalist urbanization', pp. 119–46 in C. Pickvance (ed.) *Urban Sociology: critical essays*. Tavistock, London.

Lombardo, S. (1987). 'Esplendor y ocaso colonial de la ciudad de México', pp. 60–3 in G. Garza (ed.) *Atlas de la Ciudad de México*. Departamento del Distrito Federal and Colegio de México, Mexico DF.

Lomnitz, L. (1977). *Networks and Marginality*. Academic Press, New York.

López Acuña, D. (1980). *La salud desigual en México*. Siglo XXI Press, Mexico DF.

López Díaz, C. (1978). La intervención del estado en la formación de un asentamiento proletario: el caso de la colonia Ajusco. Licenciatura thesis, Department of Anthropology, Universidad Iberoamericana, Mexico DF.

Lowe, S. (1986). *Urban Social Movements: the city after Castells*. Macmillan, Basingstoke.

Lujambio, A. (1995). *Federalismo y congreso en el cambio político de México*. UNAM, Mexico DF.

Lustig, N. (1992). *Mexico: the remaking of an economy*. Brookings Institute, Washington, DC.

Lynch, K. (1981). *A Theory of Good City Form*. MIT Press, Cambridge, MA.

Makin, J. (1984). Self-help housing in Mexico City, and the role of the state. Unpublished PhD thesis, Heriot Watt University, Edinburgh.

Mantecón, A. and Reyes Domínguez, G. (1993). *Los usos de la identidad barrial: Tepito 1970–1984*. Universidad Autónoma de México, Mexico.

Martin, R. (1987). The new economics and politics of regional restructuring: the British experience. Paper presented at the international conference on 'Regional Policy at the Cross Roads', University of Leuven, 22–24 April.

Martínez Assad, C. (1996). *¿Cuál destino para el DF? Ciudadanos, partidos y gobierno por el control de la capital*. Oceano, Mexico DF.

Massey, D. and Allen, J. (eds) (1984). *Geography Matters*. Oxford University Press, Oxford.

Mattos, C. de (1979). 'Plans versus planning in Latin American Experience', *CEPAL Review*, 8.

Mele, P. (1987). Urban growth, illegality and local power in the city of Puebla. Paper presented to the annual conference of the Institute of British Geographers, 9 January, Portsmouth.

Mendoza, J. (1995). The characteristics and behavior of street vendors: a case study in Mexico City. Unpublished PhD dissertation, Business School of the University of Texas at Austin.

Mesa Lago, C. (1978). *Social Security in Latin America: pressure groups, stratification and inequality*. University of Pittsburgh Press, Pittsburgh, PA.

Mexico, BNH (1952). *El problema de la habitación en la Ciudad de México*. BNH report, Mexico DF.

Mexico, COPLAMAR (1982). *Necesidades esenciales en México: Salud*. Siglo XXI, Mexico DF.

Mexico, DDF (1980). *Plan de desarrollo urbano: plan general del plan director, versión abreviada*. DDF publication, Mexico DF.

Mexico, DDF (1982). *Sistema de planificación urbana del Distrito Federal*. DDF publication, Mexico DF.

Mexico, RHP (Renovación Habitacional Popular) (1986). *Programa operativo*. RHP Agency publication, Mexico DF.

Mexico, RHP (1988). *Housing reconstruction program: a memoire*. RHP Agency Report, Mexico DF.

Mexico, SAHOP (1978). *Plan nacional de desarrollo urbano, versión abreviada.* Agency publication, Mexico DF.

Mexico, SAHOP (1979). La incorporación de los procesos que generan los asentamientos irregulares a la planeación de los centros de población. SAHOP, DGCP, Mexico DF.

Mexico, SEDESOL (1994). *Solidaridad: seis años de trabajo.* SEDESOL publication, Mexico DF.

Mexico, SEDESOL (1996). *Programa nacional de desarrollo urbano 1995–2000.* SEDESOL publication, Mexico DF.

Mexico, SPP (1983). *Plan nacional de desarrollo, 1983–88.* SPP publication, Mexico DF.

Meyer, L. (1987). 'Sistema de gobierno y evolución política hasta 1940', pp. 372–5, in G. Garza (ed.) *Atlas de la Ciudad de México.* Departamento del Distrito Federal and Colegio de México, Mexico DF.

Middlebrook, K. (1995). *The Paradox of Revolution: labor, the state, and authoritarianism in Mexico.* Johns Hopkins University Press, Baltimore, MD.

Midgley, J. (1984). *Social Security, Inequality and the Third World.* Wiley, Chichester.

Mizrahi, Y. (1994). 'Rebels without a cause? The politics of entrepreneurs in Chihuahua', *Journal of Latin American Studies,* 26: 137–58.

Mizrahi, Y. (1995). 'Entrepreneurs in the opposition: modes of political participation in Chihuahua', pp. 81–96 in V. Rodríguez and P. Ward (eds) *Opposition Government in Mexico.* University of New Mexico Press, Albuquerque, NM.

Molinar Horcasitas, J. (1991). *El tiempo de la legitimidad. Elecciones, autoritanismo y democracia en México.* Cal y Arena, Mexico DF.

Monnet, J. (1995). *Usos e imágenes del centro histórico de la Ciudad de México.* Depto. del D.F. and Centro de Estudios Mexicanos y Centroamericanos, Mexico DF.

Montaño, J. (1976). *Los pobres de la ciudad de México en los asentamientos espontáneos.* Siglo XXI, Mexico DF.

Moore, R. (1978). 'Urban problems and policy responses for Metropolitan Guayaquil', pp. 181–204 in W. Cornelius and R. Kemper (eds) *Latin American Urban Research.* Sage, Beverley Hills, CA.

Morales, M.D. (1987). La expansión de la Ciudad de México (1858–1910)', pp. 64–8 in G. Garza (ed.) *Atlas de la Ciudad de México.* Departamento del Distrito Federal and Colegio de México, Mexico DF.

Morris, S. (1995). *Political Reformism in Mexico: an overview of contemporary Mexican politics.* Lynne Rienner, Boulder, CO.

Morse, R. (1971). 'Trends and issues in Latin American urban research, 1965–70', *Latin American Research Review,* 6: 3–52.

Moser, C. (1989). 'Gender planning in the Third world: meeting practical and strategic gender needs', *World Development,* 17: 1799–825.

Mumford, L. (1938). *The Culture of Cities.* Secker and Warburg, London.

Muñoz, H. and Oliveira, O. de (1976). 'Migración, oportunidades de empleo y diferencias de ingreso en la Ciudad de México', *Revista Mexicana de Sociología,* 1: 51–83.

Muñoz, H., Oliviera, O. and Stern, C. (eds) (1977). *Migración y marginalidad ocupacional.* Universidad Nacional Autónoma de México, Mexico DF.

Navarrete, I. Martínez de (1970). 'La distribución del ingreso en México: tendencias y perspectivas', pp. 15–71 in D. Ibarra (ed.) *El perfil de México en 1980.* Vol. 1. Siglo XXI, Mexico DF.

Navarro Alvarez Tostado, E. (1997). Revitalización del Centro Histórico de la Cd. de México. Proyecto Alameda, 1991–1995. Paper presented at the XVII Annual

Institute of Latin American Studies Student Association Conference on Latin America, Austin, Texas, 1 March 1997.

Navarro Benítez, B. (1988a). 'Sistemas de transporte y metropolización en la ciudad de México', pp. 143–60 in O. Terrazas and E. Preciat (eds) *Estructura territorial de la Ciudad de México*. Plaza y Valdés and Departamento del Distrito Federal, Mexico City.

Navarro Benítez, B. (1988b). 'El transporte público en la zona metropolitana de la Ciudad de México', *Vivienda*, 13: 34–47.

Navarro Benítez, B. (1989). *El traslado masivo de la fuerza de trabajo en la Ciudad de México*. Plaza y Valdés and DDF, Mexico DF.

Navarro Benítez, B. (1993). 'Dialéctica contradictoria del transporte', pp. 175–91 in A. Bassols Batalla, G. González Salazar and J. Delgadillo Macías (eds) *Zona metropolitana de la ciudad de México, complejo geográfico, socioecónomico y político: qué fue, qué es y qué pasa*. Instituto de Investigaciones Económicas, Universidad Nacional Autónoma de México, Mexico DF.

Needler, M. (1982). *Mexican Politics: the containment of conflict*. Praeger, New York.

Negrete Salas, M.E. and Salazar, H. (1987). 'Dinámica de crecimiento de la población de la ciudad de México (1900–1980)', pp. 125–8 in G. Garza (ed.) *Atlas de la Ciudad de México*. Departamento del Distrito Federal and Colegio de México, Mexico DF.

Newman, O. (1972). *Defensible Space*. Macmillan, New York.

Noelle, L. and Tejeda, C. (1993). *Catálogo guía de arquitectura contemporánea, Ciudad de México*. Fomento Cultural Banamex, AC, Mexico DF.

O'Connor, J. (1973). *The Fiscal Crisis of the State*. St Martin's Press, New York.

O'Connor, J. (1984). *The Accumulation Crisis*. Basil Blackwells, Oxford.

O'Donnell, G. (1974). 'Corporatism and the question of the state', pp. 47–87 in J. Malloy (ed.) *Authoritarianism and Corporatism in Latin America*. University of Pittsburgh Press, Pittsburgh, PA.

Offner, J. (1984). *Law and Politics in Aztec Texcoco*. Cambridge University Press, Cambridge.

Oliveira, O. de and García, B. (1987). 'El mercado de trabajo en la ciudad de México', pp. 140–5 in G. Garza (ed.) *Atlas de la Ciudad de México*. Departamento del Distrito Federal and Colegio de México, Mexico DF.

Orellana, C. (1973). 'Mixtec migrants in Mexico City: a case study of urbanization', *Human Organization*, 32: 273–83.

Padgett, L.V. (1966). *The Mexican Political System*. Houghton Mifflin, Boston, MA.

Padilla Aragón, E. (1981). *México: hacia el crecimiento con distribución del ingreso*. Siglo XXI, Mexico DF.

Palma, G. (1978). 'Dependency: a formal theory of underdevelopment or a methodology for the analysis of concrete situations of underdevelopment?' *World Development*, 6: 881–924.

Partida, V. (1987a). 'El proceso de migración a la ciudad de México', pp. 134–40 in G. Garza (ed.) *Atlas de la Ciudad de México*. Departamento del Distrito Federal and Colegio de México, Mexico DF.

Partida, V. (1987b). 'Proyecciones de la población de la zona metropolitana de la Ciudad de México', pp. 410–14 in G. Garza (ed.) *Atlas de la Ciudad de México*. Departamento del Distrito Federal and Colegio de México, Mexico DF.

Pastor, M. and Wise, C. (1997), 'State policy, distribution and neoliteral reform in Mexico'. *Journal of Latin American Studies*, 29: 419–56.

Paz, O. (1961). *The Labyrinth of Solitude*. Grove Press, New York.

Perlman, J. (1976). *The Myth of Marginality*. University of California Press, Berkeley, CA.

Perló, M. (1988). Historia de las obras, planes y problemas hidráulicos en el Distrito Federal. Mimeo.

Pezzoli, K. (1989). Irregular settlement and the politics of land allocation in Mexico City: the case of Ajusco. Mimeo.

Phillips. D. (1990). *Health and Health Care in the Third World*. Longman, New York.

Pichardo Pagaza, I. (1990). *Primer Informe de Gobierno*. Gobierno del Estado de México, Toluca.

Pickvance, C. (ed.) (1976). *Urban Sociology: critical essays*. Tavistock, London.

Pommier, P. (1982). 'The place of Mexico City in the nation's growth: employment trends and policies', *International Labour Review*, 121: 345–60.

Pradilla, E. (1988). 'Crisis y arqitectura de subsistencia en México', pp. 45–77 in O. Terrazas and E. Preciat (eds) *Estructura territorial de la Ciudad de México*. Plaza y Valdés and Departamento del Distrito Federal, Mexico City.

Pradilla, E. (1995). 'La política territorial y la configuración urbana-regional', pp. 131–51 in A.G. Aguilar (ed.) *Desarrollo regional y urbano: tendencias y alternativas*, vol. II. Juan Pablos Editor, SA, Mexico, UNAM and U. de Guadalajara.

Prieto Inzunza, E. and Delgado Lamas, R. (1995). Cronología histórica mínima de la Zona Sur de la Alameda. Paper presented at the International Research Workshop 'The cultural patrimony of Mexican inner-cities: towards equitable conservation policies and practices'. The Mexican Center, University of Texas at Austin, 8–9 December 1995.

Puente, S. (1987). 'Estructura industrial y participación de la zona metropolitana de la ciudad de México en el producto interno bruto', pp. 92–5 in G. Garza (ed.) *Atlas de la Ciudad de México*. Departamento del Distrito Federal and Colegio de México, Mexico DF.

Purcell, S. and Purcell, J. (1980). 'State and society in Mexico', *World Politics*, 32: 194–227.

Ramírez Saíz, J.M. (1983). *Carácter y contradicciones de la ley general de asentamientos humanos*. Instituto de Investigaciones Sociales, UNAM, Mexico DF.

Rapoport, A. (1988). 'Spontaneous settlements as vernacular design', pp. 51–77 in C. Patton (ed.) *Spontaneous Shelter: international perspectives and prospects*. Temple University Press, Philadelphia, PA.

Ray, T. (1969). *The Politics of the Barrio*. University of California Press, Berkeley, CA.

Reynoso, V.M. (1994). 'Estructura interna y lucha de fracciones. La propuesta de reforma a los Estatutos del Partido Acción Nacional (1991–1992)', pp. 52–61 in J. Reyes del Campillo, E. Sandoval Forero and M.A. Carrillo (eds) *Partidos, elecciones y cultura política mexicana contemporánea*. UAEM, UAM-Xochimilco and COMECSO, Mexico DF.

Ricalde, H. and Sánchez, F. (1984). *Arquitectura Mexicana: Siglo XX*, pp. 48–80. Asociación de Ingenieros y Arquitectos de México AC, Mexico DF.

Richardson, H. (1973). *The Economics of Urban Size*. Saxon House and Lexington Books, New York.

Richardson, H. (1976). 'The arguments for very large cities reconsidered: a comment', *Urban Studies*, 13: 307–10.

Riofrío, G. (1996). 'Lima: Mega-city and mega-problem', pp. 155–72 in A. Gilbert (ed.) *The Mega-city in Latin America*. United Nations University Press, Tokyo.

Roberts, B. (1978). *Cities of Peasants: the political economy of urbanization*. Edward Arnold, London.

Roberts, B. (1994). *The Making of Citizens: cities of peasants revisited*. Edward Arnold, London.

Rodríguez, V. (1987). The politics of decentralization in Mexico. Unpublished PhD dissertation, University of California, Berkeley.

Rodríguez, V. (1992). 'Mexico's decentralization in the 1980s: promises, promises, promises . . .', pp. 127–43 in A. Morris and S. Lowder (eds) *Decentralization in Latin America*. Praeger, New York.

Rodríguez, V. (1993). 'The politics of decentralization in Mexico: from *municipio libre* to *Solidaridad*', *Bulletin of Latin American Research*, 12: 133–45.

Rodríguez, V. (1995). 'Municipal autonomy and the politics of intergovernmental finance: is it different for the opposition?' pp. 153–72 in V. Rodríguez and P. Ward (eds) *Opposition Government in Mexico*. University of New Mexico Press, Albuquerque, NM.

Rodríguez, V. (1997). *Decentralization in Mexico: from* municipio libre *to* solidaridad *to* nuevo federalismo. Westview Press, Boulder, CO.

Rodríguez, V. and Ward, P. (1992). *Policymaking, Politics, and Urban Governance in Chihuahua: the experience of recent panista governments*. LBJ School of Public Affairs, US–Mexican Studies Policy Report 3, Austin, TX.

Rodríguez, V. and Ward, P. (1994a). 'Disentangling the PRI from the government in Mexico', *Mexican Studies/Estudios Mexicanos*, 10: 163–86.

Rodríguez, V. and Ward, P. (1994b). *Political Change in Baja California: democracy in the making?* UCSD Center for US–Mexican Studies, Monograph Series, No. 40, San Diego, CA.

Rodríguez, V. and Ward, P. (eds) (1995). *Opposition Government in Mexico*. University of New Mexico Press, Albuquerque, NM.

Rodríguez, V. and Ward, P. (1996). 'The New PRI: recasting its identity', pp. 92–112 in R. Aitken, N. Craske, G. Jones and D. Stansfield (eds) *Dismantling the Mexican State?* Macmillan, London.

Rodríguez, V., Ward, P. *et al*. (1996). *New Federalism, State and Local Government in Mexico: memoria/synthesis of the bi-national conference*. Mexican Center of the Institute of Latin American Studies, Austin, TX.

Rodríguez Kuri, A. (1996). *La experiencia olvidada, el ayuntamiento de México: política y gobierno, 1876–1912*. Universidad Autonómoa Metropolitana, and El Colegio de México, Mexico DF.

Rodwin, L. (1969). *Planning Urban Growth and Regional Development*. MIT Press, Cambridge, MA.

Roett, R. (1993). 'At the crossroads: liberalization in Mexico', pp. 1–13 in R. Roett, (ed.) *Political and Economic Liberalization in Mexico: at a critical juncture?* Lynne Rienner, Boulder, CO.

Roth, G. (1987). *The Private Provision of Public Services*. Oxford University Press and the World Bank, Washington, DC.

Rowland, A. and Gordon, P. (1996). 'Mexico City: no longer a Leviathan?' pp. 173–202 in A. Gilbert (ed.) *The Mega-City in Latin America*. United Nations University Press, Tokyo.

Roxborough, I. (1979). *Theories of Underdevelopment*. Macmillan, Basingstoke.

Rubalcava, R.M. and Schteingart, M. (1985). 'Diferenciación socioespacial intraurbana en el área metropolitana de la ciudad de México', *Estudios Sociológicos*, 9.

Rubalcava, R.M. and Schteingart, M. (1987). 'Estructura urbana y diferenciación socioespacial en la zona metropolitana de la ciudad de México (1970–80)', pp. 108–15 in G. Garza (ed.) *Atlas de la Ciudad de México*. Departamento del Distrito Federal and Colegio de México, Mexico DF.

Rubio, L. (1993). 'Economic reform and political change in Mexico', pp. 35–50 in R.

Roett (ed.) *Political and Economic Liberalization in Mexico: at a critical juncture?* Lynne Rienner, Boulder, CO.

Salas Páez, C. (1992). 'Actividad económica y empleo en el area metropolitana de la Cd. de México: 1970–1990', pp. 86–93 in Consejo Nacional de Población. *La Zona metropolitana de la ciudad de México: problemática actual y perspectivas demográficas y urbanas.* CONAPO, Mexico DF.

Saldívar, A. (1981). *Ideología y política del estado mexicano 1970–76.* 2nd edn. Siglo XXI, Mexico DF.

Sánchez Almanza, A. (1993). 'Crecimiento y distribución territorial de la población en la zona metropolitana de la ciudad de México', pp. 103–27 in A. Bassols Batalla, G. González Salazar and J. Delgadillo Macías (eds) *Zona metropolitana de la ciudad de México, complejo geográfico, socioecónomico y político: qué fue, qué es y qué pasa.* Instituto de Investigaciones Económicas, Universidad Nacional Autónoma de México, Mexico DF.

Sanders, W., Parsons, J. and Santley, R. (1979). *The Basin of Mexico: ecological processes in the evolution of a civilization.* Academic Press, New York.

Sassen, S. (1991). *The Global City.* Princeton University Press, Princeton, NJ.

Sassen, S. (1996). *Losing Control? Sovereignty in an Age of Globalization.* Princeton University Press, Princeton, NJ.

Saunders, P. (1979). *Urban Politics: a sociological interpretation.* Hutchinson, London.

Saunders, P. (1986). *Social Theory and the Urban Question.* 2nd edn. Hutchinson, London.

Scarpaci, J. and Gutman, M. (1995). *Buscando lo común*: land use patterns in seven Latin American *cascos históricos.* Paper presented at the International Research Workshop 'The cutural patrimony of Mexican inner-cities: towards equitable conservation policies and practices'. The Mexican Center, University of Texas at Austin, 8–9 December 1995.

Scarpaci, J., Segre, R. and Coyula, M. (1997). *Havana: two faces of the Antilean Metropolis.* World Cities Series. Wiley, Chichester.

Schafer, R. (1966). *Mexico, Mutual Adjustment Planning.* Syracuse University Press, Syracuse, NY.

Schers, D. (1972). The popular sector of the PRI in Mexico. Unpublished PhD dissertation, University of New Mexico.

Schnore, L. (1966). 'On the spatial structure of cities in the two Americas', in P. Hauser and L. Schnore (eds) *The Study of Urbanization.* Wiley, New York.

Schteingart, M. (1987). 'Expansión urbana, conflictos sociales y deterioro ambiental en la Ciudad de México. El caso del Ajusco', *Estudios demográficos y urbanos,* 2: 449–78.

Scobie, J. (1974). *Buenos Aires: plaza to suburb 1870–1910.* Oxford University Press, New York.

Scott, I. (1982). *Urban and Spatial Development in Mexico.* Johns Hopkins University Press, Baltimore, MD.

Scott, R. (1964). *Mexican Government in Transition.* University of Illinois Press, Champaigne, IL.

Selby, H., Murphy, A. and Lorenzen, S. (1990). *The Mexican Urban Household: organizing for self-defense.* University of Texas Press, Austin, TX.

Shaiken, H. (1990). *Mexico in the Global Economy: high technology and work organization in export industries.* Center for US–Mexican Studies, UCSD, San Diego, CA.

Sigg, A. (1993). 'De la ideología confesional a la ideología nacional: el PAN y sus presidentes, 1962–82', pp. 143–70 in *La transción interrumpida: Mexico, 1968–1988.* Nueva Imagen, Mexico.

Simmie, J. (1986). General Editor's Preface to S. Lowe, *Urban social movements: the city after Castells*. Macmillan, Basingstoke.

Skinner, R. and Rodell, M. (eds) (1983). *People, Poverty and Shelter: problems of self-help housing in the Third World*. Methuen, London.

Sklair, L. (1988). 'Mexico's *maquiladora* programme: a critical evaluation', in G. Philip (ed.) *The Mexican Economy*. Routledge, London.

Sklair, L. (1989). *Assembling for Development: the maquila industry in Mexico and the United States*. Unwin Hyman, Boston, MA.

Smith, N. (1996). *The New Urban Frontier: gentrification and the revanchist city*. Routledge, London.

Smith, P. (1979). *Labyrinths of Power: political recruitment in twentieth century Mexico*. Princeton University Press, Princeton, NJ.

Smith, P. (1996). *The Talons of the Eagle: dynamics of US–Latin American relations*. Oxford University Press, New York.

Sobrino, L.J. (1992). 'Estructura ocupacional del sector servicios en la Cd. de México: 1960–1988', pp. 95–17 in Consejo Nacional de Población. *La zona metropolitana de la ciudad de México: problemática actual y perspectivas demográficas y urbanas*. CONAPO, Mexico DF.

Soustelle, J. (1971). *The Four Suns*. André Deutsch, London.

Stanislawski, D. (1947). 'Early Spanish town planning in the New World', *Geographical Review*, 37: 94–105.

Stern, C. (1977). 'Cambios en los volúmenes de migrantes provenientes de distintas zonas geoeconómicas', pp. 115–28 in C. Stern *et al.* (eds) *Migración y desigualdad social en la Ciudad de México*. UNAM/El Colegio de México, Mexico.

Stolarski, N. (1982). *La vivienda en el Distrito Federal: situación y perspectivas*. General Directorate of Planning, Mexico DDF.

Story, D. (1986). *Industry, the State, and Public Policy*. University of Texas Press, Austin, TX.

Suárez Pareyón, A. (1978). 'La colonia Guerrero: un caso de deterioro en la Ciudad de México', *Arquitectura Autogobierno*, 9: 36–44.

Sutherland, L. (1985). Informal paratransit in Mexico City. Unpublished PhD dissertation, University of Zurich.

Tamayo, S. (1995). Identidad colectiva y patrimonio cultural en el centro histórico de la Ciudad de México. Paper presented at the International Research Workshop 'The cultural patrimony of Mexican inner-cities: towards equitable conservation policies and practices'. The Mexican Center, University of Texas at Austin, 8–9 December 1995.

Teichman, J. (1988). *Policy Making in Mexico: from boom to crisis*. Allen & Unwin, Boston, MA.

Tejeda, C. (1995). Program for the improvement of popular commerce in the historic center of Mexico City. Paper presented at the International Research Workshop 'The cutural patrimony of Mexican inner-cities: towards equitable conservation policies and practices'. The Mexican Center, University of Texas at Austin, 8–9 December 1995.

Tello, C. (1978). *La política económica en México, 1970–1976*. Siglo XXI, Mexico DF.

Tenorio-Trillo, M. (1996). *Mexico at the World's Fairs: crafting a modern nation*. University of California Press, Berkeley, CA.

Townroe, P. and Keen, D. (1984). 'Polarization reversal in the State of São Paulo, Brazil', *Regional Studies*, 18: 45–54.

Tuirán Gutiérrez, R. (1992). 'Los hogares frente a la crisis: Cd. de México: 1985–88', pp. 179–201 in Consejo Nacional de Población. *La zona metropolitana de la ciudad de México: problemática actual y perspectivas demográficas y urbanas.* CONAPO, Mexico DF.

Turner, J. (1963). 'Dwelling resources in South America', *Architectural Design*, 37: 360–93.

Turner, J. (1968a). 'Housing priorities, settlement patterns and urban development in modernizing countries', *Journal of the American Institute of Planners*, 34: 354–63.

Turner, J. (1968b). 'The squatter settlement: architecture that works', *Architectural Design*, 38: 355–60.

Turner, J. (1969). 'Uncontrolled urban settlements: problems and policies', pp. 507–31 in G. Breese (ed.) *The City in Newly Developing Countries*. Prentice Hall, Englewood Cliffs, NJ.

Turner, J. (ed.) (1972). Government policy and lower-income housing systems in Mexico City. Agency Report to AURIS, Mimeo, Mexico City and Cambridge, MA.

Turner, J. (1976). *Housing by People*. Marion Boyars, London.

UNCHS (United Nations Centre for Human Settlements) (1982). *Survey of Slum and Squatter Settlements*. Tycooly, Dublin.

UNCHS (United Nations Centre for Human Settlements) (1996). *An Urbanizing World: global report on human settlements 1996*. Oxford University Press for UNCHS, Oxford.

UNDIESA (1991). *Population Growth and Policies in Mega-Cities: Mexico City*. Population Policy Paper No. 32, United Nations Department of International Economic and Social Affairs.

Unikel, L. (1972). *La dinámica del crecimiento de la Ciudad de México*. Fundación para Estudios de Población, Mexico DF.

Unikel, L. and Lavell, A. (1979). 'El problema urbano regional en México', *Gaceta UNAM*, cuarta época, vol. 3, suplemento número 20, 9 de agosto.

United Nations (1980). *Yearbook of National Accounts Statistics*. United Nations, New York.

Valencia, E. (1965). *La Merced: estudio ecológico y social de una zona de la Ciudad de México*. Instituto Nacional de Antropología e Historia, Mexico DF.

Valiant, G. (1972). *Aztecs of Mexico: origin, rise and fall of the Aztec Nation*. Penguin, Harmondsworth.

Varley, A. (1985a). 'Ya somos dueños'. Ejido land regularization and development in Mexico City. Unpublished PhD Thesis, University of London.

Varley, A. (1985b). 'Urbanization and agrarian law: the case of Mexico City', *Bulletin of Latin American Research*, 4: 1–16.

Varley, A. (1987). 'The relationship between tenure legalization and housing improvements: evidence from Mexico City', *Development and Change*, 18: 463–81.

Varley, A. (1989). 'Settlement, illegality, and legalization: the need for reassessment', pp. 143–74 in P. Ward (ed.) *Corruption, Development and Inequality*. Routledge, London.

Varley, A. (1993). 'Clientelism or technocracy? The politics of urban land regularisation', pp. 249–76 in N. Harvey (ed.) *Mexico: dilemmas of transition*. British Academic Press and Institute of Latin American Studies, London.

Varley, A. (1996). 'Delivering the goods: Solidarity, land regularisation and urban services', pp. 204–24 in R. Aitken, N. Craske, G. Jones and D. Stansfield (eds) *Dismantling the Mexican State?* Macmillan, London.

Vaughn, D. and Feindt, W. (1973). 'Initial settlement and intra-urban movement of migrants in Monterrey, Mexico', *Journal of the American Institute of Planners*, 39: 388–401.

Venegas, L. (1995). 'Political culture and women of the popular sector in Cd. Juárez, 1983–1986', pp. 97–112 in V. Rodríguez and P. Ward (eds) *Opposition Government in Mexico*. University of New Mexico Press, Albuquerque, NM.

Vernez, G. (1973). The residential movements of low-income families; the case of Bogotá, Colombia. Mimeo, New York City Rand Institute.

Vicencio, G. (1996). 'The PAN's administration in Baja California: the struggle for a free and sovereign state', pp. 113–29 in R. Aitken, N. Craske, G. Jones and D. Stansfield (eds) *Dismantling the Mexican State?* Macmillan, London.

Vidrio, M. (1987). 'El transporte de la Ciudad de México en el siglo XIX', pp. 68–71 in G. Garza (ed.) *Atlas de la Ciudad de México*. Departamento del Distrito Federal and Colegio de México, Mexico DF.

Villegas, J. (1988). 'Zona metropolitana de la Ciudad de México: localización y estructura de la actividad industrial', pp. 161–88 in O. Terrazas and E. Preciat (eds) *Estructura territorial de la Ciudad de México*. Plaza y Valdés and Departamento del Distrito Federal, Mexico City.

Wallerstein, I. (1974). *The Modern World System: capitalist agriculture and the origins of the European world economy in the sixteenth century*. Academic Press, New York.

Ward, P. (1976a). In search of a home: social and economic characteristics of squatter settlements and the role of self-help housing in Mexico City. Unpublished PhD Thesis, University of Liverpool.

Ward, P. (1976b). 'The squatter settlement as slum or housing solution: the evidence from Mexico City', *Land Economics*, 52: 330–46.

Ward, P. (1976c). 'Intra-city migration to squatter settlements in Mexico City', *Geoforum*, 7: 369–82.

Ward, P. (1978). 'Self-help housing in Mexico: social and economic determinants of success', *Town Planning Review*, 49: 38–50.

Ward, P. (1981a). 'Political pressure for urban services: the response of two Mexico City administrations', *Development and Change*, 12: 379–407.

Ward, P. (1981b). 'Mexico City', pp. 28–64 in M. Pacione (ed.) *Urban Problems and Planning in Third World Cities*. Croom Helm, London.

Ward, P. (1982). 'Informal housing: conventional wisdoms reappraised', *Built Environment*, 8: 85–94.

Ward, P. (1986). *Welfare Politics in Mexico: papering over the cracks*. Allen & Unwin, London.

Ward, P. (1989a). 'Land values and valorisation processes in Latin American cities: a research agenda', *Bulletin of Latin American Research*, 8: 47–66.

Ward, P. (1989b). 'Political mediation and illegal settlement in Mexico City', pp. 135–55 in A. Gilbert (ed.) *Housing and Land in Urban Mexico*. Monograph Series No. 31, Centre for US–Mexican Studies, University of California at San Diego.

Ward, P. (1989c). 'Government without democracy in Mexico City: defending the high ground', pp. 307–24 in W. Cornelius, J. Gentleman and P. Smith (eds) *Mexico's Alternative Political Futures*. Center for US–Mexican Studies, University of California, Monograph Series, San Diego, CA.

Ward, P. (1990). 'Mexico', in W. van Vliet (ed.) *International Handbook of Housing Policies and Practices*. Greenwood Press, Westport, CT.

Ward, P. (1993). 'The Latin American inner city: differences of degree or of kind?' *Environment and Planning A*, 25: 1131–60.

Ward, P. (1995). 'Policy-making and policy implementation among non-PRI governments: the PAN in Ciudad Juárez and in Chihuahua', pp. 135–52 in V. Rodríguez and P. Ward (eds) *Opposition Government in Mexico*. University of New Mexico Press, Albuquerque, NM.

Ward, P. (1996). 'Contemporary issues in the government and administration of Latin American mega-cities', pp. 53–72 in A. Gilbert (ed.) *The Mega-City in Latin America*. United Nations University Press, New York.

Ward, P. (1998). 'From machine politics to the politics of technocracy: charting the decline of partisanship in the Mexican municipality', *Bulletin of Latin American Research*, in press.

Ward, P. and Macoloo, C. (1992). 'Articulation theory and self-help housing practice in the 1990s', *International Journal of Urban and Regional Research*, 6: 60–80.

Ward, P. and Melligan, S. (1985). 'Urban renovation and the impact upon low-income families in Mexico City', *Urban Studies*, 22: 199–207.

Ward, P., Jiménez, E. and Jones, G. (1994). 'Measuring residential land-price changes and affordability', pp. 159–78 in G. Jones and P. Ward (eds) *Methodology for Land and Housing Market Analysis*. University College Press, London.

Weisskoff, R. and Figueroa, A. (1976). 'Traversing the social pyramid: a comparative review of income distribution in Latin America', *Latin American Research Review*, 2: 71–112.

Whitehead, L. (1980). 'Mexico from bust to boom: a political evaluation of the 1976–79 stabilization program', *World Development*, 8: 843–63.

Whitehead, L. (1984). Politics of economic management. Seminar presentation, 'Mexico 1984' conference held at the Institute of Latin American Studies, London, 4–5 June.

Whitehead, L. (1994). 'Prospects for a "transition" from authoritarian rule in Mexico', pp. 327–46 in M. Cook, K. Middlebrook and J. Molinar (eds) *The Politics of Economic Restructuring: state–society relations and regime change in Mexico*. Center for US–Mexican Studies, UCSD, San Diego, CA.

Wilson, P. (1992). *Exports and Local Development: Mexico's new maquiladoras*. University of Texas Press, Austin, TX.

World Bank (1972). *Urbanization*. Sector Policy Paper. World Bank, Washington, DC.

World Bank (1991). *Urban Policy and Economic Development: an agenda for the 1990s*. World Bank, Washington, DC.

World Health Organisation (WHO) (1978). *Primary Health Care*. WHO, Geneva.

World Health Organisation (WHO) (1981). *Global Strategy for Health for all by the year 2000*. WHO, Geneva.

Wynia, G. (1972). *Politics and Planners: economic development policy in Central America*. University of Wisconsin Press, Madison, WI.

Yescas Martínez, I. (1994). 'Oaxaca: designación o elección de gobernadores', pp. 84–91 in J. Reyes del Campillo, E. Sandoval Forero and M.A. Carrillo (eds) *Partidos, elecciones y cultura política mexicana contemporánea*. UAEM, UAM-Xochimilco and COMECSO, Mexico DF.

Zedillo, E. (1995). *First State of the Nation Report*. Presidencia de la República, Mexico DF.

Zorrilla-Vázquez, E. (1996). *Mexico at the Crossroads*. Tecnología Avanzada, Mexico DF.

BIBLIOGRAPHY

Aguilar Martínez, G. (1995). 'Dinámica metropolitana y terciarización del empleo en México. 1970–1990', pp. 75–97 in A.G. Aguilar (ed.) *Desarrollo regional y urbano: tendencias y alternativas*, tomo II. UNAM and U de G., Juan Pablos Editor, SA, Mexico.

Aguilar, A.G. and Rodríguez, F. (1995). 'Tendencias de desconcentración urbana en México, 1970–1990', pp. 75–100 in A. Aguilar, L.J. Castro Castro and E. Juárez Aguirre (eds) *El desarrollo urbano de México a fines del siglo XX*. Instituto de Estudios Urbanos de Nuevo León, Mexico, Nuevo León.

Arizpe, L. (1978). *Migraciones, etnicismo y cambio económico: un estudio sobre migrantes campesinas a la Cd. de México*. El Colegio de México, Mexico DF.

Azuela, A. and Duhau, E. (eds) (1993). *Gestión urbana y cambio institucional*. Universidad Autónoma Metropolitana, Azcapotzalco, Mexico DF.

Basáñez, M. (1993). 'Is Mexico headed towards its fifth crisis?' pp. 95–116 in R. Roett (ed.) *Political and Economic Liberalization in Mexico: at a critical juncture?* Lynne Rienner Publishers, Boulder, CO.

Bataillon, C. and D'Arc, H. (1973). *La Ciudad de México*. Sepsetentas, Mexico DF.

Borja, J. (1992). 'Past, present, and future of local government in Latin America', pp. 130–44 in R. Morse and J. Hardoy (eds) *Rethinking the Latin American City*. Johns Hopkins University Press, Baltimore, MD.

Bustamante Lemus, C. (1993). 'Crecimiento metropolitano y políticas urbanas, 1970–1992', pp. 128–53 in A. Bassols Batalla, G. González Salazar, and J. Delgadillo Macías (eds) *Zona metropolitana de la ciudad de México, complejo geográfico, socioecónomico y político: qué fue, qué es y qué pasa*. Instituto de Investigaciones Económicas, Universidad Nacional Autónoma de México, Mexico DF.

Cárdenas Zepeda, A. and Santos Zavala, J. (1996). 'El caso de Tlanepantla, Estado de México', pp. 329–432 in E. Cabero (ed.) *Los dilemas de la modernización municipal: estudios sobre la gestión hacendaria en municipios urbanos de México*. Miguel Angel Porrúa, Mexico DF.

Connolly, P. (1984). 'Finanzas públicas y el estado local: el caso del D.D.F.' *Revista de ciencias sociales y humanidades – UAM*', 11: 57–91.

Connolly, P. (1988). 'Productividad y relaciones laborales en la industria de la construcción', *Vivienda*, 13: 82–99.

Connolly, P. (1993). 'La reestructuración económica de la ciudad de México', pp. 45–70 in R. Coulomb and E. Duhau (eds) *Dinámica urbana y procesos socio-políticos*. Programa observatorio de la Cd. de México 1970–1988. UAM and CENVI, Mexico DF.

COPEVI (1977). *Investigación sobre vivienda: las políticas habitacionales del estado mexicano*. COPEVI AC, Mexico DF.

Coulomb, R. (ed.) (1992). *Pobreza urbana, autogestión y política*. CENVI, Mexico DF.

Coulomb, R. and Duhau, E. (eds) (1993). *Dinámica urbana y procesos socio-políticos*. Programa observatorio de la Cd. de México 1970–1988. UAM and CENVI, Mexico DF.

De la Madrid, M. (1982). *Los grandes retos de la Ciudad de México*. Grijalbo, Mexico DF.

Dear, M. (1988). 'The post-modern challenge: reconstructing human geography', *Transactions of the Institute of British Geographers*, 13: 262–74.

Delgado, J. (1992). 'Tendencias megalopolitanas de la Cd. de México', pp. 51–70 in Consejo Nacional de Población. *La zona metropolitana de la ciudad de México: problemática actual y perspectivas demográficas y urbanas*. CONAPO, Mexico DF.

Domínguez, J. and McCann, J. (1996). *Democratizing Mexico: public opinion and electoral choices*. Johns Hopkins University Press, Baltimore, MD.

Dornbusch, R. (1990). 'Mexico's economy at the crossroads', *Journal of International Affairs*, 43: 313–26.

Duhau, E. (1993). 'Planeación urbana y políticas medio ambientales', pp. 186–206 in R. Coulomb and E. Duhau (eds) *Dinámica urbana y procesos socio-politicos*. Programa observatorio de la Cd. de México 1970–1988. UAM and CENVI, Mexico DF.

Durand, J. (1983). *La ciudad invade el ejido*. Ediciones de la Casa Chata, Mexico DF.

Foro Nacional (1995). *Foro Nacional: Hacia un Auténtico Federalísmo*. Memoria de la reunión en Guadalajara, 29–31 March 1995.

Friedmann, J. (1995). 'Where we stand: a decade of world city research', pp. 21–47 in P. Knox and P. Taylor (eds) *World Cities in a World System*. Cambridge University Press, Cambridge.

García, B., Muñoz, H. and de Oliveira, O. (1994). *Trabajo femenino y vida familar en México*. El Colegio de México, DF.

Garza, G. (ed.) (1995). *Atlas de Monterrey*. Gobierno del Estado de Nuevo León and El Colegio de México, Monterrey.

Gilbert, A. (1991). 'Self-help housing during recession: the Mexican experience', pp. 221–41 in M. González de la Rocha and A. Escobar (eds) *Social Responses to Mexico's Economic Crisis of the 1980s*. Center for US–Mexican Studies, UCSD, Contemporary Perspectives Series 1, La Jolla, San Diego, CA.

Gilbert, A. (1994). *The Latin American City*. Latin American Bureau, London.

González Block, M.A. (1991). 'Economic crisis and the decentralization of health services in Mexico', pp. 67–90 in M. González de la Rocha and A. Escobar (eds) *Social Responses to Mexico's Economic Crisis of the 1980s*. Center for US–Mexican Studies, UCSD, Contemporary Perspectives Series 1, La Jolla, San Diego CA.

González de la Rocha, M. and Escobar, A. (eds) (1991). *Social Responses to Mexico's Economic Crisis of the 1980s*. Center for US–Mexican Studies, UCSD, Contemporary Perspectives Series 1, La Jolla, San Diego, CA.

Gottdiener, M. (1994). (2nd edn) *The Social Production of Urban Space*. University of Texas Press, Austin, TX.

Graizbord, B. and Arias, R. (1988). 'Prospectiva del crecimiento de la zona metropolitana de la ciudad de México', *Vivienda*, 13: 100–7.

Gutiérrez Guzmán, F. (1992). 'Las fuentes de la información demográfica para la ZMCM', pp. 17–20 in CONAPO, *La zona metropolitana de la ciudad de México: problemática actual y perspectivas demográficas y urbanas*. CONAPO, Mexico DF.

Harvey, D. (1992). 'Social justice, postmodernism and the city', *International Journal of Urban and Regional Research*, 16: 588–601.

Jáuregui, E. (1971). *Mesoclima de la Ciudad de México*. UNAM, Instituto de Geografia, Mexico DF.

King, A. (ed.) (1996). *Re-presenting the City: ethnicity, capital and culture in the 21st century metropolis*. Macmillan, London.

Knight, A. (1994). 'Cardenism: juggernaut or jalopy?' *Journal of Latin American Studies*, 26: 73–107.

Knight, A. (1996). 'Salinas and social liberalism in historical context', pp. 1–23 in R. Aitken, N. Craske, G. Jones and D. Stansfield (eds) *Dismantling the Mexican State?* Macmillan, London.

Kouyoumdjian, A. (1988). 'The Miguel De la Madrid *sexenio*: major reforms or foundation for disaster?' pp. 78–94 in G. Philip (ed.) *The Mexican Economy*. Routledge, London.

Logan, J. and Molotch, H. (1987). *Urban Fortunes: the political economy of place*. University of California Press, Berkeley, CA.

Luna Pichardo, M.A. and Gómez Olvera, R. (1992). 'Límites al crecimiento de la zona metropolitana de la Cd. de México', pp. 35–49 in Consejo Nacional de Población. *La zona metropolitana de la ciudad de México: problemática actual y perspectivas demográficas y urbanas*. CONAPO, Mexico DF.

Marcuse, P. (1994). 'Not chaos but walls: postmodernism and the partitioned city', in S. Watson and K. Gibson (eds) *Postmodern Cities and Space*. Blackwells, Oxford.

Mele, P. (1994). *Puebla: urbanización y políticas urbanas*. Benemérita Universidad Autónoma de Puebla, and UAM–Azcapotzalco, Puebla and Mexico DF.

Mexico, INVI (1958). *Las colonias populares de la Ciudad de México: problemas y soluciones*. INVI publication, Mexico DF.

Meyer, L. (1989). 'En México, perestroika sin glasnost', *Excélsior*, 13 December.

Micheli, J. (1994). *Nueva manufactura globalización y producción de automóviles en México*. Universidad Nacional Autónoma de México, Mexico DF.

Molinar Horcasitas, J. and Weldon, J. (1994). 'Electoral determinants and consequences of National Solidarity', pp. 123–42 in W. Cornelius, A. Craig and J. Fox (eds) *Transforming State–Society Relations in Mexico: the National Solidarity strategy*. Center for US–Mexican Studies, UCSD, La Jolla, San Diego, CA.

Moreno Toscano, A. (1979). 'La "crisis" en la ciudad', pp. 152–76 in P. González Casanova and E. Florescano (eds) *Mexico Hoy*. Siglo XXI, Mexico DF.

Negrete Salas, M.E. (1995). 'Evolución de las zonas metropolitanas en México', pp. 19–46 in C. Garrocho and J. Sobrino (eds) *Sistemas metropolitanos: nuevos enfoques y prospectiva*. El Colegio Mexiquense and SEDESOL, Mexico.

Nord. B. (1996). *Mexico City's Alternative Futures*. University Press of America, Lanham.

Nuñez, O. (1983). 'Causas sociales y políticas en las movilizaciones de los colonos en el D.F., 1970–73', *Tabique*, 2: 3–33.

Pansters, W. (1996). 'Citizens with dignity: opposition and government in San Luis Potosí, 1938–93', pp. 244–66 in R. Aitken, N. Craske, G. Jones and D. Stansfield (eds) *Dismantling the Mexican State?* Macmillan, London.

Peña, G. de la, Durán, J.M., Escobar, A. and García de Alba, J. (eds) (1990). *Crisis, conflicto y sobrevivencia: estudios sobre la sociedad urbana en México*. Universidad de Guadalajara and CIESAS, Guadalajara.

Perló, M. (1980). Los problemas financieros de la Cd. de México. *El Día*, 7 June 1984.

Perló, M. (ed.) (1990). *La modernización de las ciudades en México*. Universidad Nacional Autónoma de México, Mexico DF.

Perló, M. (no date). De cómo perdió la Cd. de México su municipalidad sin obtener un cambio ni una democracia de manzana. Mimeo, Mexico DF.

Rodríguez Araujo, O. (1979). *La reforma política y los partidos en México*. Siglo XXI, Mexico DF.

Rotenberg, R. and McDonogh, G. (1993). *The Cultural Meaning of Urban Space*. Bergin and Garvey, London.

Schteingart, M. (1988). 'Mexico City', pp. 268–93 in M. Dogan and J. Kasada (eds) *Megacities*. Vol. 2. Sage, Beverly Hills, CA.

Schteingart, M. (ed.) (1991). *Espacio y vivienda en la Ciudad de México*. El Colegio de México, Mexico DF.

Schulz, D. and Williams, E. (1995). 'Crisis or transformation? The struggle for the soul of Mexico', pp. 1–28 in D. Schulz and E. Williams (eds) *Mexico Faces the 21st Century*. Praeger, Westport, CT.

Sepúlveda, I. (1995). 'Mexico's political transition; the emergence of civil socity', pp. 145–58 in D. Schulz and E. Williams (eds) *Mexico Faces the 21st Century*. Praeger, Westport, CT.

Sobrino, J. and Garrocho, C. (1995). *Pobreza, política social y participación ciudadana*. El Colegio Mexiquense, AC and SEDESOL, Mexico.

Suárez Dávila, F. (1994). *Convención en el purgatorio sobre el futuro de México*. Cal y Arena, Mexico DF.

Villa, M. and Rodríguez, J. (1996). 'Demographic trends in Latin America's metropolises, 1950–1990', pp. 25–52 in A. Gilbert (ed.) *The Mega-City in Latin America*. United Nations University Press, Tokyo.

Whitehead, L. (1981). 'On "governability" in Mexico', *Bulletin of Latin American Research*, 1: 27–47.

Williams, M. (1993). 'El cambio en la estructura y localización de las actividades económicas del área metropolitana de la Cd. de México, 1970–1988', in R. Coulomb and E. Duhau (eds) *Dinámica urbana y procesos socio-políticos*. Programa observatorio de la Cd. de México 1970–1988. UAM and CENVI, Mexico DF.

World Bank (with UNDP and UNCHS) (1990). *Urban Management Program Phase 2: capacity building for urban management in the 1990s*. World Bank, Washington, DC.

Zedillo, E. (1996). *Second State of the Nation Report*. Presidencia de la República, Mexico DF.

Ziccardi, A. (1995). 'Gobiernos locales: entre la globalización y la ciudadanía: reflexiones sobre las transformaciones recientes en el Distrito Federal', pp. 145–62 in A.G. Aguilar (ed.) *Desarrollo regional y urbano: tendencias y alternativas*. Vol. I. UNAM and U. de G., Juan Pablos Editor, SA, Mexico.

INDEX